A PROPHET WITHOUT HONOR

by

E. G. White

"A prophet is not without honour, save in his own country, and in his own house."

Matthew 13:57

Another fine Audio Visual Production

This volume contains excerpts from the best-selling classic *Desire of Ages* by the same author.

COVER CREDITS:
Cover art by James Arrabito. Copyright © 1984 by Audio Visual Productions, Inc. All rights reserved. Cover layout and design by Charles Wheeling.

ISBN: 0-916547-03-5

Printed in U.S.A.

Contents

Chapter 1

IMMANUEL

"His NAME shall be called Immanuel, . . . God with us."

"The light of the knowledge of the glory of God" is seen "in the face of Jesus Christ." From the days of eternity the Lord Jesus Christ was one with the Father; He was "the image of God," the image of His greatness and majesty, "the outshining of His glory." It was to manifest this glory that He came to our world. To this sin-darkened earth He came to reveal the light of God's love,—to be "God with us." Therefore it was prophesied of Him, "His name shall be called Immanuel."

By coming to dwell with us, Jesus was to reveal God both to men and to angels. He was the Word of God,—God's thought made audible. In His prayer for His disciples He says, "I have declared unto them Thy name,"—"merciful and gracious, long-suffering, and abundant in goodness and truth,"—"that the love wherewith Thou hast loved Me may be in them, and I in them." But not alone for His earthborn children was this revelation given. Our little world is the lesson book of the universe. God's wonderful purpose of grace, the mystery of redeeming love, is the theme into which "angels desire to look," and it will be their study throughout endless ages. Both the redeemed and the unfallen beings will find in the cross of Christ their science and their song. It will be seen that the glory shining in the face of Jesus is the glory of self-sacrificing love. In the light from Calvary it will be seen that the law of self-renouncing love is the law of life for earth and heaven; that the love which "seeketh not her own" has its source in the heart of God; and that in the meek and lowly One is manifested the character of Him who dwelleth in the light which no man can approach unto.

In the beginning, God was revealed in all the works of creation. It was Christ that spread the heavens, and laid

1

the foundations of the earth. It was His hand that hung the worlds in space, and fashioned the flowers of the field. "His strength setteth fast the mountains." "The sea is His, and He made it." Ps. 65:6; 95:5. It was He that filled the earth with beauty, and the air with song. And upon all things in earth, and air, and sky, He wrote the message of the Father's love.

Now sin has marred God's perfect work, yet that hand-writing remains. Even now all created things declare the glory of His excellence. There is nothing, save the selfish heart of man, that lives unto itself. No bird that cleaves the air, no animal that moves upon the ground, but minis-ters to some other life. There is no leaf of the forest, or lowly blade of grass, but has its ministry. Every tree and shrub and leaf pours forth that element of life without which neither man nor animal could live; and man and an-imal, in turn, minister to the life of tree and shrub and leaf. The flowers breathe fragrance and unfold their beau-ty in blessing to the world. The sun sheds its light to glad-den a thousand worlds. The ocean, itself the source of all our springs and fountains, receives the streams from every land, but takes to give. The mists ascending from its bosom fall in showers to water the earth, that it may bring forth and bud.

The angels of glory find their joy in giving,—giving love and tireless watchcare to souls that are fallen and unholy. Heavenly beings woo the hearts of men; they bring to this dark world light from the courts above; by gentle and pa-tient ministry they move upon the human spirit, to bring the lost into a fellowship with Christ which is even closer than they themselves can know.

But turning from all lesser representations, we behold God in Jesus. Looking unto Jesus we see that it is the glory of our God to give. "I do nothing of Myself," said Christ; "the living Father hath sent Me, and I live by the Father." "I seek not Mine own glory," but the glory of Him that sent Me. John 8:28; 6:57; 8:50; 7:18. In these words is set forth the great principle which is the law of life for the universe. All things Christ received from God, but He took to give. So in the heavenly courts, in His min-istry for all created beings: through the beloved Son, the Father's life flows out to all; through the Son it returns, in praise and joyous service, a tide of love, to the great Source of all. And thus through Christ the circuit of beneficence is complete, representing the character of the great Giver, the law of life.

In heaven itself this law was broken. Sin originated in self-seeking. Lucifer, the covering cherub, desired to be first in heaven. He sought to gain control of heavenly beings, to draw them away from their Creator, and to win their homage to himself. Therefore he misrepresented God, attributing to Him the desire for self-exaltation. With his own evil characteristics he sought to invest the loving Creator. Thus he deceived angels. Thus he deceived men. He led them to doubt the word of God, and to distrust His goodness. Because God is a God of justice and terrible majesty, Satan caused them to look upon Him as severe and unforgiving. Thus he drew men to join him in rebellion against God, and the night of woe settled down upon the world.

The earth was dark through misapprehension of God. That the gloomy shadows might be lightened, that the world might be brought back to God, Satan's deceptive power was to be broken. This could not be done by force. The exercise of force is contrary to the principles of God's government; He desires only the service of love; and love cannot be commanded; it cannot be won by force or authority. Only by love is love awakened. To know God is to love Him; His character must be manifested in contrast to the character of Satan. This work only one Being in all the universe could do. Only He who knew the height and depth of the love of God could make it known. Upon the world's dark night the Sun of Righteousness must rise, "with healing in His wings." Mal. 4:2.

The plan for our redemption was not an afterthought, a plan formulated after the fall of Adam. It was a revelation of "the mystery which hath been kept in silence through times eternal." Rom. 16:25, R. V. It was an unfolding of the principles that from eternal ages have been the foundation of God's throne. From the beginning, God and Christ knew of the apostasy of Satan, and of the fall of man through the deceptive power of the apostate. God did not ordain that sin should exist, but He foresaw its existence, and made provision to meet the terrible emergency. So great was His love for the world, that He covenanted to give His only-begotten Son, "that whosoever believeth in Him should not perish, but have everlasting life." John 3:16.

Lucifer had said, "I will exalt my throne above the stars

of God; . . . I will be like the Most High." Isa. 14:13, 14. But Christ, "being in the form of God, counted it not a thing to be grasped to be on an equality with God, but emptied Himself, taking the form of a servant, being made in the likeness of men." Phil. 2:6, 7, R. V., margin.

This was a voluntary sacrifice. Jesus might have remained at the Father's side. He might have retained the glory of heaven, and the homage of the angels. But He chose to give back the scepter into the Father's hands, and to step down from the throne of the universe, that He might bring light to the benighted, and life to the perishing.

Nearly two thousand years ago, a voice of mysterious import was heard in heaven, from the throne of God, "Lo, I come." "Sacrifice and offering Thou wouldest not, but a body hast Thou prepared Me. . . . Lo, I come (in the volume of the Book it is written of Me,) to do Thy will, O God." Heb. 10:5-7. In these words is announced the fulfillment of the purpose that had been hidden from eternal ages. Christ was about to visit our world, and to become incarnate. He says, "A body hast Thou prepared Me." Had He appeared with the glory that was His with the Father before the world was, we could not have endured the light of His presence. That we might behold it and not be destroyed, the manifestation of His glory was shrouded. His divinity was veiled with humanity,—the invisible glory in the visible human form.

This great purpose had been shadowed forth in types and symbols. The burning bush, in which Christ appeared to Moses, revealed God. The symbol chosen for the representation of the Deity was a lowly shrub, that seemingly had no attractions. This enshrined the Infinite. The all-merciful God shrouded His glory in a most humble type, that Moses could look upon it and live. So in the pillar of cloud by day and the pillar of fire by night, God communicated with Israel, revealing to men His will, and imparting to them His grace. God's glory was subdued, and His majesty veiled, that the weak vision of finite men might behold it. So Christ was to come in "the body of our humiliation" (Phil. 3:21, R. V.), "in the likeness of men." In the eyes of the world He possessed no beauty that they should desire Him; yet He was the incarnate God, the light of heaven and earth. His glory was veiled, His greatness and majesty were hidden, that He might draw near to sorrowful, tempted men.

God commanded Moses for Israel, "Let them make Me a sanctuary; that I may dwell among them" (Ex. 25:8), and He abode in the sanctuary, in the midst of His people. Through all their weary wandering in the desert, the symbol of His presence was with them. So Christ set up His tabernacle in the midst of our human encampment. He pitched His tent by the side of the tents of men, that He might dwell among us, and make us familiar with His divine character and life. "The Word became flesh, and tabernacled among us (and we beheld His glory, glory as of the Only Begotten from the Father), full of grace and truth." John 1:14, R. V., margin.

Since Jesus came to dwell with us, we know that God is acquainted with our trials, and sympathizes with our griefs. Every son and daughter of Adam may understand that our Creator is the friend of sinners. For in every doctrine of grace, every promise of joy, every deed of love, every divine attraction presented in the Saviour's life on earth, we see "God with us."

Satan represents God's law of love as a law of selfishness. He declares that it is impossible for us to obey its precepts. The fall of our first parents, with all the woe that has resulted, he charges upon the Creator, leading men to look upon God as the author of sin, and suffering, and death. Jesus was to unveil this deception. As one of us He was to give an example of obedience. For this He took upon Himself our nature, and passed through our experiences. "In all things it behooved Him to be made like unto His brethren." Heb. 2:17. If we had to bear anything which Jesus did not endure, then upon this point Satan would represent the power of God as insufficient for us. Therefore Jesus was "in all points tempted like as we are." Heb. 4:15. He endured every trial to which we are subject. And He exercised in His own behalf no power that is not freely offered to us. As man, He met temptation, and overcame in the strength given Him from God. He says, "I delight to do Thy will, O My God: yea, Thy law is within My heart." Ps. 40:8. As He went about doing good, and healing all who were afflicted by Satan, He made plain to men the character of God's law and the nature of His service. His life testifies that it is possible for us also to obey the law of God.

By His humanity, Christ touched humanity; by His divinity, He lays hold upon the throne of God. As the Son of man, He gave us an example of obedience; as the Son of God, He gives us power to obey. It was Christ who from the bush on Mount Horeb spoke to Moses saying, "I AM THAT I AM. . . . Thus shalt thou say unto the children of Israel, I AM hath sent me unto you." Ex. 3:14. This was the pledge of Israel's deliverance. So when He came "in the likeness of men," He declared Himself the I AM. The Child of Bethlehem, the meek and lowly Saviour, is God "manifest in the flesh." 1 Tim. 3:16. And to us He says: "I AM the Good Shepherd." "I AM the living Bread." "I AM the Way, the Truth, and the Life." "All power is given unto Me in heaven and in earth." John 10:11; 6:51; 14:6; Matt. 28:18. I AM the assurance of every promise. I AM; be not afraid. "God with us" is the surety of our deliverance from sin, the assurance of our power to obey the law of heaven.

In stooping to take upon Himself humanity, Christ revealed a character the opposite of the character of Satan. But He stepped still lower in the path of humiliation. "Being found in fashion as a man, He humbled Himself, and became obedient unto death, even the death of the cross." Phil. 2:8. As the high priest laid aside his gorgeous pontifical robes, and officiated in the white linen dress of the common priest, so Christ took the form of a servant, and offered sacrifice, Himself the priest, Himself the victim. "He was wounded for our transgressions, He was bruised for our iniquities: the chastisement of our peace was upon Him." Isa. 53:5.

Christ was treated as we deserve, that we might be treated as He deserves. He was condemned for our sins, in which He had no share, that we might be justified by His righteousness, in which we had no share. He suffered the death which was ours, that we might receive the life which was His. "With His stripes we are healed."

By His life and His death, Christ has achieved even more than recovery from the ruin wrought through sin. It was Satan's purpose to bring about an eternal separation between God and man; but in Christ we become more closely united to God than if we had never fallen. In taking our nature, the Saviour has bound Himself to humanity by a tie that is never to be broken. Through the eternal ages He is linked with us. "God so loved the world, that He gave His only-begotten Son." John 3:16. He gave Him not only to bear our sins, and to die as our sacrifice; He gave Him to the fallen race. To assure us of His immutable counsel of peace, God gave His only-begotten Son to become one of the human family, forever to retain His human nature. This is the pledge that God will fulfill His word. "Unto *us* a child is born, unto *us* a son is given: and the government shall be upon His shoulder." God has adopted human nature in the person of His Son, and has carried the same into the highest heaven. It is the "Son of man" who shares the throne of the universe. It is the "Son of man" whose name shall be called, "Wonderful, Counselor, The mighty God, The everlasting Father, The Prince of Peace." Isa. 9:6. The I AM is the Daysman between God and humanity, laying His hand upon both. He who is "holy, harmless, undefiled, separate from sinners," is not ashamed to call us brethren. Heb. 7:26; 2:11. In Christ the family of earth and the family of heaven are bound together. Christ glorified is our brother. Heaven is enshrined in humanity, and humanity is enfolded in the bosom of Infinite Love.

Of His people God says, "They shall be as the stones of a crown, lifted up as an ensign upon His land. For how great is His goodness, and how great is His beauty!" Zech. 9:16, 17. The exaltation of the redeemed will be an eternal testimony to God's mercy. "In the ages to come," He will "show the exceeding riches of His grace in His kindness toward us through Christ Jesus." "To the intent that . . . unto the principalities and the powers in the heavenly places might be made known . . . the manifold wisdom of God, according to the eternal purpose which He purposed in Christ Jesus our Lord." Eph. 2:7; 3:10, 11, R. V.

Through Christ's redeeming work the government of God stands justified. The Omnipotent One is made known as the God of love. Satan's charges are refuted, and his character unveiled. Rebellion can never again arise. Sin can never again enter the universe. Through eternal ages all are secure from apostasy. By love's self-sacrifice, the inhabitants of earth and heaven are bound to their Creator in bonds of indissoluble union.

The work of redemption will be complete. In the place where sin abounded, God's grace much more abounds. The earth itself, the very field that Satan claims as his, is to be not only ransomed but exalted. Our little world, under the curse of sin the one dark blot in His glorious creation, will be honored above all other worlds in the universe of God. Here, where the Son of God tabernacled in humanity; where the King of glory lived and suffered and died,—here, when He shall make all things new, the tabernacle of God shall be with men, "and He will dwell with them, and they shall be His people, and God Himself shall be with them, and be their God." And through endless ages as the redeemed walk in the light of the Lord, they will praise Him for His unspeakable Gift,—

"Immanuel, God with us."

Chapter 2

NIGHT WATCHERS

THE KING OF glory stooped low to take humanity. Rude and forbidding were His earthly surroundings. His glory was veiled, that the majesty of His outward form might not become an object of attraction. He shunned all outward display. Riches, worldly honor, and human greatness can never save a soul from death; Jesus purposed that no attraction of an earthly nature should call men to His side. Only the beauty of heavenly truth must draw those who would follow Him. The character of the Messiah had long been foretold in prophecy, and He desired men to accept Him upon the testimony of the word of God.

The angels had wondered at the glorious plan of redemption. They watched to see how the people of God would receive His Son, clothed in the garb of humanity. Angels came to the land of the chosen people. Other nations were dealing in fables and worshiping false gods. To the land where the glory of God had been revealed, and the light of prophecy had shone, the angels came. They came unseen to Jerusalem, to the appointed expositors of the Sacred Oracles, and the ministers of God's house. Already to Zacharias the priest, as he ministered before the altar, the nearness of Christ's coming had been announced. Already the forerunner was born, his mission attested by miracle and prophecy. The tidings of his birth and the wonderful significance of his mission had been spread abroad. Yet Jerusalem was not preparing to welcome her Redeemer.

With amazement the heavenly messengers beheld the indifference of that people whom God had called to communicate to the world the light of sacred truth. The Jewish nation had been preserved as a witness that Christ was to

This chapter is based on Luke 2:1-20.

9

be born of the seed of Abraham and of David's line; yet they knew not that His coming was now at hand. In the temple the morning and the evening sacrifice daily pointed to the Lamb of God; yet even here was no preparation to receive Him. The priests and teachers of the nation knew not that the greatest event of the ages was about to take place. They rehearsed their meaningless prayers, and performed the rites of worship to be seen by men, but in their strife for riches and worldly honor they were not prepared for the revelation of the Messiah. The same indifference pervaded the land of Israel. Hearts selfish and world-engrossed were untouched by the joy that thrilled all heaven. Only a few were longing to behold the Unseen. To these heaven's embassy was sent.

Angels attend Joseph and Mary as they journey from their home in Nazareth to the city of David. The decree of imperial Rome for the enrollment of the peoples of her vast dominion has extended to the dwellers among the hills of Galilee. As in old time Cyrus was called to the throne of the world's empire that he might set free the captives of the Lord, so Caesar Augustus is made the agent for the fulfillment of God's purpose in bringing the mother of Jesus to Bethlehem. She is of the lineage of David, and the Son of David must be born in David's city. Out of Bethlehem, said the prophet, "shall He come forth . . . that is to be ruler in Israel; whose goings forth have been from of old, from the days of eternity." Micah 5:2, margin. But in the city of their royal line, Joseph and Mary are unrecognized and unhonored. Weary and homeless, they traverse the entire length of the narrow street, from the gate of the city to the eastern extremity of the town, vainly seeking a resting place for the night. There is no room for them at the crowded inn. In a rude building where the beasts are sheltered, they at last find refuge, and here the Redeemer of the world is born.

Men know it not, but the tidings fill heaven with rejoicing. With a deeper and more tender interest the holy beings from the world of light are drawn to the earth. The whole world is brighter for His presence. Above the hills of Bethlehem are gathered an innumerable throng of angels. They wait the signal to declare the glad news to the world. Had the leaders in Israel been true to their trust, they might have shared the joy of heralding the birth of Jesus. But now they are passed by.

God declares, "I will pour water upon him that is

thirsty, and floods upon the dry ground." "Unto the upright there ariseth light in the darkness." Isa. 44:3; Ps. 112:4. To those who are seeking for light, and who accept it with gladness, the bright rays from the throne of God will shine.

In the fields where the boy David had led his flock, shepherds were still keeping watch by night. Through the silent hours they talked together of the promised Saviour, and prayed for the coming of the King to David's throne. "And, lo, the angel of the Lord came upon them, and the glory of the Lord shone round about them: and they were sore afraid. And the angel said unto them, Fear not: for, behold, I bring you good tidings of great joy, which shall be to all people. For unto you is born this day in the city of David a Saviour, which is Christ the Lord."

At these words, visions of glory fill the minds of the listening shepherds. The Deliverer has come to Israel! Power, exaltation, triumph, are associated with His coming. But the angel must prepare them to recognize their Saviour in poverty and humiliation. "This shall be a sign unto you," he says; "Ye shall find the babe wrapped in swaddling clothes, lying in a manger."

The heavenly messenger had quieted their fears. He had told them how to find Jesus. With tender regard for their human weakness, he had given them time to become accustomed to the divine radiance. Then the joy and glory could no longer be hidden. The whole plain was lighted up with the bright shining of the hosts of God. Earth was hushed, and heaven stooped to listen to the song,—

> "Glory to God in the highest,
> And on earth peace, good will toward men."

Oh that today the human family could recognize that song! The declaration then made, the note then struck, will swell to the close of time, and resound to the ends of the earth. When the Sun of Righteousness shall arise, with healing in His wings, that song will be re-echoed by the voice of a great multitude, as the voice of many waters, saying, "Alleluia: for the Lord God omnipotent reigneth." Rev. 19:6.

As the angels disappeared, the light faded away, and the shadows of night once more fell on the hills of Bethlehem. But the brightest picture ever beheld by human eyes remained in the memory of the shepherds. "And it came to pass, as the angels were gone away from them into heaven, the shepherds said one to another, Let us now go even unto Bethlehem, and see this thing which is come to pass, which the Lord hath made known unto us. And they came with haste, and found Mary, and Joseph, and the babe lying in a manger."

Departing with great joy, they made known the things they had seen and heard. "And all they that heard it wondered at those things which were told them by the shepherds. But Mary kept all these things, and pondered them in her heart. And the shepherds returned, glorifying and praising God."

Heaven and earth are no wider apart today than when shepherds listened to the angels' song. Humanity is still as much the object of heaven's solicitude as when common men of common occupations met angels at noonday, and talked with the heavenly messengers in the vineyards and the fields. To us in the common walks of life, heaven may be very near. Angels from the courts above will attend the steps of those who come and go at God's command.

The story of Bethlehem is an exhaustless theme. In it is hidden "the depth of the riches both of the wisdom and knowledge of God," Rom. 11:33. We marvel at the Saviour's sacrifice in exchanging the throne of heaven for the manger, and the companionship of adoring angels for the beasts of the stall. Human pride and self-sufficiency stand rebuked in His presence. Yet this was but the beginning of His wonderful condescension. It would have been an almost infinite humiliation for the Son of God to take man's nature, even when Adam stood in his innocence in Eden. But Jesus accepted humanity when the race had been weakened by four thousand years of sin. Like every child of Adam He accepted the results of the working of the great law of heredity. What these results were is shown in the history of His earthly ancestors. He came with such a heredity to share our sorrows and temptations, and to give us the example of a sinless life.

Satan in heaven had hated Christ for His position in the courts of God. He hated Him the more when he himself was dethroned. He hated Him who pledged Himself to redeem a race of sinners. Yet into the world where Satan claimed dominion God permitted His Son to come, a helpless babe, subject to the weakness of humanity. He permitted Him to meet life's peril in common with every human soul, to fight the battle as every child of humanity must fight it, at the risk of failure and eternal loss.

The heart of the human father yearns over his son. He looks into the face of his little child, and trembles at the thought of life's peril. He longs to shield his dear one from Satan's power, to hold him back from temptation and conflict. To meet a bitterer conflict and a more fearful risk, God gave His only-begotten Son, that the path of life might be made sure for our little ones. "Herein is love." Wonder, O heavens! and be astonished, O earth!

Chapter 3

THE DEDICATION

ABOUT FORTY days after the birth of Christ, Joseph and Mary took Him to Jerusalem, to present Him to the Lord, and to offer sacrifice. This was according to the Jewish law, and as man's substitute Christ must conform to the law in every particular. He had already been subjected to the rite of circumcision, as a pledge of His obedience to the law.

As an offering for the mother, the law required a lamb of the first year for a burnt offering, and a young pigeon or a turtledove for a sin offering. But the law provided that if the parents were too poor to bring a lamb, a pair of turtledoves or two young pigeons, one for a burnt offering, the other for a sin offering, might be accepted.

The offerings presented to the Lord were to be without blemish. These offerings represented Christ, and from this it is evident that Jesus Himself was free from physical deformity. He was the "lamb without blemish and without spot." 1 Peter 1:19. His physical structure was not marred by any defect; His body was strong and healthy. And throughout His lifetime He lived in conformity to nature's laws. Physically as well as spiritually, He was an example of what God designed all humanity to be through obedience to His laws.

The dedication of the first-born had its origin in the earliest times. God had promised to give the First-born of heaven to save the sinner. This gift was to be acknowledged in every household by the consecration of the first-born son. He was to be devoted to the priesthood, as a representative of Christ among men.

In the deliverance of Israel from Egypt, the dedication of the first-born was again commanded. While the children

This chapter is based on Luke 2:21-38.

14

of Israel were in bondage to the Egyptians, the Lord directed Moses to go to Pharaoh, king of Egypt, and say, "Thus saith the Lord, Israel is My son, even My first-born: and I say unto thee, Let My son go, that he may serve Me: and if thou refuse to let him go, behold, I will slay thy son, even thy first-born." Ex. 4:22, 23.

Moses delivered his message; but the proud king's answer was, "Who is the Lord, that I should obey His voice to let Israel go? I know not the Lord, neither will I let Israel go." Ex. 5:2. The Lord worked for His people by signs and wonders, sending terrible judgments upon Pharaoh. At length the destroying angel was bidden to slay the first-born of man and beast among the Egyptians. That the Israelites might be spared, they were directed to place upon their doorposts the blood of a slain lamb. Every house was to be marked, that when the angel came on his mission of death, he might pass over the homes of the Israelites.

After sending this judgment upon Egypt, the Lord said to Moses, "Sanctify unto Me all the first-born, . . . both of man and of beast: it is Mine;" "for on the day that I smote all the first-born in the land of Egypt I hallowed unto Me all the first-born in Israel, both man and beast: Mine shall they be: I am the Lord." Ex. 13:2; Num. 3:13. After the tabernacle service was established, the Lord chose the tribe of Levi in the place of the first-born of all Israel to minister in the sanctuary. But the first-born were still to be regarded as the Lord's, and were to be bought back by a ransom.

Thus the law for the presentation of the first-born was made particularly significant. While it was a memorial of the Lord's wonderful deliverance of the children of Israel, it prefigured a greater deliverance, to be wrought out by the only-begotten Son of God. As the blood sprinkled on the doorposts had saved the first-born of Israel, so the blood of Christ has power to save the world.

What meaning then was attached to Christ's presentation! But the priest did not see through the veil; he did not read the mystery beyond. The presentation of infants was a common scene. Day after day the priest received the redemption money as the babes were presented to the Lord. Day after day he went through the routine of his work, giving little heed to the parents or children, unless he saw some indication of the wealth or high rank of the parents. Joseph and Mary were poor; and when they came with their child, the priests saw only a man and woman dressed as Galileans, and in the humblest garments. There was nothing in their appearance to attract attention, and they presented only the offering made by the poorer classes.

The priest went through the ceremony of his official work. He took the child in his arms, and held it up before the altar. After handing it back to its mother, he inscribed the name "Jesus" on the roll of the first-born. Little did he think, as the babe lay in his arms, that it was the Majesty of heaven, the King of glory. The priest did not think that this babe was the One of whom Moses had written, "A Prophet shall the Lord your God raise up unto you of your brethren, like unto me; Him shall ye hear in all things whatsoever He shall say unto you." Acts 3:22. He did not think that this babe was He whose glory Moses had asked to see. But One greater than Moses lay in the priest's arms; and when he enrolled the child's name, he was enrolling the name of One who was the foundation of the whole Jewish economy. That name was to be its death warrant; for the system of sacrifices and offerings was waxing old; the type had almost reached its antitype, the shadow its substance.

The Shekinah had departed from the sanctuary, but in the Child of Bethlehem was veiled the glory before which angels bow. This unconscious babe was the promised seed, to whom the first altar at the gate of Eden pointed. This was Shiloh, the peace giver. It was He who declared Himself to Moses as the I AM. It was He who in the pillar of cloud and of fire had been the guide of Israel. This was He whom seers had long foretold. He was the Desire of all nations, the Root and the Offspring of David, and the Bright and Morning Star. The name of that helpless little babe, inscribed in the roll of Israel, declaring Him our brother, was the hope of fallen humanity. The child for whom the redemption money had been paid was He who was to pay the ransom for the sins of the whole world. He was the true "high priest over the house of God," the head of "an unchangeable priesthood," the intercessor at "the right hand of the Majesty on high." Heb. 10:21; 7:24; 1:3.

Spiritual things are spiritually discerned. In the temple the Son of God was dedicated to the work He had come to do. The priest looked upon Him as he would upon any other child. But though he neither saw nor felt anything unusual, God's act in giving His Son to the world was acknowledged. This occasion did not pass without some recognition of Christ. "There was a man in Jerusalem, whose name was Simeon; and the same man was just and devout, waiting for the Consolation of Israel: and the Holy Ghost was upon him. And it was revealed unto him by the Holy Ghost, that he should not see death, before he had seen the Lord's Christ."

As Simeon enters the temple, he sees a family presenting their first-born son before the priest. Their appearance bespeaks poverty; but Simeon understands the warnings of the Spirit, and he is deeply impressed that the infant being presented to the Lord is the Consolation of Israel, the One he has longed to see. To the astonished priest, Simeon appears like a man enraptured. The child has been returned to Mary, and he takes it in his arms and presents it to God, while a joy that he has never before felt enters his soul. As he lifts the infant Saviour toward heaven, he says, "Lord, now lettest Thou Thy servant depart in peace, according to Thy word: for mine eyes have seen Thy salvation, which Thou hast prepared before the face of all people; a light to lighten the Gentiles, and the glory of Thy people Israel."

The spirit of prophecy was upon this man of God, and while Joseph and Mary stood by, wondering at his words, he blessed them, and said unto Mary, "Behold, this child is set for the fall and rising again of many in Israel; and for a sign which shall be spoken against; (yea, a sword shall pierce through thy own soul also,) that the thoughts of many hearts may be revealed."

Anna also, a prophetess, came in and confirmed Simeon's testimony concerning Christ. As Simeon spoke, her face lighted up with the glory of God, and she poured out her heartfelt thanks that she had been permitted to behold Christ the Lord.

These humble worshipers had not studied the prophecies in vain. But those who held positions as rulers and priests in Israel, though they too had before them the precious utterances of prophecy, were not walking in the way of the Lord, and their eyes were not open to behold the Light of life.

So it is still. Events upon which the attention of all heaven is centered are undiscerned, their very occurrence is unnoticed, by religious leaders, and worshipers in the house of God. Men acknowledge Christ in history, while they turn away from the living Christ. Christ in His word

calling to self-sacrifice, in the poor and suffering who plead
for relief, in the righteous cause that involves poverty and
toil and reproach, is no more readily received today than
He was eighteen hundred years ago.

Mary pondered the broad and far-reaching prophecy of
Simeon. As she looked upon the child in her arms, and recalled the words spoken by the shepherds of Bethlehem,
she was full of grateful joy and bright hope. Simeon's
words called to her mind the prophetic utterances of
Isaiah: "There shall come forth a rod out of the stem of
Jesse, and a Branch shall grow out of his roots: and the
Spirit of the Lord shall rest upon Him, the spirit of wisdom and understanding, the spirit of counsel and might,
the spirit of knowledge and of the fear of the Lord. . . .
And righteousness shall be the girdle of His loins, and
faithfulness the girdle of His reins." "The people that
walked in darkness have seen a great light: they that dwell
in the land of the shadow of death, upon them hath the
light shined. . . . For unto us a child is born, unto us a son
is given: and the government shall be upon His shoulder:
and His name shall be called Wonderful, Counselor, The
mighty God, The everlasting Father, the Prince of Peace."
Isa. 11:1-5; 9:2-6.

Yet Mary did not understand Christ's mission. Simeon
had prophesied of Him as a light to lighten the Gentiles,
as well as a glory to Israel. Thus the angels had announced
the Saviour's birth as tidings of joy to all peoples. God was
seeking to correct the narrow, Jewish conception of the
Messiah's work. He desired men to behold Him, not merely as the deliverer of Israel, but as the Redeemer of the
world. But many years must pass before even the mother
of Jesus would understand His mission.

Mary looked forward to the Messiah's reign on David's
throne, but she saw not the baptism of suffering by which
it must be won. Through Simeon it is revealed that the
Messiah is to have no unobstructed passage through the
world. In the words to Mary, "A sword shall pierce
through thy own soul also," God in His tender mercy gives
to the mother of Jesus an intimation of the anguish that already for His sake she had begun to bear.

"Behold," Simeon had said, "this child is set for the fall
and rising again of many in Israel; and for a sign which
shall be spoken against." They must fall who would rise
again. We must fall upon the Rock and be broken before
we can be uplifted in Christ. Self must be dethroned, pride

must be humbled, if we would know the glory of the spiritual kingdom. The Jews would not accept the honor that is reached through humiliation. Therefore they would not receive their Redeemer. He was a sign that was spoken against.

"That the thoughts of many hearts may be revealed." In the light of the Saviour's life, the hearts of all, even from the Creator to the prince of darkness, are revealed. Satan has represented God as selfish and oppressive, as claiming all, and giving nothing, as requiring the service of His creatures for His own glory, and making no sacrifice for their good. But the gift of Christ reveals the Father's heart. It testifies that the thoughts of God toward us are "thoughts of peace, and not of evil." Jer. 29:11. It declares that while God's hatred of sin is as strong as death, His love for the sinner is stronger than death. Having undertaken our redemption, He will spare nothing, however dear, which is necessary to the completion of His work. No truth essential to our salvation is withheld, no miracle of mercy is neglected, no divine agency is left unemployed. Favor is heaped upon favor, gift upon gift. The whole treasury of heaven is open to those He seeks to save. Having collected the riches of the universe, and laid open the resources of infinite power, He gives them all into the hands of Christ, and says, All these are for man. Use these gifts to convince him that there is no love greater than Mine in earth or heaven. His greatest happiness will be found in loving Me.

At the cross of Calvary, love and selfishness stood face to face. Here was their crowning manifestation. Christ had lived only to comfort and bless, and in putting Him to death, Satan manifested the malignity of his hatred against God. He made it evident that the real purpose of his rebellion was to dethrone God, and to destroy Him through whom the love of God was shown.

By the life and the death of Christ, the thoughts of men also are brought to view. From the manger to the cross, the life of Jesus was a call to self-surrender, and to fellowship in suffering. It unveiled the purposes of men. Jesus came with the truth of heaven, and all who were listening to the voice of the Holy Spirit were drawn to Him. The worshipers of self belonged to Satan's kingdom. In their attitude toward Christ, all would show on which side they stood. And thus everyone passes judgment on himself.

In the day of final judgment, every lost soul will under-

stand the nature of his own rejection of truth. The cross
will be presented, and its real bearing will be seen by every
mind that has been blinded by transgression. Before the vision of Calvary with its mysterious Victim, sinners will
stand condemned. Every lying excuse will be swept away.
Human apostasy will appear in its heinous character. Men
will see what their choice has been. Every question of
truth and error in the long-standing controversy will then
have been made plain. In the judgment of the universe,
God will stand clear of blame for the existence or continu-
ance of evil. It will be demonstrated that the divine decrees
are not accessory to sin. There was no defect in God's
government, no cause for disaffection. When the thoughts
of all hearts shall be revealed, both the loyal and the rebel-
lious will unite in declaring, "Just and true are Thy ways,
Thou King of saints. Who shall not fear Thee, O Lord,
and glorify Thy name? . . . for Thy judgments are made
manifest." Rev. 15:3, 4.

Chapter 4

KINGS FROM THE EAST

"Now WHEN Jesus was born in Bethlehem of Judea in the days of Herod the king, behold, there came wise men from the East to Jerusalem, saying, Where is He that is born King of the Jews? for we have seen His star in the East, and are come to worship Him."

The wise men from the East were philosophers. They belonged to a large and influential class that included men of noble birth, and comprised much of the wealth and learning of their nation. Among these were many who imposed on the credulity of the people. Others were upright men who studied the indications of Providence in nature, and who were honored for their integrity and wisdom. Of this character were the wise men who came to Jesus.

The light of God is ever shining amid the darkness of heathenism. As these magi studied the starry heavens, and sought to fathom the mystery hidden in their bright paths, they beheld the glory of the Creator. Seeking clearer knowledge, they turned to the Hebrew Scriptures. In their own land were treasured prophetic writings that predicted the coming of a divine teacher. Balaam belonged to the magicians, though at one time a prophet of God; by the Holy Spirit he had foretold the prosperity of Israel and the appearing of the Messiah; and his prophecies had been handed down by tradition from century to century. But in the Old Testament the Saviour's advent was more clearly revealed. The magi learned with joy that His coming was near, and that the whole world was to be filled with a knowledge of the glory of the Lord.

The wise men had seen a mysterious light in the heavens upon that night when the glory of God flooded the hills of Bethlehem. As the light faded, a luminous star appeared, and lingered in the sky. It was not a fixed star nor a planet, and the phenomenon excited the keenest interest. That star was a distant company of shining angels, but of this the wise men were ignorant. Yet they were impressed that the star was of special import to them. They consulted priests and philosophers, and searched the scrolls of the ancient records. The prophecy of Balaam had declared, "There shall come a Star out of Jacob, and a Scepter shall rise out of Israel." Num. 24:17. Could this strange star have been sent as a harbinger of the Promised One? The magi had welcomed the light of heaven-sent truth; now it was shed upon them in brighter rays. Through dreams they were instructed to go in search of the newborn Prince.

As by faith Abraham went forth at the call of God, "not knowing whither he went" (Heb. 11:8); as by faith Israel followed the pillar of cloud to the Promised Land, so did these Gentiles go forth to find the promised Saviour. The Eastern country abounded in precious things, and the magi did not set out empty-handed. It was the custom to offer presents as an act of homage to princes or other personages of rank, and the richest gifts the land afforded were borne as an offering to Him in whom all the families of the earth were to be blessed. It was necessary to journey by night in order to keep the star in view; but the travelers beguiled the hours by repeating traditional sayings and prophetic utterances concerning the One they sought. At every pause for rest they searched the prophecies; and the conviction deepened that they were divinely guided. While they had the star before them as an outward sign, they had also the inward evidence of the Holy Spirit, which was impressing their hearts, and inspiring them with hope. The journey, though long, was a happy one to them.

They have reached the land of Israel, and are descending the Mount of Olives, with Jerusalem in sight, when, lo, the star that has guided them all the weary way rests above the temple, and after a season fades from their view. With eager steps they press onward, confidently expecting the Messiah's birth to be the joyful burden of every tongue. But their inquiries are in vain. Entering the holy city, they repair to the temple. To their amazement they find none who seem to have a knowledge of the newborn king. Their questions call forth no expressions of joy, but rather of surprise and fear, not unmingled with contempt.

The priests are rehearsing traditions. They extol their religion and their own piety, while they denounce the Greeks and Romans as heathen, and sinners above others. The wise men are not idolaters, and in the sight of God they stand far higher than do these, His professed worshipers; yet they are looked upon by the Jews as heathen. Even among the appointed guardians of the Holy Oracles their eager questionings touch no chord of sympathy.

The arrival of the magi was quickly noised throughout Jerusalem. Their strange errand created an excitement among the people, which penetrated to the palace of King Herod. The wily Edomite was aroused at the intimation of a possible rival. Countless murders had stained his pathway to the throne. Being of alien blood, he was hated by the people over whom he ruled. His only security was the favor of Rome. But this new Prince had a higher claim. He was born to the kingdom.

Herod suspected the priests of plotting with the strangers to excite a popular tumult and unseat him from the throne. He concealed his mistrust, however, determined to thwart their schemes by superior cunning. Summoning the chief priests and the scribes, he questioned them as to the teaching of their sacred books in regard to the place of the Messiah's birth.

This inquiry from the usurper of the throne, and made at the request of strangers, stung the pride of the Jewish teachers. The indifference with which they turned to the rolls of prophecy enraged the jealous tyrant. He thought them trying to conceal their knowledge of the matter. With an authority they dared not disregard, he commanded them to make close search, and to declare the birthplace of their expected King. "And they said unto him, In Bethlehem of Judea: for thus it is written by the prophet,

"And thou Bethlehem, land of Judah,
    Art in nowise least among the princes of Judah:
    For out of thee shall come forth a governor,
    Which shall be shepherd of My people Israel."

                                                R. V.

Herod now invited the magi to a private interview. A tempest of wrath and fear was raging in his heart, but he preserved a calm exterior, and received the strangers courteously. He inquired at what time the star had appeared, and professed to hail with joy the intimation of the birth of Christ. He bade his visitors, "Search diligently for the young child; and when ye have found Him, bring me word again, that I may come and worship Him also." So saying, he dismissed them to go on their way to Bethlehem.

The priests and elders of Jerusalem were not as ignorant concerning the birth of Christ as they pretended. The report of the angels' visit to the shepherds had been brought to Jerusalem, but the rabbis had treated it as unworthy of their notice. They themselves might have found Jesus, and might have been ready to lead the magi to His birthplace; but instead of this, the wise men came to call their attention to the birth of the Messiah. "Where is He that is born King of the Jews?" they said; "for we have seen His star in the East, and are come to worship Him."

Now pride and envy closed the door against the light. If the reports brought by the shepherds and the wise men were credited, they would place the priests and rabbis in a most unenviable position, disproving their claim to be the exponents of the truth of God. These learned teachers would not stoop to be instructed by those whom they termed heathen. It could not be, they said, that God had passed them by, to communicate with ignorant shepherds or uncircumcised Gentiles. They determined to show their contempt for the reports that were exciting King Herod and all Jerusalem. They would not even go to Bethlehem to see whether these things were so. And they led the people to regard the interest in Jesus as a fanatical excitement. Here began the rejection of Christ by the priests and rabbis. From this point their pride and stubbornness grew into a settled hatred of the Saviour. While God was opening the door to the Gentiles, the Jewish leaders were closing the door to themselves.

The wise men departed alone from Jerusalem. The shadows of night were falling as they left the gates, but to their great joy they again saw the star, and were directed to Bethlehem. They had received no such intimation of the lowly estate of Jesus as was given to the shepherds. After the long journey they had been disappointed by the indifference of the Jewish leaders, and had left Jerusalem less confident than when they entered the city. At Bethlehem they found no royal guard stationed to protect the newborn King. None of the world's honored men were in attendance. Jesus was cradled in a manger. His parents, uneducated peasants, were His only guardians. Could this be He of whom it was written, that He should "raise up the tribes of Jacob," and "restore the preserved of Israel;" that

He should be "a light to the Gentiles," and for "salvation unto the end of the earth"? Isa. 49:6.

"When they were come into the house, they saw the young child with Mary His mother, and fell down, and worshiped Him." Beneath the lowly guise of Jesus, they recognized the presence of Divinity. They gave their hearts to Him as their Saviour, and then poured out their gifts,— "gold, and frankincense, and myrrh." What a faith was theirs! It might have been said of the wise men from the East, as afterward of the Roman centurion, "I have not found so great faith, no, not in Israel." Matt. 8:10.

The wise men had not penetrated Herod's design toward Jesus. When the object of their journey was accomplished, they prepared to return to Jerusalem, intending to acquaint him with their success. But in a dream they received a divine message to hold no further communication with him. Avoiding Jerusalem, they set out for their own country by another route.

In like manner Joseph received warning to flee into Egypt with Mary and the child. And the angel said, "Be thou there until I bring thee word: for Herod will seek the young child to destroy Him." Joseph obeyed without delay, setting out on the journey by night for greater security.

Through the wise men, God had called the attention of the Jewish nation to the birth of His Son. Their inquiries in Jerusalem, the popular interest excited, and even the jealousy of Herod, which compelled the attention of the priests and rabbis, directed minds to the prophecies concerning the Messiah, and to the great event that had just taken place.

Satan was bent on shutting out the divine light from the world, and he used his utmost cunning to destroy the Saviour. But He who never slumbers nor sleeps was watching over His beloved Son. He who had rained manna from heaven for Israel and had fed Elijah in the time of famine provided in a heathen land a refuge for Mary and the child Jesus. And through the gifts of the magi from a heathen country, the Lord supplied the means for the journey into Egypt and the sojourn in a land of strangers.

The magi had been among the first to welcome the Redeemer. Their gift was the first that was laid at His feet. And through that gift, what privilege of ministry was theirs! The offering from the heart that loves, God delights to honor, giving it highest efficiency in service for Him. If we have given our hearts to Jesus, we also shall bring our gifts to Him. Our gold and silver, our most precious earthly possessions, our highest mental and spiritual endowments, will be freely devoted to Him who loved us, and gave Himself for us.

Herod in Jerusalem impatiently awaited the return of the wise men. As time passed, and they did not appear, his suspicions were roused. The unwillingness of the rabbis to point out the Messiah's birthplace seemed to indicate that they had penetrated his design, and that the magi had purposely avoided him. He was maddened at the thought. Craft had failed, but there was left the resort to force. He would make an example of this child-king. Those haughty Jews should see what they might expect in their attempts to place a monarch on the throne.

Soldiers were at once sent to Bethlehem, with orders to put to death all the children of two years and under The quiet homes of the city of David witnessed those scenes of horror that, six hundred years before, had been opened to the prophet. "In Ramah was there a voice heard, lamentation, and weeping, and great mourning, Rachel weeping for her children, and would not be comforted, because they are not."

This calamity the Jews had brought upon themselves. If they had been walking in faithfulness and humility before God, He would in a signal manner have made the wrath of the king harmless to them. But they had separated themselves from God by their sins, and had rejected the Holy Spirit, which was their only shield. They had not studied the Scriptures with a desire to conform to the will of God. They had searched for prophecies which could be interpreted to exalt themselves, and to show how God despised all other nations. It was their proud boast that the Messiah was to come as a king, conquering His enemies, and treading down the heathen in His wrath. Thus they had excited the hatred of their rulers. Through their misrepresentation of Christ's mission, Satan had purposed to compass the destruction of the Saviour; but instead of this, it returned upon their own heads.

This act of cruelty was one of the last that darkened the reign of Herod. Soon after the slaughter of the innocents, he was himself compelled to yield to that doom which none can turn aside. He died a fearful death.

Joseph, who was still in Egypt, was now bidden by an angel of God to return to the land of Israel. Regarding

Jesus as the heir of David's throne, Joseph desired to make his home in Bethlehem; but learning that Archelaus reigned in Judea in his father's stead, he feared that the father's designs against Christ might be carried out by the son. Of all the sons of Herod, Archelaus most resembled him in character. Already his succession to the government had been marked by a tumult in Jerusalem, and the slaughter of thousands of Jews by the Roman guards.

Again Joseph was directed to a place of safety. He returned to Nazareth, his former home, and here for nearly thirty years Jesus dwelt, "that it might be fulfilled which was spoken by the prophets, He shall be called a Nazarene." Galilee was under the control of a son of Herod, but it had a much larger admixture of foreign inhabitants than Judea. Thus there was less interest in matters relating especially to the Jews, and the claims of Jesus would be less likely to excite the jealousy of those in power.

Such was the Saviour's reception when He came to the earth. There seemed to be no place of rest or safety for the infant Redeemer. God could not trust His beloved Son with men, even while carrying forward His work for their salvation. He commissioned angels to attend Jesus and protect Him till He should accomplish His mission on earth, and die by the hands of those whom He came to save.

Chapter 5

GROWING UP

THE CHILDHOOD and youth of Jesus were spent in a little mountain village. There was no place on earth that would not have been honored by His presence. The palaces of kings would have been privileged in receiving Him as a guest. But He passed by the homes of wealth, the courts of royalty, and the renowned seats of learning, to make His home in obscure and despised Nazareth.

Wonderful in its significance is the brief record of His early life: "The child grew, and waxed strong in spirit, filled with wisdom: and the grace of God was upon Him." In the sunlight of His Father's countenance, Jesus "increased in wisdom and stature, and in favor with God and man." Luke 2:52. His mind was active and penetrating, with a thoughtfulness and wisdom beyond His years. Yet His character was beautiful in its symmetry. The powers of mind and body developed gradually, in keeping with the laws of childhood.

As a child, Jesus manifested a peculiar loveliness of disposition. His willing hands were ever ready to serve others. He manifested a patience that nothing could disturb, and a truthfulness that would never sacrifice integrity. In principle firm as a rock, His life revealed the grace of unselfish courtesy.

With deep earnestness the mother of Jesus watched the unfolding of His powers, and beheld the impress of perfection upon His character. With delight she sought to encourage that bright, receptive mind. Through the Holy Spirit she received wisdom to co-operate with the heavenly agencies in the development of this child, who could claim only God as His Father.

From the earliest times the faithful in Israel had given

much care to the education of the youth. The Lord had directed that even from babyhood the children should be taught of His goodness and His greatness, especially as revealed in His law, and shown in the history of Israel. Song and prayer and lessons from the Scriptures were to be adapted to the opening mind. Fathers and mothers were to instruct their children that the law of God is an expression of His character, and that as they received the principles of the law into the heart, the image of God was traced on mind and soul. Much of the teaching was oral; but the youth also learned to read the Hebrew writings; and the parchment rolls of the Old Testament Scriptures were open to their study.

In the days of Christ the town or city that did not provide for the religious instruction of the young was regarded as under the curse of God. Yet the teaching had become formal. Tradition had in a great degree supplanted the Scriptures. True education would lead the youth to "seek the Lòrd, if haply they might feel after Him, and find Him." Acts 17:27. But the Jewish teachers gave their attention to matters of ceremony. The mind was crowded with material that was worthless to the learner, and that would not be recognized in the higher school of the courts above. The experience which is obtained through a personal acceptance of God's word had no place in the educational system. Absorbed in the round of externals, the students found no quiet hours to spend with God. They did not hear His voice speaking to the heart. In their search after knowledge, they turned away from the Source of wisdom. The great essentials of the service of God were neglected. The principles of the law were obscured. That which was regarded as superior education was the greatest hindrance to real development. Under the training of the rabbis the powers of the youth were repressed. Their minds became cramped and narrow.

The child Jesus did not receive instruction in the synagogue schools. His mother was His first human teacher. From her lips and from the scrolls of the prophets, He learned of heavenly things. The very words which He Himself had spoken to Moses for Israel He was now taught at His mother's knee. As He advanced from childhood to youth, He did not seek the schools of the rabbis. He needed not the education to be obtained from such sources; for God was His instructor.

The question asked during the Saviour's ministry, "How

knoweth this man letters, having never learned?" does not indicate that Jesus was unable to read, but merely that He had not received a rabbinical education. John 7:15. Since He gained knowledge as we may do, His intimate acquaintance with the Scriptures shows how diligently His early years were given to the study of God's word. And spread out before Him was the great library of God's created works. He who had made all things studied the lessons which His own hand had written in earth and sea and sky. Apart from the unholy ways of the world, He gathered stores of scientific knowledge from nature. He studied the life of plants and animals, and the life of man. From His earliest years He was possessed of one purpose; He lived to bless others. For this He found resources in nature; new ideas of ways and means flashed into His mind as He studied plant life and animal life. Continually He was seeking to draw from things seen illustrations by which to present the living oracles of God. The parables by which, during His ministry, He loved to teach His lessons of truth show how open His spirit was to the influences of nature, and how He had gathered the spiritual teaching from the surroundings of His daily life.

Thus to Jesus the significance of the word and the works of God was unfolded, as He was trying to understand the reason of things. Heavenly beings were His attendants, and the culture of holy thoughts and communings was His. From the first dawning of intelligence He was constantly growing in spiritual grace and knowledge of truth.

Every child may gain knowledge as Jesus did. As we try to become acquainted with our heavenly Father through His word, angels will draw near, our minds will be strengthened, our characters will be elevated and refined. We shall become more like our Saviour. And as we behold the beautiful and grand in nature, our affections go out after God. While the spirit is awed, the soul is invigorated by coming in contact with the Infinite through His works. Communion with God through prayer develops the mental and moral faculties, and the spiritual powers strengthen as we cultivate thoughts upon spiritual things.

The life of Jesus was a life in harmony with God. While He was a child, He thought and spoke as a child; but no trace of sin marred the image of God within Him. Yet He was not exempt from temptation. The inhabitants of Nazareth were proverbial for their wickedness. The low estimate in which they were generally held is shown by Nathanael's question, "Can there any good thing come out of Nazareth?" John 1:46. Jesus was placed where His character would be tested. It was necessary for Him to be constantly on guard in order to preserve His purity. He was subject to all the conflicts which we have to meet, that He might be an example to us in childhood, youth, and manhood.

Satan was unwearied in his efforts to overcome the Child of Nazareth. From His earliest years Jesus was guarded by heavenly angels, yet His life was one long struggle against the powers of darkness. That there should be upon the earth one life free from the defilement of evil was an offense and a perplexity to the prince of darkness. He left no means untried to ensnare Jesus. No child of humanity will ever be called to live a holy life amid so fierce a conflict with temptation as was our Saviour.

The parents of Jesus were poor, and dependent upon their daily toil. He was familiar with poverty, self-denial, and privation. This experience was a safeguard to Him. In His industrious life there were no idle moments to invite temptation. No aimless hours opened the way for corrupting associations. So far as possible, He closed the door to the tempter. Neither gain nor pleasure, applause nor censure, could induce Him to consent to a wrong act. He was wise to discern evil, and strong to resist it.

Christ was the only sinless one who ever dwelt on earth; yet for nearly thirty years He lived among the wicked inhabitants of Nazareth. This fact is a rebuke to those who think themselves dependent upon place, fortune, or prosperity, in order to live a blameless life. Temptation, poverty, adversity, is the very discipline needed to develop purity and firmness.

Jesus lived in a peasant's home, and faithfully and cheerfully acted His part in bearing the burdens of the household. He had been the Commander of heaven, and angels had delighted to fulfill His word; now He was a willing servant, a loving, obedient son. He learned a trade, and with His own hands worked in the carpenter's shop with Joseph. In the simple garb of a common laborer He walked the streets of the little town, going to and returning from His humble work. He did not employ His divine power to lessen His burdens or to lighten His toil.

As Jesus worked in childhood and youth, mind and body were developed. He did not use His physical powers recklessly, but in such a way as to keep them in health, that He might do the best work in every line. He was not willing to be defective, even in the handling of tools. He was perfect as a workman, as He was perfect in character. By His own example He taught that it is our duty to be industrious, that our work should be performed with exactness and thoroughness, and that such labor is honorable. The exercise that teaches the hands to be useful and trains the young to bear their share of life's burdens gives physical strength, and develops every faculty. All should find something to do that will be beneficial to themselves and helpful to others. God appointed work as a blessing, and only the diligent worker finds the true glory and joy of life. The approval of God rests with loving assurance upon children and youth who cheerfully take their part in the duties of the household, sharing the burdens of father and mother. Such children will go out from the home to be useful members of society.

Throughout His life on earth, Jesus was an earnest and constant worker. He expected much; therefore He attempted much. After He had entered on His ministry, He said, "I must work the works of Him that sent Me, while it is day: the night cometh, when no man can work." John 9:4. Jesus did not shirk care and responsibility, as do many who profess to be His followers. It is because they seek to evade this discipline that so many are weak and inefficient. They may possess precious and amiable traits, but they are nerveless and almost useless when difficulties are to be met or obstacles surmounted. The positiveness and energy, the solidity and strength of character, manifested in Christ are to be developed in us, through the same discipline that He endured. And the grace that He received is for us.

So long as He lived among men, our Saviour shared the lot of the poor. He knew by experience their cares and hardships, and He could comfort and encourage all humble workers. Those who have a true conception of the teaching of His life will never feel that a distinction must be made between classes, that the rich are to be honored above the worthy poor.

Jesus carried into His labor cheerfulness and tact. It requires much patience and spirituality to bring Bible religion into the home life and into the workshop, to bear the strain of worldly business, and yet keep the eye single to the glory of God. This is where Christ was a helper. He was never so full of worldly care as to have no time or thought for heavenly things. Often He expressed the gladness of His heart by singing psalms and heavenly songs. Often the dwellers in Nazareth heard His voice raised in praise and thanksgiving to God. He held communion with heaven in song; and as His companions complained of weariness from labor, they were cheered by the sweet melody from His lips. His praise seemed to banish the evil angels, and, like incense, fill the place with fragrance. The minds of His hearers were carried away from their earthly exile, to the heavenly home.

Jesus was the fountain of healing mercy for the world; and through all those secluded years at Nazareth, His life flowed out in currents of sympathy and tenderness. The aged, the sorrowing, and the sin-burdened, the children at play in their innocent joy, the little creatures of the groves, the patient beasts of burden,—all were happier for His presence. He whose word of power upheld the worlds would stoop to relieve a wounded bird. There was nothing beneath His notice, nothing to which He disdained to minister.

Thus as He grew in wisdom and stature, Jesus increased in favor with God and man. He drew the sympathy of all hearts by showing Himself capable of sympathizing with all. The atmosphere of hope and courage that surrounded Him made Him a blessing in every home. And often in the synagogue on the Sabbath day He was called upon to read the lesson from the prophets, and the hearts of the hearers thrilled as a new light shone out from the familiar words of the sacred text.

Yet Jesus shunned display. During all the years of His stay in Nazareth, He made no exhibition of His miraculous power. He sought no high position and assumed no titles. His quiet and simple life, and even the silence of the Scriptures concerning His early years, teach an important lesson. The more quiet and simple the life of the child,— the more free from artificial excitement, and the more in harmony with nature,—the more favorable is it to physical and mental vigor and to spiritual strength.

Jesus is our example. There are many who dwell with interest upon the period of His public ministry, while they pass unnoticed the teaching of His early years. But it is in His home life that He is the pattern for all children and youth. The Saviour condescended to poverty, that He might teach how closely we in a humble lot may walk with God. He lived to please, honor, and glorify His Father in the common things of life. His work began in consecrating the lowly trade of the craftsmen who toil for their daily bread. He was doing God's service just as much when laboring at the carpenter's bench as when working miracles for the multitude. And every youth who follows Christ's example of faithfulness and obedience in His lowly home may claim those words spoken of Him by the Father through the Holy Spirit, "Behold My Servant, whom I uphold; Mine Elect, in whom My soul delighteth." Isa. 42:1.

Chapter 6

COUSINS

TIDINGS OF THE wilderness prophet and his wonderful announcement spread throughout Galilee. The message reached the peasants in the remotest hill towns, and the fisher folk by the sea, and in these simple, earnest hearts found its truest response. In Nazareth it was told in the carpenter shop that had been Joseph's, and One recognized the call. His time had come. Turning from His daily toil, He bade farewell to His mother, and followed in the steps of His countrymen who were flocking to the Jordan.

Jesus and John the Baptist were cousins, and closely related by the circumstances of their birth; yet they had had no direct acquaintance with each other. The life of Jesus had been spent at Nazareth in Galilee; that of John, in the wilderness of Judea. Amid widely different surroundings they had lived in seclusion, and had had no communication with other. Providence had ordered this. No occasion was to be given for the charge that they had conspired together to support each other's claims.

John was acquainted with the events that had marked the birth of Jesus. He had heard of the visit to Jerusalem in His boyhood, and of what had passed in the school of the rabbis. He knew of His sinless life, and believed Him to be the Messiah; but of this he had no positive assurance. The fact that Jesus had for so many years remained in obscurity, giving no special evidence of His mission, gave occasion for doubt as to whether He could be the Promised One. The Baptist, however, waited in faith, believing that in God's own time all would be made plain. It had been revealed to him that the Messiah would seek baptism at his hands, and that a sign of His divine charac-

This chapter is based on Matt. 3:13-17; Mark 1:9-11; Luke 3:21, 22.

35

ter should then be given. Thus he would be enabled to present Him to the people.

When Jesus came to be baptized, John recognized in Him a purity of character that he had never before perceived in any man. The very atmosphere of His presence was holy and awe-inspiring. Among the multitudes that had gathered about him at the Jordan, John had heard dark tales of crime, and had met souls bowed down with the burden of myriad sins; but never had he come in contact with a human being from whom there breathed an influence so divine. All this was in harmony with what had been revealed to John regarding the Messiah. Yet he shrank from granting the request of Jesus. How could he, a sinner, baptize the Sinless One? And why should He who needed no repentance submit to a rite that was a confession of guilt to be washed away?

As Jesus asked for baptism, John drew back, exclaiming, "I have need to be baptized of Thee, and comest Thou to me?" With firm yet gentle authority, Jesus answered, "Suffer it to be so now: for thus it becometh us to fulfill all righteousness." And John, yielding, led the Saviour down into the Jordan, and buried Him beneath the water. "And straightway coming up out of the water," Jesus "saw the heavens opened, and the Spirit like a dove descending upon Him."

Jesus did not receive baptism as a confession of guilt on His own account. He identified Himself with sinners, taking the steps that we are to take, and doing the work that we must do. His life of suffering and patient endurance after His baptism was also an example to us.

Upon coming up out of the water, Jesus bowed in prayer on the river bank. A new and important era was opening before Him. He was now, upon a wider stage, entering on the conflict of His life. Though He was the Prince of Peace, His coming must be as the unsheathing of a sword. The kingdom He had come to establish was the opposite of that which the Jews desired. He who was the foundation of the ritual and economy of Israel would be looked upon as its enemy and destroyer. He who had proclaimed the law upon Sinai would be condemned as a transgressor. He who had come to break the power of Satan would be denounced as Beelzebub. No one upon earth had understood Him, and during His ministry He must still walk alone. Throughout His life His mother and His brothers did not comprehend His mission. Even His disciples did not understand Him. He had dwelt in eternal light, as one with God, but His life on earth must be spent in solitude.

As one with us, He must bear the burden of our guilt and woe. The Sinless One must feel the shame of sin. The peace lover must dwell with strife, the truth must abide with falsehood, purity with vileness. Every sin, every discord, every defiling lust that transgression had brought, was torture to His spirit.

Alone He must tread the path; alone He must bear the burden. Upon Him who had laid off His glory and accepted the weakness of humanity the redemption of the world must rest. He saw and felt it all, but His purpose remained steadfast. Upon His arm depended the salvation of the fallen race, and He reached out His hand to grasp the hand of Omnipotent Love.

The Saviour's glance seems to penetrate heaven as He pours out His soul in prayer. Well He knows how sin has hardened the hearts of men, and how difficult it will be for them to discern His mission, and accept the gift of salvation. He pleads with the Father for power to overcome their unbelief, to break the fetters with which Satan has enthralled them, and in their behalf to conquer the destroyer. He asks for the witness that God accepts humanity in the person of His Son.

Never before have the angels listened to such a prayer. They are eager to bear to their loved Commander a message of assurance and comfort. But no; the Father Himself will answer the petition of His Son. Direct from the throne issue the beams of His glory. The heavens are opened, and upon the Saviour's head descends a dovelike form of purest light,—fit emblem of Him, the meek and lowly One.

Of the vast throng at the Jordan, few except John discerned the heavenly vision. Yet the solemnity of the divine Presence rested upon the assembly. The people stood silently gazing upon Christ. His form was bathed in the light that ever surrounds the throne of God. His upturned face was glorified as they had never before seen the face of man. From the open heavens a voice was heard saying, "This is My beloved Son, in whom I am well pleased."

These words of confirmation were given to inspire faith in those who witnessed the scene, and to strengthen the Saviour for His mission. Notwithstanding that the sins of a guilty world were laid upon Christ, notwithstanding the humiliation of taking upon Himself our fallen nature, the voice from heaven declared Him to be the Son of the Eternal.

John had been deeply moved as he saw Jesus bowed as a suppliant, pleading with tears for the approval of the Father. As the glory of God encircled Him, and the voice from heaven was heard, John recognized the token which God had promised. He knew that it was the world's Redeemer whom he had baptized. The Holy Spirit rested upon him, and with outstretched hand pointing to Jesus, he cried, "Behold the Lamb of God, which taketh away the sin of the world."

None among the hearers, and not even the speaker himself, discerned the import of these words, "the Lamb of God." Upon Mount Moriah, Abraham had heard the question of his son, "My father, . . . where is the lamb for a burnt offering?" The father answered, "My son, God will provide Himself a lamb for a burnt offering." Gen. 22:7, 8. And in the ram divinely provided in the place of Isaac, Abraham saw a symbol of Him who was to die for the sins of men. The Holy Spirit through Isaiah, taking up the illustration, prophesied of the Saviour, "He is brought as a lamb to the slaughter," "and the Lord hath laid on Him the iniquity of us all" (Isa. 53:7, 6); but the people of Israel had not understood the lesson. Many of them regarded the sacrificial offerings much as the heathen looked upon their sacrifices,—as gifts by which they themselves might propitiate the Deity. God desired to teach them that from His own love comes the gift which reconciles them to Himself.

And the word that was spoken to Jesus at the Jordan, "This is My beloved Son, in whom I am well pleased," embraces humanity. God spoke to Jesus as our representative. With all our sins and weaknesses, we are not cast aside as worthless. "He hath made us accepted in the Beloved." Eph. 1:6. The glory that rested upon Christ is a pledge of the love of God for us. It tells us of the power of prayer, —how the human voice may reach the ear of God, and our petitions find acceptance in the courts of heaven. By sin, earth was cut off from heaven, and alienated from its communion; but Jesus has connected it again with the sphere of glory. His love has encircled man, and reached the highest heaven. The light which fell from the open portals upon the head of our Saviour will fall upon us as we pray for help to resist temptation. The voice which spoke to Jesus says to every believing soul, This is My beloved child, in whom I am well pleased.

"Beloved, now are we the sons of God, and it doth not yet appear what we shall be: but we know that, when He shall appear, we shall be like Him; for we shall see Him as He is." 1 John 3:2. Our Redeemer has opened the way so that the most sinful, the most needy, the most oppressed and despised, may find access to the Father. All may have a home in the mansions which Jesus has gone to prepare. "These things saith He that is holy, He that is true, He that hath the key of David, He that openeth, and no man shutteth; and shutteth, and no man openeth; . . . behold, I have set before thee an open door, and no man can shut it." Rev. 3:7, 8.

Chapter 7

TEMPTED

"AND JESUS being full of the Holy Ghost returned from Jordan, and was led by the Spirit into the wilderness." The words of Mark are still more significant. He says, "Immediately the Spirit driveth Him into the wilderness. And He was there in the wilderness forty days, tempted of Satan; and was with the wild beasts." "And in those days He did eat nothing."

When Jesus was led into the wilderness to be tempted, He was led by the Spirit of God. He did not invite temptation. He went to the wilderness to be alone, to contemplate His mission and work. By fasting and prayer He was to brace Himself for the bloodstained path He must travel. But Satan knew that the Saviour had gone into the wilderness, and he thought this the best time to approach Him.

Mighty issues for the world were at stake in the conflict between the Prince of light and the leader of the kingdom of darkness. After tempting man to sin, Satan claimed the earth as his, and styled himself the prince of this world. Having conformed to his own nature the father and mother of our race, he thought to establish here his empire. He declared that men had chosen him as their sovereign. Through his control of men, he held dominion over the world. Christ had come to disprove Satan's claim. As the Son of man, Christ would stand loyal to God. Thus it would be shown that Satan had not gained complete control of the human race, and that his claim to the world was false. All who desired deliverance from his power would be set free. The dominion that Adam had lost through sin would be recovered.

Since the announcement to the serpent in Eden, "I will put enmity between thee and the woman, and between thy

This chapter is based on Matt. 4:1-11; Mark 1:12, 13; Luke 4:1-13.

seed and her seed" (Gen. 3:15), Satan had known that he
did not hold absolute sway over the world. There was seen
in men the working of a power that withstood his dominion. With intense interest he watched the sacrifices offered
by Adam and his sons. In these ceremonies he discerned
a symbol of communion between earth and heaven. He set
himself to intercept this communion. He misrepresented
God, and misinterpreted the rites that pointed to the Saviour. Men were led to fear God as one who delighted in
their destruction. The sacrifices that should have revealed
His love were offered only to appease His wrath. Satan excited the evil passions of men, in order to fasten his rule
upon them. When God's written word was given, Satan
studied the prophecies of the Saviour's advent. From generation to generation he worked to blind the people to these
prophecies, that they might reject Christ at His coming.

At the birth of Jesus, Satan knew that One had come with
a divine commission to dispute his dominion. He trembled
at the angel's message attesting the authority of the newborn King. Satan well knew the position that Christ had
held in heaven as the Beloved of the Father. That the Son of
God should come to this earth as a man filled him with
amazement and with apprehension. He could not fathom
the mystery of this great sacrifice. His selfish soul could not
understand such love for the deceived race. The glory and
peace of heaven, and the joy of communion with God, were
but dimly comprehended by men; but they were well known
to Lucifer, the covering cherub. Since he had lost heaven,
he was determined to find revenge by causing others to
share his fall. This he would do by causing them to under-
value heavenly things, and to set the heart upon things of
earth.

Not without hindrance was the Commander of heaven
to win the souls of men to His kingdom. From the time
when He was a babe in Bethlehem, He was continually assailed by the evil one. The image of God was manifest in
Christ, and in the councils of Satan it was determined that
He should be overcome. No human being had come into
the world and escaped the power of the deceiver. The
forces of the confederacy of evil were set upon His track
to engage in warfare against Him, and if possible to prevail
over Him.

At the Saviour's baptism, Satan was among the witnesses. He saw the Father's glory overshadowing His Son.
He heard the voice of Jehovah testifying to the divinity of

Jesus. Ever since Adam's sin, the human race had been cut off from direct communion with God; the intercourse between heaven and earth had been through Christ; but now that Jesus had come "in the likeness of sinful flesh" (Rom. 8:3), the Father Himself spoke. He had before communicated with humanity *through* Christ; now He communicated with humanity *in* Christ. Satan had hoped that God's abhorrence of evil would bring an eternal separation between heaven and earth. But now it was manifest that the connection between God and man had been restored.

Satan saw that he must either conquer or be conquered. The issues of the conflict involved too much to be entrusted to his confederate angels. He must personally conduct the warfare. All the energies of apostasy were rallied against the Son of God. Christ was made the mark of every weapon of hell.

Many look on this conflict between Christ and Satan as having no special bearing on their own life; and for them it has little interest. But within the domain of every human heart this controversy is repeated. Never does one leave the ranks of evil for the service of God without encountering the assaults of Satan. The enticements which Christ resisted were those that we find it so difficult to withstand. They were urged upon Him in as much greater degree as His character is superior to ours. With the terrible weight of the sins of the world upon Him, Christ withstood the test upon appetite, upon the love of the world, and upon that love of display which leads to presumption. These were the temptations that overcame Adam and Eve, and that so readily overcome us.

Satan had pointed to Adam's sin as proof that God's law was unjust, and could not be obeyed. In our humanity, Christ was to redeem Adam's failure. But when Adam was assailed by the tempter, none of the effects of sin were upon him. He stood in the strength of perfect manhood, possessing the full vigor of mind and body. He was surrounded with the glories of Eden, and was in daily communion with heavenly beings. It was not thus with Jesus when He entered the wilderness to cope with Satan. For four thousand years the race had been decreasing in physical strength, in mental power, and in moral worth; and Christ took upon Him the infirmities of degenerate humanity. Only thus could He rescue man from the lowest depths of his degradation.

Many claim that it was impossible for Christ to be overcome by temptation. Then He could not have been placed in Adam's position; He could not have gained the victory that Adam failed to gain. If we have in any sense a more trying conflict than had Christ, then He would not be able to succor us. But our Saviour took humanity, with all its liabilities. He took the nature of man, with the possibility of yielding to temptation. We have nothing to bear which He has not endured.

With Christ, as with the holy pair in Eden, appetite was the ground of the first great temptation. Just where the ruin began, the work of our redemption must begin. As by the indulgence of appetite Adam fell, so by the denial of appetite Christ must overcome. "And when He had fasted forty days and forty nights, He was afterward an hungred. And when the tempter came to Him, he said, If Thou be the Son of God, command that these stones be made bread. But He answered and said, It is written, Man shall not live by bread alone, but by every word that proceedeth out of the mouth of God."

From the time of Adam to that of Christ, self-indulgence had increased the power of the appetites and passions, until they had almost unlimited control. Thus men had become debased and diseased, and of themselves it was impossible for them to overcome. In man's behalf, Christ conquered by enduring the severest test. For our sake He exercised a self-control stronger than hunger or death. And in this first victory were involved other issues that enter into all our conflicts with the powers of darkness.

When Jesus entered the wilderness, He was shut in by the Father's glory. Absorbed in communion with God, He was lifted above human weakness. But the glory departed, and He was left to battle with temptation. It was pressing upon Him every moment. His human nature shrank from the conflict that awaited Him. For forty days He fasted and prayed. Weak and emaciated from hunger, worn and haggard with mental agony, "His visage was so marred more than any man, and His form more than the sons of men." Isa. 52:14. Now was Satan's opportunity. Now he supposed that he could overcome Christ.

There came to the Saviour, as if in answer to His prayers, one in the guise of an angel from heaven. He claimed to have a commission from God to declare that Christ's fast was at an end. As God had sent an angel to

stay the hand of Abraham from offering Isaac, so, satisfied
with Christ's willingness to enter the bloodstained path,
the Father had sent an angel to deliver Him; this was the
message brought to Jesus. The Saviour was faint from
hunger, He was craving for food, when Satan came suddenly upon Him. Pointing to the stones which strewed the
desert, and which had the appearance of loaves, the
tempter said, "If Thou be the Son of God, command that
these stones be made bread."

Though he appears as an angel of light, these first words
betray his character. "If Thou be the Son of God." Here is
the insinuation of distrust. Should Jesus do what Satan
suggests, it would be an acceptance of the doubt. The
tempter plans to overthrow Christ by the same means that
were so successful with the human race in the beginning.
How artfully had Satan approached Eve in Eden! "Yea,
hath God said, Ye shall not eat of every tree of the garden?" Gen. 3:1. Thus far the tempter's words were truth;
but in his manner of speaking them there was a disguised
contempt for the words of God. There was a covert nega-
tive, a doubt of the divine truthfulness. Satan sought to in-
still into the mind of Eve the thought that God would not
do as He had said; that the withholding of such beautiful
fruit was a contradiction of His love and compassion for
man. So now the tempter seeks to inspire Christ with his
own sentiments. "If Thou be the Son of God." The words
rankle with bitterness in his mind. In the tones of his voice
is an expression of utter incredulity. Would God treat His
own Son thus? Would He leave Him in the desert with
wild beasts, without food, without companions, without
comfort? He insinuates that God never meant His Son to
be in such a state as this. "If Thou be the Son of God,"
show Thy power by relieving Thyself of this pressing
hunger. Command that this stone be made bread.

The words from heaven, "This is My beloved Son, in
whom I am well pleased" (Matt. 3:17), were still sounding in the ears of Satan. But he was determined to make
Christ disbelieve this testimony. The word of God was
Christ's assurance of His divine mission. He had come to
live as a man among men, and it was the word that declared His connection with heaven. It was Satan's purpose
to cause Him to doubt that word. If Christ's confidence in
God could be shaken, Satan knew that the victory in the
whole controversy would be his. He could overcome Jesus.
He hoped that under the force of despondency and ex-

treme hunger, Christ would lose faith in His Father, and
work a miracle in His own behalf. Had He done this, the
plan of salvation would have been broken.

When Satan and the Son of God first met in conflict,
Christ was the commander of the heavenly hosts; and
Satan, the leader of revolt in heaven, was cast out. Now
their condition is apparently reversed, and Satan makes the
most of his supposed advantage. One of the most powerful
of the angels, he says, has been banished from heaven. The
appearance of Jesus indicates that He is that fallen angel,
forsaken by God, and deserted by man. A divine being
would be able to sustain his claim by working a miracle;
"if Thou be the Son of God, command this stone that it be
made bread." Such an act of creative power, urges the
tempter, would be conclusive evidence of divinity. It
would bring the controversy to an end.

Not without a struggle could Jesus listen in silence to
the archdeceiver. But the Son of God was not to prove
His divinity to Satan, or to explain the reason of His humiliation. By conceding to the demands of the rebel, nothing for the good of man or the glory of God would be
gained. Had Christ complied with the suggestion of the
enemy, Satan would still have said, Show me a sign that I
may believe you to be the Son of God. Evidence would
have been worthless to break the power of rebellion in his
heart. And Christ was not to exercise divine power for His
own benefit. He had come to bear trial as we must do,
leaving us an example of faith and submission. Neither
here nor at any subsequent time in His earthly life did He
work a miracle in His own behalf. His wonderful works
were all for the good of others. Though Jesus recognized
Satan from the beginning, He was not provoked to enter
into controversy with him. Strengthened with the memory
of the voice from heaven, He rested in His Father's love.
He would not parley with temptation.

Jesus met Satan with the words of Scripture. "It is written," He said. In every temptation the weapon of His warfare was the word of God. Satan demanded of Christ a
miracle as a sign of His divinity. But that which is greater
than all miracles, a firm reliance upon a "Thus saith the
Lord," was a sign that could not be controverted. So long
as Christ held to this position, the tempter could gain no
advantage.

It was in the time of greatest weakness that Christ was
assailed by the fiercest temptations. Thus Satan thought to

prevail. By this policy he had gained the victory over men. When strength failed, and the will power weakened, and faith ceased to repose in God, then those who had stood long and valiantly for the right were overcome. Moses was wearied with the forty years' wandering of Israel, when for the moment his faith let go its hold upon infinite power. He failed just upon the borders of the Promised Land. So with Elijah, who had stood undaunted before King Ahab, who had faced the whole nation of Israel, with the four hundred and fifty prophets of Baal at their head. After that terrible day upon Carmel, when the false prophets had been slain, and the people had declared their allegiance to God, Elijah fled for his life before the threats of the idolatrous Jezebel. Thus Satan has taken advantage of the weakness of humanity. And he will still work in the same way. Whenever one is encompassed with clouds, perplexed by circumstances, or afflicted by poverty or distress, Satan is at hand to tempt and annoy. He attacks our weak points of character. He seeks to shake our confidence in God, who suffers such a condition of things to exist. We are tempted to distrust God, to question His love. Often the tempter comes to us as he came to Christ, arraying before us our weakness and infirmities. He hopes to discourage the soul, and to break our hold on God. Then he is sure of his prey. If we would meet him as Jesus did, we should escape many a defeat. By parleying with the enemy, we give him an advantage.

When Christ said to the tempter, "Man shall not live by bread alone, but by every word that proceedeth out of the mouth of God," He repeated the words that, more than fourteen hundred years before, He had spoken to Israel: "The Lord thy God led thee these forty years in the wilderness. . . . And He humbled thee, and suffered thee to hunger, and fed thee with manna, which thou knewest not, neither did thy fathers know; that He might make thee know that man doth not live by bread only, but by every word that proceedeth out of the mouth of the Lord doth man live." Deut. 8:2, 3. In the wilderness, when all means of sustenance failed, God sent His people manna from heaven; and a sufficient and constant supply was given. This provision was to teach them that while they trusted in God and walked in His ways He would not forsake them. The Saviour now practiced the lesson He had taught to Israel. By the word of God succor had been given to the Hebrew host, and by the same word it would be given to

Jesus. He awaited God's time to bring relief. He was in the wilderness in obedience to God, and He would not obtain food by following the suggestions of Satan. In the presence of the witnessing universe, He testified that it is a less calamity to suffer whatever may befall than to depart in any manner from the will of God.

"Man shall not live by bread alone, but by every word of God." Often the follower of Christ is brought where he cannot serve God and carry forward his worldly enterprises. Perhaps it appears that obedience to some plain requirement of God will cut off his means of support. Satan would make him believe that he must sacrifice his conscientious convictions. But the only thing in our world upon which we can rely is the word of God. "Seek ye first the kingdom of God, and His righteousness; and all these things shall be added unto you." Matt. 6:33. Even in this life it is not for our good to depart from the will of our Father in heaven. When we learn the power of His word, we shall not follow the suggestions of Satan in order to obtain food or to save our lives. Our only questions will be, What is God's command? and what His promise? Knowing these, we shall obey the one, and trust the other.

In the last great conflict of the controversy with Satan those who are loyal to God will see every earthly support cut off. Because they refuse to break His law in obedience to earthly powers, they will be forbidden to buy or sell. It will finally be decreed that they shall be put to death. See Rev. 13:11-17. But to the obedient is given the promise, "He shall dwell on high: his place of defense shall be the munitions of rocks: bread shall be given him; his waters shall be sure." Isa. 33:16. By this promise the children of God will live. When the earth shall be wasted with famine, they shall be fed. "They shall not be ashamed in the evil time: and in the days of famine they shall be satisfied." Ps. 37:19. To that time of distress the prophet Habakkuk looked forward, and his words express the faith of the church: "Although the fig tree shall not blossom, neither shall fruit be in the vines; the labor of the olive shall fail, and the fields shall yield no meat; the flock shall be cut off from the fold, and there shall be no herd in the stalls: yet I will rejoice in the Lord, I will joy in the God of my salvation." Hab. 3:17, 18.

Of all the lessons to be learned from our Lord's first great temptation none is more important than that bearing upon the control of the appetites and passions. In all ages, temptations appealing to the physical nature have been most effectual in corrupting and degrading mankind. Through intemperance, Satan works to destroy the mental and moral powers that God gave to man as a priceless endowment. Thus it becomes impossible for men to appreciate things of eternal worth. Through sensual indulgence, Satan seeks to blot from the soul every trace of likeness to God.

The uncontrolled indulgence and consequent disease and degradation that existed at Christ's first advent will again exist, with intensity of evil, before His second coming. Christ declares that the condition of the world will be as in the days before the Flood, and as in Sodom and Gomorrah. Every imagination of the thoughts of the heart will be evil continually. Upon the very verge of that fearful time we are now living, and to us should come home the lesson of the Saviour's fast. Only by the inexpressible anguish which Christ endured can we estimate the evil of unrestrained indulgence. His example declares that our only hope of eternal life is through bringing the appetites and passions into subjection to the will of God.

In our own strength it is impossible for us to deny the clamors of our fallen nature. Through this channel Satan will bring temptation upon us. Christ knew that the enemy would come to every human being, to take advantage of hereditary weakness, and by his false insinuations to ensnare all whose trust is not in God. And by passing over the ground which man must travel, our Lord has prepared the way for us to overcome. It is not His will that we should be placed at a disadvantage in the conflict with Satan. He would not have us intimidated and discouraged by the assaults of the serpent. "Be of good cheer," He says; "I have overcome the world." John 16:33.

Let him who is struggling against the power of appetite look to the Saviour in the wilderness of temptation. See Him in His agony upon the cross, as He exclaimed, "I thirst." He has endured all that it is possible for us to bear. His victory is ours.

Jesus rested upon the wisdom and strength of His heavenly Father. He declares, "The Lord God will help Me; therefore shall I not be confounded: . . . and I know that I shall not be ashamed. . . . Behold, the Lord God will help Me." Pointing to His own example, He says to us, "Who is among you that feareth the Lord, . . . that walketh in darkness, and hath no light? let him trust in the name of the Lord, and stay upon his God." Isa. 50:7-10.

"The prince of this world cometh," said Jesus, "and hath nothing in Me." John 14:30. There was in Him nothing that responded to Satan's sophistry. He did not consent to sin. Not even by a thought did He yield to temptation. So it may be with us. Christ's humanity was united with divinity; He was fitted for the conflict by the indwelling of the Holy Spirit. And He came to make us partakers of the divine nature. So long as we are united to Him by faith, sin has no more dominion over us. God reaches for the hand of faith in us to direct it to lay fast hold upon the divinity of Christ, that we may attain to perfection of character.

And how this is accomplished, Christ has shown us. By what means did He overcome in the conflict with Satan? By the word of God. Only by the word could He resist temptation. "It is written," He said. And unto us are given "exceeding great and precious promises: that by these ye might be partakers of the divine nature, having escaped the corruption that is in the world through lust." 2 Peter 1:4. Every promise in God's word is ours. "By every word that proceedeth out of the mouth of God" are we to live. When assailed by temptation, look not to circumstances or to the weakness of self, but to the power of the word. All its strength is yours. "Thy word," says the psalmist, "have I hid in mine heart, that I might not sin against Thee." "By the word of Thy lips I have kept me from the paths of the destroyer." Ps. 119:11; 17:4.

Chapter 8

THE VICTORY

"THEN THE devil taketh Him up into the holy city, and setteth Him on a pinnacle of the temple, and saith unto Him, If Thou be the Son of God, cast Thyself down: for it is written,—

"He shall give His angels charge concerning Thee:
And in their hands they shall bear Thee up,
Lest at any time Thou dash Thy foot against a stone."

Satan now supposes that he has met Jesus on His own ground. The wily foe himself presents words that proceeded from the mouth of God. He still appears as an angel of light, and he makes it evident that he is acquainted with the Scriptures, and understands the import of what is written. As Jesus before used the word of God to sustain His faith, the tempter now uses it to countenance his deception. He claims that he has been only testing the fidelity of Jesus, and he now commends His steadfastness. As the Saviour has manifested trust in God, Satan urges Him to give still another evidence of His faith.

But again the temptation is prefaced with the insinuation of distrust, "*If* Thou be the Son of God." Christ was tempted to answer the "if;" but He refrained from the slightest acceptance of the doubt. He would not imperil His life in order to give evidence to Satan.

The tempter thought to take advantage of Christ's humanity, and urge Him to presumption. But while Satan can solicit, he cannot compel to sin. He said to Jesus, "Cast Thyself down," knowing that he could not cast Him down; for God would interpose to deliver Him. Nor could Satan force Jesus to cast Himself down. Unless Christ

This chapter is based on Matt. 4:5-11; Mark 1:12, 13; Luke 4:5-13.

50

should consent to temptation, He could not be overcome. Not all the power of earth or hell could force Him in the slightest degree to depart from the will of His Father.

The tempter can never compel us to do evil. He cannot control minds unless they are yielded to his control. The will must consent, faith must let go its hold upon Christ, before Satan can exercise his power upon us. But every sinful desire we cherish affords him a foothold. Every point in which we fail of meeting the divine standard is an open door by which he can enter to tempt and destroy us. And every failure or defeat on our part gives occasion for him to reproach Christ.

When Satan quoted the promise, "He shall give His angels charge over Thee," he omitted the words, "to keep Thee in all Thy ways;" that is, in all the ways of God's choosing. Jesus refused to go outside the path of obedience. While manifesting perfect trust in His Father, He would not place Himself, unbidden, in a position that would necessitate the interposition of His Father to save Him from death. He would not force Providence to come to His rescue, and thus fail of giving man an example of trust and submission.

Jesus declared to Satan, "It is written again, Thou shalt not tempt the Lord thy God." These words were spoken by Moses to the children of Israel when they thirsted in the desert, and demanded that Moses should give them water, exclaiming, "Is the Lord among us, or not?" Exodus 17:7. God had wrought marvelously for them; yet in trouble they doubted Him, and demanded evidence that He was with them. In their unbelief they sought to put Him to the test. And Satan was urging Christ to do the same thing. God had already testified that Jesus was His Son; and now to ask for proof that He was the Son of God would be putting God's word to the test,—tempting Him. And the same would be true of asking for that which God had not promised. It would manifest distrust, and be really proving, or tempting, Him. We should not present our petitions to God to *prove* whether He will fulfill His word, but *because* He will fulfill it; not to prove that He loves us, but because He loves us. "Without faith it is impossible to please Him: for he that cometh to God must believe that He is, and that He is a rewarder of them that diligently seek Him." Heb. 11:6.

But faith is in no sense allied to presumption. Only he who has true faith is secure against presumption. For presumption is Satan's counterfeit of faith. Faith claims God's promises, and brings forth fruit in obedience. Presumption also claims the promises, but uses them as Satan did, to excuse transgression. Faith would have led our first parents to trust the love of God, and to obey His commands. Presumption. led them to transgress His law, believing that His great love would save them from the consequence of their sin. It is not faith that claims the favor of Heaven without complying with the conditions on which mercy is to be granted. Genuine faith has its foundation in the promises and provisions of the Scriptures.

Often when Satan has failed of exciting distrust, he succeeds in leading us to presumption. If he can cause us to place ourselves unnecessarily in the way of temptation, he knows that the victory is his. God will preserve all who walk in the path of obedience; but to depart from it is to venture on Satan's ground. There we are sure to fall. The Saviour has bidden us, "Watch ye and pray, lest ye enter into temptation." Mark 14:38. Meditation and prayer would keep us from rushing unbidden into the way of danger, and thus we should be saved from many a defeat.

Yet we should not lose courage when assailed by temptation. Often when placed in a trying situation we doubt that the Spirit of God has been leading us. But it was the Spirit's leading that brought Jesus into the wilderness to be tempted by Satan. When God brings us into trial, He has a purpose to accomplish for our good. Jesus did not presume on God's promises by going unbidden into temptation, neither did He give up to despondency when temptation came upon Him. Nor should we. "God is faithful, who will not suffer you to be tempted above that ye are able; but will with the temptation also make a way to escape, that ye may be able to bear it." He says, "Offer unto God thanksgiving; and pay thy vows unto the Most High: and call upon Me in the day of trouble: I will deliver thee, and thou shalt glorify Me." 1 Cor. 10:13; Ps. 50:14, 15.

Jesus was victor in the second temptation, and now Satan manifests himself in his true character. But he does not appear as a hideous monster, with cloven feet and bat's wings. He is a mighty angel, though fallen. He avows himself the leader of rebellion and the god of this world

Placing Jesus upon a high mountain, Satan caused the kingdoms of the world, in all their glory, to pass in panoramic view before Him. The sunlight lay on templed cities, marble palaces, fertile fields, and fruit-laden vineyards. The traces of evil were hidden. The eyes of Jesus, so lately greeted by gloom and desolation, now gazed upon a scene of unsurpassed loveliness and prosperity. Then the tempter's voice was heard: "All this power will I give Thee, and the glory of them: for that is delivered unto me; and to whomsoever I will I give it. If Thou therefore wilt worship me, all shall be Thine."

Christ's mission could be fulfilled only through suffering. Before Him was a life of sorrow, hardship, and conflict, and an ignominious death. He must bear the sins of the whole world. He must endure separation from His Father's love. Now the tempter offered to yield up the power he had usurped. Christ might deliver Himself from the dreadful future by acknowledging the supremacy of Satan. But to do this was to yield the victory in the great controversy. It was in seeking to exalt himself above the Son of God that Satan had sinned in heaven. Should he prevail now, it would be the triumph of rebellion.

When Satan declared to Christ, The kingdom and glory of the world are delivered unto me, and to whomsoever I will I give it, he stated what was true only in part, and he declared it to serve his own purpose of deception. Satan's dominion was that wrested from Adam, but Adam was the vicegerent of the Creator. His was not an independent rule. The earth is God's, and He has committed all things to His Son. Adam was to reign subject to Christ. When Adam betrayed his sovereignty into Satan's hands, Christ still remained the rightful King. Thus the Lord had said to King Nebuchadnezzar, "The Most High ruleth in the kingdom of men, and giveth it to whomsoever He will." Dan. 4:17. Satan can exercise his usurped authority only as God permits.

When the tempter offered to Christ the kingdom and glory of the world, he was proposing that Christ should yield up the real kingship of the world, and hold dominion subject to Satan. This was the same dominion upon which the hopes of the Jews were set. They desired the kingdom of this world. If Christ had consented to offer them such a kingdom, they would gladly have received Him. But the curse of sin, with all its woe, rested upon it. Christ declared to the tempter, "Get thee behind Me, Satan: for it is written, Thou shalt worship the Lord thy God, and Him only shalt thou serve."

By the one who had revolted in heaven the kingdoms of this world were offered Christ, to buy His homage to the principles of evil; but He would not be bought; He had come to establish a kingdom of righteousness, and He would not abandon His purpose. With the same temptation Satan approaches men, and here he has better success than with Christ. To men he offers the kingdom of this world on condition that they will acknowledge his supremacy. He requires that they sacrifice integrity, disregard conscience, indulge selfishness. Christ bids them seek first the kingdom of God, and His righteousness; but Satan walks by their side and says: Whatever may be true in regard to life eternal, in order to make a success in this world you must serve me. I hold your welfare in my hands. I can give you riches, pleasures, honor, and happiness. Hearken to my counsel. Do not allow yourselves to be carried away with whimsical notions of honesty or self-sacrifice. I will prepare the way before you. Thus multitudes are deceived. They consent to live for the service of self, and Satan is satisfied. While he allures them with the hope of worldly dominion, he gains dominion over the soul. But he offers that which is not his to bestow, and which is soon to be wrested from him. In return he beguiles them of their title to the inheritance of the sons of God.

Satan had questioned whether Jesus was the Son of God. In his summary dismissal he had proof that he could not gainsay. Divinity flashed through suffering humanity. Satan had no power to resist the command. Writhing with humiliation and rage, he was forced to withdraw from the presence of the world's Redeemer. Christ's victory was as complete as had been the failure of Adam.

So we may resist temptation, and force Satan to depart from us. Jesus gained the victory through submission and faith in God, and by the apostle He says to us, "Submit yourselves therefore to God. Resist the devil, and he will flee from you. Draw nigh to God, and He will draw nigh to you." James 4:7, 8. We cannot save ourselves from the tempter's power; he has conquered humanity, and when we try to stand in our own strength, we shall become a prey to his devices; but "the name of the Lord is a strong tower: the righteous runneth into it, and is safe." Prov. 18:10. Satan trembles and flees before the weakest soul who finds refuge in that mighty name.

After the foe had departed, Jesus fell exhausted to the earth, with the pallor of death upon His face. The angels of heaven had watched the conflict, beholding their loved Commander as He passed through inexpressible suffering to make a way of escape for us. He had endured the test, greater than we shall ever be called to endure. The angels now ministered to the Son of God as He lay like one dying. He was strengthened with food, comforted with the message of His Father's love and the assurance that all heaven triumphed in His victory. Warming to life again, His great heart goes out in sympathy for man, and He goes forth to complete the work He has begun; to rest not until the foe is vanquished, and our fallen race redeemed.

Never can the cost of our redemption be realized until the redeemed shall stand with the Redeemer before the throne of God. Then as the glories of the eternal home burst upon our enraptured senses we shall remember that Jesus left all this for us, that He not only became an exile from the heavenly courts, but for us took the risk of failure and eternal loss. Then we shall cast our crowns at His feet, and raise the song, "Worthy is the Lamb that was slain to receive power, and riches, and wisdom, and strength, and honor, and glory, and blessing." Rev. 5:12.

Chapter 9

FOLLOWERS

JOHN THE Baptist was now preaching and baptizing at Bethabara, beyond Jordan. It was not far from this spot that God had stayed the river in its flow until Israel had passed over. A little distance from here the stronghold of Jericho had been overthrown by the armies of heaven. The memory of these events was at this time revived, and gave a thrilling interest to the Baptist's message. Would not He who had wrought so wonderfully in ages past again manifest His power for Israel's deliverance? Such was the thought stirring the hearts of the people who daily thronged the banks of the Jordan.

The preaching of John had taken so deep a hold on the nation as to demand the attention of the religious authorities. The danger of insurrection caused every popular gathering to be looked upon with suspicion by the Romans, and whatever pointed toward an uprising of the people excited the fears of the Jewish rulers. John had not recognized the authority of the Sanhedrin by seeking their sanction for his work; and he had reproved rulers and people, Pharisees and Sadducees alike. Yet the people followed him eagerly. The interest in his work seemed to be continually increasing. Though he had not deferred to them, the Sanhedrin accounted that, as a public teacher, he was under their jurisdiction.

This body was made up of members chosen from the priesthood, and from the chief rulers and teachers of the nation. The high priest was usually the president. All its members were to be men advanced in years, though not aged; men of learning, not only versed in Jewish religion and history, but in general knowledge. They were to be without physical blemish, and must be married men, and

This chapter is based on John 1:19-51.

fathers, as being more likely than others to be humane and considerate. Their place of meeting was an apartment connected with the temple at Jerusalem. In the days of Jewish independence the Sanhedrin was the supreme court of the nation, possessing secular as well as ecclesiastical authority. Though now subordinated by the Roman governors, it still exercised a strong influence in civil as well as religious matters.

The Sanhedrin could not well defer an investigation of John's work. There were some who recalled the revelation made to Zacharias in the temple, and the father's prophecy that had pointed to his child as the Messiah's herald. In the tumults and changes of thirty years, these things had in a great measure been lost sight of. They were now called to mind by the excitement concerning the ministry of John.

It was long since Israel had had a prophet, long since such a reformation as was now in progress had been witnessed. The demand for confession of sin seemed new and startling. Many among the leaders would not go to hear John's appeals and denunciations, lest they should be led to disclose the secrets of their own lives. Yet his preaching was a direct announcement of the Messiah. It was well known that the seventy weeks of Daniel's prophecy, covering the Messiah's advent, were nearly ended; and all were eager to share in that era of national glory which was then expected. Such was the popular enthusiasm that the Sanhedrin would soon be forced either to sanction or to reject John's work. Already their power over the people was waning. It was becoming a serious question how to maintain their position. In the hope of arriving at some conclusion, they dispatched to the Jordan a deputation of priests and Levites to confer with the new teacher.

A multitude were gathered, listening to his words, when the delegates approached. With an air of authority designed to impress the people and to command the deference of the prophet the haughty rabbis came. With a movement of respect, almost of fear, the crowd opened to let them pass. The great men, in their rich robes, in the pride of rank and power, stood before the prophet of the wilderness.

"Who art thou?" they demanded.

Knowing what was in their thoughts, John answered, "I am not the Christ."

"What then? Art thou Elias?"

"I am not."

"Art thou that prophet?"

"No."

"Who art thou? that we may give an answer to them that sent us. What sayest thou of thyself?"

"I am the voice of one crying in the wilderness, Make straight the way of the Lord, as said the prophet Esaias."

The scripture to which John referred is that beautiful prophecy of Isaiah: "Comfort ye, comfort ye My people, saith your God. Speak ye comfortably to Jerusalem, and cry unto her, that her appointed time is accomplished, that her iniquity is pardoned. . . . The voice of him that crieth in the wilderness, Prepare ye the way of the Lord, make straight in the desert a highway for our God. Every valley shall be exalted, and every mountain and hill shall be made low: and the crooked shall be made straight, and the rough places plain: and the glory of the Lord shall be revealed, and all flesh shall see it together." Isa. 40:1-5, margin.

Anciently, when a king journeyed through the less frequented parts of his dominion, a company of men was sent ahead of the royal chariot to level the steep places and to fill up the hollows, that the king might travel in safety and without hindrance. This custom is employed by the prophet to illustrate the work of the gospel. "Every valley shall be exalted, and every mountain and hill shall be made low." When the Spirit of God, with its marvelous awakening power, touches the soul, it abases human pride. Worldly pleasure and position and power are seen to be worthless. "Imaginations, and every high thing that exalteth itself against the knowledge of God" are cast down; every thought is brought into captivity "to the obedience of Christ." 2 Cor. 10:5. Then humility and self-sacrificing love, so little valued among men, are exalted as alone of worth. This is the work of the gospel, of which John's message was a part.

The rabbis continued their questioning: "Why baptizest thou then, if thou be not that Christ, nor Elias, neither that prophet?" The words "that prophet" had reference to Moses. The Jews had been inclined to the belief that Moses would be raised from the dead, and taken to heaven. They did not know that he had already been raised. When the Baptist began his ministry, many thought that he might be the prophet Moses risen from the dead, for he seemed to have a thorough knowledge of the prophecies and of the history of Israel.

It was believed also that before the Messiah's advent, Elijah would personally appear. This expectation John met in his denial; but his words had a deeper meaning. Jesus afterward said, referring to John, "If ye are willing to receive it, this is Elijah, which is to come." Matt. 11:14, R. V. John came in the spirit and power of Elijah, to do such a work as Elijah did. If the Jews had received him, it would have been accomplished for them. But they did not receive his message. To them he was not Elijah. He could not fulfill for them the mission he came to accomplish.

Many of those gathered at the Jordan had been present at the baptism of Jesus; but the sign then given had been manifest to but few among them. During the preceding months of the Baptist's ministry, many had refused to heed the call to repentance. Thus they had hardened their hearts and darkened their understanding. When Heaven bore testimony to Jesus at His baptism, they perceived it not. Eyes that had never been turned in faith to Him that is invisible beheld not the revelation of the glory of God; ears that had never listened to His voice heard not the words of witness. So it is now. Often the presence of Christ and the ministering angels is manifest in the assemblies of the people, and yet there are many who know it not. They discern nothing unusual. But to some the Saviour's presence is revealed. Peace and joy animate their hearts. They are comforted, encouraged, and blessed.

The deputies from Jerusalem had demanded of John, "Why baptizest thou?" and they were awaiting his answer. Suddenly, as his glance swept over the throng, his eye kindled, his face was lighted up, his whole being was stirred with deep emotion. With outstretched hands he cried, "I baptize in water: in the midst of you standeth One whom ye know not, even He that cometh after me, the latchet of whose shoe I am not worthy to unloose." R. V., margin.

The message was distinct and unequivocal, to be carried back to the Sanhedrin. The words of John could apply to no other than the long-promised One. The Messiah was among them! In amazement priests and rulers gazed about them, hoping to discover Him of whom John had spoken. But He was not distinguishable among the throng.

When at the baptism of Jesus, John pointed to Him as the Lamb of God, a new light was shed upon the Mes-

siah's work. The prophet's mind was directed to the words
of Isaiah, "He is brought as a lamb to the slaughter." Isa.
53:7. During the weeks that followed, John with new interest studied the prophecies and the teaching of the sacrificial service. He did not distinguish clearly the two phases
of Christ's work,—as a suffering sacrifice and a conquering king,—but he saw that His coming had a deeper significance than priests or people had discerned. When he
beheld Jesus among the throng on His return from the
desert, he confidently looked for Him to give the people
some sign of His true character. Almost impatiently he
waited to hear the Saviour declare His mission; but no
word was spoken, no sign given. Jesus did not respond to
the Baptist's announcement of Him, but mingled with the
disciples of John, giving no outward evidence of His special work, and taking no measures to bring Himself to
notice.

The next day John sees Jesus coming. With the light of
the glory of God resting upon him, the prophet stretches
out his hands, declaring, "Behold, the Lamb of God,
which taketh away the sin of the world! This is He of
whom I said, After me cometh a man which is become before me. . . . And I knew Him not; but that He should be
made manifest to Israel, for this cause came I baptizing in
water. . . . I have beheld the Spirit descending as a dove
out of heaven; and it abode upon Him. And I knew Him
not: but He that sent me to baptize in water, He said unto
me, Upon whomsoever thou shalt see the Spirit descending, and abiding upon Him, the same is He that baptizeth
with the Holy Spirit. And I have seen, and have borne witness that this is the Son of God." R. V., margin.

Was this the Christ? With awe and wonder the people
looked upon the One just declared to be the Son of God.
They had been deeply moved by the words of John. He
had spoken to them in the name of God. They had listened to him day after day as he reproved their sins, and
daily the conviction that he was sent of Heaven had
strengthened. But who was this One greater than John the
Baptist? In His dress and bearing there was nothing that
betokened rank. He was apparently a simple personage,
clad like themselves in the humble garments of the poor.

There were in the throng some who at Christ's baptism
had beheld the divine glory, and had heard the voice of
God. But since that time the Saviour's appearance had

greatly changed. At His baptism they had seen His countenance transfigured in the light of heaven; now, pale, worn, and emaciated, He had been recognized only by the prophet John.

But as the people looked upon Him, they saw a face where divine compassion was blended with conscious power. Every glance of the eye, every feature of the countenance, was marked with humility, and expressive of unutterable love. He seemed to be surrounded by an atmosphere of spiritual influence. While His manners were gentle and unassuming, He impressed men with a sense of power that was hidden, yet could not be wholly concealed. Was this the One for whom Israel had so long waited?

Jesus came in poverty and humiliation, that He might be our example as well as our Redeemer. If He had appeared with kingly pomp, how could He have taught humility? how could He have presented such cutting truths as in the Sermon on the Mount? Where would have been the hope of the lowly in life had Jesus come to dwell as a king among men?

To the multitude, however, it seemed impossible that the One designated by John should be associated with their lofty anticipations. Thus many were disappointed, and greatly perplexed.

The words which the priests and rabbis so much desired to hear, that Jesus would now restore the kingdom to Israel, had not been spoken. For such a king they had been waiting and watching; such a king they were ready to receive. But one who sought to establish in their hearts a kingdom of righteousness and peace, they would not accept.

On the following day, while two disciples were standing near, John again saw Jesus among the people. Again the face of the prophet was lighted up with glory from the Unseen, as he cried, "Behold the Lamb of God!" The words thrilled the hearts of the disciples. They did not fully understand them. What meant the name that John had given Him,—"the Lamb of God"? John himself had not explained it.

Leaving John, they went to seek Jesus. One of the two was Andrew, the brother of Simon; the other was John the evangelist. These were Christ's first disciples. Moved by an irresistible impulse, they followed Jesus,—anxious to speak with Him, yet awed and silent, lost in the overwhelming significance of the thought, "Is this the Messiah?"

Jesus knew that the disciples were following Him. They

were the first fruits of His ministry, and there was joy in the heart of the divine Teacher as these souls responded to His grace. Yet turning, He asked only, "What seek ye?" He would leave them free to turn back or to speak of their desire.

Of one purpose only were they conscious. One presence filled their thought. They exclaimed, "Rabbi, . . . where dwellest *Thou?*" In a brief interview by the wayside they could not receive that for which they longed. They desired to be alone with Jesus, to sit at His feet, and hear His words.

"He saith unto them, Come and see. They came and saw where He dwelt, and abode with Him that day."

If John and Andrew had possessed the unbelieving spirit of the priests and rulers, they would not have been found as learners at the feet of Jesus. They would have come to Him as critics, to judge His words. Many thus close the door to the most precious opportunities. But not so did these first disciples. They had responded to the Holy Spirit's call in the preaching of John the Baptist. Now they recognized the voice of the heavenly Teacher. To them the words of Jesus were full of freshness and truth and beauty. A divine illumination was shed upon the teaching of the Old Testament Scriptures. The many-sided themes of truth stood out in new light.

It is contrition and faith and love that enable the soul to receive wisdom from heaven. Faith working by love is the key of knowledge, and everyone that loveth "knoweth God." 1 John 4:7.

The disciple John was a man of earnest and deep affection, ardent, yet comtemplative. He had begun to discern the glory of Christ,—not the worldly pomp and power for which he had been taught to hope, but "the glory as of the Only-begotten of the Father, full of grace and truth." John 1:14. He was absorbed in contemplation of the wondrous theme.

Andrew sought to impart the joy that filled his heart. Going in search of his brother Simon, he cried, "We have found the Messias." Simon waited for no second bidding. He also had heard the preaching of John the Baptist, and he hastened to the Saviour. The eye of Christ rested upon him, reading his character and his life history. His impulsive nature, his loving, sympathetic heart, his ambition and self-confidence, the history of his fall, his repentance, his labors, and his martyr death,—the Saviour read it all, and

He said, "Thou art Simon the son of Jona: thou shalt be called Cephas, which is by interpretation, A stone."

"The day following Jesus would go forth into Galilee, and findeth Philip, and saith unto him, Follow Me." Philip obeyed the command, and straightway he also became a worker for Christ.

Philip called Nathanael. The latter had been among the throng when the Baptist pointed to Jesus as the Lamb of God. As Nathanael looked upon Jesus, he was disappointed. Could this man, who bore the marks of toil and poverty, be the Messiah? Yet Nathanael could not decide to reject Jesus, for the message of John had brought conviction to his heart.

At the time when Philip called him, Nathanael had withdrawn to a quiet grove to meditate upon the announcement of John and the prophecies concerning the Messiah. He prayed that if the one announced by John was the deliverer, it might be made known to him, and the Holy Spirit rested upon him with assurance that God had visited His people and raised up a horn of salvation for them. Philip knew that his friend was searching the prophecies, and while Nathanael was praying under a fig tree, Philip discovered his retreat. They had often prayed together in this secluded spot hidden by the foliage.

The message, "We have found Him, of whom Moses in the law, and the prophets, did write," seemed to Nathanael a direct answer to his prayer. But Philip had yet a trembling faith. He added doubtfully, "Jesus of Nazareth, the son of Joseph." Again prejudice arose in Nathanael's heart. He exclaimed, "Can there any good thing come out of Nazareth?"

Philip entered into no controversy. He said, "Come and see. Jesus saw Nathanael coming to Him, and saith of him, Behold an Israelite indeed, in whom is no guile!" In surprise Nathanael exclaimed, "Whence knowest Thou me? Jesus answered and said unto him, Before that Philip called thee, when thou wast under the fig tree, I saw thee."

It was enough. The divine Spirit that had borne witness to Nathanael in his solitary prayer under the fig tree now spoke to him in the words of Jesus. Though in doubt, and yielding somewhat to prejudice, Nathanael had come to Christ with an honest desire for truth, and now his desire was met. His faith went beyond that of the one who had brought him to Jesus. He answered and said, "Rabbi, Thou art the Son of God; Thou art the King of Israel."

If Nathanael had trusted to the rabbis for guidance, he would never have found Jesus. It was by seeing and judging for himself that he became a disciple. So in the case of many today whom prejudice withholds from good. How different would be the result if they would "come and see"!

While they trust to the guidance of human authority, none will come to a saving knowledge of the truth. Like Nathanael, we need to study God's word for ourselves, and pray for the enlightenment of the Holy Spirit. He who saw Nathanael under the fig tree will see us in the secret place of prayer. Angels from the world of light are near to those who in humility seek for divine guidance.

With the calling of John and Andrew and Simon, of Philip and Nathanael, began the foundation of the Christian church. John directed two of his disciples to Christ. Then one of these, Andrew, found his brother, and called him to the Saviour. Philip was then called, and he went in search of Nathanael. These examples should teach us the importance of personal effort, of making direct appeals to our kindred, friends, and neighbors. There are those who for a lifetime have professed to be acquainted with Christ, yet who have never made a personal effort to bring even one soul to the Saviour. They leave all the work for the minister. He may be well qualified for his calling, but he cannot do that which God has left for the members of the church.

There are many who need the ministration of loving Christian hearts. Many have gone down to ruin who might have been saved if their neighbors, common men and women, had put forth personal effort for them. Many are waiting to be personally addressed. In the very family, the neighborhood, the town, where we live, there is work for us to do as missionaries for Christ. If we are Christians, this work will be our delight. No sooner is one converted than there is born within him a desire to make known to others what a precious friend he has found in Jesus. The saving and sanctifying truth cannot be shut up in his heart.

All who are consecrated to God will be channels of light. God makes them His agents to communicate to others the riches of His grace. His promise is, "I will make them and the places round about My hill a blessing; and I will cause the shower to come down in his season; there shall be showers of blessing." Ezek. 34:26.

Philip said to Nathanael, "Come and see." He did not

ask him to accept another's testimony, but to behold Christ for himself. Now that Jesus has ascended to heaven, His disciples are His representatives among men, and one of the most effective ways of winning souls to Him is in exemplifying His character in our daily life. Our influence upon others depends not so much upon what we say as upon what we are. Men may combat and defy our logic, they may resist our appeals; but a life of disinterested love is an argument they cannot gainsay. A consistent life, characterized by the meekness of Christ, is a power in the world.

The teaching of Christ was the expression of an inwrought conviction and experience, and those who learn of Him become teachers after the divine order. The word of God, spoken by one who is himself sanctified through it, has a life-giving power that makes it attractive to the hearers, and convicts them that it is a living reality. When one has received the truth in the love of it, he will make this manifest in the persuasion of his manner and the tones of his voice. He makes known that which he himself has heard, seen, and handled of the word of life, that others may have fellowship with him through the knowledge of Christ. His testimony, from lips touched with a live coal from off the altar, is truth to the receptive heart, and works sanctification upon the character.

And he who seeks to give light to others will himself be blessed. "There shall be showers of blessing." "He that watereth shall be watered also himself." Prov. 11:25. God could have reached His object in saving sinners without our aid; but in order for us to develop a character like Christ's, we must share in His work. In order to enter into His joy,—the joy of seeing souls redeemed by His sacrifice,—we must participate in His labors for their redemption.

Nathanael's first expression of his faith, so full and earnest and sincere, fell like music on the ears of Jesus. And He "answered and said unto him, Because I said unto thee, I saw thee under the fig tree, believest thou? thou shalt see greater things than these." The Saviour looked forward with joy to His work in preaching good tidings to the meek, binding up the brokenhearted, and proclaiming liberty to the captives of Satan. At thought of the precious blessings He had brought to men, Jesus added, "Verily, verily, I say unto you, Hereafter ye shall see heaven open, and the angels of God ascending and descending upon the Son of man."

Here Christ virtually says, On the bank of the Jordan the heavens were opened, and the Spirit descended like a dove upon Me. That scene was but a token that I am the Son of God. If you believe on Me as such, your faith shall be quickened. You shall see that the heavens are opened, and are never to be closed. I have opened them to you. The angels of God are ascending, bearing the prayers of the needy and distressed to the Father above, and descending, bringing blessing and hope, courage, help, and life, to the children of men.

The angels of God are ever passing from earth to heaven, and from heaven to earth. The miracles of Christ for the afflicted and suffering were wrought by the power of God through the ministration of the angels. And it is through Christ, by the ministration of His heavenly messengers, that every blessing comes from God to us. In taking upon Himself humanity, our Saviour unites His interests with those of the fallen sons and daughters of Adam, while through His divinity He grasps the throne of God. And thus Christ is the medium of communication of men with God, and of God with men.

[illegible faded text at top of page]

Chapter 10

WATER TO WINE

JESUS DID NOT begin His ministry by some great work before the Sanhedrin at Jerusalem. At a household gathering in a little Galilean village His power was put forth to add to the joy of a wedding feast. Thus He showed His sympathy with men, and His desire to minister to their happiness. In the wilderness of temptation He Himself had drunk the cup of woe. He came forth to give to men the cup of blessing, by His benediction to hallow the relations of human life.

From the Jordan, Jesus had returned to Galilee. There was to be a marriage at Cana, a little town not far from Nazareth; the parties were relatives of Joseph and Mary; and Jesus, knowing of this family gathering, went to Cana, and with His disciples was invited to the feast.

Again He met His mother, from whom He had for some time been separated. Mary had heard of the manifestation at the Jordan, at His baptism. The tidings had been carried to Nazareth, and had brought to her mind afresh the scenes that for so many years had been hidden in her heart. In common with all Israel, Mary was deeply stirred by the mission of John the Baptist. Well she remembered the prophecy given at his birth. Now his connection with Jesus kindled her hopes anew. But tidings had reached her also of the mysterious departure of Jesus to the wilderness, and she was oppressed with troubled forebodings.

From the day when she heard the angel's announcement in the home at Nazareth Mary had treasured every evidence that Jesus was the Messiah. His sweet, unselfish life assured her that He could be no other than the Sent of God. Yet there came to her also doubts and disappointments, and she had longed for the time when His glory

This chapter is based on John 2:1-11.

should be revealed. Death had separated her from Joseph, who had shared her knowledge of the mystery of the birth of Jesus. Now there was no one to whom she could confide her hopes and fears. The past two months had been very sorrowful. She had been parted from Jesus, in whose sympathy she found comfort; she pondered upon the words of Simeon, "A sword shall pierce through thy own soul also" (Luke 2:35); she recalled the three days of agony when she thought Jesus lost to her forever; and with an anxious heart she awaited His return.

At the marriage feast she meets Him, the same tender, dutiful son. Yet He is not the same. His countenance is changed. It bears the traces of His conflict in the wilderness, and a new expression of dignity and power gives evidence of His heavenly mission. With Him is a group of young men, whose eyes follow Him with reverence, and who call Him Master. These companions recount to Mary what they have seen and heard at the baptism and elsewhere. They conclude by declaring, "We have found Him, of whom Moses in the law, and the prophets, did write." John 1:45.

As the guests assemble, many seem to be preoccupied with some topic of absorbing interest. A suppressed excitement pervades the company. Little groups converse together in eager but quiet tones, and wondering glances are turned upon the Son of Mary. As Mary had heard the disciples' testimony in regard to Jesus, she had been gladdened with the assurance that her long-cherished hopes were not in vain. Yet she would have been more than human if there had not mingled with this holy joy a trace of the fond mother's natural pride. As she saw the many glances bent upon Jesus, she longed to have Him prove to the company that He was really the Honored of God. She hoped there might be opportunity for Him to work a miracle before them.

It was the custom of the times for marriage festivities to continue several days. On this occasion, before the feast ended it was found that the supply of wine had failed. This discovery caused much perplexity and regret. It was unusual to dispense with wine on festive occasions, and its absence would seem to indicate a want of hospitality. As a relative of the parties, Mary had assisted in the arrangements for the feast, and she now spoke to Jesus, saying, "They have no wine." These words were a suggestion that

He might supply their need. But Jesus answered, "Woman, what have I to do with thee? Mine hour is not yet come."

This answer, abrupt as it seems to us, expressed no coldness or discourtesy. The Saviour's form of address to His mother was in accordance with Oriental custom. It was used toward persons to whom it was desired to show respect. Every act of Christ's earthly life was in harmony with the precept He Himself had given, "Honor thy father and thy mother." Ex. 20:12. On the cross, in His last act of tenderness toward His mother, Jesus again addressed her in the same way, as He committed her to the care of His best-loved disciple. Both at the marriage feast and upon the cross, the love expressed in tone and look and manner interpreted His words.

At His visit to the temple in His boyhood, as the mystery of His lifework opened before Him, Christ had said to Mary, "Wist ye not that I must be about My Father's business?" Luke 2:49. These words struck the keynote of His whole life and ministry. Everything was held in abeyance to His work, the great work of redemption which He had come into the world to accomplish. Now He repeated the lesson. There was danger that Mary would regard her relationship to Jesus as giving her a special claim upon Him, and the right, in some degree, to direct Him in His mission. For thirty years He had been to her a loving and obedient son, and His love was unchanged; but He must now go about His Father's work. As Son of the Most High, and Saviour of the world, no earthly ties must hold Him from His mission, or influence His conduct. He must stand free to do the will of God. This lesson is also for us. The claims of God are paramount even to the ties of human relationship. No earthly attraction should turn our feet from the path in which He bids us walk.

The only hope of redemption for our fallen race is in Christ; Mary could find salvation only through the Lamb of God. In herself she possessed no merit. Her connection with Jesus placed her in no different spiritual relation to Him from that of any other human soul. This is indicated in the Saviour's words. He makes clear the distinction between His relation to her as the Son of man and as the Son of God. The tie of kinship between them in no way placed her on an equality with Him.

The words, "Mine hour is not yet come," point to the fact that every act of Christ's life on earth was in fulfillment of the plan that had existed from the days of eternity. Before He came to earth, the plan lay out before Him, perfect in all its details. But as He walked among men, He was guided, step by step, by the Father's will. He did not hesitate to act at the appointed time. With the same submission He waited until the time had come.

In saying to Mary that His hour had not yet come, Jesus was replying to her unspoken thought,—to the expectation she cherished in common with her people. She hoped that He would reveal Himself as the Messiah, and take the throne of Israel. But the time had not come. Not as a King, but as "a Man of Sorrows, and acquainted with grief," had Jesus accepted the lot of humanity.

But though Mary had not a right conception of Christ's mission, she trusted Him implicitly. To this faith Jesus responded. It was to honor Mary's trust, and to strengthen the faith of His disciples, that the first miracle was performed. The disciples were to encounter many and great temptations to unbelief. To them the prophecies had made it clear beyond all controversy that Jesus was the Messiah. They looked for the religious leaders to receive Him with confidence even greater than their own. They declared among the people the wonderful works of Christ and their own confidence in His mission, but they were amazed and bitterly disappointed by the unbelief, the deep-seated prejudice, and the enmity to Jesus, displayed by the priests and rabbis. The Saviour's early miracles strengthened the disciples to stand against this opposition.

In nowise disconcerted by the words of Jesus, Mary said to those serving at table, "Whatsoever He saith unto you, do it." Thus she did what she could to prepare the way for the work of Christ.

Beside the doorway stood six large stone water jars, and Jesus bade the servants fill these with water. It was done. Then as the wine was wanted for immediate use, He said, "Draw out now, and bear unto the governor of the feast." Instead of the water with which the vessels had been filled, there flowed forth wine. Neither the ruler of the feast nor the guests generally were aware that the supply of wine had failed. Upon tasting that which the servants brought, the ruler found it superior to any he had ever before drunk, and very different from that served at the beginning of the feast. Turning to the bridegroom, he said, "Every man at the beginning doth set forth good wine; and when men have well drunk, then that which is worse: but thou hast kept the good wine until now."

As men set forth the best wine first, then afterward that which is worse, so does the world with its gifts. That which it offers may please the eye and fascinate the senses, but it proves to be unsatisfying. The wine turns to bitterness, the gaiety to gloom. That which was begun with songs and mirth ends in weariness and disgust. But the gifts of Jesus are ever fresh and new. The feast that He provides for the soul never fails to give satisfaction and joy. Each new gift increases the capacity of the receiver to appreciate and enjoy the blessings of the Lord. He gives grace for grace. There can be no failure of supply. If you abide in Him, the fact that you receive a rich gift today insures the reception of a richer gift tomorrow. The words of Jesus to Nathanael express the law of God's dealing with the children of faith. With every fresh revelation of His love, He declares to the receptive heart, "Believest thou? thou shalt see greater things than these." John 1:50.

The gift of Christ to the marriage feast was a symbol. The water represented baptism into His death; the wine, the shedding of His blood for the sins of the world. The water to fill the jars was brought by human hands, but the word of Christ alone could impart to it life-giving virtue. So with the rites which point to the Saviour's death. It is only by the power of Christ, working through faith, that they have efficacy to nourish the soul.

The word of Christ supplied ample provision for the feast. So abundant is the provision of His grace to blot out the iniquities of men, and to renew and sustain the soul.

At the first feast He attended with His disciples, Jesus gave them the cup that symbolized His work for their salvation. At the last supper He gave it again, in the institution of that sacred rite by which His death was to be shown forth "till He come." 1 Cor. 11:26. And the sorrow of the disciples at parting from their Lord was comforted with the promise of reunion, as He said, "I will not drink henceforth of this fruit of the vine, until that day when I drink it new with you in My Father's kingdom." Matt. 26:29.

The wine which Christ provided for the feast, and that which He gave to the disciples as a symbol of His own blood, was the pure juice of the grape. To this the prophet Isaiah refers when he speaks of the new wine "in the cluster," and says, "Destroy it not; for a blessing is in it." Isa. 65:8.

It was Christ who in the Old Testament gave the warning to Israel, "Wine is a mocker, strong drink is raging: and whosoever is deceived thereby is not wise." Prov. 20:1. And He Himself provided no such beverage. Satan tempts men to indulgence that will becloud reason and benumb the spiritual perceptions, but Christ teaches us to bring the lower nature into subjection. His whole life was an example of self-denial. In order to break the power of appetite, He suffered in our behalf the severest test that humanity could endure. It was Christ who directed that John the Baptist should drink neither wine nor strong drink. It was He who enjoined similar abstinence upon the wife of Manoah. And He pronounced a curse upon the man who should put the bottle to his neighbor's lips. Christ did not contradict His own teaching. The unfermented wine which He provided for the wedding guests was a wholesome and refreshing drink. Its effect was to bring the taste into harmony with a healthful appetite.

As the guests at the feast remarked upon the quality of the wine, inquiries were made that drew from the servants an account of the miracle. The company were for a time too much amazed to think of Him who had performed the wonderful work. When at length they looked for Him, it was found that He had withdrawn so quietly as to be unnoticed even by His disciples.

The attention of the company was now turned to the disciples. For the first time they had the opportunity of acknowledging their faith in Jesus. They told what they had seen and heard at the Jordan, and there was kindled in many hearts the hope that God had raised up a deliverer for His people. The news of the miracle spread through all that region, and was carried to Jerusalem. With new interest the priests and elders searched the prophecies pointing to Christ's coming. There was eager desire to learn the mission of this new teacher, who appeared among the people in so unassuming a manner.

The ministry of Christ was in marked contrast to that of the Jewish elders. Their regard for tradition and formalism had destroyed all real freedom of thought or action. They lived in continual dread of defilement. To avoid contact with the "unclean," they kept aloof, not only from the Gentiles, but from the majority of their own people, seeking neither to benefit them nor to win their friendship. By dwelling constantly on these matters, they had dwarfed their minds and narrowed the orbit of their lives. Their example encouraged egotism and intolerance among all classes of the people.

Jesus began the work of reformation by coming into close sympathy with humanity. While He showed the greatest reverence for the law of God, He rebuked the pretentious piety of the Pharisees, and tried to free the people from the senseless rules that bound them. He was seeking to break down the barriers which separated the different classes of society, that He might bring men together as children of one family. His attendance at the marriage feast was designed to be a step toward effecting this.

God had directed John the Baptist to dwell in the wilderness, that he might be shielded from the influence of the priests and rabbis, and be prepared for a special mission. But the austerity and isolation of his life were not an example for the people. John himself had not directed his hearers to forsake their former duties. He bade them give evidence of their repentance by faithfulness to God in the place where He had called them.

Jesus reproved self-indulgence in all its forms, yet He was social in His nature. He accepted the hospitality of all classes, visiting the homes of the rich and the poor, the learned and the ignorant, and seeking to elevate their thoughts from questions of commonplace life to those things that are spiritual and eternal. He gave no license to dissipation, and no shadow of worldly levity marred His conduct; yet He found pleasure in scenes of innocent happiness, and by His presence sanctioned the social gathering. A Jewish marriage was an impressive occasion, and its joy was not displeasing to the Son of man. By attending this feast, Jesus honored marriage as a divine institution.

In both the Old and the New Testament, the marriage relation is employed to represent the tender and sacred union that exists between Christ and His people. To the mind of Jesus the gladness of the wedding festivities pointed forward to the rejoicing of that day when He shall bring home His bride to the Father's house, and the redeemed with the Redeemer shall sit down to the marriage supper of the Lamb. He says, "As the bridegroom rejoiceth over the bride, so shall thy God rejoice over thee." "Thou shalt no more be termed Forsaken; . . . but thou shalt be called My Delight; . . . for the Lord delighteth in thee." "He will rejoice over thee with joy; He will rest in His love, He will joy over thee with singing." Isa. 62:5, 4, margin; Zeph. 3:17. When the vision of heavenly things

was granted to John the apostle, he wrote: "I heard as it
were the voice of a great multitude, and as the voice of
many waters, and as the voice of mighty thunderings, saying, Alleluia: for the Lord God omnipotent reigneth. Let us
be glad and rejoice, and give honor to Him: for the marriage of the Lamb is come, and His wife hath made herself
ready." "Blessed are they which are called unto the marriage supper of the Lamb." Rev. 19:6, 7, 9.

Jesus saw in every soul one to whom must be given the
call to His kingdom. He reached the hearts of the people
by going among them as one who desired their good. He
sought them in the public streets, in private houses, on the
boats, in the synagogue, by the shores of the lake, and at
the marriage feast. He met them at their daily vocations,
and manifested an interest in their secular affairs. He carried His instruction into the household, bringing families
in their own homes under the influence of His divine presence. His strong personal sympathy helped to win hearts.
He often repaired to the mountains for solitary prayer, but
this was a preparation for His labor among men in active
life. From these seasons He came forth to relieve the sick,
to instruct the ignorant, and to break the chains from the
captives of Satan.

It was by personal contact and association that Jesus
trained His disciples. Sometimes He taught them, sitting
among them on the mountainside; sometimes beside the
sea, or walking with them by the way, He revealed the
mysteries of the kingdom of God. He did not sermonize as
men do today. Wherever hearts were open to receive the
divine message, He unfolded the truths of the way of salvation. He did not command His disciples to do this or
that, but said, "Follow Me." On His journeys through
country and cities He took them with Him, that they
might see how He taught the people. He linked their interest with His, and they united with Him in the work.

The example of Christ in linking Himself with the interests of humanity should be followed by all who preach His
word, and by all who have received the gospel of His
grace. We are not to renounce social communion. We
should not seclude ourselves from others. In order to
reach all classes, we must meet them where they are. They
will seldom seek us of their own accord. Not alone from
the pulpit are the hearts of men touched by divine truth.
There is another field of labor, humbler, it may be, but
fully as promising. It is found in the home of the lowly,

and in the mansion of the great; at the hospitable board, and in gatherings for innocent social enjoyment.

As disciples of Christ we shall not mingle with the world from a mere love of pleasure, to unite with them in folly. Such associations can result only in harm. We should never give sanction to sin by our words or our deeds, our silence or our presence. Wherever we go, we are to carry Jesus with us, and to reveal to others the preciousness of our Saviour. But those who try to preserve their religion by hiding it within stone walls lose precious opportunities of doing good. Through the social relations, Christianity comes in contact with the world. Everyone who has received the divine illumination is to brighten the pathway of those who know not the Light of life.

We should all become witnesses for Jesus. Social power, sanctified by the grace of Christ, must be improved in winning souls to the Saviour. Let the world see that we are not selfishly absorbed in our own interests, but that we desire others to share our blessings and privileges. Let them see that our religion does not make us unsympathetic or exacting. Let all who profess to have found Christ, minister as He did for the benefit of men.

We should never give to the world the false impression that Christians are a gloomy, unhappy people. If our eyes are fixed on Jesus, we shall see a compassionate Redeemer, and shall catch light from His countenance. Wherever His Spirit reigns, there peace abides. And there will be joy also, for there is a calm, holy trust in God.

Christ is pleased with His followers when they show that, though human, they are partakers of the divine nature. They are not statues, but living men and women. Their hearts, refreshed by the dews of divine grace, open and expand to the Sun of Righteousness. The light that shines upon them they reflect upon others in works that are luminous with the love of Christ.

Chapter 11

MONEY CHANGERS

"AFTER THIS He went down to Capernaum, He, and His mother, and His brethren, and His disciples: and they continued there not many days. And the Jews' Passover was at hand, and Jesus went up to Jerusalem."

In this journey, Jesus joined one of the large companies that were making their way to the capital. He had not yet publicly announced His mission, and He mingled unnoticed with the throng. Upon these occasions, the coming of the Messiah, to which such prominence had been given by the ministry of John, was often the theme of conversation. The hope of national greatness was dwelt upon with kindling enthusiasm. Jesus knew that this hope was to be disappointed, for it was founded on a misinterpretation of the Scriptures. With deep earnestness He explained the prophecies, and tried to arouse the people to a closer study of God's word.

The Jewish leaders had instructed the people that at Jerusalem they were to be taught to worship God. Here during the Passover week large numbers assembled, coming from all parts of Palestine, and even from distant lands. The temple courts were filled with a promiscuous throng. Many were unable to bring with them the sacrifices that were to be offered up as typifying the one great Sacrifice. For the convenience of these, animals were bought and sold in the outer court of the temple. Here all classes of people assembled to purchase their offerings. Here all foreign money was exchanged for the coin of the sanctuary.

Every Jew was required to pay yearly a half shekel as "a ransom for his soul;" and the money thus collected was used for the support of the temple. Ex. 30:12-16. Besides

This chapter is based on John 2:12-22.

76

this, large sums were brought as freewill offerings, to be deposited in the temple treasury. And it was required that all foreign coin should be changed for a coin called the temple shekel, which was accepted for the service of the sanctuary. The money changing gave opportunity for fraud and extortion, and it had grown into a disgraceful traffic, which was a source of revenue to the priests.

The dealers demanded exorbitant prices for the animals sold, and they shared their profits with the priests and rulers, who thus enriched themselves at the expense of the people. The worshipers had been taught to believe that if they did not offer sacrifice, the blessing of God would not rest on their children or their lands. Thus a high price for the animals could be secured; for after coming so far, the people would not return to their homes without performing the act of devotion for which they had come.

A great number of sacrifices were offered at the time of the Passover, and the sales at the temple were very large. The consequent confusion indicated a noisy cattle market rather than the sacred temple of God. There could be heard sharp bargaining, the lowing of cattle, the bleating of sheep, the cooing of doves, mingled with the chinking of coin and angry disputation. So great was the confusion that the worshipers were disturbed, and the words addressed to the Most High were drowned in the uproar that invaded the temple. The Jews were exceedingly proud of their piety. They rejoiced over their temple, and regarded a word spoken in its disfavor as blasphemy; they were very rigorous in the performance of ceremonies connected with it; but the love of money had overruled their scruples. They were scarcely aware how far they had wandered from the original purpose of the service instituted by God Himself.

When the Lord descended upon Mount Sinai, the place was consecrated by His presence. Moses was commanded to put bounds around the mount and sanctify it, and the word of the Lord was heard in warning: "Take heed to yourselves, that ye go not up into the mount, or touch the border of it: whosoever toucheth the mount shall be surely put to death: there shall not an hand touch it, but he shall surely be stoned, or shot through; whether it be beast or man, it shall not live." Ex. 19:12, 13. Thus was taught the lesson that wherever God manifests His presence, the place is holy. The precincts of God's temple should have been regarded as sacred. But in the strife for gain, all this was lost sight of.

The priests and rulers were called to be the representatives of God to the nation; they should have corrected the abuses of the temple court. They should have given to the people an example of integrity and compassion. Instead of studying their own profit, they should have considered the situation and needs of the worshipers, and should have been ready to assist those who were not able to buy the required sacrifices. But this they did not do. Avarice had hardened their hearts.

There came to this feast those who were suffering, those who were in want and distress. The blind, the lame, the deaf, were there. Some were brought on beds. Many came who were too poor to purchase the humblest offering for the Lord, too poor even to buy food with which to satisfy their own hunger. These were greatly distressed by the statements of the priests. The priests boasted of their piety; they claimed to be the guardians of the people; but they were without sympathy or compassion. The poor, the sick, the dying, made their vain plea for favor. Their suffering awakened no pity in the hearts of the priests.

As Jesus came into the temple, He took in the whole scene. He saw the unfair transactions. He saw the distress of the poor, who thought that without shedding of blood there would be no forgiveness for their sins. He saw the outer court of His temple converted into a place of unholy traffic. The sacred enclosure had become one vast exchange.

Christ saw that something must be done. Numerous ceremonies were enjoined upon the people without the proper instruction as to their import. The worshipers offered their sacrifices without understanding that they were typical of the only perfect Sacrifice. And among them, unrecognized and unhonored, stood the One symbolized by all their service. He had given directions in regard to the offerings. He understood their symbolical value, and He saw that they were now perverted and misunderstood. Spiritual worship was fast disappearing. No link bound the priests and rulers to their God. Christ's work was to establish an altogether different worship.

With searching glance, Christ takes in the scene before Him as He stands upon the steps of the temple court. With prophetic eye He looks into futurity, and sees not only years, but centuries and ages. He sees how priests and rulers will turn the needy from their right, and forbid that the gospel shall be preached to the poor. He sees how the love of God will be concealed from sinners, and men will make merchandise of His grace. As He beholds the scene, indignation, authority, and power are expressed in His countenance. The attention of the people is attracted to Him. The eyes of those engaged in their unholy traffic are riveted upon His face. They cannot withdraw their gaze. They feel that this Man reads their inmost thoughts, and discovers their hidden motives. Some attempt to conceal their faces, as if their evil deeds were written upon their countenances, to be scanned by those searching eyes.

The confusion is hushed. The sound of traffic and bargaining has ceased. The silence becomes painful. A sense of awe overpowers the assembly. It is as if they were arraigned before the tribunal of God to answer for their deeds. Looking upon Christ, they behold divinity flash through the garb of humanity. The Majesty of heaven stands as the Judge will stand at the last day,—not now encircled with the glory that will then attend Him, but with the same power to read the soul. His eye sweeps over the multitude, taking in every individual. His form seems to rise above them in commanding dignity, and a divine light illuminates His countenance. He speaks, and His clear, ringing voice—the same that upon Mount Sinai proclaimed the law that priests and rulers are transgressing—is heard echoing through the arches of the temple: "Take these things hence; make not My Father's house an house of merchandise."

Slowly descending the steps, and raising the scourge of cords gathered up on entering the enclosure, He bids the bargaining company depart from the precincts of the temple. With a zeal and severity He has never before manifested, He overthrows the tables of the money-changers. The coin falls, ringing sharply upon the marble pavement. None presume to question His authority. None dare stop to gather up their ill-gotten gain. Jesus did not smite them with the whip of cords, but in His hand that simple scourge seems terrible as a flaming sword. Officers of the temple, speculating priests, brokers and cattle traders, with their sheep and oxen, rush from the place, with the one thought of escaping from the condemnation of His presence.

A panic sweeps over the multitude, who feel the overshadowing of His divinity. Cries of terror escape from hundreds of blanched lips. Even the disciples tremble.

They are awestruck by the words and manner of Jesus, so unlike His usual demeanor. They remember that it is written of Him, "The zeal of Thine house hath eaten Me up." Ps. 69:9. Soon the tumultuous throng with their merchandise are far removed from the temple of the Lord. The courts are free from unholy traffic, and a deep silence and solemnity settles upon the scene of confusion. The presence of the Lord, that of old sanctified the mount, has now made sacred the temple reared in His honor.

In the cleansing of the temple, Jesus was announcing His mission as the Messiah, and entering upon His work. That temple, erected for the abode of the divine Presence, was designed to be an object lesson for Israel and for the world. From eternal ages it was God's purpose that every created being, from the bright and holy seraph to man, should be a temple for the indwelling of the Creator. Because of sin, humanity ceased to be a temple for God. Darkened and defiled by evil, the heart of man no longer revealed the glory of the Divine One. But by the incarnation of the Son of God, the purpose of Heaven is fulfilled. God dwells in humanity, and through saving grace the heart of man becomes again His temple. God designed that the temple at Jerusalem should be a continual witness to the high destiny open to every soul. But the Jews had not understood the significance of the building they regarded with so much pride. They did not yield themselves as holy temples for the Divine Spirit. The courts of the temple at Jerusalem, filled with the tumult of unholy traffic, represented all too truly the temple of the heart, defiled by the presence of sensual passion and unholy thoughts. In cleansing the temple from the world's buyers and sellers, Jesus announced His mission to cleanse the heart from the defilement of sin,—from the earthly desires, the selfish lusts, the evil habits, that corrupt the soul. "The Lord, whom ye seek, shall suddenly come to His temple, even the Messenger of the covenant, whom ye delight in: behold, He shall come, saith the Lord of hosts. But who may abide the day of His coming? and who shall stand when He appeareth? for He is like a refiner's fire, and like fullers' soap: and He shall sit as a refiner and purifier of silver: and He shall purify the sons of Levi, and purge them as gold and silver." Mal. 3:1-3.

"Know ye not that ye are the temple of God, and that the Spirit of God dwelleth in you? If any man defile the temple of God, him shall God destroy; for the temple of

God is holy, which temple ye are." 1 Cor. 3:16, 17. No man can of himself cast out the evil throng that have taken possession of the heart. Only Christ can cleanse the soul temple. But He will not force an entrance. He comes not into the heart as to the temple of old; but He says, "Behold, I stand at the door, and knock: if any man hear My voice, and open the door, I will come in to him." Rev. 3:20. He will come, not for one day merely; for He says, "I will dwell in them, and walk in them; . . . and they shall be My people." He will subdue our iniquities; and Thou wilt cast all their sins into the depths of the sea." 2 Cor. 6:16; Micah 7:19. His presence will cleanse and sanctify the soul, so that it may be a holy temple unto the Lord, and "an habitation of God through the Spirit." Eph. 2:21, 22.

Overpowered with terror, the priests and rulers had fled from the temple court, and from the searching glance that read their hearts. In their flight they met others on their way to the temple, and bade them turn back, telling them what they had seen and heard. Christ looked upon the fleeing men with yearning pity for their fear, and their ignorance of what constituted true worship. In this scene He saw symbolized the dispersion of the whole Jewish nation for their wickedness and impenitence.

And why did the priests flee from the temple? Why did they not stand their ground? He who commanded them to go was a carpenter's son, a poor Galilean, without earthly rank or power. Why did they not resist Him? Why did they leave the gain so ill acquired, and flee at the command of One whose outward appearance was so humble?

Christ spoke with the authority of a king, and in His appearance, and in the tones of His voice, there was that which they had no power to resist. At the word of command they realized, as they had never realized before, their true position as hypocrites and robbers. When divinity flashed through humanity, not only did they see indignation on Christ's countenance; they realized the import of His words. They felt as if before the throne of the eternal Judge, with their sentence passed on them for time and for eternity. For a time they were convinced that Christ was a prophet; and many believed Him to be the Messiah. The Holy Spirit flashed into their minds the utterances of the prophets concerning Christ. Would they yield to this conviction?

Repent they would not. They knew that Christ's sympathy for the poor had been aroused. They knew that they had been guilty of extortion in their dealings with the people. Because Christ discerned their thoughts they hated Him. His public rebuke was humiliating to their pride, and they were jealous of His growing influence with the people. They determined to challenge Him as to the power by which He had driven them forth, and who gave Him this power.

Slowly and thoughtfully, but with hate in their hearts, they returned to the temple. But what a change had taken place during their absence! When they fled, the poor remained behind; and these were now looking to Jesus, whose countenance expressed His love and sympathy. With tears in His eyes, He said to the trembling ones around Him: Fear not; I will deliver thee, and thou shalt glorify Me. For this cause came I into the world.

The people pressed into Christ's presence with urgent, pitiful appeals: Master, bless me. His ear heard every cry. With pity exceeding that of a tender mother He bent over the suffering little ones. All received attention. Everyone was healed of whatever disease he had. The dumb opened their lips in praise; the blind beheld the face of their Restorer. The hearts of the sufferers were made glad.

As the priests and temple officials witnessed this great work, what a revelation to them were the sounds that fell on their ears! The people were relating the story of the pain they had suffered, of their disappointed hopes, of painful days and sleepless nights. When the last spark of hope seemed to be dead, Christ had healed them. The burden was so heavy, one said; but I have found a helper. He is the Christ of God, and I will devote my life to His service. Parents said to their children, He has saved your life; lift up your voice and praise Him. The voices of children and youth, fathers and mothers, friends and spectators, blended in thanksgiving and praise. Hope and gladness filled their hearts. Peace came to their minds. They were restored soul and body, and they returned home, proclaiming everywhere the matchless love of Jesus.

At the crucifixion of Christ, those who had thus been healed did not join with the rabble throng in crying, "Crucify Him, crucify Him." Their symapthies were with Jesus; for they had felt His great sympathy and wonderful power. They knew Him to be their Saviour; for He had given them health of body and soul. They listened to the preaching of the apostles, and the entrance of God's word into their hearts gave them understanding. They became agents of God's mercy, and instruments of His salvation.

The crowd that had fled from the temple court after a time slowly drifted back. They had partially recovered from the panic that had seized them, but their faces expressed irresolution and timidity. They looked with amazement on the works of Jesus, and were convicted that in Him the prophecies concerning the Messiah were fulfilled. The sin of the desecration of the temple rested, in a great degree, upon the priests. It was by their arrangement that the court had been turned into a market place. The people were comparatively innocent. They were impressed by the divine authority of Jesus; but with them the influence of the priests and rulers was paramount. They regarded Christ's mission as an innovation, and questioned His right to interfere with what was permitted by the authorities of the temple. They were offended because the traffic had been interrupted, and they stifled the convictions of the Holy Spirit.

Above all others the priests and rulers should have seen in Jesus the anointed of the Lord; for in their hands were the sacred scrolls that described His mission, and they knew that the cleansing of the temple was a manifestation of more than human power. Much as they hated Jesus, they could not free themselves from the thought that He might be a prophet sent by God to restore the sanctity of the temple. With a deference born of this fear, they went to Him with the inquiry, "What sign showest Thou unto us, seeing that Thou doest these things?"

Jesus had shown them a sign. In flashing light into their hearts, and in doing before them the works which the Messiah was to do, He had given convincing evidence of His character. Now when they asked for a sign, He answered them by a parable, showing that He read their malice, and saw to what lengths it would lead them. "Destroy this temple," He said, "and in three days I will raise it up."

In these words His meaning was twofold. He referred not only to the destruction of the Jewish temple and worship, but to His own death,—the destruction of the temple of His body. This the Jews were already plotting. As the priests and rulers returned to the temple, they had proposed to kill Jesus, and thus rid themselves of the troubler. Yet when He set before them their purpose, they did not understand Him. They took His words as applying only to the temple at Jerusalem, and with indignation exclaimed,

"Forty and six years was this temple in building, and wilt Thou rear it up in three days?" Now they felt that Jesus had justified their unbelief, and they were confirmed in their rejection of Him.

Christ did not design that His words should be understood by the unbelieving Jews, nor even by His disciples at this time. He knew that they would be misconstrued by His enemies, and would be turned against Him. At His trial they would be brought as an accusation, and on Calvary they would be flung at Him as a taunt. But to explain them now would give His disciples a knowledge of His sufferings, and bring upon them sorrow which as yet they were not able to bear. And an explanation would prematurely disclose to the Jews the result of their prejudice and unbelief. Already they had entered upon a path which they would steadily pursue until He should be led as a lamb to the slaughter.

It was for the sake of those who should believe on Him that these words of Christ were spoken. He knew that they would be repeated. Being spoken at the Passover, they would come to the ears of thousands, and be carried to all parts of the world. After He had risen from the dead, their meaning would be made plain. To many they would be conclusive evidence of His divinity.

Because of their spiritual darkness, even the disciples of Jesus often failed of comprehending His lessons. But many of these lessons were made plain to them by subsequent events. When He walked no more with them, His words were a stay to their hearts.

As referring to the temple at Jerusalem, the Saviour's words, "Destroy this temple, and in three days I will raise it up," had a deeper meaning than the hearers perceived. Christ was the foundation and life of the temple. Its services were typical of the sacrifice of the Son of God. The priesthood was established to represent the mediatorial character and work of Christ. The entire plan of sacrificial worship was a foreshadowing of the Saviour's death to redeem the world. There would be no efficacy in these offerings when the great event toward which they had pointed for ages was consummated.

Since the whole ritual economy was symbolical of Christ, it had no value apart from Him. When the Jews sealed their rejection of Christ by delivering Him to death, they rejected all that gave significance to the temple and its services. Its sacredness had departed. It was doomed to destruction. From that day sacrificial offerings and the service connected with them were meaningless. Like the offering of Cain, they did not express faith in the Saviour. In putting Christ to death, the Jews virtually destroyed their temple. When Christ was crucified, the inner veil of the temple was rent in twain from top to bottom, signifying that the great final sacrifice had been made, and that the system of sacrificial offerings was forever at an end.

"In three days I will raise it up." In the Saviour's death the powers of darkness seemed to prevail, and they exulted in their victory. But from the rent sepulcher of Joseph, Jesus came forth a conqueror. "Having spoiled principalities and powers, He made a show of them openly, triumphing over them." Col. 2:15. By virtue of His death and resurrection He became the minister of the "true tabernacle, which the Lord pitched, and not man." Heb. 8:2. Men reared the Jewish tabernacle; men builded the Jewish temple; but the sanctuary above, of which the earthly was a type, was built by no human architect. "Behold the Man whose name is The Branch; . . . He shall build the temple of the Lord; and He shall bear the glory, and shall sit and rule upon His throne; and He shall be a priest upon His throne." Zech. 6:12, 13.

The sacrificial service that had pointed to Christ passed away; but the eyes of men were turned to the true sacrifice for the sins of the world. The earthly priesthood ceased; but we look to Jesus, the minister of the new covenant, and "to the blood of sprinkling, that speaketh better things than that of Abel." "The way into the holiest of all was not yet made manifest, while as the first tabernacle was yet standing: . . . but Christ being come an high priest of good things to come, by a greater and more perfect tabernacle, not made with hands, . . . by His own blood He entered in once into the holy place, having obtained eternal redemption for us." Heb. 12:24; 9:8-12.

"Wherefore He is able also to save them to the uttermost that come unto God by Him, seeing He ever liveth to make intercession for them." Heb. 7:25. Though the ministration was to be removed from the earthly to the heavenly temple; though the sanctuary and our great high priest would be invisible to human sight, yet the disciples were to suffer no loss thereby. They would realize no break in their communion, and no diminution of power because of the Saviour's absence. While Jesus ministers in the sanctuary above, He is still by His Spirit the minister of the church on earth. He is withdrawn from the eye of sense, but His parting promise is fulfilled, "Lo, I am with you alway, even unto the end of the world." Matt. 28:20. While He delegates His power to inferior ministers, His energizing presence is still with His church.

"Seeing then that we have a great high priest, . . . Jesus, the Son of God, let us hold fast our profession. For we have not an high priest which cannot be touched with the feeling of our infirmities; but was in all points tempted like as we are, yet without sin. Let us therefore come boldly unto the throne of grace, that we may obtain mercy, and find grace to help in time of need." Heb. 4:14-16.

Chapter 12

NIGHT MEETING

NICODEMUS HELD a high position of trust in the Jewish nation. He was highly educated, and possessed talents of no ordinary character, and he was an honored member of the national council. With others, he had been stirred by the teaching of Jesus. Though rich, learned, and honored, he had been strangely attracted by the humble Nazarene. The lessons that had fallen from the Saviour's lips had greatly impressed him, and he desired to learn more of these wonderful truths.

Christ's exercise of authority in the cleansing of the temple had roused the determined hatred of the priests and rulers. They feared the power of this stranger. Such boldness on the part of an obscure Galilean was not to be tolerated. They were bent on putting an end to His work. But not all were agreed in this purpose. There were some that feared to oppose One who was so evidently moved upon by the Spirit of God. They remembered how prophets had been slain for rebuking the sins of the leaders in Israel. They knew that the bondage of the Jews to a heathen nation was the result of their stubbornness in rejecting reproofs from God. They feared that in plotting against Jesus the priests and rulers were following in the steps of their fathers, and would bring fresh calamities upon the nation. Nicodemus shared these feelings. In a council of the Sanhedrin, when the course to be pursued toward Jesus was considered, Nicodemus advised caution and moderation. He urged that if Jesus was really invested with authority from God, it would be perilous to reject His warnings. The priests dared not disregard this counsel, and for the time they took no open measures against the Saviour.

Since hearing Jesus, Nicodemus had anxiously studied

the prophecies relating to the Messiah; and the more he searched, the stronger was his conviction that this was the One who was to come. With many others in Israel he had been greatly distressed by the profanation of the temple. He was a witness of the scene when Jesus drove out the buyers and the sellers; he beheld the wonderful manifesta tion of divine power; he saw the Saviour receiving the poor and healing the sick; he saw their looks of joy, and heard their words of praise; and he could not doubt that Jesus of Nazareth was the Sent of God.

He greatly desired an interview with Jesus, but shrank from seeking Him openly. It would be too humiliating for a ruler of the Jews to acknowledge himself in sympathy with a teacher as yet so little known. And should his visit come to the knowledge of the Sanhedrin, it would draw upon him their scorn and denunciation. He resolved upon a secret interview, excusing this on the ground that if he were to go openly, others might follow his example. Learning by special inquiry the Saviour's place of retire- ment in the Mount of Olives, he waited until the city was hushed in slumber, and then sought Him.

In the presence of Christ, Nicodemus felt a strange ti- midity, which he endeavored to conceal under an air of composure and dignity. "Rabbi," he said, "we know that Thou art a teacher come from God: for no man can do these miracles that Thou doest, except God be with him." By speaking of Christ's rare gifts as a teacher, and also of His wonderful power to perform miracles, he hoped to pave the way for his interview. His words were designed to express and to invite confidence; but they really expressed unbelief. He did not acknowledge Jesus to be the Messiah, but only a teacher sent from God.

Instead of recognizing this salutation, Jesus bent His eyes upon the speaker, as if reading his very soul. In His infinite wisdom He saw before Him a seeker after truth. He knew the object of this visit, and with a desire to deep- en the conviction already resting upon His listener's mind, He came directly to the point, saying solemnly, yet kindly, "Verily, verily, I say unto thee, Except a man be born from above, he cannot see the kingdom of God." margin.

Nicodemus had come to the Lord thinking to enter into a discussion with Him, but Jesus laid bare the foundation principles of truth. He said to Nicodemus, It is not theo- retical knowledge you need so much as spiritual regeneration. You need not to have your curiosity satisfied, but to have a new heart. You must receive a new life from above before you can appreciate heavenly things. Until this change takes place, making all things new, it will result in no saving good for you to discuss with Me My authority or My mission.

Nicodemus had heard the preaching of John the Baptist concerning repentance and baptism, and pointing the people to One who should baptize with the Holy Spirit. He himself had felt that there was a lack of spirituality among the Jews, that, to a great degree, they were controlled by bigotry and worldly ambition. He had hoped for a better state of things at the Messiah's coming. Yet the heart-searching message of the Baptist had failed to work in him conviction of sin. He was a strict Pharisee, and prided himself on his good works. He was widely esteemed for his benevolence and his liberality in sustaining the temple service, and he felt secure of the favor of God. He was startled at the thought of a kingdom too pure for him to see in his present state.

The figure of the new birth, which Jesus had used, was not wholly unfamiliar to Nicodemus. Converts from heathenism to the faith of Israel were often compared to children just born. Therefore he must have perceived that the words of Christ were not to be taken in a literal sense. But by virtue of his birth as an Israelite he regarded himself as sure of a place in the kingdom of God. He felt that he needed no change. Hence his surprise at the Saviour's words. He was irritated by their close application to himself. The pride of the Pharisee was struggling against the honest desire of the seeker after truth. He wondered that Christ should speak to him as He did, not respecting his position as ruler in Israel.

Surprised out of his self-possession, he answered Christ in words full of irony, "How can a man be born when he is old?" Like many others when cutting truth is brought home to the conscience, he revealed the fact that the natural man receiveth not the things of the Spirit of God. There is in him nothing that responds to spiritual things; for spiritual things are spiritually discerned.

But the Saviour did not meet argument with argument. Raising His hand with solemn, quiet dignity, He pressed the truth home with greater assurance, "Verily, verily, I say unto thee, Except a man be born of water and of the Spirit, he cannot enter into the kingdom of God." Nicodemus knew that Christ here referred to water baptism and the renewing of the heart by the Spirit of God. He was convinced that he was in the presence of the One whom John the Baptist had foretold.

Jesus continued: "That which is born of the flesh is flesh; and that which is born of the Spirit is spirit." By nature the heart is evil, and "who can bring a clean thing out of an unclean? not one." Job 14:4. No human invention can find a remedy for the sinning soul. "The carnal mind is enmity against God: for it is not subject to the law of God, neither indeed can be." "Out of the heart proceed evil thoughts, murders, adulteries, fornications, thefts, false witness, blasphemies." Rom. 8:7; Matt. 15:19. The fountain of the heart must be purified before the streams can become pure. He who is trying to reach heaven by his own works in keeping the law is attempting an impossibility. There is no safety for one who has merely a legal religion, a form of godliness. The Christian's life is not a modification or improvement of the old, but a transformation of nature. There is a death to self and sin, and a new life altogether. This change can be brought about only by the effectual working of the Holy Spirit.

Nicodemus was still perplexed, and Jesus used the wind to illustrate His meaning: "The wind bloweth where it listeth. and thou hearest the sound thereof, but canst not tell whence it cometh, and whither it goeth: so is everyone that is born of the Spirit."

The wind is heard among the branches of the trees, rustling the leaves and flowers; yet it is invisible, and no man knows whence it comes or whither it goes. So with the work of the Holy Spirit upon the heart. It can no more be explained than can the movements of the wind. A person may not be able to tell the exact time or place, or to trace all the circumstances in the process of conversion; but this does not prove him to be unconverted. By an agency as unseen as the wind, Christ is constantly working upon the heart. Little by little, perhaps unconsciously to the receiver, impressions are made that tend to draw the soul to Christ. These may be received through meditating upon Him, through reading the Scriptures, or through hearing the word from the living preacher. Suddenly, as the Spirit comes with more direct appeal, the soul gladly surrenders itself to Jesus. By many this is called sudden conversion; but it is the result of long wooing by the Spirit of God,—a patient, protracted process.

While the wind is itself invisible, it produces effects that are seen and felt. So the work of the Spirit upon the soul will reveal itself in every act of him who has felt its saving power. When the Spirit of God takes possession of the heart, it transforms the life. Sinful thoughts are put away, evil deeds are renounced; love, humility, and peace take the place of anger, envy, and strife. Joy takes the place of sadness, and the countenance reflects the light of heaven. No one sees the hand that lifts the burden, or beholds the light descend from the courts above. The blessing comes when by faith the soul surrenders itself to God. Then that power which no human eye can see creates a new being in the image of God.

It is impossible for finite minds to comprehend the work of redemption. Its mystery exceeds human knowledge; yet he who passes from death to life realizes that it is a divine reality. The beginning of redemption we may know here through a personal experience. Its results reach through the eternal ages.

While Jesus was speaking, some gleams of truth penetrated the ruler's mind. The softening, subduing influence of the Holy Spirit impressed his heart. Yet he did not fully understand the Saviour's words. He was not so much impressed by the necessity of the new birth as by the manner of its accomplishment. He said wonderingly, "How can these things be?"

"Art thou a master of Israel, and knowest not these things?" Jesus asked. Surely one entrusted with the religious instruction of the people should not be ignorant of truths so important. His words conveyed the lesson that instead of feeling irritated over the plain words of truth, Nicodemus should have had a very humble opinion of himself, because of his spiritual ignorance. Yet Christ spoke with such solemn dignity, and both look and tone expressed such earnest love, that Nicodemus was not offended as he realized his humiliating condition.

But as Jesus explained that His mission on earth was to establish a spiritual instead of a temporal kingdom, His hearer was troubled. Seeing this, Jesus added, "If I have told you earthly things, and ye believe not, how shall ye believe, if I tell you of heavenly things?" If Nicodemus could not receive Christ's teaching, illustrating the work of grace upon the heart, how could he comprehend the nature of His glorious heavenly kingdom? Not discerning the nature of Christ's work on earth, he could not understand His work in heaven.

The Jews whom Jesus had driven from the temple claimed to be children of Abraham, but they fled from the Saviour's presence because they could not endure the glory of God which was manifested in Him. Thus they gave evidence that they were not fitted by the grace of God to participate in the sacred services of the temple. They were zealous to maintain an appearance of holiness, but they neglected holiness of heart. While they were sticklers for the letter of the law, they were constantly violating its spirit. Their great need was that very change which Christ had been explaining to Nicodemus,—a new moral birth, a cleansing from sin, and a renewing of knowledge and holiness.

There was no excuse for the blindness of Israel in regard to the work of regeneration. Under the inspiration of the Holy Spirit, Isaiah had written, "We are all as an unclean thing, and all our righteousnesses are as filthy rags." David had prayed, "Create in me a clean heart, O God; and renew a right spirit within me." And through Ezekiel the promise had been given, "A new heart also will I give you, and a new spirit will I put within you: and I will take away the stony heart out of your flesh, and I will give you an heart of flesh. And I will put My Spirit within you, and cause you to walk in My statutes." Isa. 64:6; Ps. 51:10; Ezek. 36:26, 27.

Nicodemus had read these scriptures with a clouded mind; but he now began to comprehend their meaning. He saw that the most rigid obedience to the mere letter of the law as applied to the outward life could entitle no man to enter the kingdom of heaven. In the estimation of men, his life had been just and honorable; but in the presence of Christ he felt that his heart was unclean, and his life unholy.

Nicodemus was being drawn to Christ. As the Saviour explained to him concerning the new birth, he longed to have this change wrought in himself. By what means could it be accomplished? Jesus answered the unspoken question: "As Moses lifted up the serpent in the wilderness, even so must the Son of man be lifted up: that whosoever believeth in Him should not perish, but have eternal life."

Here was ground with which Nicodemus was familiar. The symbol of the uplifted serpent made plain to him the Saviour's mission. When the people of Israel were dying from the sting of the fiery serpents, God directed Moses to make a serpent of brass, and place it on high in the midst of the congregation. Then the word was sounded throughout the encampment that all who would look upon the serpent should live. The people well knew that in itself the serpent had no power to help them. It was a symbol of Christ. As the image made in the likeness of the destroying serpents was lifted up for their healing, so One made "in the likeness of sinful flesh" was to be their Redeemer. Rom. 8:3. Many of the Israelites regarded the sacrificial service as having in itself virtue to set them free from sin. God desired to teach them that it had no more value than that serpent of brass. It was to lead their minds to the Saviour. Whether for the healing of their wounds or the pardon of their sins, they could do nothing for themselves but show their faith in the Gift of God. They were to look and live.

Those who had been bitten by the serpents might have delayed to look. They might have questioned how there could be efficacy in that brazen symbol. They might have demanded a scientific explanation. But no explanation was given. They must accept the word of God to them through Moses. To refuse to look was to perish.

Not through controversy and discussion is the soul enlightened. We must look and live. Nicodemus received the lesson, and carried it with him. He searched the Scriptures in a new way, not for the discussion of a theory, but in order to receive life for the soul. He began to see the kingdom of heaven as he submitted himself to the leading of the Holy Spirit.

There are thousands today who need to learn the same truth that was taught to Nicodemus by the uplifted serpent. They depend on their obedience to the law of God to commend them to His favor. When they are bidden to look to Jesus, and believe that He saves them solely through His grace, they exclaim, "How can these things be?"

Like Nicodemus, we must be willing to enter into life in the same way as the chief of sinners. Than Christ, "there is none other name under heaven given among men, whereby we must be saved." Acts 4:12. Through faith we receive the grace of God; but faith is not our Saviour. It earns nothing. It is the hand by which we lay hold upon Christ, and appropriate His merits, the remedy for sin. And we cannot even repent without the aid of the Spirit of God. The Scripture says of Christ, "Him hath God exalted with His right hand to be a Prince and a Saviour, for to give repentance to Israel, and forgiveness of sins." Acts 5:31. Repentance comes from Christ as truly as does pardon.

How, then, are we to be saved? "As Moses lifted up the serpent in the wilderness," so the Son of man has been lifted up, and everyone who has been deceived and bitten by the serpent may look and live. "Behold the Lamb of God, which taketh away the sin of the world." John 1:29. The light shining from the cross reveals the love of God. His love is drawing us to Himself. If we do not resist this drawing, we shall be led to the foot of the cross in repentance for the sins that have crucified the Saviour. Then the Spirit of God through faith produces a new life in the soul. The thoughts and desires are brought into obedience to the will of Christ. The heart, the mind, are created anew in the image of Him who works in us to subdue all things to Himself. Then the law of God is written in the mind and heart, and we can say with Christ, "I delight to do Thy will, O my God." Ps. 40:8.

In the interview with Nicodemus, Jesus unfolded the plan of salvation and His mission to the world. In none of His subsequent discourses did He explain so fully, step by step, the work necessary to be done in the hearts of all who would inherit the kingdom of heaven. At the very beginning of His ministry He opened the truth to a member of the Sanhedrin, to the mind that was most receptive, and to an appointed teacher of the people. But the leaders of Israel did not welcome the light. Nicodemus hid the truth in his heart, and for three years there was little apparent fruit.

But Jesus was acquainted with the soil into which He cast the seed. The words spoken at night to one listener in the lonely mountain were not lost. For a time Nicodemus did not publicly acknowledge Christ, but he watched His life, and pondered His teachings. In the Sanhedrin council he repeatedly thwarted the schemes of the priests to destroy Him. When at last Jesus was lifted up on the cross, Nicodemus remembered the teaching upon Olivet: "As Moses lifted up the serpent in the wilderness, even so must the Son of man be lifted up: that whosoever believeth in Him should not perish, but have eternal life." The light from that secret interview illumined the cross upon Calvary, and Nicodemus saw in Jesus the world's Redeemer.

After the Lord's ascension, when the disciples were scattered by persecution, Nicodemus came boldly to the front.

He employed his wealth in sustaining the infant church that the Jews had expected to be blotted out at the death of Christ. In the time of peril he who had been so cautious and questioning was firm as a rock, encouraging the faith of the disciples, and furnishing means to carry forward the work of the gospel. He was scorned and persecuted by those who had paid him reverence in other days. He became poor in this world's goods; yet he faltered not in the faith which had its beginning in that night conference with Jesus.

Nicodemus related to John the story of that interview, and by his pen it was recorded for the instruction of millions. The truths there taught are as important today as they were on that solemn night in the shadowy mountain, when the Jewish ruler came to learn the way of life from the lowly Teacher of Galilee.

Chapter 13

A SAMARITAN WOMAN

ON THE WAY to Galilee Jesus passed through Samaria. It was noon when He reached the beautiful Vale of Shechem. At the opening of this valley was Jacob's well. Wearied with His journey, He sat down here to rest while His disciples went to buy food.

The Jews and the Samaritans were bitter enemies, and as far as possible avoided all dealing with each other. To trade with the Samaritans in case of necessity was indeed counted lawful by the rabbis; but all social intercourse with them was condemned. A Jew would not borrow from a Samaritan, nor receive a kindness, not even a morsel of bread or a cup of water. The disciples, in buying food, were acting in harmony with the custom of their nation. But beyond this they did not go. To ask a favor of the Samaritans, or in any way seek to benefit them, did not enter into the thought of even Christ's disciples.

As Jesus sat by the well side, He was faint from hunger and thirst. The journey since morning had been long, and now the sun of noontide beat upon Him. His thirst was increased by the thought of the cool, refreshing water so near, yet inaccessible to Him; for He had no rope nor water jar, and the well was deep. The lot of humanity was His, and He waited for someone to come to draw.

A woman of Samaria approached, and seeming unconscious of His presence, filled her pitcher with water. As she turned to go away, Jesus asked her for a drink. Such a favor no Oriental would withhold. In the East, water was called "the gift of God." To offer a drink to the thirsty traveler was held to be a duty so sacred that the Arabs of the desert would go out of their way in order to perform it. The hatred between Jews and Samaritans prevented the

This chapter is based on John 4:1-42.

woman from offering a kindness to Jesus; but the Saviour was seeking to find the key to this heart, and with the tact born of divine love, He asked, not offered, a favor. The offer of a kindness might have been rejected; but trust awakens trust. The King of heaven came to this outcast soul, asking a service at her hands. He who made the ocean, who controls the waters of the great deep, who opened the springs and channels of the earth, rested from His weariness at Jacob's well, and was dependent upon a stranger's kindness for even the gift of a drink of water.

The woman saw that Jesus was a Jew. In her surprise she forgot to grant His request, but tried to learn the reason for it. "How is it," she said, "that Thou, being a Jew, askest drink of me, which am a woman of Samaria?"

Jesus answered, "If thou knewest the gift of God, and who it is that saith to thee, Give Me to drink; thou wouldest have asked of Him, and He would have given thee living water." You wonder that I should ask of you even so small a favor as a draught of water from the well at our feet. Had you asked of Me, I would have given you to drink of the water of everlasting life.

The woman had not comprehended the words of Christ, but she felt their solemn import. Her light, bantering manner began to change. Supposing that Jesus spoke of the well before them, she said, "Sir, Thou hast nothing to draw with, and the well is deep: from whence then hast Thou that living water? Art Thou greater than our father Jacob, which gave us the well, and drank thereof himself?" She saw before her only a thirsty traveler, wayworn and dusty. In her mind she compared Him with the honored patriarch Jacob. She cherished the feeling, which is so natural, that no other well could be equal to that provided by the fathers. She was looking backward to the fathers, forward to the Messiah's coming, while the Hope of the fathers, the Messiah Himself, was beside her, and she knew Him not. How many thirsting souls are today close by the living fountain, yet looking far away for the wellsprings of life! "Say not in thine heart, Who shall ascend into heaven? (that is, to bring Christ down from above:) or, Who shall descend into the deep? (that is, to bring up Christ again from the dead.) . . . The word is nigh thee, even in thy mouth, and in thy heart: . . . if thou shalt confess with thy mouth the Lord Jesus, and shalt believe in thine heart that God hath raised Him from the dead, thou shalt be saved." Rom. 10:6-9.

Jesus did not immediately answer the question in regard to Himself, but with solemn earnestness He said, "Whosoever drinketh of this water shall thirst again: but whosoever drinketh of the water that I shall give him shall never thirst; but the water that I shall give him shall be in him a well of water springing up into everlasting life."

He who seeks to quench his thirst at the fountains of this world will drink only to thirst again. Everywhere men are unsatisfied. They long for something to supply the need of the soul. Only One can meet that want. The need of the world, "The Desire of all nations," is Christ. The divine grace which He alone can impart, is as living water, purifying, refreshing, and invigorating the soul.

Jesus did not convey the idea that merely one draft of the water of life would suffice the receiver. He who tastes of the love of Christ will continually long for more; but he seeks for nothing else. The riches, honors, and pleasures of the world do not attract him. The constant cry of his heart is, More of Thee. And He who reveals to the soul its necessity is waiting to satisfy its hunger and thirst. Every human resource and dependence will fail. The cisterns will be emptied, the pools become dry; but our Redeemer is an inexhaustible fountain. We may drink, and drink again, and ever find a fresh supply. He in whom Christ dwells has within himself the fountain of blessing,—"a well of water springing up into everlasting life." From this source he may draw strength and grace sufficient for all his needs.

As Jesus spoke of the living water, the woman looked upon Him with wondering attention. He had aroused her interest, and awakened a desire for the gift of which He spoke. She perceived that it was not the water of Jacob's well to which He referred; for of this she used continually, drinking, and thirsting again. "Sir," she said, "give me this water, that I thirst not, neither come hither to draw."

Jesus now abruptly turned the conversation. Before this soul could receive the gift He longed to bestow, she must be brought to recognize her sin and her Saviour. He "saith unto her, Go, call thy husband, and come hither." She answered, "I have no husband." Thus she hoped to prevent all questioning in that direction. But the Saviour continued, "Thou hast well said, I have no husband: for thou hast had five husbands; and he whom thou now hast is not thy husband: in that saidst thou truly."

The listener trembled. A mysterious hand was turning the pages of her life history, bringing to view that which she had hoped to keep forever hidden. Who was He that could read the secrets of her life? There came to her thoughts of eternity, of the future judgment, when all that is now hidden shall be revealed. In its light, conscience was awakened.

She could deny nothing; but she tried to evade all mention of a subject so unwelcome. With deep reverence, she said, "Sir, I perceive that Thou art a prophet." Then, hoping to silence conviction, she turned to points of religious controversy. If this was a prophet, surely He could give her instruction concerning these matters that had been so long disputed.

Patiently Jesus permitted her to lead the conversation whither she would. Meanwhile He watched for the opportunity of again bringing the truth home to her heart. "Our fathers worshiped in this mountain," she said, "and ye say, that in Jerusalem is the place where men ought to worship." Just in sight was Mount Gerizim. Its temple was demolished, and only the altar remained. The place of worship had been a subject of contention between the Jews and the Samaritans. Some of the ancestors of the latter people had once belonged to Israel; but because of their sins, the Lord suffered them to be overcome by an idolatrous nation. For many generations they were intermingled with idolaters, whose religion gradually contaminated their own. It is true they held that their idols were only to remind them of the living God, the Ruler of the universe; nevertheless the people were led to reverence their graven images.

When the temple at Jerusalem was rebuilt in the days of Ezra, the Samaritans wished to join the Jews in its erection. This privilege was refused them, and a bitter animosity sprang up between the two peoples. The Samaritans built a rival temple on Mount Gerizim. Here they worshiped in accordance with the Mosaic ritual, though they did not wholly renounce idolatry. But disasters attended them, their temple was destroyed by their enemies, and they seemed to be under a curse; yet they still clung to their traditions and their forms of worship. They would not acknowledge the temple at Jerusalem as the house of God, nor admit that the religion of the Jews was superior to their own.

In answer to the woman, Jesus said, "Believe Me, the hour cometh, when ye shall neither in this mountain, nor yet at Jerusalem, worship the Father. Ye worship ye know not what: we know what we worship: for salvation is of the Jews." Jesus had shown that He was free from Jewish prejudice against the Samaritans. Now He sought to break down the prejudice of this Samaritan against the Jews. While referring to the fact that the faith of the Samaritans was corrupted with idolatry, He declared that the great truths of redemption had been committed to the Jews, and that from among them the Messiah was to appear In the Sacred Writings they had a clear presentation of the character of God and the principles of His government. Jesus classed Himself with the Jews as those to whom God had given a knowledge of Himself.

He desired to lift the thoughts of His hearer above matters of form and ceremony, and questions of controversy. "The hour cometh," He said, "and now is, when the true worshipers shall worship the Father in spirit and in truth: for the Father seeketh such to worship Him. God is a Spirit: and they that worship Him must worship Him in spirit and in truth."

Here is declared the same truth that Jesus had revealed to Nicodemus when He said, "Except a man be born from above, he cannot see the kingdom of God." John 3:3, margin. Not by seeking a holy mountain or a sacred temple are men brought into communion with heaven. Religion is not to be confined to external forms and ceremonies. The religion that comes from God is the only religion that will lead to God. In order to serve Him aright, we must be born of the divine Spirit. This will purify the heart and renew the mind, giving us a new capacity for knowing and loving God. It will give us a willing obedience to all His requirements. This is true worship. It is the fruit of the working of the Holy Spirit. By the Spirit every sincere prayer is indited, and such prayer is acceptable to God. Wherever a soul reaches out after God, there the Spirit's working is manifest, and God will reveal Himself to that soul. For such worshipers He is seeking. He waits to receive them, and to make them His sons and daughters.

As the woman talked with Jesus, she was impressed with His words. Never had she heard such sentiments from the priests of her own people or from the Jews. As the past of her life had been spread out before her, she had been made sensible of her great want. She realized her soul thirst, which the waters of the well of Sychar could never satisfy. Nothing that had hitherto come in contact with her had so awakened her to a higher need. Jesus had convinced her that He read the secrets of her life; yet she felt that He was her friend, pitying and loving her. While the very purity of His presence condemned her sin, He had spoken no word of denunciation, but had told her of His grace, that could renew the soul. She began to have some conviction of His character. The question arose in her mind, Might not this be the long-looked-for Messiah? She said to Him, "I know that Messias cometh, which is called Christ: when He is come, He will tell us all things." Jesus answered, "I that speak unto thee am He."

As the woman heard these words, faith sprang up in her heart. She accepted the wonderful announcement from the lips of the divine Teacher.

This woman was in an appreciative state of mind. She was ready to receive the noblest revelation; for she was interested in the Scriptures, and the Holy Spirit had been preparing her mind to receive more light. She had studied the Old Testament promise, "The Lord thy God will raise up unto thee a Prophet from the midst of thee, of thy brethren, like unto me; unto Him ye shall hearken." Deut. 18:15. She longed to understand this prophecy. Light was already flashing into her mind. The water of life, the spiritual life which Christ gives to every thirsty soul, had begun to spring up in her heart. The Spirit of the Lord was working with her.

The plain statement made by Christ to this woman could not have been made to the self-righteous Jews. Christ was far more reserved when He spoke to them. That which had been withheld from the Jews, and which the disciples were afterward enjoined to keep secret, was revealed to her. Jesus saw that she would make use of her knowledge in bringing others to share His grace.

When the disciples returned from their errand, they were surprised to find their Master speaking with the woman. He had not taken the refreshing draught that He desired, and He did not stop to eat the food His disciples had brought. When the woman had gone, the disciples entreated Him to eat. They saw Him silent, absorbed, as in rapt meditation. His face was beaming with light, and they feared to interrupt His communion with heaven. But they knew that He was faint and weary, and thought it their duty to remind Him of His physical necessities. Jesus recognized their loving interest, and He said, "I have meat to eat that ye know not of."

The disciples wondered who could have brought Him

food; but He explained, "My meat is to do the will of Him that sent Me, and to accomplish His work." R. V. As His words to the woman had aroused her conscience, Jesus rejoiced. He saw her drinking of the water of life, and His own hunger and thirst were satisfied. The accomplishment of the mission which He had left heaven to perform strengthened the Saviour for His labor, and lifted Him above the necessities of humanity. To minister to a soul hungering and thirsting for the truth was more grateful to Him than eating or drinking. It was a comfort, a refreshment, to Him. Benevolence was the life of His soul.

Our Redeemer thirsts for recognition. He hungers for the sympathy and love of those whom He has purchased with His own blood. He longs with inexpressible desire that they should come to Him and have life. As the mother watches for the smile of recognition from her little child, which tells of the dawning of intelligence, so does Christ watch for the expression of grateful love, which shows that spiritual life is begun in the soul.

The woman had been filled with joy as she listened to Christ's words. The wonderful revelation was almost overpowering. Leaving her waterpot, she returned to the city, to carry the message to others. Jesus knew why she had gone. Leaving her waterpot spoke unmistakably as to the effect of His words. It was the earnest desire of her soul to obtain the living water; and she forgot her errand to the well, she forgot the Saviour's thirst, which she had purposed to supply. With heart overflowing with gladness, she hastened on her way, to impart to others the precious light she had received.

"Come, see a man, which told me all things that ever I did," she said to the men of the city. "Is not this the Christ?" Her words touched their hearts. There was a new expression on her face, a change in her whole appearance. They were interested to see Jesus. "Then they went out of the city, and came unto Him."

As Jesus still sat at the well side, He looked over the fields of grain that were spread out before Him, their tender green touched by the golden sunlight. Pointing His disciples to the scene, He employed it as a symbol: "Say not ye, There are yet four months, and then cometh harvest? behold, I say unto you, Lift up your eyes, and look on the fields; for they are white already to harvest." And as He spoke, He looked on the groups that were coming to the well. It was four months to the time for harvesting the grain, but here was a harvest ready for the reaper.

"He that reapeth," He said, "receiveth wages, and gathereth fruit unto life eternal: that both he that soweth and he that reapeth may rejoice together. And herein is that saying true, One soweth, and another reapeth." Here Christ points out the sacred service owed to God by those who receive the gospel. They are to be His living agencies. He requires their individual service. And whether we sow or reap, we are working for God. One scatters the seed; another gathers in the harvest; and both the sower and the reaper receive wages. They rejoice together in the reward of their labor.

Jesus said to the disciples, "I sent you to reap that whereon ye bestowed no labor: other men labored, and ye are entered into their labors." The Saviour was here looking forward to the great ingathering on the day of Pentecost. The disciples were not to regard this as the result of their own efforts. They were entering into other men's labors. Ever since the fall of Adam Christ had been committing the seed of the word to His chosen servants, to be sown in human hearts. And an unseen agency, even an omnipotent power, had worked silently but effectually to produce the harvest. The dew and rain and sunshine of God's grace had been given, to refresh and nourish the seed of truth. Christ was about to water the seed with His own blood. His disciples were privileged to be laborers together with God. They were coworkers with Christ and with the holy men of old. By the outpouring of the Holy Spirit at Pentecost, thousands were to be converted in a day. This was the result of Christ's sowing, the harvest of His work.

In the words spoken to the woman at the well, good seed had been sown, and how quickly the harvest was received. The Samaritans came and heard Jesus, and believed on Him. Crowding about Him at the well, they plied Him with questions, and eagerly received His explanations of many things that had been obscure to them. As they listened, their perplexity began to clear away. They were like a people in great darkness tracing up a sudden ray of light till they had found the day. But they were not satisfied with this short conference. They were anxious to hear more, and to have their friends also listen to this wonderful teacher. They invited Him to their city, and begged Him to remain with them. For two days He tarried in Samaria, and many more believed on Him.

The Pharisees despised the simplicity of Jesus. They ignored His miracles, and demanded a sign that He was the Son of God. But the Samaritans asked no sign, and Jesus performed no miracles among them, save in revealing the secrets of her life to the woman at the well. Yet many received Him. In their new joy they said to the woman, "Now we believe, not because of thy saying: for we have heard Him ourselves, and know that this is indeed the Christ, the Saviour of the world."

The Samaritans believed that the Messiah was to come as the Redeemer, not only of the Jews, but of the world. The Holy Spirit through Moses had foretold Him as a prophet sent from God. Through Jacob it had been declared that unto Him should the gathering of the people be; and through Abraham, that in Him all the nations of the earth should be blessed. On these scriptures the people of Samaria based their faith in the Messiah. The fact that the Jews had misinterpreted the later prophets, attributing to the first advent the glory of Christ's second coming, had led the Samaritans to discard all the sacred writings except those given through Moses. But as the Saviour swept away these false interpretations, many accepted the later prophecies and the words of Christ Himself in regard to the kingdom of God.

Jesus had begun to break down the partition wall between Jew and Gentile, and to preach salvation to the world. Though He was a Jew, He mingled freely with the Samaritans, setting at nought the Pharisaic customs of His nation. In face of their prejudices He accepted the hospitality of this despised people. He slept under their roofs, ate with them at their tables,—partaking of the food prepared and served by their hands,—taught in their streets, and treated them with the utmost kindness and courtesy.

In the temple at Jerusalem a low wall separated the outer court from all other portions of the sacred building. Upon this wall were inscriptions in different languages, stating that none but Jews were allowed to pass this boundary. Had a Gentile presumed to enter the inner enclosure, he would have desecrated the temple, and would have paid the penalty with his life. But Jesus, the originator of the temple and its service, drew the Gentiles to Him by the tie of human sympathy, while His divine grace brought to them the salvation which the Jews rejected.

The stay of Jesus in Samaria was designed to be a blessing to His disciples, who were still under the influence of Jewish bigotry. They felt that loyalty to their own nation required them to cherish enmity toward the Samaritans. They wondered at the conduct of Jesus. They could not refuse to follow His example, and during the two days in Samaria, fidelity to Him kept their prejudices under control; yet in heart they were unreconciled. They were slow to learn that their contempt and hatred must give place to pity and sympathy. But after the Lord's ascension, His lessons came back to them with a new meaning. After the outpouring of the Holy Spirit, they recalled the Saviour's look, His words, the respect and tenderness of His bearing toward these despised strangers. When Peter went to preach in Samaria, he brought the same spirit into his own work. When John was called to Ephesus and Smyrna, he remembered the experience at Shechem, and was filled with gratitude to the divine Teacher, who, foreseeing the difficulties they must meet, had given them help in His own example.

The Saviour is still carrying forward the same work as when He proffered the water of life to the woman of Samaria. Those who call themselves His followers may despise and shun the outcast ōnes; but no circumstance of birth or nationality, no condition of life, can turn away His love from the children of men. To every soul, however sinful, Jesus says, If thou hadst asked of Me, I would have given thee living water.

The gospel invitation is not to be narrowed down, and presented only to a select few, who, we suppose, will do us honor if they accept it. The message is to be given to all. Wherever hearts are open to receive the truth, Christ is ready to instruct them. He reveals to them the Father, and the worship acceptable to Him who reads the heart. For such He uses no parables. To them, as to the woman at the well, He says, "I that speak unto thee am He."

When Jesus sat down to rest at Jacob's well, He had come from Judea, where His ministry had produced little fruit. He had been rejected by the priests and rabbis, and even the people who professed to be His disciples had failed of perceiving His divine character. He was faint and weary; yet He did not neglect the opportunity of speaking to one woman, though she was a stranger, an alien from Israel, and living in open sin.

The Saviour did not wait for congregations to assemble.

Often He began His lessons with only a few gathered about Him, but one by one the passers-by paused to listen, until a multitude heard with wonder and awe the words of God through the heaven-sent Teacher. The worker for Christ should not feel that he cannot speak with the same earnestness to a few hearers as to a larger company. There may be only one to hear the message; but who can tell how far-reaching will be its influence? It seemed a small matter, even to His disciples, for the Saviour to spend His time upon a woman of Samaria. But He reasoned more earnestly and eloquently with her than with kings, councilors, or high priests. The lessons He gave to that woman have been repeated to the earth's remotest bounds.

As soon as she had found the Saviour the Samaritan woman brought others to Him. She proved herself a more effective missionary than His own disciples. The disciples saw nothing in Samaria to indicate that it was an encouraging field. Their thoughts were fixed upon a great work to be done in the future. They did not see that right around them was a harvest to be gathered. But through the woman whom they despised, a whole cityful were brought to hear the Saviour. She carried the light at once to her countrymen.

This woman represents the working of a practical faith in Christ. Every true disciple is born into the kingdom of God as a missionary. He who drinks of the living water becomes a fountain of life. The receiver becomes a giver. The grace of Christ in the soul is like a spring in the desert, welling up to refresh all, and making those who are ready to perish eager to drink of the water of life.

Chapter 14

PROPHET WITHOUT HONOR

ACROSS THE BRIGHT days of Chist's ministry in Galilee, one shadow lay. The people of Nazareth rejected Him. "Is not this the carpenter's son?" they said.

During His childhood and youth, Jesus had worshiped among His brethren in the synagogue at Nazareth. Since the opening of His ministry He had been absent from them, but they had not been ignorant of what had befallen Him. As He again appeared among them, their interest and expectation were excited to the highest pitch. Here were the familiar forms and faces of those whom He had known from infancy. Here were His mother, His brothers and sisters, and all eyes were turned upon Him as He entered the synagogue upon the Sabbath day, and took His place among the worshipers.

In the regular service for the day, the elder read from the prophets, and exhorted the people still to hope for the Coming One, who would bring in a glorious reign, and banish all oppression. He sought to encourage his hearers by rehearsing the evidence that the Messiah's coming was near. He described the glory of His advent, keeping prominent the thought that He would appear at the head of armies to deliver Israel.

When a rabbi was present at the synagogue, he was expected to deliver the sermon, and any Israelite might give the reading from the prophets. Upon this Sabbath Jesus was requested to take part in the service. He "stood up to read. And there was delivered unto Him a roll of the prophet Isaiah." Luke 4:16, 17, R. V., margin. The scripture which He read was one that was understood as referring to the Messiah:

This chapter is based on Luke 4:16-30.

"The Spirit of the Lord is upon Me,
Because He hath anointed Me to preach the gospel to the
    poor;
He hath sent Me to heal the brokenhearted,
To preach deliverance to the captives,
And recovering of sight to the blind,
To set at liberty them that are bruised,
To preach the acceptable year of the Lord."

"And He closed the roll, and gave it back to the attendant: . . . and the eyes of all in the synagogue were fastened on Him. . . . And all bare Him witness, and wondered at the words of grace which proceeded out of His mouth." Luke 4:20-22, R. V., margin.

Jesus stood before the people as a living expositor of the prophecies concerning Himself. Explaining the words He had read, He spoke of the Messiah as a reliever of the oppressed, a liberator of captives, a healer of the afflicted, restoring sight to the blind, and revealing to the world the light of truth. His impressive manner and the wonderful import of His words thrilled the hearers with a power they had never felt before. The tide of divine influence broke every barrier down; like Moses, they beheld the Invisible. As their hearts were moved upon by the Holy Spirit, they responded with fervent amens and praises to the Lord.

But when Jesus announced, "This day is this scripture fulfilled in your ears," they were suddenly recalled to think of themselves, and of the claims of Him who had been addressing them. They, Israelites, children of Abraham, had been represented as in bondage. They had been addressed as prisoners to be delivered from the power of evil; as in darkness, and needing the light of truth. Their pride was offended, and their fears were roused. The words of Jesus indicated that His work for them was to be altogether different from what they desired. Their deeds might be investigated too closely. Notwithstanding their exactness in outward ceremonies, they shrank from inspection by those clear, searching eyes.

Who is this Jesus? they questioned. He who had claimed for Himself the glory of the Messiah was the son of a carpenter, and had worked at His trade with His father Joseph. They had seen Him toiling up and down the hills, they were acquainted with His brothers and sisters, and knew His life and labors. They had seen Him develop from childhood to youth, and from youth to manhood. Al-

though His life had been spotless, they would not believe
that He was the Promised One.

What a contrast between His teaching in regard to the
new kingdom and that which they had heard from their
elder! Jesus had said nothing of delivering them from the
Romans. They had heard of His miracles, and had hoped
that His power would be exercised for their advantage, but
they had seen no indication of such purpose.

As they opened the door to doubt, their hearts became
so much the harder for having been momentarily softened.
Satan was determined that blind eyes should not that day
be opened, nor souls bound in slavery be set at liberty.
With intense energy he worked to fasten them in unbelief.
They made no account of the sign already given, when
they had been stirred by the conviction that it was their
Redeemer who addressed them.

But Jesus now gave them an evidence of His divinity by
revealing their secret thoughts. "He said unto them,
Doubtless ye will say unto Me this parable, Physician, heal
thyself: whatsoever we have heard done at Capernaum, do
also here in Thine own country. And He said, Verily I say
unto you, No prophet is acceptable in his own country.
But of a truth I say unto you, There were many widows in
Israel in the days of Elijah, when the heaven was shut up
three years and six months, when there came a great famine over all the land; and unto none of them was Elijah
sent, but only to Zarephath, in the land of Sidon, unto a
woman that was a widow. And there were many lepers in
Israel in the time of Elisha the prophet; and none of them
was cleansed, but only Naaman, the Syrian." R. V.

By this relation of events in the lives of the prophets,
Jesus met the questionings of His hearers. The servants
whom God had chosen for a special work were not allowed to labor for a hardhearted and unbelieving people.
But those who had hearts to feel and faith to believe were
especially favored with evidences of His power through
the prophets. In the days of Elijah, Israel had departed
from God. They clung to their sins, and rejected the warnings of the Spirit through the Lord's messengers. Thus they
cut themselves off from the channel by which God's blessing could come to them. The Lord passed by the homes of
Israel, and found a refuge for His servant in a heathen
land, with a woman who did not belong to the chosen people. But this woman was favored because she had followed

the light she had received, and her heart was open to the greater light that God sent her through His prophet.

It was for the same reason that in Elisha's time the lepers of Israel were passed by. But Naaman, a heathen nobleman, had been faithful to his convictions of right, and had felt his great need of help. He was in a condition to receive the gifts of God's grace. He was not only cleansed from his leprosy, but blessed with a knowledge of the true God.

Our standing before God depends, not upon the amount of light we have received, but upon the use we make of what we have. Thus even the heathen who choose the right as far as they can distinguish it are in a more favorable condition than are those who have had great light, and profess to serve God, but who disregard the light, and by their daily life contradict their profession.

The words of Jesus to His hearers in the synagogue struck at the root of their self-righteousness, pressing home upon them the bitter truth that they had departed from God and forfeited their claim to be His people. Every word cut like a knife as their real condition was set before them. They now scorned the faith with which Jesus had at first inspired them. They would not admit that He who had sprung from poverty and lowliness was other than a common man.

Their unbelief bred malice. Satan controlled them, and in wrath they cried out against the Saviour. They had turned from Him whose mission it was to heal and restore; now they manifested the attributes of the destroyer.

When Jesus referred to the blessings given to the Gentiles, the fierce national pride of His hearers was aroused, and His words were drowned in a tumult of voices. These people had prided themselves on keeping the law; but now that their prejudices were offended, they were ready to commit murder. The assembly broke up, and laying hands upon Jesus, they thrust Him from the synagogue, and out of the city. All seemed eager for His destruction. They hurried Him to the brow of a precipice, intending to cast Him down headlong. Shouts and maledictions filled the air. Some were casting stones at Him, when suddenly He disappeared from among them. The heavenly messengers who had been by His side in the synagogue were with Him in the midst of that maddened throng. They shut Him in from His enemies, and conducted Him to a place of safety.

So angels protected Lot, and led him out safely from the

midst of Sodom. So they protected Elisha in the little mountain city. When the encircling hills were filled with the horses and chariots of the king of Syria, and the great host of his armed men, Elisha beheld the nearer hill slopes covered with the armies of God,—horses and chariots of fire round about the servant of the Lord.

So, in all ages, angels have been near to Christ's faithful followers. The vast confederacy of evil is arrayed against all who would overcome; but Christ would have us look to the things which are not seen, to the armies of heaven encamped about all who love God, to deliver them. From what dangers, seen and unseen, we have been preserved through the interposition of the angels, we shall never know, until in the light of eternity we see the providences of God. Then we shall know that the whole family of heaven was interested in the family here below, and that messengers from the throne of God attended our steps from day to day.

When Jesus in the synagogue read from the prophecy, He stopped short of the final specification concerning the Messiah's work. Having read the words, "To proclaim the acceptable year of the Lord," He omitted the phrase, "and the day of vengeance of our God." Isa. 61:2. This was just as much truth as was the first of the prophecy, and by His silence Jesus did not deny the truth. But this last expression was that upon which His hearers delighted to dwell, and which they were desirous of fulfilling. They denounced judgments against the heathen, not discerning that their own guilt was even greater than that of others. They themselves were in deepest need of the mercy they were so ready to deny to the heathen. That day in the synagogue, when Jesus stood among them, was their opportunity to accept the call of Heaven. He who "delighteth in mercy" (Micah 7:18) would fain have saved them from the ruin which their sins were inviting.

Not without one more call to repentance could He give them up. Toward the close of His ministry in Galilee, He again visited the home of His childhood. Since His rejection there, the fame of His preaching and His miracles had filled the land. None now could deny that He possessed more than human power. The people of Nazareth knew that He went about doing good, and healing all that were oppressed by Satan. About them were whole villages where there was not a moan of sickness in any house; for He had passed through them, and healed all their sick. The mercy revealed in every act of His life testified to His divine anointing.

Again as they listened to His words the Nazarenes were moved by the Divine Spirit. But even now they would not admit that this Man, who had been brought up among them, was other or greater than themselves. Still there rankled the bitter memory that while He had claimed for Himself to be the Promised One, He had really denied them a place with Israel; for He had shown them to be less worthy of God's favor than a heathen man and woman. Hence though they questioned, "Whence hath this Man this wisdom, and these mighty works?" they would not receive Him as the Christ of God. Because of their unbelief, the Saviour could not work many miracles among them. Only a few hearts were open to His blessing, and reluctantly He departed, never to return.

Unbelief, having once been cherished, continued to control the men of Nazareth. So it controlled the Sanhedrin and the nation. With priests and people, the first rejection of the demonstration of the Holy Spirit's power was the beginning of the end. In order to prove that their first resistance was right, they continued ever after to cavil at the words of Christ. Their rejection of the Spirit culminated in the cross of Calvary, in the destruction of their city, in the scattering of the nation to the winds of heaven.

Oh, how Christ longed to open to Israel the precious treasures of the truth! But such was their spiritual blindness that it was impossible to reveal to them the truths relating to His kingdom. They clung to their creed and their useless ceremonies when the truth of Heaven awaited their acceptance. They spent their money for chaff and husks, when the bread of life was within their reach. Why did they not go to the word of God, and search diligently to know whether they were in error? The Old Testament Scriptures stated plainly every detail of Christ's ministry, and again and again He quoted from the prophets, and declared. "Today is this scripture fulfilled in your ears." If they had honestly searched the Scriptures. bringing their theories to the test of God's word, Jesus need not have wept over their impenitence. He need not have declared, "Behold, your house is left unto you desolate." Luke 13:35. They might have been acquainted with the evidence of His Messiahship, and the calamity that laid their proud city in ruins might have been averted. But the minds of the Jews had become narrowed by their unreasoning bigotry.

The lessons of Christ revealed their deficiencies of character, and demanded repentance. If they accepted His teachings, their practices must be changed, and their cherished hopes relinquished. In order to be honored by Heaven, they must sacrifice the honor of men. If they obeyed the words of this new rabbi, they must go contrary to the opinions of the great thinkers and teachers of the time.

Truth was unpopular in Christ's day. It is unpopular in our day. It has been unpopular ever since Satan first gave man a disrelish for it by presenting fables that lead to self-exaltation. Do we not today meet theories and doctrines that have no foundation in the word of God? Men cling as tenaciously to them as did the Jews to their traditions.

The Jewish leaders were filled with spiritual pride. Their desire for the glorification of self manifested itself even in the service of the sanctuary. They loved the highest seats in the synagogue. They loved greetings in the market places, and were gratified with the sound of their titles on the lips of men. As real piety declined, they became more jealous for their traditions and ceremonies.

Because their understanding was darkened by selfish prejudice, they could not harmonize the power of Christ's convicting words with the humility of His life. They did not appreciate the fact that real greatness can dispense with outward show. This Man's poverty seemed wholly inconsistent with His claim to be the Messiah. They questioned, If He was what He claimed to be, why was He so unpretending? If He was satisfied to be without the force of arms, what would become of their nation? How could the power and glory so long anticipated bring the nations as subjects to the city of the Jews? Had not the priests taught that Israel was to bear rule over all the earth? and could it be possible that the great religious teachers were in error?

But it was not simply the absence of outward glory in His life that led the Jews to reject Jesus. He was the embodiment of purity, and they were impure. He dwelt among men an example of spotless integrity. His blameless life flashed light upon their hearts. His sincerity revealed their insincerity. It made manifest the hollowness of their pretentious piety, and discovered iniquity to them in its odious character. Such a light was unwelcome.

If Christ had called attention to the Pharisees, and had extolled their learning and piety, they would have hailed Him with joy. But when He spoke of the kingdom of heaven as a dispensation of mercy for all mankind, He was presenting a phase of religion they would not tolerate. Their own example and teaching had never been such as to make the service of God seem desirable. When they saw Jesus giving attention to the very ones they hated and repulsed, it stirred up the worst passions of their proud hearts. Notwithstanding their proud boast that under the "Lion of the tribe of Judah" (Rev. 5:5), Israel should be exalted to pre-eminence over all nations, they could have borne the disappointment of their ambitious hopes better than they could bear Christ's reproof of their sins, and the reproach they felt even from the presence of His purity.

Chapter 15

BESIDE THE SEA

CHRIST SELDOM gathered His disciples alone to receive His words. He did not choose for His audience those only who knew the way of life. It was His work to reach the multitudes who were in ignorance and error. He gave His lessons of truth where they could reach the darkened understanding. He Himself was the Truth, standing with girded loins and hands ever outstretched to bless, and in words of warning, entreaty, and encouragement, seeking to uplift all who would come unto Him.

The Sermon on the Mount, though given especially to the disciples, was spoken in the hearing of the multitude. After the ordination of the apostles, Jesus went with them to the seaside. Here in the early morning the people had begun to assemble. Besides the usual crowds from the Galilean towns, there were people from Judea, and even from Jerusalem itself; from Perea, from Decapolis, from Idumea, away to the south of Judea; and from Tyre and Sidon, the Phoenician cities on the shore of the Mediterranean. "When they had heard what great things He did," they "came to hear Him, and to be healed of their diseases: . . . there went virtue out of Him, and healed them all." Mark 3:8; Luke 6:17-19.

The narrow beach did not afford even standing room within reach of His voice for all who desired to hear Him, and Jesus led the way back to the mountainside. Reaching a level space that offered a pleasant gathering place for the vast assembly, He seated Himself on the grass, and the disciples and the multitude followed His example.

The disciples' place was always next to Jesus. The people constantly pressed upon Him, yet the disciples understood that they were not to be crowded away from His

This chapter is based on Matt. 5; 6; 7.

presence. They sat close beside Him, that they might not lose a word of His instruction. They were attentive listeners, eager to understand the truths they were to make known to all lands and all ages.

With a feeling that something more than usual might be expected, they now pressed about their Master. They believed that the kingdom was soon to be established, and from the events of the morning they gathered assurance that some announcement concerning it was about to be made. A feeling of expectancy pervaded the multitude also, and eager faces gave evidence of the deep interest. As the people sat upon the green hillside, awaiting the words of the divine Teacher, their hearts were filled with thoughts of future glory. There were scribes and Pharisees who looked forward to the day when they should have dominion over the hated Romans, and possess the riches and splendor of the world's great empire. The poor peasants and fishermen hoped to hear the assurance that their wretched hovels, the scanty food, the life of toil, and fear of want were to be exchanged for mansions of plenty and days of ease. In place of the one coarse garment which was their covering by day, and their blanket at night, they hoped that Christ would give them the rich and costly robes of their conquerors. All hearts thrilled with the proud hope that Israel was soon to be honored before the nations as the chosen of the Lord, and Jerusalem exalted as the head of a universal kingdom.

Christ disappointed the hope of worldly greatness. In the Sermon on the Mount He sought to undo the work that had been wrought by false education, and to give His hearers a right conception of His kingdom and of His own character. Yet He did not make a direct attack on the errors of the people. He saw the misery of the world on account of sin, yet He did not present before them a vivid delineation of their wretchedness. He taught them of something infinitely better than they had known. Without combating their ideas of the kingdom of God, He told them the conditions of entrance therein, leaving them to draw their own conclusions as to its nature. The truths He taught are no less important to us than to the multitude that followed Him. We no less than they need to learn the foundation principles of the kingdom of God.

Christ's first words to the people on the mount were words of blessing. Happy are they, He said, who recognize their spiritual poverty, and feel their need of redemption.

The gospel is to be preached to the poor. Not to the spiritually proud, those who claim to be rich and in need of nothing, is it revealed, but to those who are humble and contrite. One fountain only has been opened for sin, a fountain for the poor in spirit.

The proud heart strives to earn salvation; but both our title to heaven and our fitness for it are found in the righteousness of Christ. The Lord can do nothing toward the recovery of man until, convinced of his own weakness, and stripped of all self-sufficiency, he yields himself to the control of God. Then he can receive the gift that God is waiting to bestow. From the soul that feels his need, nothing is withheld. He has unrestricted access to Him in whom all fullness dwells. "For thus saith the high and lofty One that inhabiteth eternity, whose name is Holy; I dwell in the high and holy place, with him also that is of a contrite and humble spirit, to revive the spirit of the humble, and to revive the heart of the contrite ones." Isa. 57:15.

"Blessed are they that mourn: for they shall be comforted." By these words Christ does not teach that mourning in itself has power to remove the guilt of sin. He gives no sanction to pretense or to voluntary humility. The mourning of which He speaks does not consist in melancholy and lamentation. While we sorrow on account of sin, we are to rejoice in the precious privilege of being children of God.

We often sorrow because our evil deeds bring unpleasant consequences to ourselves; but this is not repentance. Real sorrow for sin is the result of the working of the Holy Spirit. The Spirit reveals the ingratitude of the heart that has slighted and grieved the Saviour, and brings us in contrition to the foot of the cross. By every sin Jesus is wounded afresh; and as we look upon Him whom we have pierced, we mourn for the sins that have brought anguish upon Him. Such mourning will lead to the renunciation of sin.

The worldling may pronounce this sorrow a weakness; but it is the strength which binds the penitent to the Infinite One with links that cannot be broken. It shows that the angels of God are bringing back to the soul the graces that were lost through hardness of heart and transgression. The tears of the penitent are only the raindrops that precede the sunshine of holiness. This sorrow heralds a joy which will be a living fountain in the soul. "Only acknowledge thine iniquity, that thou hast transgressed against the Lord thy God;" "and I will not cause Mine anger to fall upon you: for I am merciful, saith the Lord." Jer.

3:13, 12. "Unto them that mourn in Zion," He has appointed to give "beauty for ashes, the oil of joy for mourning, the garment of praise for the spirit of heaviness." Isa. 61:3.

And for those also who mourn in trial and sorrow there is comfort. The bitterness of grief and humiliation is better than the indulgences of sin. Through affliction God reveals to us the plague spots in our characters, that by His grace we may overcome our faults. Unknown chapters in regard to ourselves are opened to us, and the test comes, whether we will accept the reproof and the counsel of God. When brought into trial, we are not to fret and complain. We should not rebel, or worry ourselves out of the hand of Christ. We are to humble the soul before God. The ways of the Lord are obscure to him who desires to see things in a light pleasing to himself. They appear dark and joyless to our human nature. But God's ways are ways of mercy and the end is salvation. Elijah knew not what he was doing when in the desert he said that he had had enough of life, and prayed that he might die. The Lord in His mercy did not take him at his word. There was yet a great work for Elijah to do; and when his work was done, he was not to perish in discouragement and solitude in the wilderness. Not for him the descent into the dust of death, but the ascent in glory, with the convoy of celestial chariots, to the throne on high.

God's word for the sorrowing is, "I have seen his ways, and will heal him: I will lead him also, and restore comforts unto him and to his mourners." "I will turn their mourning into joy, and will comfort them, and make them rejoice from their sorrow." Isa. 57:18; Jer. 31:13.

"Blessed are the meek." The difficulties we have to encounter may be very much lessened by that meekness which hides itself in Christ. If we possess the humility of our Master, we shall rise above the slights, the rebuffs, the annoyances, to which we are daily exposed, and they will cease to cast a gloom over the spirit. The highest evidence of nobility in a Christian is self-control. He who under abuse or cruelty fails to maintain a calm and trustful spirit robs God of His right to reveal in him His own perfection of character. Lowliness of heart is the strength that gives victory to the followers of Christ; it is the token of their connection with the courts above.

"Though the Lord be high, yet hath He respect unto the lowly." Ps. 138:6. Those who reveal the meek and lowly

spirit of Christ are tenderly regarded by God. They may
be looked upon with scorn by the world, but they are of
great value in His sight. Not only the wise, the great, the
beneficent, will gain a passport to the heavenly courts; not
only the busy worker, full of zeal and restless activity. No;
the poor in spirit, who crave the presence of an abiding
Christ, the humble in heart, whose highest ambition is to
do God's will,—these will gain an abundant entrance.
They will be among that number who have washed their
robes and made them white in the blood of the Lamb.
"Therefore are they before the throne of God, and serve
Him day and night in His temple: and He that sitteth on
the throne shall dwell among them." Rev. 7:15.

"Blessed are they which do hunger and thirst after righteousness." The sense of unworthiness will lead the heart to
hunger and thirst for righteousness, and this desire will not
be disappointed. Those who make room in their hearts for
Jesus will realize His love. All who long to bear the likeness of the character of God shall be satisfied. The Holy
Spirit never leaves unassisted the soul who is looking unto
Jesus. He takes of the things of Christ and shows them
unto him. If the eye is kept fixed on Christ, the work of
the Spirit ceases not until the soul is conformed to His
image. The pure element of love will expand the soul, giving it a capacity for higher attainments, for increased
knowledge of heavenly things, so that it will not rest short
of the fullness. "Blessed are they which do hunger and
thirst after righteousness; for they shall be filled."

The merciful shall find mercy, and the pure in heart
shall see God. Every impure thought defiles the soul, im-
pairs the moral sense, and tends to obliterate the impressions of the Holy Spirit. It dims the spiritual vision, so that
men cannot behold God. The Lord may and does forgive
the repenting sinner; but though forgiven, the soul is
marred. All impurity of speech or of thought must be
shunned by him who would have clear discernment of
spiritual truth.

But the words of Christ cover more than freedom from
sensual impurity, more than freedom from that ceremonial
defilement which the Jews so rigorously shunned. Selfishness prevents us from beholding God. The self-seeking
spirit judges of God as altogether such a one as itself.
Until we have renounced this, we cannot understand Him
who is love. Only the unselfish heart, the humble and
trustful spirit, shall see God as "merciful and gracious,

long-suffering, and abundant in goodness and truth." Ex. 34:6.

"Blessed are the peacemakers." The peace of Christ is born of truth. It is harmony with God. The world is at enmity with the law of God; sinners are at enmity with their Maker; and as a result they are at enmity with one another. But the psalmist declares, "Great peace have they which love Thy law: and nothing shall offend them." Ps. 119:165. Men cannot manufacture peace. Human plans for the purification and uplifting of individuals or of society will fail of producing peace, because they do not reach the heart. The only power that can create or perpetuate true peace is the grace of Christ. When this is implanted in the heart, it will cast out the evil passions that cause strife and dissension. "Instead of the thorn shall come up the fir tree, and instead of the brier shall come up the myrtle tree;" and life's desert "shall rejoice, and blossom as the rose." Isa. 55:13; 35:1.

The multitudes were amazed at this teaching, which was so at variance with the precepts and example of the Pharisees. The people had come to think that happiness consisted in the possession of the things of this world, and that fame and the honor of men were much to be coveted. It was very pleasing to be called "Rabbi," and to be extolled as wise and religious, having their virtues paraded before the public. This was regarded as the crown of happiness. But in the presence of that vast throng, Jesus declared that earthly gain and honor were all the reward such persons would ever receive. He spoke with certainty, and a convincing power attended His words. The people were silenced, and a feeling of fear crept over them. They looked at one another doubtfully. Who of them would be saved if this Man's teachings were true? Many were convicted that this remarkable Teacher was actuated by the Spirit of God, and that the sentiments He uttered were divine.

After explaining what constitutes true happiness, and how it may be obtained, Jesus more definitely pointed out the duty of His disciples, as teachers chosen of God to lead others into the path of righteousness and eternal life. He knew that they would often suffer from disappointment and discouragement, that they would meet with decided opposition, that they would be insulted, and their testimony rejected. Well He knew that in the fulfillment of their mission, the humble men who listened so attentively to His words were to bear calumny, torture, imprisonment, and death, and He continued:

"Blessed are they which are persecuted for righteousness' sake: for theirs is the kingdom of heaven. Blessed are ye, when men shall revile you, and persecute you, and shall say all manner of evil against you, falsely, for My sake. Rejoice, and be exceeding glad: for great is your reward in heaven: for so persecuted they the prophets which were before you."

The world loves sin, and hates righteousness, and this was the cause of its hostility to Jesus. All who refuse His infinite love will find Christianity a disturbing element. The light of Christ sweeps away the darkness that covers their sins, and the need of reform is made manifest. While those who yield to the influence of the Holy Spirit begin war with themselves, those who cling to sin war against the truth and its representatives.

Thus strife is created, and Christ's followers are accused as troublers of the people. But it is fellowship with God that brings them the world's enmity. They are bearing the reproach of Christ. They are treading the path that has been trodden by the noblest of the earth. Not with sorrow, but with rejoicing, should they meet persecution. Each fiery trial is God's agent for their refining. Each is fitting them for their work as colaborers with Him. Each conflict has its place in the great battle for righteousness, and each will add to the joy of their final triumph. Having this in view, the test of their faith and patience will be cheerfully accepted rather than dreaded and avoided. Anxious to fulfill their obligation to the world, fixing their desire upon the approval of God, His servants are to fulfill every duty, irrespective of the fear or the favor of men.

"Ye are the salt of the earth," Jesus said. Do not withdraw yourselves from the world in order to escape persecution. You are to abide among men, that the savor of the divine love may be as salt to preserve the world from corruption.

Hearts that respond to the influence of the Holy Spirit are the channels through which God's blessing flows. Were those who serve God removed from the earth, and His Spirit withdrawn from among men, this world would be left to desolation and destruction, the fruit of Satan's dominion. Though the wicked know it not, they owe even the blessings of this life to the presence, in the world, of God's people whom they despise and oppress. But if Christians are such in name only, they are like the salt that has lost its savor. They have no influence for good in the world. Through their misrepresentation of God they are worse than unbelievers.

"Ye are the light of the world." The Jews thought to confine the benefits of salvation to their own nation; but Christ showed them that salvation is like the sunshine. It belongs to the whole world. The religion of the Bible is not to be confined between the covers of a book, nor within the walls of a church. It is not to be brought out occasionally for our own benefit, and then to be carefully laid aside again. It is to sanctify the daily life, to manifest itself in every business transaction and in all our social relations.

True character is not shaped from without, and put on; it radiates from within. If we wish to direct others in the path of righteousness, the principles of righteousness must be enshrined in our own hearts. Our profession of faith may proclaim the theory of religion, but it is our practical piety that holds forth the word of truth. The consistent life, the holy conversation, the unswerving integrity, the active, benevolent spirit, the godly example,—these are the mediums through which light is conveyed to the world.

Jesus had not dwelt on the specifications of the law, but He did not leave His hearers to conclude that He had come to set aside its requirements. He knew that spies stood ready to seize upon every word that might be wrested to serve their purpose. He knew the prejudice that existed in the minds of many of His hearers, and He said nothing to unsettle their faith in the religion and institutions that had been committed to them through Moses. Christ Himself had given both the moral and the ceremonial law. He did not come to destroy confidence in His own instruction. It was because of His great reverence for the law and the prophets that He sought to break through the wall of traditional requirements which hemmed in the Jews. While He set aside their false interpretations of the law, He carefully guarded His disciples against yielding up the vital truths committed to the Hebrews.

The Pharisees prided themselves on their obedience to the law; yet they knew so little of its principles through everyday practice that to them the Saviour's words sounded like heresy. As He swept away the rubbish under which the truth had been buried, they thought He was sweeping away the truth itself. They whispered to one another that

He was making light of the law. He read their thoughts, and answered them, saying,—

"Think not that I am come to destroy the law, or the prophets: I am not come to destroy, but to fulfill." Here Jesus refutes the charge of the Pharisees. His mission to the world is to vindicate the sacred claims of that law which they charge Him with breaking. If the law of God could have been changed or abrogated, then Christ need not have suffered the consequences of our transgression. He came to explain the relation of the law to man, and to illustrate its precepts by His own life of obedience.

God has given us His holy precepts, because He loves mankind. To shield us from the results of transgression, He reveals the principles of righteousness. The law is an expression of the thought of God; when received in Christ, it becomes our thought. It lifts us above the power of natural desires and tendencies, above temptations that lead to sin. God desires us to be happy, and He gave us the precepts of the law that in obeying them we might have joy. When at Jesus' birth the angels sang,—

"Glory to God in the highest,
And on earth peace, good will toward men" (Luke 2:14),

they were declaring the principles of the law which He had come to magnify and make honorable.

When the law was proclaimed from Sinai, God made known to men the holiness of His character, that by contrast they might see the sinfulness of their own. The law was given to convict them of sin, and reveal their need of a Saviour. It would do this as its principles were applied to the heart by the Holy Spirit. This work it is still to do. In the life of Christ the principles of the law are made plain; and as the Holy Spirit of God touches the heart, as the light of Christ reveals to men their need of His cleansing blood and His justifying righteousness, the law is still an agent in bringing us to Christ, that we may be justified by faith. "The law of the Lord is perfect, converting the soul." Ps. 19:7.

"Till heaven and earth pass," said Jesus, "one jot or one tittle shall in nowise pass from the law, till all be fulfilled." The sun shining in the heavens, the solid earth upon which you dwell, are God's witnesses that His law is changeless and eternal. Though they may pass away, the divine precepts shall endure. "It is easier for heaven and earth to pass, than one tittle of the law to fail." Luke 16:17. The system of types that pointed to Jesus as the Lamb of God was to be abolished at His death; but the precepts of the Decalogue are as immutable as the throne of God.

Since "the law of the Lord is perfect," every variation from it must be evil. Those who disobey the commandments of God, and teach others to do so, are condemned by Christ. The Saviour's life of obedience maintained the claims of the law; it proved that the law could be kept in humanity, and showed the excellence of character that obedience would develop. All who obey as He did are likewise declaring that the law is "holy, and just, and good." Rom. 7:12. On the other hand, all who break God's commandments are sustaining Satan's claim that the law is unjust, and cannot be obeyed. Thus they second the deceptions of the great adversary, and cast dishonor upon God. They are the children of the wicked one, who was the first rebel against God's law. To admit them into heaven would again bring in the elements of discord and rebellion, and imperil the well-being of the universe. No man who willfully disregards one principle of the law shall enter the kingdom of heaven.

The rabbis counted their righteousness a passport to heaven; but Jesus declared it to be insufficient and unworthy. External ceremonies and a theoretical knowledge of truth constituted Pharisaical righteousness. The rabbis claimed to be holy through their own efforts in keeping the law; but their works had divorced righteousness from religion. While they were punctilious in ritual observances, their lives were immoral and debased. Their so-called righteousness could never enter the kingdom of heaven.

The greatest deception of the human mind in Christ's day was that a mere assent to the truth constitutes righteousness. In all human experience a theoretical knowledge of the truth has been proved to be insufficient for the saving of the soul. It does not bring forth the fruits of righteousness. A jealous regard for what is termed theological truth often accompanies a hatred of genuine truth as made manifest in life. The darkest chapters of history are burdened with the record of crimes committed by bigoted religionists. The Pharisees claimed to be children of Abraham, and boasted of their possession of the oracles of God; yet these advantages did not preserve them from selfishness, malignity, greed for gain, and the basest hypocrisy. They thought themselves the greatest religionists of the world, but their so-called orthodoxy led them to crucify the Lord of glory.

The same danger still exists. Many take it for granted that they are Christians, simply because they subscribe to certain theological tenets. But they have not brought the truth into practical life. They have not believed and loved it, therefore they have not received the power and grace that come through sanctification of the truth. Men may profess faith in the truth; but if it does not make them sincere, kind, patient, forbearing, heavenly-minded, it is a curse to its possessors, and through their influence it is a curse to the world.

The righteousness which Christ taught is conformity of heart and life to the revealed will of God. Sinful men can become righteous only as they have faith in God and maintain a vital connection with Him. Then true godliness will elevate the thoughts and ennoble the life. Then the external forms of religion accord with the Christian's internal purity. Then the ceremonies required in the service of God are not meaningless rites, like those of the hypocritical Pharisees.

Jesus takes up the commandments separately, and explains the depth and breadth of their requirement. Instead of removing one jot of their force, He shows how far-reaching their principles are, and exposes the fatal mistake of the Jews in their outward show of obedience. He declares that by the evil thought or the lustful look the law of God is transgressed. One who becomes a party to the least injustice is breaking the law and degrading his own moral nature. Murder first exists in the mind. He who gives hatred a place in his heart is setting his feet in the path of the murderer, and his offerings are abhorrent to God.

The Jews cultivated a spirit of retaliation. In their hatred of the Romans they gave utterance to hard denunciations, and pleased the wicked one by manifesting his attributes. Thus they were training themselves to do the terrible deeds to which he led them on. In the religious life of the Pharisees there was nothing to recommend piety to the Gentiles. Jesus bade them not to deceive themselves with the thought that they could in heart rise up against their oppressors, and cherish the longing to avenge their wrongs.

It is true there is an indignation that is justifiable, even in the followers of Christ. When they see that God is dishonored, and His service brought into disrepute, when they see the innocent oppressed, a righteous indignation stirs the soul. Such anger, born of sensitive morals, is not a sin. But those who at any supposed provocation feel at liberty to indulge anger or resentment are opening the heart to Satan. Bitterness and animosity must be banished from the soul if we would be in harmony with heaven.

The Saviour goes farther than this. He says, "If thou bring thy gift to the altar, and there rememberest that thy brother hath aught against thee; leave there thy gift before the altar, and go thy way; first be reconciled to thy brother, and then come and offer thy gift." Many are zealous in religious services, while between them and their brethren are unhappy differences which they might reconcile. God requires them to do all in their power to restore harmony. Until they do this, He cannot accept their services. The Christian's duty in this matter is clearly pointed out.

God pours His blessings upon all. "He maketh His sun to rise on the evil and on the good, and sendeth rain on the just and on the unjust." He is "kind unto the unthankful and to the evil." Luke 6:35. He bids us to be like Him. "Bless them that curse you," said Jesus; "do good to them that hate you, . . . that ye may be the children of your Father which is in heaven." These are the principles of the law, and they are the wellsprings of life.

God's ideal for His children is higher than the highest human thought can reach. "Be ye therefore perfect, even as your Father which is in heaven is perfect." This command is a promise. The plan of redemption contemplates our complete recovery from the power of Satan. Christ always separates the contrite soul from sin. He came to destroy the works of the devil, and He has made provision that the Holy Spirit shall be imparted to every repentant soul, to keep him from sinning.

The tempter's agency is not to be accounted an excuse for one wrong act. Satan is jubilant when he hears the professed followers of Christ making excuses for their deformity of character. It is these excuses that lead to sin. There is no excuse for sinning. A holy temper, a Christlike life, is accessible to every repenting, believing child of God.

The ideal of Christian character is Christlikeness. As the Son of man was perfect in His life, so His followers are to be perfect in their life. Jesus was in all things made like unto His brethren. He became flesh, even as we are. He was hungry and thirsty and weary. He was sustained by food and refreshed by sleep. He shared the lot of man; yet He was the blameless Son of God. He was God in the flesh. His character is to be ours. The Lord says of those who believe in Him, "I will dwell in them, and walk in them; and I will be their God, and they shall be My people." 2 Cor. 6:16.

Christ is the ladder that Jacob saw, the base resting on the earth, and the topmost round reaching to the gate of heaven, to the very threshold of glory. If that ladder had failed by a single step of reaching the earth, we should have been lost. But Christ reaches us where we are. He took our nature and overcame, that we through taking His nature might overcome. Made "in the likeness of sinful flesh" (Rom. 8:3), He lived a sinless life. Now by His divinity He lays hold upon the throne of heaven, while by His humanity He reaches us. He bids us by faith in Him attain to the glory of the character of God. Therefore are we to be perfect, even as our "Father which is in heaven is perfect."

Jesus had shown in what righteousness consists, and had pointed to God as its source. Now He turned to practical duties. In almsgiving, in prayer, in fasting, He said, let nothing be done to attract attention or win praise to self. Give in sincerity, for the benefit of the suffering poor. In prayer, let the soul commune with God. In fasting, go not with the head bowed down, and heart filled with thoughts of self. The heart of the Pharisee is a barren and profitless soil, in which no seeds of divine life can flourish. It is he who yields himself most unreservedly to God that will render Him the most acceptable service. For through fellowship with God men become workers together with Him in presenting His character in humanity.

The service rendered in sincerity of heart has great recompense. "Thy Father which seeth in secret Himself shall reward thee openly." By the life we live through the grace of Christ the character is formed. The original loveliness begins to be restored to the soul. The attributes of the character of Christ are imparted, and the image of the Divine begins to shine forth. The faces of men and women who walk and work with God express the peace of heaven. They are surrounded with the atmosphere of heaven. For these souls the kingdom of God has begun. They have Christ's joy, the joy of being a blessing to humanity. They have the honor of being accepted for the Master's use; they are trusted to do His work in His name.

"No man can serve two masters." We cannot serve God with a divided heart. Bible religion is not one influence among many others; its influence is to be supreme, pervading and controlling every other. It is not to be like a dash of color brushed here and there upon the canvas, but it is to pervade the whole life, as if the canvas were dipped into the color, until every thread of the fabric were dyed a deep, unfading hue.

"If therefore thine eye be single, thy whole body shall be full of light. But if thine eye be evil, thy whole body shall be full of darkness." Purity and steadfastness of purpose are the conditions of receiving light from God. He who desires to know the truth must be willing to accept all that it reveals. He can make no compromise with error. To be wavering and halfhearted in allegiance to truth is to choose the darkness of error and satanic delusion.

Worldly policy and the undeviating principles of righteousness do not blend into each other imperceptibly, like the colors of the rainbow. Between the two a broad, clear line is drawn by the eternal God. The likeness of Christ stands out as distinct from that of Satan as midday in contrast with midnight. And only those who live the life of Christ are His coworkers. If one sin is cherished in the soul, or one wrong practice retained in the life, the whole being is contaminated. The man becomes an instrument of unrighteousness.

All who have chosen God's service are to rest in His care. Christ pointed to the birds flying in the heavens, to the flowers of the field, and bade His hearers consider these objects of God's creation. "Are not ye of much more value than they?" He said. Matt. 6:26, R. V. The measure of divine attention bestowed on any object is proportionate to its rank in the scale of being. The little brown sparrow is watched over by Providence. The flowers of the field, the grass that carpets the earth, share the notice and care of our heavenly Father. The great Master Artist has taken thought for the lilies, making them so beautiful that they outshine the glory of Solomon. How much more does He care for man, who is the image and glory of God. He longs to see His children reveal a character after His similitude. As the sunbeam imparts to the flowers their varied and delicate tints, so does God impart to the soul the beauty of His own character.

All who choose Christ's kingdom of love and righteousness and peace, making its interest paramount to all other, are linked to the world above, and every blessing needed for this life is theirs. In the book of God's providence, the volume of life, we are each given a page. That page contains every particular of our history; even the hairs of the head are numbered. God's children are never absent from His mind.

"Be not therefore anxious for the morrow." Matt. 6:34, R. V. We are to follow Christ day by day. God does not bestow help for tomorrow. He does not give His children all the directions for their life journey at once, lest they should become confused. He tells them just as much as they can remember and perform. The strength and wisdom imparted are for the present emergency. "If any of you lack wisdom,"—for today,—"let him ask of God, that giveth to all men liberally, and upbraideth not; and it shall be given him." James 1:5.

"Judge not, that ye be not judged." Do not think yourself better than other men, and set yourself up as their judge. Since you cannot discern motive, you are incapable of judging another. In criticizing him, you are passing sentence upon yourself; for you show that you are a participant with Satan, the accuser of the brethren. The Lord says, "Examine yourselves, whether ye be in the faith; prove your own selves." This is our work. "If we would judge ourselves, we should not be judged." 2 Cor. 13:5; 1 Cor. 11:31.

The good tree will produce good fruit. If the fruit is unpalatable and worthless, the tree is evil. So the fruit borne in the life testifies as to the condition of the heart and the excellence of the character. Good works can never purchase salvation, but they are an evidence of the faith that acts by love and purifies the soul. And though the eternal reward is not bestowed because of our merit, yet it will be in proportion to the work that has been done through the grace of Christ.

Thus Christ set forth the principles of His kingdom, and showed them to be the great rule of life. To impress the lesson He adds an illustration. It is not enough, He says, for you to hear My words. By obedience you must make them the foundation of your character. Self is but shifting sand. If you build upon human theories and inventions, your house will fall. By the winds of temptation, the tempests of trial, it will be swept away. But these principles that I have given will endure. Receive Me; build on My words.

"Everyone therefore which heareth these words of Mine, and doeth them, shall be likened unto a wise man, which built his house upon the rock: and the rain descended, and the floods came, and the winds blew, and beat upon that house; and it fell not: for it was founded upon the rock." Matt. 7:24, 25, R. V.

Chapter 16

THE CENTURION

CHRIST HAD said to the nobleman whose son He healed, "Except ye see signs and wonders, ye will not believe." John 4:48. He was grieved that His own nation should require these outward signs of His Messiahship. Again and again He had marveled at their unbelief. But He marveled at the faith of the centurion who came to Him. The centurion did not question the Saviour's power. He did not even ask Him to come in person to perform the miracle. "Speak the word only," he said, "and my servant shall be healed."

The centurion's servant had been stricken with palsy, and lay at the point of death. Among the Romans the servants were slaves, bought and sold in the market places, and treated with abuse and cruelty; but the centurion was tenderly attached to his servant, and greatly desired his recovery. He believed that Jesus could heal him. He had not seen the Saviour, but the reports he heard had inspired him with faith. Notwithstanding the formalism of the Jews, this Roman was convinced that their religion was superior to his own. Already he had broken through the barriers of national prejudice and hatred that separated the conquerors from the conquered people. He had manifested respect for the service of God, and had shown kindness to the Jews as His worshipers. In the teaching of Christ, as it had been reported to him, he found that which met the need of the soul. All that was spiritual within him responded to the Saviour's words. But he felt unworthy to come into the presence of Jesus, and he appealed to the Jewish elders to make request for the healing of his servant. They were acquainted with the Great Teacher, and would, he

This chapter is based on Matt. 8:5-13; Luke 7:1-17.

thought, know how to approach Him so as to win His favor.

As Jesus entered Capernaum, He was met by a delegation of the elders, who told Him of the centurion's desire. They urged "that he was worthy for whom He should do this: for he loveth our nation, and he has built us a synagogue."

Jesus immediately set out for the officer's home; but, pressed by the multitude, He advanced slowly. The news of His coming preceded Him, and the centurion, in his self-distrust, sent Him the message, "Lord, trouble not Thyself: for I am not worthy that Thou shouldest enter under my roof." But the Saviour kept on His way, and the centurion, venturing at last to approach Him, completed the message, saying, "Neither thought I myself worthy to come unto Thee;" "but speak the word only, and my servant shall be healed. For I am a man under authority, having soldiers under me: and I say to this man, Go, and he goeth; and to another, Come, and he cometh; and to my servant, Do this, and he doeth it." As I represent the power of Rome, and my soldiers recognize my authority as supreme, so dost Thou represent the power of the Infinite God, and all created things obey Thy word. Thou canst command the disease to depart, and it shall obey Thee. Thou canst summon Thy heavenly messengers, and they shall impart healing virtue. Speak but the word, and my servant shall be healed.

"When Jesus heard these things, He marveled at him, and turned Him about, and said unto the people that followed Him, I say unto you, I have not found so great faith, no, not in Israel." And to the centurion He said, "As thou hast believed, so be it done unto thee. And his servant was healed in the selfsame hour."

The Jewish elders who recommended the centurion to Christ had shown how far they were from possessing the spirit of the gospel. They did not recognize that our great need is our only claim on God's mercy. In their self-righteousness they commended the centurion because of the favor he had shown to "our nation." But the centurion said of himself, "I am not worthy." His heart had been touched by the grace of Christ. He saw his own unworthiness; yet he feared not to ask help. He trusted not to his own goodness; his argument was his great need. His faith took hold upon Christ in His true character. He did not believe in Him merely as a worker of miracles, but as the friend and Saviour of mankind.

It is thus that every sinner may come to Christ. "Not by works of righteousness which we have done, but according to His mercy He saved us." Titus 3:5. When Satan tells you that you are a sinner, and cannot hope to receive blessing from God, tell him that Christ came into the world to save sinners. We have nothing to recommend us to God; but the plea that we may urge now and ever is our utterly helpless condition that makes His redeeming power a necessity. Renouncing all self-dependence, we may look to the cross of Calvary and say,—

> "In my hand no price I bring;
> Simply to Thy cross I cling."

The Jews had been instructed from childhood concerning the work of the Messiah. The inspired utterances of patriarchs and prophets and the symbolic teaching of the sacrificial service had been theirs. But they had disregarded the light; and now they saw in Jesus nothing to be desired. But the centurion, born in heathenism, educated in the idolatry of imperial Rome, trained as a soldier, seemingly cut off from spiritual life by his education and surroundings, and still further shut out by the bigotry of the Jews, and by the contempt of his own countrymen for the people of Israel,—this man perceived the truth to which the children of Abraham were blinded. He did not wait to see whether the Jews themselves would receive the One who claimed to be their Messiah. As the "Light, which lighteth every man that cometh into the world" (John 1:9) had shone upon him, he had, though afar off, discerned the glory of the Son of God.

To Jesus this was an earnest of the work which the gospel was to accomplish among the Gentiles. With joy He looked forward to the gathering of souls from all nations to His kingdom. With deep sadness He pictured to the Jews the result of their rejection of His grace: "I say unto you, That many shall come from the east and west, and shall sit down with Abraham, and Isaac, and Jacob, in the kingdom of heaven. But the children of the kingdom shall be cast out into outer darkness: there shall be weeping and gnashing of teeth." Alas, how many are still preparing for the same fatal disappointment! While souls in heathen darkness accept His grace, how many there are in Christian lands upon whom the light shines only to be disregarded.

More than twenty miles from Capernaum, on a table-land overlooking the wide, beautiful plain of Esdraelon, lay the village of Nain, and thither Jesus next bent His steps. Many of His disciples and others were with Him, and all along the way the people came, longing for His words of love and pity, bringing their sick for His healing, and ever with the hope that He who wielded such wondrous power would make Himself known as the King of Israel. A multitude thronged His steps, and it was a glad, expectant company that followed Him up the rocky path toward the gate of the mountain village.

As they draw near, a funeral train is seen coming from the gates. With slow, sad steps it is proceeding to the place of burial. On an open bier carried in front is the body of the dead, and about it are the mourners, filling the air with their wailing cries. All the people of the town seem to have gathered to show their respect for the dead and their sympathy with the bereaved.

It was a sight to awaken sympathy. The deceased was the only son of his mother, and she a widow. The lonely mourner was following to the grave her sole earthly support and comfort. "When the Lord saw her, He had compassion on her." As she moved on blindly, weeping, noting not His presence, He came close beside her, and gently said, "Weep not." Jesus was about to change her grief to joy, yet He could not forbear this expression of tender sympathy.

"He came and touched the bier;" to Him even contact with death could impart no defilement. The bearers stood still, and the lamentations of the mourners ceased. The two companies gathered about the bier, hoping against hope. One was present who had banished disease and vanquished demons; was death also subject to His power?

In clear, authoritative voice the words are spoken, "Young man, I say unto thee, Arise." That voice pierces the ears of the dead. The young man opens his eyes. Jesus takes him by the hand, and lifts him up. His gaze falls upon her who has been weeping beside him, and mother and son unite in a long, clinging, joyous embrace. The multitude look on in silence, as if spellbound. "There came a fear on all." Hushed and reverent they stood for a little time, as if in the very presence of God. Then they "glorified God, saying, That a great prophet is risen up among us; and, That God hath visited His people." The funeral train returned to Nain as a triumphal procession. "And this rumor of Him went forth throughout all Judea, and throughout all the region round about."

He who stood beside the sorrowing mother at the gate of Nain, watches with every mourning one beside the bier. He is touched with sympathy for our grief. His heart, that loved and pitied, is a heart of unchangeable tenderness. His word, that called the dead to life, is no less efficacious now than when spoken to the young man of Nain. He says, "All power is given unto Me in heaven and in earth." Matt. 28:18. That power is not diminished by the lapse of years, nor exhausted by the ceaseless activity of His overflowing grace. To all who believe on Him He is still a living Saviour.

Jesus changed the mother's grief to joy when He gave back her son; yet the youth was but called forth to this earthly life, to endure its sorrows, its toils, and its perils, and to pass again under the power of death. But Jesus comforts our sorrow for the dead with a message of infinite hope: "I am He that liveth, and was dead; and, behold, I am alive forevermore, . . . and have the keys of hell and of death." "Forasmuch then as the children are partakers of flesh and blood, He also Himself likewise took part of the same; that through death He might destroy him that had the power of death, that is, the devil; and deliver them who through fear of death were all their lifetime subject to bondage." Rev. 1:18; Heb. 2:14, 15.

Satan cannot hold the dead in his grasp when the Son of God bids them live. He cannot hold in spiritual death one soul who in faith receives Christ's word of power. God is saying to all who are dead in sin, "Awake thou that sleepest, and arise from the dead." Eph. 5:14. That word is eternal life. As the word of God which bade the first man live, still gives us life; as Christ's word, "Young man, I say unto thee, Arise," gave life to the youth of Nain, so that word, "Arise from the dead," is life to the soul that receives it. God "hath delivered us from the power of darkness, and hath translated us into the kingdom of His dear Son." Col. 1:13. It is all offered us in His word. If we receive the word, we have the deliverance.

And "if the Spirit of Him that raised up Jesus from the dead dwell in you, He that raised up Christ from the dead shall also quicken your mortal bodies by His Spirit that dwelleth in you." "For the Lord Himself shall descend from heaven with a shout, with the voice of the Archangel, and with the trump of God: and the dead in Christ shall rise first: then we which are alive and remain shall be caught up together with them in the clouds, to meet the Lord in the air: and so shall we ever be with the Lord." Rom. 8:11; 1 Thess. 4:16, 17. This is the word of comfort wherewith He bids us comfort one another.

SOMETHING WITHOUT

Chapter 17

"WHAT MANNER OF MAN IS THIS?"

IT HAD BEEN an eventful day in the life of Jesus. Beside the Sea of Galilee He had spoken His first parables, by familiar illustrations again explaining to the people the nature of His kingdom and the manner in which it was to be established. He had likened His own work to that of the sower; the development of His kingdom to the growth of the mustard seed and the effect of leaven in the measure of meal. The great final separation of the righteous and the wicked He had pictured in the parables of the wheat and tares and the fishing net. The exceeding preciousness of the truths He taught had been illustrated by the hidden treasure and the pearl of great price, while in the parable of the householder He taught His disciples how they were to labor as His representatives.

All day He had been teaching and healing; and as evening came on the crowds still pressed upon Him. Day after day He had ministered to them, scarcely pausing for food or rest. The malicious criticism and misrepresentation with which the Pharisees constantly pursued Him made His labors much more severe and harassing; and now the close of the day found Him so utterly wearied that He determined to seek retirement in some solitary place across the lake.

The eastern shore of Gennesaret was not uninhabited, for there were towns here and there beside the lake; yet it was a desolate region when compared with the western side. It contained a population more heathen than Jewish, and had little communication with Galilee. Thus it offered Jesus the seclusion He sought, and He now bade His disciples accompany Him thither.

After He had dismissed the multitude, they took Him,

This chapter is based on Matt. 8:23-34; Mark 4:35-41; 5:1-20; Luke 8:22-39.

even "as He was," into the boat, and hastily set off. But they were not to depart alone. There were other fishing boats lying near the shore, and these were quickly crowded with people who followed Jesus, eager still to see and hear Him.

The Saviour was at last relieved from the pressure of the multitude, and, overcome with weariness and hunger, He lay down in the stern of the boat, and soon fell asleep. The evening had been calm and pleasant, and quiet rested upon the lake; but suddenly darkness overspread the sky, the wind swept wildly down the mountain gorges along the eastern shore, and a fierce tempest burst upon the lake.

The sun had set, and the blackness of night settled down upon the stormy sea. The waves, lashed into fury by the howling winds, dashed fiercely over the disciples' boat, and threatened to engulf it. Those hardy fishermen had spent their lives upon the lake, and had guided their craft safely through many a storm; but now their strength and skill availed nothing. They were helpless in the grasp of the tempest, and hope failed them as they saw that their boat was filling.

Absorbed in their efforts to save themselves, they had forgotten that Jesus was on board. Now, seeing their labor vain and only death before them, they remembered at whose command they had set out to cross the sea. In Jesus was their only hope. In their helplessness and despair they cried, "Master, Master!" But the dense darkness hid Him from their sight. Their voices were drowned by the roaring of the tempest, and there was no reply. Doubt and fear assailed them. Had Jesus forsaken them? Was He who had conquered disease and demons, and even death, powerless to help His disciples now? Was He unmindful of them in their distress?

Again they call, but there is no answer except the shrieking of the angry blast. Already their boat is sinking. A moment, and apparently they will be swallowed up by the hungry waters.

Suddenly a flash of lightning pierces the darkness, and they see Jesus lying asleep, undisturbed by the tumult. In amazement and despair they exclaim, "Master, carest Thou not that we perish?" How can He rest so peacefully while they are in danger and battling with death?

Their cry arouses Jesus. As the lightning's glare reveals Him, they see the peace of heaven in His face; they read

in His glance self-forgetful, tender love, and, their hearts
turning to Him, cry, "Lord, save us: we perish."

Never did a soul utter that cry unheeded. As the disciples grasp their oars to make a last effort, Jesus rises. He
stands in the midst of His disciples, while the tempest
rages, the waves break over them, and the lightning illuminates His countenance. He lifts His hand, so often employed in deeds of mercy, and says to the angry sea,
"Peace, be still."

The storm ceases. The billows sink to rest. The clouds
roll away, and the stars shine forth. The boat rests upon a
quiet sea. Then turning to His disciples, Jesus asks sorrowfully, "Why are ye fearful? have ye not yet faith?" R. V.

A hush fell upon the disciples. Even Peter did not attempt to express the awe that filled his heart. The boats
that had set out to accompany Jesus had been in the same
peril with that of the disciples. Terror and despair had
seized their occupants; but the command of Jesus brought
quiet to the scene of tumult. The fury of the storm had
driven the boats into close proximity, and all on board beheld the miracle. In the calm that followed, fear was forgotten. The people whispered among themselves, "What
manner of man is this, that even the winds and the sea
obey Him?"

When Jesus was awakened to meet the storm, He was in
perfect peace. There was no trace of fear in word or look,
for no fear was in His heart. But He rested not in the possession of almighty power. It was not as the "Master of
earth and sea and sky" that He reposed in quiet. That
power He had laid down, and He says, "I can of Mine
own self do nothing." John 5:30. He trusted in the Father's might. It was in faith—faith in God's love and care
—that Jesus rested, and the power of that word which
stilled the storm was the power of God.

As Jesus rested by faith in the Father's care, so we are
to rest in the care of our Saviour. If the disciples had trusted in Him, they would have been kept in peace. Their fear
in the time of danger revealed their unbelief. In their efforts to save themselves, they forgot Jesus; and it was only
when, in despair of self-dependence, they turned to Him
that He could give them help.

How often the disciples' experience is ours! When the
tempests of temptation gather, and the fierce lightnings
flash, and the waves sweep over us, we battle with the

storm alone, forgetting that there is One who can help us We trust to our own strength till our hope is lost, and we are ready to perish. Then we remember Jesus, and if we call upon Him to save us, we shall not cry in vain. Though He sorrowfully reproves our unbelief and self-confidence, He never fails to give us the help we need. Whether on the land or on the sea, if we have the Saviour in our hearts, there is no need of fear. Living faith in the Redeemer will smooth the sea of life, and will deliver us from danger in the way that He knows to be best.

There is another spiritual lesson in this miracle of the stilling of the tempest. Every man's experience testifies to the truth of the words of Scripture, "The wicked are like the troubled sea, when it cannot rest. . . . There is no peace, saith my God, to the wicked." Isa. 57:20, 21. Sin has destroyed our peace. While self is unsubdued, we can find no rest. The masterful passions of the heart no human power can control. We are as helpless here as were the disciples to quiet the raging storm. But He who spoke peace to the billows of Galilee has spoken the word of peace for every soul. However fierce the tempest, those who turn to Jesus with the cry, "Lord, save us," will find deliverance. His grace, that reconciles the soul to God, quiets the strife of human passion, and in His love the heart is at rest. "He maketh the storm a calm, so that the waves thereof are still. Then are they glad because they be quiet; so He bringeth them unto their desired haven." Ps. 107:29, 30. "Being justified by faith, we have peace with God through our Lord Jesus Christ." "The work of righteousness shall be peace; and the effect of righteousness quietness and assurance forever." Rom. 5:1; Isa. 32:17.

In the early morning the Saviour and His companions came to shore, and the light of the rising sun touched sea and land as with the benediction of peace. But no sooner had they stepped upon the beach than their eyes were greeted by a sight more terrible than the fury of the tempest. From some hiding place among the tombs, two madmen rushed upon them as if to tear them in pieces. Hanging about these men were parts of chains which they had broken in escaping from confinement. Their flesh was torn and bleeding where they had cut themselves with sharp stones. Their eyes glared out from their long and matted hair, the very likeness of humanity seemed to have been blotted out by the demons that possessed them, and they looked more like wild beasts than like men.

The disciples and their companions fled in terror; but presently they noticed that Jesus was not with them, and they turned to look for Him. He was standing where they had left Him. He who had stilled the tempest, who had before met Satan and conquered him, did not flee before these demons. When the men, gnashing their teeth, and foaming at the mouth, approached Him, Jesus raised that hand which had beckoned the waves to rest, and the men could come no nearer. They stood raging but helpless before Him.

With authority He bade the unclean spirits come out of them. His words penetrated the darkened minds of the unfortunate men. They realized dimly that One was near who could save them from the tormenting demons. They fell at the Saviour's feet to worship Him; but when their lips were opened to entreat His mercy, the demons spoke through them, crying vehemently, "What have I to do with Thee, Jesus, Thou Son of God most high? I beseech Thee, torment me not."

Jesus asked, "What is thy name?" And the answer was, "My name is Legion: for we are many." Using the afflicted men as mediums of communication, they besought Jesus not to send them out of the country. Upon a mountainside not far distant a great herd of swine was feeding. Into these the demons asked to be allowed to enter, and Jesus suffered them. Immediately a panic seized the herd. They rushed madly down the cliff, and, unable to check themselves upon the shore, plunged into the lake and perished.

Meanwhile a marvelous change had come over the demoniacs. Light had shone into their minds. Their eyes beamed with intelligence. The countenances, so long deformed into the image of Satan, became suddenly mild, the bloodstained hands were quiet, and with glad voices the men praised God for their deliverance.

From the cliff the keepers of the swine had seen all that had occurred, and they hurried away to publish the news to their employers and to all the people. In fear and amazement the whole population flocked to meet Jesus. The two demoniacs had been the terror of the country. No one had been safe to pass the place where they were; for they would rush upon every traveler with the fury of demons. Now these men were clothed and in their right mind, sitting at the feet of Jesus, listening to His words, and glorifying the name of Him who had made them whole. But the people who beheld this wonderful scene did not rejoice. The loss of the swine seemed to them of greater moment than the deliverance of these captives of Satan.

It was in mercy to the owners of the swine that this loss had been permitted to come upon them. They were absorbed in earthly things, and cared not for the great interests of spiritual life. Jesus desired to break the spell of selfish indifference, that they might accept His grace. But regret and indignation for their temporal loss blinded their eyes to the Saviour's mercy.

The manifestation of supernatural power aroused the superstitions of the people, and excited their fears. Further calamities might follow from having this Stranger among them. They apprehended financial ruin, and determined to be freed from His presence. Those who had crossed the lake with Jesus told of all that had happened on the preceding night, of their peril in the tempest, and how the wind and the sea had been stilled. But their words were without effect. In terror the people thronged about Jesus, beseeching Him to depart from them, and He complied, taking ship at once for the opposite shore.

The people of Gergesa had before them the living evidence of Christ's power and mercy. They saw the men who had been restored to reason; but they were so fearful of endangering their earthly interests that He who had vanquished the prince of darkness before their eyes was treated as an intruder, and the Gift of heaven was turned from their doors. We have not the opportunity of turning from the person of Christ as had the Gergesenes; but still there are many who refuse to obey His word, because obedience would involve the sacrifice of some worldly interest. Lest His presence shall cause them pecuniary loss, many reject His grace, and drive His Spirit from them.

But far different was the feeling of the restored demoniacs. They desired the company of their deliverer. In His presence they felt secure from the demons that had tormented their lives and wasted their manhood. As Jesus was about to enter the boat, they kept close to His side, knelt at His feet, and begged Him to keep them near Him, where they might ever listen to His words. But Jesus bade them go home and tell what great things the Lord had done for them.

Here was a work for them to do,—to go to a heathen home, and tell of the blessing they had received from

Jesus. It was hard for them to be separated from the Saviour. Great difficulties were sure to beset them in association with their heathen countrymen. And their long isolation from society seemed to have disqualified them for the work He had indicated. But as soon as Jesus pointed out their duty they were ready to obey. Not only did they tell their own households and neighbors about Jesus, but they went throughout Decapolis, everywhere declaring His power to save, and describing how He had freed them from the demons. In doing this work they could receive a greater blessing than if, merely for benefit to themselves, they had remained in His presence. It is in working to spread the good news of salvation that we are brought near to the Saviour.

The two restored demoniacs were the first missionaries whom Christ sent to preach the gospel in the region of Decapolis. For a few moments only these men had been privileged to hear the teachings of Christ. Not one sermon from His lips had ever fallen upon their ears. They could not instruct the people as the disciples who had been daily with Christ were able to do. But they bore in their own persons the evidence that Jesus was the Messiah. They could tell what they knew; what they themselves had seen, and heard, and felt of the power of Christ. This is what everyone can do whose heart has been touched by the grace of God. John, the beloved disciple, wrote: "That which was from the beginning, which we have heard, which we have seen with our eyes, which we have looked upon, and our hands have handled, of the Word of life; . . . that which we have seen and heard declare we unto you." 1 John 1:1-3. As witnesses for Christ, we are to tell what we know, what we ourselves have seen and heard and felt. If we have been following Jesus step by step, we shall have something right to the point to tell concerning the way in which He has led us. We can tell how we have tested His promise, and found the promise true. We can bear witness to what we have known of the grace of Christ. This is the witness for which our Lord calls, and for want of which the world is perishing.

Though the people of Gergesa had not received Jesus, He did not leave them to the darkness they had chosen. When they bade Him depart from them, they had not heard His words. They were ignorant of that which they were rejecting. Therefore He again sent the light to them, and by those to whom they would not refuse to listen.

In causing the destruction of the swine, it was Satan's purpose to turn the people away from the Saviour, and prevent the preaching of the gospel in that region. But this very occurrence roused the whole country as nothing else could have done, and directed attention to Christ. Though the Saviour Himself departed, the men whom He had healed remained as witnesses to His power. Those who had been mediums of the prince of darkness became channels of light, messengers of the Son of God. Men marveled as they listened to the wondrous news. A door was opened to the gospel throughout that region. When Jesus returned to Decapolis, the people flocked about Him, and for three days, not merely the inhabitants of one town, but thousands from all the surrounding region, heard the message of salvation. Even the power of demons is under the control of our Saviour, and the working of evil is overruled for good.

The encounter with the demoniacs of Gergesa had a lesson for the disciples. It showed the depths of degradation to which Satan is seeking to drag the whole human race, and the mission of Christ to set men free from his power. Those wretched beings, dwelling in the place of graves, possessed by demons, in bondage to uncontrolled passions and loathsome lusts, represent what humanity would become if given up to satanic jurisdiction. Satan's influence is constantly exerted upon men to distract the senses, control the mind for evil, and incite to violence and crime. He weakens the body, darkens the intellect, and debases the soul. Whenever men reject the Saviour's invitation, they are yielding themselves to Satan. Multitudes in every department in life, in the home, in business, and even in the church, are doing this today. It is because of this that violence and crime have overspread the earth, and moral darkness, like the pall of death, enshrouds the habitations of men. Through his specious temptations Satan leads men to worse and worse evils, till utter depravity and ruin are the result. The only safeguard against his power is found in the presence of Jesus. Before men and angels Satan has been revealed as man's enemy and destroyer; Christ, as man's friend and deliverer. His Spirit will develop in man all that will ennoble the character and dignify the nature. It will build man up for the glory of God in body and soul and spirit. "For God hath not given us the spirit of fear; but of power, and of love, and of a sound mind." 2 Tim. 1:7. He has called us "to the obtaining of the glory"—

character—"of our Lord Jesus Christ;" has called us to be "conformed to the image of His Son." 2 Thess. 2:14; Rom. 8:29.

And souls that have been degraded into instruments of Satan are still through the power of Christ transformed into messengers of righteousness, and sent forth by the Son of God to tell what "great things the Lord hath done for thee, and hath had compassion on thee."

clear. [?] our Lord, Jesus Christ, [?] called us to be
conformed to the image of His Son. 2 Cor. 3:18;
Rom. 8:29.

And [?] that have been degraded into instruments of
Satan are still through the power of Christ transformed
into messengers of righteousness and sent forth by the Son
of God, to tell what "great things the Lord hath done for
thee, and hath had compassion on thee."

Chapter 18

THE TOUCH OF FAITH

RETURNING FROM Gergesa to the western shore, Jesus
found a multitude gathered to receive Him, and they greeted Him with joy. He remained by the seaside for a time,
teaching and healing, and then repaired to the house of
Levi-Matthew to meet the publicans at the feast. Here
Jairus, the ruler of the synagogue, found Him.

This elder of the Jews came to Jesus in great distress,
and cast himself at His feet, exclaiming, "My little daughter lieth at the point of death: I pray Thee, come and lay
Thy hands on her, that she may be healed; and she shall
live."

Jesus set out at once with the ruler for his home.
Though the disciples had seen so many of His works of
mercy, they were surprised at His compliance with the entreaty of the haughty rabbi; yet they accompanied their
Master, and the people followed, eager and expectant.

The ruler's house was not far distant, but Jesus and His
companions advanced slowly, for the crowd pressed Him
on every side. The anxious father was impatient of delay;
but Jesus, pitying the people, stopped now and then to relieve some suffering one, or to comfort a troubled heart.

While they were still on the way, a messenger pressed
through the crowd, bearing to Jairus the news that his
daughter was dead, and it was useless to trouble the Master further. The word caught the ear of Jesus. "Fear not,"
He said; "believe only, and she shall be made whole."

Jairus pressed closer to the Saviour, and together they
hurried to the ruler's home. Already the hired mourners
and flute players were there, filling the air with their clam-
or. The presence of the crowd and the tumult jarred upon
the spirit of Jesus. He tried to silence them, saying, "Why

This chapter is based on Matt. 9:18-26; Mark 5:21-43; Luke 8:40-56.

make ye this ado, and weep? the damsel is not dead, but sleepeth." They were indignant at the words of the Stranger. They had seen the child in the embrace of death, and they laughed Him to scorn. Requiring them all to leave the house, Jesus took with Him the father and mother of the maiden, and the three disciples, Peter, James, and John, and together they entered the chamber of death.

Jesus approached the bedside, and, taking the child's hand in His own, He pronounced softly, in the familiar language of her home, the words, "Damsel, I say unto thee, arise."

Instantly a tremor passed through the unconscious form. The pulses of life beat again. The lips unclosed with a smile. The eyes opened widely as if from sleep, and the maiden gazed with wonder on the group beside her. She arose, and her parents clasped her in their arms, and wept for joy.

On the way to the ruler's house, Jesus had met, in the crowd, a poor woman who for twelve years had suffered from a disease that made her life a burden. She had spent all her means upon physicians and remedies, only to be pronounced incurable. But her hopes revived when she heard of the cures that Christ performed. She felt assured that if she could only go to Him she would be healed. In weakness and suffering she came to the seaside where He was teaching, and tried to press through the crowd, but in vain. Again she followed Him from the house of Levi-Matthew, but was still unable to reach Him. She had begun to despair, when, in making His way through the multitude, He came near where she was.

The golden opportunity had come. She was in the presence of the Great Physician! But amid the confusion she could not speak to Him, nor catch more than a passing glimpse of His figure. Fearful of losing her one chance of relief, she pressed forward, saying to herself, "If I may but touch His garment, I shall be whole." As He was passing, she reached forward, and succeeded in barely touching the border of His garment. But in that moment she knew that she was healed. In that one touch was concentrated the faith of her life, and instantly her pain and feebleness gave place to the vigor of perfect health.

With a grateful heart she then tried to withdraw from the crowd; but suddenly Jesus stopped, and the people halted with Him. He turned, and looking about asked in a voice distinctly heard above the confusion of the multitude, "Who touched Me?" The people answered this query with a look of amazement. Jostled upon all sides, and rudely pressed hither and thither, as He was, it seemed a strange inquiry.

Peter, ever ready to speak, said, "Master, the multitude throng Thee and press Thee, and sayest Thou, Who touched Me?" Jesus answered, "Somebody hath touched Me: for I perceive that virtue is gone out of Me." The Saviour could distinguish the touch of faith from the casual contact of the careless throng. Such trust should not be passed without comment. He would speak to the humble woman words of comfort that would be to her a well-spring of joy,—words that would be a blessing to His followers to the close of time.

Looking toward the woman, Jesus insisted on knowing who had touched Him. Finding concealment vain, she came forward tremblingly, and cast herself at His feet. With grateful tears she told the story of her suffering, and how she had found relief. Jesus gently said, "Daughter, be of good comfort: thy faith hath made thee whole; go in peace." He gave no opportunity for superstition to claim healing virtue for the mere act of touching His garments. It was not through the outward contact with Him, but through the faith which took hold on His divine power, that the cure was wrought.

The wondering crowd that pressed close about Christ realized no accession of vital power. But when the suffering woman put forth her hand to touch Him, believing that she would be made whole, she felt the healing virtue. So in spiritual things. To talk of religion in a casual way, to pray without soul hunger and living faith, avails nothing. A nominal faith in Christ, which accepts Him merely as the Saviour of the world, can never bring healing to the soul. The faith that is unto salvation is not a mere intellectual assent to the truth. He who waits for entire knowledge before he will exercise faith cannot receive blessing from God. It is not enough to believe *about* Christ; we must believe *in* Him. The only faith that will benefit us is that which embraces Him as a personal Saviour; which appropriates His merits to ourselves. Many hold faith as an opinion. Saving faith is a transaction by which those who receive Christ join themselves in covenant relation with God. Genuine faith is life. A living faith means an increase of vigor, a confiding trust, by which the soul becomes a conquering power.

After healing the woman, Jesus desired her to acknowledge the blessing she had received. The gifts which the gospel offers are not to be secured by stealth or enjoyed in secret. So the Lord calls upon us for confession of His goodness. "Ye are My witnesses, saith the Lord, that I am God." Isa. 43:12.

Our confession of His faithfulness is Heaven's chosen agency for revealing Christ to the world. We are to acknowledge His grace as made known through the holy men of old; but that which will be most effectual is the testimony of our own experience. We are witnesses for God as we reveal in ourselves the working of a power that is divine. Every individual has a life distinct from all others, and an experience differing essentially from theirs. God desires that our praise shall ascend to Him, marked by our own individuality. These precious acknowledgments to the praise of the glory of His grace, when supported by a Christlike life, have an irresistible power that works for the salvation of souls.

When the ten lepers came to Jesus for healing, He bade them go and show themselves to the priest. On the way they were cleansed, but only one of them returned to give Him glory. The others went their way, forgetting Him who had made them whole. How many are still doing the same thing! The Lord works continually to benefit mankind. He is ever imparting His bounties. He raises up the sick from beds of languishing, He delivers men from peril which they do not see, He commissions heavenly angels to save them from calamity, to guard them from "the pestilence that walketh in darkness" and "the destruction that wasteth at noonday" (Ps. 91:6); but their hearts are unimpressed. He has given all the riches of heaven to redeem them, and yet they are unmindful of His great love. By their ingratitude they close their hearts against the grace of God. Like the heath in the desert they know not when good cometh, and their souls inhabit the parched places of the wilderness.

It is for our own benefit to keep every gift of God fresh in our memory. Thus faith is strengthened to claim and to receive more and more. There is greater encouragement for us in the least blessing we ourselves receive from God than in all the accounts we can read of the faith and experience of others. The soul that responds to the grace of God shall be like a watered garden. His health shall spring forth speedily; his light shall rise in obscurity, and the glory of the Lord shall be seen upon him. Let us then re-member the loving-kindness of the Lord, and the multi-tude of His tender mercies. Like the people of Israel, let us set up our stones of witness, and inscribe upon them the precious story of what God has wrought for us. And as we review His dealings with us in our pilgrimage, let us, out of hearts melted with gratitude, declare, "What shall I render unto the Lord for all His benefits toward me? I will take the cup of salvation, and call upon the name of the Lord. I will pay my vows unto the Lord now in the pres-ence of all His people." Ps. 116:12-14.

Chapter 19

BREAD BASKETS

CHRIST HAD retired to a secluded place with His disciples, but this rare season of peaceful quietude was soon broken. The disciples thought they had retired where they would not be disturbed; but as soon as the multitude missed the divine Teacher, they inquired, "Where is He?" Some among them had noticed the direction in which Christ and His disciples had gone. Many went by land to meet them, while others followed in their boats across the water. The Passover was at hand, and, from far and near, bands of pilgrims on their way to Jerusalem gathered to see Jesus. Additions were made to their number, until there were assembled five thousand men besides women and children. Before Christ reached the shore, a multitude were waiting for Him. But He landed unobserved by them, and spent a little time apart with the disciples.

From the hillside He looked upon the moving multitude, and His heart was stirred with sympathy. Interrupted as He was, and robbed of His rest, He was not impatient. He saw a greater necessity demanding His attention as He watched the people coming and still coming. He "was moved with compassion toward them, because they were as sheep not having a shepherd." Leaving His retreat, He found a convenient place where He could minister to them. They received no help from the priests and rulers; but the healing waters of life flowed from Christ as He taught the multitude the way of salvation.

The people listened to the words of mercy flowing so freely from the lips of the Son of God. They heard the gracious words, so simple and so plain that they were as the balm of Gilead to their souls. The healing of His di-

This chapter is based on Matt. 14:13-21; Mark 6:32-44; Luke 9:10-17; John 6:1-13.

151

vine hand brought gladness and life to the dying, and ease and health to those suffering with disease. The day seemed to them like heaven upon earth, and they were utterly unconscious of how long it had been since they had eaten anything.

At length the day was far spent. The sun was sinking in the west, and yet the people lingered. Jesus had labored all day without food or rest. He was pale from weariness and hunger, and the disciples besought Him to cease from His toil. But He could not withdraw Himself from the multitude that pressed upon Him.

The disciples finally came to Him, urging that for their own sake the people should be sent away. Many had come from far, and had eaten nothing since morning. In the surrounding towns and villages they might be able to buy food. But Jesus said, "Give ye them to eat," and then, turning to Philip, questioned, "Whence shall we buy bread, that these may eat?" This He said to test the faith of the disciple. Philip looked over the sea of heads, and thought how impossible it would be to provide food to satisfy the wants of such a crowd. He answered that two hundred pennyworth of bread would not be nearly enough to divide among them, so that each might have a little. Jesus inquired how much food could be found among the company. "There is a lad here," said Andrew, "which hath five barley loaves, and two small fishes: but what are they among so many?" Jesus directed that these be brought to Him. Then He bade the disciples seat the people on the grass in parties of fifty or a hundred, to preserve order, and that all might witness what He was about to do. When this was accomplished, Jesus took the food, "and looking up to heaven, He blessed, and brake, and gave the loaves to His disciples, and the disciples to the multitude." "And they did all eat, and were filled. And they took up twelve baskets full of the fragments, and of the fishes."

He who taught the people the way to secure peace and happiness was just as thoughtful of their temporal necessities as of their spiritual need. The people were weary and faint. There were mothers with babes in their arms, and little children clinging to their skirts. Many had been standing for hours. They had been so intensely interested in Christ's words that they had not once thought of sitting down, and the crowd was so great that there was danger of their trampling on one another. Jesus would give them a chance to rest, and He bade them sit down. There was much grass in the place, and all could rest in comfort.

Christ never worked a miracle except to supply a genuine necessity, and every miracle was of a character to lead the people to the tree of life, whose leaves are for the healing of the nations. The simple food passed round by the hands of the disciples contained a whole treasure of lessons. It was humble fare that had been provided; the fishes and barley loaves were the daily food of the fisher folk about the Sea of Galilee. Christ could have spread before the people a rich repast, but food prepared merely for the gratification of appetite would have conveyed no lesson for their good. Christ taught them in this lesson that the natural provisions of God for man had been perverted. And never did people enjoy the luxurious feasts prepared for the gratification of perverted taste as this people enjoyed the rest and the simple food which Christ provided so far from human habitations.

If men today were simple in their habits, living in harmony with nature's laws, as did Adam and Eve in the beginning, there would be an abundant supply for the needs of the human family. There would be fewer imaginary wants, and more opportunities to work in God's ways. But selfishness and the indulgence of unnatural taste have brought sin and misery into the world, from excess on the one hand, and from want on the other.

Jesus did not seek to attract the people to Him by gratifying the desire for luxury. To that great throng, weary and hungry after the long, exciting day, the simple fare was an assurance not only of His power, but of His tender care for them in the common needs of life. The Saviour has not promised His followers the luxuries of the world; their fare may be plain, and even scanty; their lot may be shut in by poverty; but His word is pledged that their need shall be supplied, and He has promised that which is far better than worldly good,—the abiding comfort of His own presence.

In feeding the five thousand, Jesus lifts the veil from the world of nature, and reveals the power that is constantly exercised for our good. In the production of earth's harvest God is working a miracle every day. Through natural agencies the same work is accomplished that was wrought in the feeding of the multitude. Men prepare the soil and sow the seed, but it is the life from God that causes the seed to germinate. It is God's rain and air and sunshine that cause it to put forth, "first the blade, then the ear, after that the full corn in the ear." Mark 4:28. It is God who is every day feeding millions from earth's harvest fields. Men are called upon to co-operate with God in the care of the grain and the preparation of the loaf, and because of this they lose sight of the divine agency. They do not give God the glory due unto His holy name. The working of His power is ascribed to natural causes or to human instrumentality. Man is glorified in place of God, and His gracious gifts are perverted to selfish uses, and made a curse instead of a blessing. God is seeking to change all this. He desires that our dull senses shall be quickened to discern His merciful kindness and to glorify Him for the working of His power. He desires us to recognize Him in His gifts, that they may be, as He intended, a blessing to us. It was to accomplish this purpose that the miracles of Christ were performed.

After the multitude had been fed, there was an abundance of food left. But He who had all the resources of infinite power at His command said, "Gather up the fragments that remain, that nothing be lost." These words meant more than putting the bread into the baskets. The lesson was twofold. Nothing is to be wasted. We are to let slip no temporal advantage. We should neglect nothing that will tend to benefit a human being. Let everything be gathered up that will relieve the necessity of earth's hungry ones. And there should be the same carefulness in spiritual things. When the baskets of fragments were collected, the people thought of their friends at home. They wanted them to share in the bread that Christ had blessed. The contents of the baskets were distributed among the eager throng, and were carried away into all the region round about. So those who were at the feast were to give to others the bread that comes down from heaven, to satisfy the hunger of the soul. They were to repeat what they had learned of the wonderful things of God. Nothing was to be lost. Not one word that concerned their eternal salvation was to fall useless to the ground.

The miracle of the loaves teaches a lesson of dependence upon God. When Christ fed the five thousand, the food was not nigh at hand. Apparently He had no means at His command. Here He was, with five thousand men, besides women and children, in the wilderness. He had not invited the large multitude to follow Him; they came without invitation or command; but He knew that after they had listened so long to His instruction, they would feel hungry and faint; for He was one with them in their need of food. They were far from home, and the night was close at hand. Many of them were without means to purchase food. He who for their sake had fasted forty days in the wilderness would not suffer them to return fasting to their homes. The providence of God had placed Jesus where He was; and He depended on His heavenly Father for the means to relieve the necessity.

And when we are brought into strait places, we are to depend on God. We are to exercise wisdom and judgment in every action of life, that we may not, by reckless movements, place ourselves in trial. We are not to plunge into difficulties, neglecting the means God has provided, and misusing the faculties He has given us. Christ's workers are to obey His instructions implicitly. The work is God's, and if we would bless others His plans must be followed. Self cannot be made a center; self can receive no honor. If we plan according to our own ideas, the Lord will leave us to our own mistakes. But when, after following His directions, we are brought into strait places, He will deliver us. We are not to give up in discouragement, but in every emergency we are to seek help from Him who has infinite resources at His command. Often we shall be surrounded with trying circumstances, and then, in the fullest confidence, we must depend upon God. He will keep every soul that is brought into perplexity through trying to keep the way of the Lord.

Christ has bidden us, through the prophet, "Deal thy bread to the hungry," and "satisfy the afflicted soul;" "when thou seest the naked, that thou cover him," and "bring the poor that are cast out to thy house." Isa. 58:7-10. He has bidden us, "Go ye into all the world, and preach the gospel to every creature." Mark 16:15. But how often our hearts sink, and faith fails us, as we see how great is the need, and how small the means in our hands. Like Andrew looking upon the five barley loaves and the two little fishes, we exclaim, "What are they among so many?" Often we hesitate, unwilling to give all that we have, fearing to spend and to be spent for others. But Jesus has bidden us, "Give ye them to eat." His command is a promise; and behind it is the same power that fed the multitude beside the sea.

In Christ's act of supplying the temporal necessities of a hungry multitude is wrapped up a deep spiritual lesson for all His workers. Christ received from the Father; He imparted to the disciples; they imparted to the multitude; and the people to one another. So all who are united to Christ will receive from Him the bread of life, the heavenly food, and impart it to others.

In full reliance upon God, Jesus took the small store of loaves; and although there was but a small portion for His own family of disciples, He did not invite them to eat, but began to distribute to them, bidding them serve the people. The food multiplied in His hands; and the hands of the disciples, reaching out to Christ Himself the Bread of Life, were never empty. The little store was sufficient for all. After the wants of the people had been supplied, the fragments were gathered up, and Christ and His disciples ate together of the precious, Heaven-supplied food.

The disciples were the channel of communication between Christ and the people. This should be a great encouragement to His disciples today. Christ is the great center, the source of all strength. His disciples are to receive their supplies from Him. The most intelligent, the most spiritually minded, can bestow only as they receive. Of themselves they can supply nothing for the needs of the soul. We can impart only that which we receive from Christ; and we can receive only as we impart to others. As we continue imparting, we continue to receive; and the more we impart, the more we shall receive. Thus we may be constantly believing, trusting, receiving, and imparting.

The work of building up the kingdom of Christ will go forward, though to all appearance it moves slowly and impossibilities seem to testify against advance. The work is of God, and He will furnish means, and will send helpers, true, earnest disciples, whose hands also will be filled with food for the starving multitude. God is not unmindful of those who labor in love to give the word of life to perishing souls, who in their turn reach forth their hands for food for other hungry souls.

In our work for God there is danger of relying too largely upon what man with his talents and ability can do. Thus we lose sight of the one Master Worker. Too often the worker for Christ fails to realize his personal responsibility. He is in danger of shifting his burden upon organizations, instead of relying upon Him who is the source of all strength. It is a great mistake to trust in human wisdom or numbers in the work of God. Successful work for Christ depends not so much on numbers or talent as upon.

pureness of purpose, the true simplicity of earnest, dependent faith. Personal responsibilities must be borne, personal duties must be taken up, personal efforts must be made for those who do not know Christ. In the place of shifting your responsibility upon someone whom you think more richly endowed than you are, work according to your ability.

When the question comes home to your heart, "Whence shall we buy bread, that these may eat?" let not your answer be the response of unbelief. When the disciples heard the Saviour's direction, "Give ye them to eat," all the difficulties arose in their minds. They questioned, Shall we go away into the villages to buy food? So now, when the people are destitute of the bread of life, the Lord's children question, Shall we send for someone from afar, to come and feed them? But what said Christ? "Make the men sit down," and He fed them there. So when you are surrounded by souls in need, know that Christ is there. Commune with Him. Bring your barley loaves to Jesus.

The means in our possession may not seem to be sufficient for the work; but if we will move forward in faith, believing in the all-sufficient power of God, abundant resources will open before us. If the work be of God, He Himself will provide the means for its accomplishment. He will reward honest, simple reliance upon Him. The little that is wisely and economically used in the service of the Lord of heaven will increase in the very act of imparting. In the hand of Christ the small supply of food remained undiminished until the famished multitude were satisfied. If we go to the Source of all strength, with our hands of faith outstretched to receive, we shall be sustained in our work, even under the most forbidding circumstances, and shall be enabled to give to others the bread of life.

The Lord says, "Give, and it shall be given unto you." "He that soweth sparingly shall reap also sparingly; and he that soweth with blessings shall reap also with blessings. . . . And God is able to make all grace abound unto you; that ye, having always all sufficiency in everything, may abound unto every good work: as it is written,—

"He hath scattered abroad, he hath given to the poor:
His righteousness abideth forever.

"And He that supplieth seed to the sower and bread for food, shall supply and multiply your seed for sowing, and increase the fruits of your righteousness: ye being enriched in everything unto all liberality, which worketh through us thanksgiving to God." Luke 6:38; 2 Cor. 9:6-11, R. V., margin.

Chapter 20

WALKING ON WATER

SEATED UPON the grassy plain, in the twilight of the spring evening, the people ate of the food that Christ had provided. The words they had heard that day had come to them as the voice of God. The works of healing they had witnessed were such as only divine power could perform. But the miracle of the loaves appealed to everyone in that vast multitude. All were sharers in its benefit. In the days of Moses, God had fed Israel with manna in the desert; and who was this that had fed them that day but He whom Moses had foretold? No human power could create from five barley loaves and two small fishes food sufficient to feed thousands of hungry people. And they said one to another, "This is of a truth that Prophet that should come into the world."

All day the conviction has strengthened. That crowning act is assurance that the long-looked-for Deliverer is among them. The hopes of the people rise higher and higher. This is He who will make Judea an earthly paradise, a land flowing with milk and honey. He can satisfy every desire. He can break the power of the hated Romans. He can deliver Judah and Jerusalem. He can heal the soldiers who are wounded in battle. He can supply whole armies with food. He can conquer the nations, and give to Israel the long-sought dominion.

In their enthusiasm the people are ready at once to crown Him king. They see that He makes no effort to attract attention or secure honor to Himself. In this He is essentially different from the priests and rulers, and they fear that He will never urge His claim to David's throne. Consulting together, they agree to take Him by force, and proclaim Him the king of Israel. The disciples unite with the

This chapter is based on Matt. 14:22-33; Mark 6:45-52; John 6:14-21.

multitude in declaring the throne of David the rightful inheritance of their Master. It is the modesty of Christ, they say, that causes Him to refuse such honor. Let the people exalt their Deliverer. Let the arrogant priests and rulers be forced to honor Him who comes clothed with the authority of God.

They eagerly arrange to carry out their purpose; but Jesus sees what is on foot, and understands, as they cannot, what would be the result of such a movement. Even now the priests and rulers are hunting His life. They accuse Him of drawing the people away from them. Violence and insurrection would follow an effort to place Him on the throne, and the work of the spiritual kingdom would be hindered. Without delay the movement must be checked. Calling His disciples, Jesus bids them take the boat and return at once to Capernaum, leaving Him to dismiss the people.

Never before had a command from Christ seemed so impossible of fulfillment. The disciples had long hoped for a popular movement to place Jesus on the throne; they could not endure the thought that all this enthusiasm should come to nothing. The multitudes that were assembling to keep the Passover were anxious to see the new prophet. To His followers this seemed the golden opportunity to establish their beloved Master on the throne of Israel. In the glow of this new ambition it was hard for them to go away by themselves, and leave Jesus alone upon that desolate shore. They protested against the arrangement; but Jesus now spoke with an authority He had never before assumed toward them. They knew that further opposition on their part would be useless, and in silence they turned toward the sea.

Jesus now commands the multitude to disperse; and His manner is so decisive that they dare not disobey. The words of praise and exaltation die on their lips. In the very act of advancing to seize Him their steps are stayed, and the glad, eager look fades from their countenances. In that throng are men of strong mind and firm determination; but the kingly bearing of Jesus, and His few quiet words of command, quell the tumult, and frustrate their designs. They recognize in Him a power above all earthly authority, and without a question they submit.

When left alone, Jesus "went up into a mountain apart to pray." For hours He continued pleading with God. Not for Himself but for men were those prayers. He prayed for power to reveal to men the divine character of His mission, that Satan might not blind their understanding and pervert their judgment. The Saviour knew that His days of personal ministry on earth were nearly ended, and that few would receive Him as their Redeemer. In travail and conflict of soul He prayed for His disciples. They were to be grievously tried. Their long-cherished hopes, based on a popular delusion, were to be disappointed in a most painful and humiliating manner. In the place of His exaltation to the throne of David they were to witness His crucifixion. This was to be indeed His true coronation. But they did not discern this, and in consequence strong temptations would come to them, which it would be difficult for them to recognize as temptations. Without the Holy Spirit to enlighten the mind and enlarge the comprehension the faith of the disciples would fail. It was painful to Jesus that their conceptions of His kingdom were, to so great a degree, limited to worldly aggrandizement and honor. For them the burden was heavy upon His heart, and He poured out His supplications with bitter agony and tears.

The disciples had not put off immediately from the land, as Jesus directed them. They waited for a time, hoping that He would come to them. But as they saw that darkness was fast gathering, they "entered into a ship, and went over the sea toward Capernaum." They had left Jesus with dissatisfied hearts, more impatient with Him than ever before since acknowledging Him as their Lord. They murmured because they had not been permitted to proclaim Him king. They blamed themselves for yielding so readily to His command. They reasoned that if they had been more persistent they might have accomplished their purpose.

Unbelief was taking possession of their minds and hearts. Love of honor had blinded them. They knew that Jesus was hated by the Pharisees, and they were eager to see Him exalted as they thought He should be. To be united with a teacher who could work mighty miracles, and yet to be reviled as deceivers, was a trial they could ill endure. Were they always to be accounted followers of a false prophet? Would Christ never assert His authority as king? Why did not He who possessed such power reveal Himself in His true character, and make their way less painful? Why had He not saved John the Baptist from a violent death? Thus the disciples reasoned until they brought upon themselves great spiritual darkness. They questioned, Could Jesus be an impostor, as the Pharisees asserted?

The disciples had that day witnessed the wonderful works of Christ. It had seemed that heaven had come down to the earth. The memory of that precious, glorious day should have filled them with faith and hope. Had they, out of the abundance of their hearts, been conversing together in regard to these things, they would not have entered into temptation. But their disappointment had absorbed their thoughts. The words of Christ, "Gather up the fragments, . . . that nothing be lost," were unheeded. Those were hours of large blessing to the disciples, but they had forgotten it all. They were in the midst of troubled waters. Their thoughts were stormy and unreasonable, and the Lord gave them something else to afflict their souls and occupy their minds. God often does this when men create burdens and troubles for themselves. The disciples had no need to make trouble. Already danger was fast approaching.

A violent tempest had been stealing upon them, and they were unprepared for it. It was a sudden contrast, for the day had been perfect; and when the gale struck them, they were afraid. They forgot their disaffection, their unbelief, their impatience. Everyone worked to keep the boat from sinking. It was but a short distance by sea from Bethsaida to the point where they expected to meet Jesus, and in ordinary weather the journey required but a few hours; but now they were driven farther and farther from the point they sought. Until the fourth watch of the night they toiled at the oars. Then the weary men gave themselves up for lost. In storm and darkness the sea had taught them their own helplessness, and they longed for the presence of their Master.

Jesus had not forgotten them. The Watcher on the shore saw those fear-stricken men battling with the tempest. Not for a moment did He lose sight of His disciples. With deepest solicitude His eyes followed the storm-tossed boat with its precious burden; for these men were to be the light of the world. As a mother in tender love watches her child, so the compassionate Master watched His disciples. When their hearts were subdued, their unholy ambition quelled, and in humility they prayed for help, it was given them.

At the moment when they believe themselves lost, a gleam of light reveals a mysterious figure approaching them upon the water. But they know not that it is Jesus. The One who has come for their help they count as an enemy. Terror overpowers them. The hands that have grasped the oars with muscles like iron let go their hold. The boat rocks at the will of the waves; all eyes are riveted on this vision of a man walking upon the white-capped billows of the foaming sea.

They think it a phantom that omens their destruction, and they cry out for fear. Jesus advances as if He would pass them; but they recognize Him, and cry out, entreating His help. Their beloved Master turns, His voice silences their fear, "Be of good cheer: it is I; be not afraid."

As soon as they could credit the wondrous fact, Peter was almost beside himself with joy. As if he could scarcely yet believe, he cried out, "Lord, if it be Thou, bid me come unto Thee on the water. And He said, Come."

Looking unto Jesus, Peter walks securely; but as in self-satisfaction he glances back toward his companions in the boat, his eyes are turned from the Saviour. The wind is boisterous. The waves roll high, and come directly between him and the Master; and he is afraid. For a moment Christ is hidden from his view, and his faith gives way. He begins to sink. But while the billows talk with death, Peter lifts his eyes from the angry waters, and fixing them upon Jesus, cries, "Lord, save me." Immediately Jesus grasps the outstretched hand, saying, "O thou of little faith, wherefore didst thou doubt?"

Walking side by side, Peter's hand in that of his Master, they stepped into the boat together. But Peter was now subdued and silent. He had no reason to boast over his fellows, for through unbelief and self-exaltation he had very nearly lost his life. When he turned his eyes from Jesus, his footing was lost, and he sank amid the waves.

When trouble comes upon us, how often we are like Peter! We look upon the waves, instead of keeping our eyes fixed upon the Saviour. Our footsteps slide, and the proud waters go over our souls. Jesus did not bid Peter come to Him that he should perish; He does not call us to follow Him, and then forsake us. "Fear not," He says; "for I have redeemed thee, I have called thee by thy name; thou art Mine. When thou passest through the waters, I will be with thee; and through the rivers, they shall not overflow thee: when thou walkest through the fire, thou shalt not be burned; neither shall the flame kindle upon thee. For I am the Lord thy God, the Holy One of Israel, thy Saviour." Isa. 43:1-3.

Jesus read the character of His disciples. He knew how sorely their faith was to be tried. In this incident on the sea He desired to reveal to Peter his own weakness,—to show that his safety was in constant dependence upon divine power. Amid the storms of temptation he could walk safely only as in utter self-distrust he should rely upon the Saviour. It was on the point where he thought himself strong that Peter was weak; and not until he discerned his weakness could he realize his need of dependence upon Christ. Had he learned the lesson that Jesus sought to teach him in that experience on the sea, he would not have failed when the great test came upon him.

Day by day God instructs His children. By the circumstances of the daily life He is preparing them to act their part upon that wider stage to which His providence has appointed them. It is the issue of the daily test that determines their victory or defeat in life's great crisis.

Those who fail to realize their constant dependence upon God will be overcome by temptation. We may now suppose that our feet stand secure, and that we shall never be moved. We may say with confidence, I know in whom I have believed; nothing can shake my faith in God and in His word. But Satan is planning to take advantage of our hereditary and cultivated traits of character, and to blind our eyes to our own necessities and defects. Only through realizing our own weakness and looking steadfastly unto Jesus can we walk securely.

No sooner had Jesus taken His place in the boat than the wind ceased, "and immediately the ship was at the land whither they went." The night of horror was succeeded by the light of dawn. The disciples, and others who also were on board, bowed at the feet of Jesus with thankful hearts, saying, "Of a truth Thou art the Son of God!"

Chapter 21

FACING DEMONS

THE ENTIRE night had been passed in the mountain; and as the sun arose, Jesus and His disciples descended to the plain. Absorbed in thought, the disciples were awed and silent. Even Peter had not a word to say. Gladly would they have lingered in that holy place which had been touched with the light of heaven, and where the Son of God had manifested His glory; but there was work to be done for the people, who were already searching far and near for Jesus.

At the foot of the mountain a large company had gathered, led hither by the disciples who had remained behind, but who knew whither Jesus had resorted. As the Saviour drew near, He charged His three companions to keep silence concerning what they had witnessed, saying, "Tell the vision to no man, until the Son of man be risen again from the dead." The revelation made to the disciples was to be pondered in their own hearts, not to be published abroad. To relate it to the multitudes would excite only ridicule or idle wonder. And even the nine apostles would not understand the scene until after Christ had risen from the dead. How slow of comprehension even the three favored disciples were, is seen in the fact that notwithstanding all that Christ had said of what was before Him, they queried among themselves what the rising from the dead should mean. Yet they asked no explanation from Jesus. His words in regard to the future had filled them with sorrow; they sought no further revelation concerning that which they were fain to believe might never come to pass.

As the people on the plain caught sight of Jesus, they ran to meet Him, greeting Him with expressions of rever-

This chapter is based on Matt. 17:9-21; Mark 9:9-29; Luke 9:37-45.

ence and joy. Yet His quick eye discerned that they were in great perplexity. The disciples appeared troubled. A circumstance had just occurred that had caused them bitter disappointment and humiliation.

While they were waiting at the foot of the mountain, a father had brought to them his son, to be delivered from a dumb spirit that tormented him. Authority over unclean spirits, to cast them out, had been conferred on the disciples when Jesus sent out the twelve to preach through Galilee. As they went forth strong in faith, the evil spirits had obeyed their word. Now in the name of Christ they commanded the torturing spirit to leave his victim; but the demon only mocked them by a fresh display of his power. The disciples, unable to account for their defeat, felt that they were bringing dishonor upon themselves and their Master. And in the crowd there were scribes who made the most of this opportunity to humiliate them. Pressing around the disciples, they plied them with questions, seeking to prove that they and their Master were deceivers. Here, the rabbis triumphantly declared, was an evil spirit that neither the disciples nor Christ Himself could conquer. The people were inclined to side with the scribes, and a feeling of contempt and scorn pervaded the crowd.

But suddenly the accusations ceased. Jesus and the three disciples were seen approaching, and with a quick revulsion of feeling the people turned to meet them. The night of communion with the heavenly glory had left its trace upon the Saviour and His companions. Upon their countenances was a light that awed the beholders. The scribes drew back in fear, while the people welcomed Jesus.

As if He had been a witness of all that had occurred, the Saviour came to the scene of conflict, and fixing His gaze upon the scribes inquired, "What question ye with them?"

But the voices so bold and defiant before were now silent. A hush had fallen upon the entire company. Now the afflicted father made his way through the crowd, and falling at the feet of Jesus, poured out the story of his trouble and disappointment.

"Master," he said, "I have brought unto Thee my son, which hath a dumb spirit; and wheresoever he taketh him, he teareth him: . . . and I spake to Thy disciples that they should cast him out; and they could not."

Jesus looked about Him upon the awe-stricken multitude, the caviling scribes, the perplexed disciples. He read the unbelief in every heart; and in a voice filled with sorrow He exclaimed, "O faithless generation, how long shall I be with you? how long shall I suffer you?" Then He bade the distressed father, "Bring thy son hither."

The boy was brought, and as the Saviour's eyes fell upon him, the evil spirit cast him to the ground in convulsions of agony. He lay wallowing and foaming, rending the air with unearthly shrieks.

Again the Prince of life and the prince of the powers of darkness had met on the field of battle,—Christ in fulfillment of His mission to "preach deliverance to the captives, . . . to set at liberty them that are bruised" (Luke 4:18), Satan seeking to hold his victim under his control. Angels of light and the hosts of evil angels, unseen, were pressing near to behold the conflict. For a moment, Jesus permitted the evil spirit to display his power, that the beholders might comprehend the deliverance about to be wrought.

The multitude looked on with bated breath, the father in an agony of hope and fear. Jesus asked, "How long is it ago since this came unto him?" The father told the story of long years of suffering, and then, as if he could endure no more, exclaimed, "If Thou canst do anything, have compassion on us, and help us." "If Thou canst!" Even now the father questioned the power of Christ.

Jesus answers, "If thou canst believe, all things are possible to him that believeth." There is no lack of power on the part of Christ; the healing of the son depends upon the father's faith. With a burst of tears, realizing his own weakness, the father casts himself upon Christ's mercy, with the cry, "Lord, I believe; help Thou mine unbelief."

Jesus turns to the suffering one, and says, "Thou dumb and deaf spirit, I charge thee, come out of him, and enter no more into him." There is a cry, an agonized struggle. The demon, in passing, seems about to rend the life from his victim. Then the boy lies motionless, and apparently lifeless. The multitude whisper, "He is dead." But Jesus takes him by the hand, and lifting him up, presents him, in perfect soundness of mind and body, to his father. Father and son praise the name of their Deliverer. The multitude are "amazed at the mighty power of God," while the scribes, defeated and crestfallen, turn sullenly away.

"If Thou canst do anything, have compassion on us, and help us." How many a sin-burdened soul has echoed that prayer. And to all, the pitying Saviour's answer is, "If thou canst believe, all things are possible to him that believeth."

It is faith that connects us with heaven, and brings us strength for coping with the powers of darkness. In Christ, God has provided means for subduing every sinful trait, and resisting every temptation, however strong. But many feel that they lack faith, and therefore they remain away from Christ. Let these souls, in their helpless unworthiness, cast themselves upon the mercy of their compassionate Saviour. Look not to self, but to Christ. He who healed the sick and cast out demons when He walked among men is the same mighty Redeemer today. Faith comes by the word of God. Then grasp His promise, "Him that cometh to Me I will in nowise cast out." John 6:37. Cast yourself at His feet with the cry, "Lord, I believe; help *Thou* mine unbelief." You can never perish while you do this—never.

In a brief space of time the favored disciples have beheld the extreme of glory and of humiliation. They have seen humanity as transfigured into the image of God, and as debased into the likeness of Satan. From the mountain where He has talked with the heavenly messengers, and has been proclaimed the Son of God by the voice from the radiant glory, they have seen Jesus descend to meet that most distressing and revolting spectacle, the maniac boy, with distorted countenance, gnashing his teeth in spasms of agony that no human power could relieve. And this mighty Redeemer, who but a few hours before stood glorified before His wondering disciples, stoops to lift the victim of Satan from the earth where he is wallowing, and in health of mind and body restores him to his father and his home.

It was an object lesson of redemption,—the Divine One from the Father's glory stooping to save the lost. It represented also the disciples' mission. Not alone upon the mountaintop with Jesus, in hours of spiritual illumination, is the life of Christ's servants to be spent. There is work for them down in the plain. Souls whom Satan has enslaved are waiting for the word of faith and prayer to set them free.

The nine disciples were yet pondering upon the bitter fact of their own failure; and when Jesus was once more alone with them, they questioned, "Why could not we cast him out?" Jesus answered them, "Because of your unbelief: for verily I say unto you, If ye have faith as a grain of mustard seed, ye shall say unto this mountain, Remove hence to yonder place; and it shall remove; and nothing shall be impossible unto you. Howbeit this kind goeth not out but by prayer and fasting." Their unbelief, that shut them out from deeper sympathy with Christ, and the carelessness with which they regarded the sacred work committed to them, had caused their failure in the conflict with the powers of darkness.

The words of Christ pointing to His death had brought sadness and doubt. And the selection of the three disciples to accompany Jesus to the mountain had excited the jealousy of the nine. Instead of strengthening their faith by prayer and meditation on the words of Christ, they had been dwelling on their discouragements and personal grievances. In this state of darkness they had undertaken the conflict with Satan.

In order to succeed in such a conflict they must come to the work in a different spirit. Their faith must be strengthened by fervent prayer and fasting, and humiliation of heart. They must be emptied of self, and be filled with the Spirit and power of God. Earnest, persevering supplication to God in faith—faith that leads to entire dependence upon God, and unreserved consecration to His work—can alone avail to bring men the Holy Spirit's aid in the battle against principalities and powers, the rulers of the darkness of this world, and wicked spirits in high places.

"If ye have faith as a grain of mustard seed," said Jesus, "ye shall say unto this mountain, Remove hence to yonder place; and it shall remove." Though the grain of mustard seed is so small, it contains that same mysterious life principle which produces growth in the loftiest tree. When the mustard seed is cast into the ground, the tiny germ lays hold of every element that God has provided for its nutriment, and it speedily develops a sturdy growth. If you have faith like this, you will lay hold upon God's word, and upon all the helpful agencies He has appointed. Thus your faith will strengthen, and will bring to your aid the power of heaven. The obstacles that are piled by Satan across your path, though apparently as insurmountable as the eternal hills, shall disappear before the demand of faith. "Nothing shall be impossible unto you."

Chapter 22

OF TRUTH AND GREATNESS

ON RETURNING to Capernaum, Jesus did not repair to the well-known resorts where He had taught the people, but with His disciples quietly sought the house that was to be His temporary home. During the remainder of His stay in Galilee it was His object to instruct the disciples rather than to labor for the multitudes.

On the journey through Galilee, Christ had again tried to prepare the minds of His disciples for the scenes before Him. He told them that He was to go up to Jerusalem to be put to death and to rise again. And He added the strange and solemn announcement that He was to be betrayed into the hands of His enemies. The disciples did not even now comprehend His words. Although the shadow of a great sorrow fell upon them, a spirit of rivalry found a place in their hearts. They disputed among themselves which should be accounted greatest in the kingdom. This strife they thought to conceal from Jesus, and they did not, as usual, press close to His side, but loitered behind, so that He was in advance of them as they entered Capernaum. Jesus read their thoughts, and He longed to counsel and instruct them. But for this He awaited a quiet hour, when their hearts should be open to receive His words.

Soon after they reached the town, the collector of the temple revenue came to Peter with the question, "Doth not your Master pay tribute?" This tribute was not a civil tax, but a religious contribution, which every Jew was required to pay annually for the support of the temple. A refusal to pay the tribute would be regarded as disloyalty to the temple,—in the estimation of the rabbis a most grievous sin. The Saviour's attitude toward the rabbinical laws, and His

This chapter is based on Matt. 17:22-27; 18:1-20; Mark 9:30-50; Luke 9:46-48.

plain reproofs to the defenders of tradition, afforded a pretext for the charge that He was seeking to overthrow the temple service. Now His enemies saw an opportunity of casting discredit upon Him. In the collector of the tribute they found a ready ally.

Peter saw in the collector's question an insinuation touching Christ's loyalty to the temple. Zealous for his Master's honor, he hastily answered, without consulting Him, that Jesus would pay the tribute.

But Peter only partially comprehended the purpose of his questioner. There were some classes who were held to be exempt from the payment of the tribute. In the time of Moses, when the Levites were set apart for the service of the sanctuary, they were given no inheritance among the people. The Lord said, "Levi hath no part nor inheritance with his brethren; the Lord is his inheritance." Deut. 10:9. In the days of Christ the priests and Levites were still regarded as especially devoted to the temple, and were not required to make the annual contribution for its support. Prophets also were exempted from this payment. In requiring the tribute from Jesus, the rabbis were setting aside His claim as a prophet or teacher, and were dealing with Him as with any commonplace person. A refusal on His part to pay the tribute would be represented as disloyalty to the temple; while, on the other hand, the payment of it would be taken as justifying their rejection of Him as a prophet.

Only a little before, Peter had acknowledged Jesus as the Son of God; but he now missed an opportunity of setting forth the character of his Master. By his answer to the collector, that Jesus would pay the tribute, he had virtually sanctioned the false conception of Him to which the priests and rulers were trying to give currency.

When Peter entered the house, the Saviour made no reference to what had taken place, but inquired, "What thinkest thou, Simon? of whom do the kings of the earth take custom or tribute? of their own children, or of strangers?" Peter answered, "Of strangers." And Jesus said, "Then are the children free." While the people of a country are taxed for the maintenance of their king, the monarch's own children are exempt. So Israel, the professed people of God, were required to maintain His service; but Jesus, the Son of God, was under no such obligation. If priests and Levites were exempt because of their connection with the temple, how much more He to whom the temple was His Father's house.

If Jesus had paid the tribute without a protest, He would virtually have acknowledged the justice of the claim, and would thus have denied His divinity. But while He saw good to meet the demand, He denied the claim upon which it was based. In providing for the payment of the tribute He gave evidence of His divine character. It was made manifest that He was one with God, and therefore was not under tribute as a mere subject of the kingdom.

"Go thou to the sea," He directed Peter, "and cast an hook, and take up the fish that first cometh up; and when thou hast opened his mouth, thou shalt find a piece of money: that take, and give unto them for Me and thee."

Though He had clothed His divinity with humanity, in this miracle He revealed His glory. It was evident that this was He who through David had declared, "Every beast of the forest is Mine, and the cattle upon a thousand hills. I know all the fowls of the mountains: and the wild beasts of the field are Mine. If I were hungry, I would not tell thee: for the world is Mine, and the fullness thereof." Ps. 50:10-12.

While Jesus made it plain that He was under no obligation to pay the tribute, He entered into no controversy with the Jews in regard to the matter; for they would have misinterpreted His words, and turned them against Him. Lest He should give offense by withholding the tribute, He did that which He could not justly be required to do. This lesson would be of great value to His disciples. Marked changes were soon to take place in their relation to the temple service, and Christ taught them not to place themselves needlessly in antagonism to established order. So far as possible, they were to avoid giving occasion for misinterpretation of their faith. While Christians are not to sacrifice one principle of truth, they should avoid controversy whenever it is possible to do so.

When Christ and the disciples were alone in the house, while Peter was gone to the sea, Jesus called the others to Him, and asked, "What was it that ye disputed among yourselves by the way?" The presence of Jesus, and His question, put the matter in an entirely different light from that in which it had appeared to them while they were contending by the way. Shame and self-condemnation kept them silent. Jesus had told them that He was to die for their sake, and their selfish ambition was in painful contrast to His unselfish love.

When Jesus told them that He was to be put to death and to rise again, He was trying to draw them into conversation in regard to the great test of their faith. Had they been ready to receive what He desired to make known to them, they would have been saved bitter anguish and despair. His words would have brought consolation in the hour of bereavement and disappointment. But although He had spoken so plainly of what awaited Him, His mention of the fact that He was soon to go to Jerusalem again kindled their hope that the kingdom was about to be set up. This had led to questioning as to who should fill the highest offices. On Peter's return from the sea, the disciples told him of the Saviour's question, and at last one ventured to ask Jesus, "Who is the greatest in the kingdom of heaven?"

The Saviour gathered His disciples about Him, and said to them, "If any man desire to be first, the same shall be last of all, and servant of all." There was in these words a solemnity and impressiveness which the disciples were far from comprehending. That which Christ discerned they could not see. They did not understand the nature of Christ's kingdom, and this ignorance was the apparent cause of their contention. But the real cause lay deeper. By explaining the nature of the kingdom, Christ might for the time have quelled their strife; but this would not have touched the underlying cause. Even after they had received the fullest knowledge, any question of precedence might have renewed the trouble. Thus disaster would have been brought to the church after Christ's departure. The strife for the highest place was the outworking of that same spirit which was the beginning of the great controversy in the worlds above, and which had brought Christ from heaven to die. There rose up before Him a vision of Lucifer, the "son of the morning," in glory surpassing all the angels that surround the throne, and united in closest ties to the Son of God. Lucifer had said, "I will be like the Most High" (Isa. 14:12, 14); and the desire for self-exaltation had brought strife into the heavenly courts, and had banished a multitude of the hosts of God. Had Lucifer really desired to be like the Most High, he would never have deserted his appointed place in heaven; for the spirit of the Most High is manifested in unselfish ministry. Lucifer desired God's power, but not His character. He sought for himself the highest place, and every being who is actuated by his spirit will do the same. Thus alienation, discord, and strife will be inevitable. Dominion becomes the prize of the strongest. The kingdom of Satan is a kingdom of force; every individual regards every other as an obstacle in the way of his own advancement, or a steppingstone on which he himself may climb to a higher place.

While Lucifer counted it a thing to be grasped to be equal with God, Christ, the Exalted One, "made Himself of no reputation, and took upon Him the form of a servant, and was made in the likeness of men: and being found in fashion as a man, He humbled Himself, and became obedient unto death, even the death of the cross." Phil. 2:7, 8. Now the cross was just before Him; and His own disciples were so filled with self-seeking—the very principle of Satan's kingdom—that they could not enter into sympathy with their Lord, or even understand Him as He spoke of His humiliation for them.

Very tenderly, yet with solemn emphasis, Jesus tried to correct the evil. He showed what is the principle that bears sway in the kingdom of heaven, and in what true greatness consists, as estimated by the standard of the courts above. Those who were actuated by pride and love of distinction were thinking of themselves, and of the rewards they were to have, rather than how they were to render back to God the gifts they had received. They would have no place in the kingdom of heaven, for they were identified with the ranks of Satan.

Before honor is humility. To fill a high place before men, Heaven chooses the worker who, like John the Baptist, takes a lowly place before God. The most childlike disciple is the most efficient in labor for God. The heavenly intelligences can co-operate with him who is seeking, not to exalt self, but to save souls. He who feels most deeply his need of divine aid will plead for it; and the Holy Spirit will give unto him glimpses of Jesus that will strengthen and uplift the soul. From communion with Christ he will go forth to work for those who are perishing in their sins. He is anointed for his mission; and he succeeds where many of the learned and intellectually wise would fail.

But when men exalt themselves, feeling that they are a necessity for the success of God's great plan, the Lord causes them to be set aside. It is made evident that the Lord is not dependent upon them. The work does not stop because of their removal from it, but goes forward with greater power.

It was not enough for the disciples of Jesus to be instructed as to the nature of His kingdom. What they needed was a change of heart that would bring them into harmony with its principles. Calling a little child to Him, Jesus set him in the midst of them; then tenderly folding the little one in His arms He said, "Except ye be converted, and become as little children, ye shall not enter into the kingdom of heaven." The simplicity, the self-forgetfulness, and the confiding love of a little child are the attributes that Heaven values. These are the characteristics of real greatness.

Again Jesus explained to the disciples that His kingdom is not characterized by earthly dignity and display. At the feet of Jesus all these distinctions are forgotten. The rich and the poor, the learned and the ignorant, meet together, with no thought of caste or worldly pre-eminence. All meet as blood-bought souls, alike dependent upon One who has redeemed them to God.

The sincere, contrite soul is precious in the sight of God. He places His own signet upon men, not by their rank, not by their wealth, not by their intellectual greatness, but by their oneness with Christ. The Lord of glory is satisfied with those who are meek and lowly in heart. "Thou hast also given me," said David, "the shield of Thy salvation: . . . and Thy gentleness"—as an element in the human character—"hath made me great." Ps. 18:35.

"Whosoever shall receive one of such children in My name," said Jesus, "receiveth Me: and whosoever shall receive Me, receiveth not Me, but Him that sent Me." "Thus saith the Lord, The heaven is My throne, and the earth is My footstool: . . . but to this man will I look, even to him that is poor and of a contrite spirit, and trembleth at My word." Isa. 66:1, 2.

The Saviour's words awakened in the disciples a feeling of self-distrust. No one had been specially pointed out in the reply; but John was led to question whether in one case his action had been right. With the spirit of a child he laid the matter before Jesus. "Master," he said, "we saw one casting out devils in Thy name, and he followeth not us: and we forbade him, because he followeth not us."

James and John had thought that in checking this man they had had in view their Lord's honor; they began to see that they were jealous for their own. They acknowledged their error, and accepted the reproof of Jesus, "Forbid him not: for there is no man which shall do a miracle in My name, that can lightly speak evil of Me." None who showed themselves in any way friendly to Christ were to be repulsed. There were many who had been deeply moved by the character and the work of Christ, and whose hearts were opening to Him in faith; and the disciples, who could not read motives, must be careful not to discourage these souls. When Jesus was no longer personally among them, and the work was left in their hands, they must not indulge a narrow, exclusive spirit, but manifest the same far-reaching sympathy which they had seen in their Master.

The fact that one does not in all things conform to our personal ideas or opinions will not justify us in forbidding him to labor for God. Christ is the Great Teacher; we are not to judge or to command, but in humility each is to sit at the feet of Jesus, and learn of Him. Every soul whom God has made willing is a channel through which Christ will reveal His pardoning love. How careful we should be lest we discourage one of God's light bearers, and thus intercept the rays that He would have shine to the world!

Harshness or coldness shown by a disciple toward one whom Christ was drawing—such an act as that of John in forbidding one to work miracles in Christ's name—might result in turning the feet into the path of the enemy, and causing the loss of a soul. Rather than for one to do this, said Jesus, "it is better for him that a millstone were hanged about his neck, and he were cast into the sea." And He added, "If thy hand cause thee to stumble, cut it off: it is good for thee to enter into life maimed, rather than having thy two hands to go into hell, into the unquenchable fire. And if thy foot cause thee to stumble, cut it off: it is good for thee to enter into life halt, rather than having thy two feet to be cast into hell." R. V.

Why this earnest language, than which none can be stronger? Because "the Son of man is come to save that which was lost." Shall His disciples show less regard for the souls of their fellow men than the Majesty of heaven has shown? Every soul has cost an infinite price, and how terrible is the sin of turning one soul away from Christ, so that for him the Saviour's love and humiliation and agony shall have been in vain.

"Woe unto the world because of occasions of stumbling! for it must needs be that the occasions come."

R. V. The world, inspired by Satan, will surely oppose the followers of Christ, and seek to destroy their faith; but woe to him who has taken Christ's name, and yet is found doing this work. Our Lord is put to shame by those who claim to serve Him, but who misrepresent His character; and multitudes are deceived, and led into false paths.

Any habit or practice that would lead into sin, and bring dishonor upon Christ, would better be put away, whatever the sacrifice. That which dishonors God cannot benefit the soul. The blessing of heaven cannot attend any man in violating the eternal principles of right. And one sin cherished is sufficient to work the degradation of the character, and to mislead others. If the foot or the hand would be cut off, or even the eye would be plucked out, to save the body from death, how much more earnest should we be to put away sin, that brings death to the soul!

In the ritual service, salt was added to every sacrifice. This, like the offering of incense, signified that only the righteousness of Christ could make the service acceptable to God. Referring to this practice, Jesus said, "Every sacrifice shall be salted with salt." "Have salt in yourselves, and have peace one with another." All who would present themselves "a living sacrifice, holy, acceptable unto God" (Rom. 12:1), must receive the saving salt, the righteousness of our Saviour. Then they become "the salt of the earth," restraining evil among men, as salt preserves from corruption. Matt. 5:13. But if the salt has lost its savor; if there is only a profession of godliness, without the love of Christ, there is no power for good. The life can exert no saving influence upon the world. Your energy and efficiency in the upbuilding of My kingdom, Jesus says, depend upon your receiving of My Spirit. You must be partakers of My grace, in order to be a savor of life unto life. Then there will be no rivalry, no self-seeking, no desire for the highest place. You will have that love which seeks not her own, but another's wealth.

Let the repenting sinner fix his eyes upon "the Lamb of God, which taketh away the sin of the world" (John 1:29); and by beholding, he becomes changed. His fear is turned to joy, his doubts to hope. Gratitude springs up. The stony heart is broken. A tide of love sweeps into the soul. Christ is in him a well of water springing up unto everlasting life. When we see Jesus, a Man of Sorrows and acquainted with grief, working to save the lost, slighted, scorned, derided, driven from city to city till His mission was accomplished; when we behold Him in Gethsemane, sweating great drops of blood, and on the cross dying in agony,—when we see this, self will no longer clamor to be recognized. Looking unto Jesus, we shall be ashamed of our coldness, our lethargy, our self-seeking. We shall be willing to be anything or nothing, so that we may do heart service for the Master. We shall rejoice to bear the cross after Jesus, to endure trial, shame, or persecution for His dear sake.

"We then that are strong ought to bear the infirmities of the weak, and not to please ourselves." Rom. 15:1. No soul who believes in Christ, though his faith may be weak, and his steps wavering as those of a little child, is to be lightly esteemed. By all that has given us advantage over another,—be it education and refinement, nobility of character, Christian training, religious experience,—we are in debt to those less favored; and, so far as lies in our power, we are to minister unto them. If we are strong, we are to stay up the hands of the weak. Angels of glory, that do always behold the face of the Father in heaven, joy in ministering to His little ones. Trembling souls, who have many objectionable traits of character, are their special charge. Angels are ever present where they are most needed, with those who have the hardest battle with self to fight, and whose surroundings are the most discouraging. And in this ministry Christ's true followers will co-operate.

If one of these little ones shall be overcome, and commit a wrong against you, then it is your work to seek his restoration. Do not wait for him to make the first effort for reconciliation. "How think ye?" said Jesus; "if a man have an hundred sheep, and one of them be gone astray, doth he not leave the ninety and nine, and goeth into the mountains, and seeketh that which is gone astray? And if so be that he find it, verily I say unto you, he rejoiceth more of that sheep, than of the ninety and nine which went not astray. Even so it is not the will of your Father which is in heaven, that one of these little ones should perish."

In the spirit of meekness, "considering thyself, lest thou also be tempted" (Gal. 6:1), go to the erring one, and "tell him his fault between thee and him alone." Do not put him to shame by exposing his fault to others; nor bring dishonor upon Christ by making public the sin or error of one who bears His name. Often the truth must be plainly spoken to the erring; he must be led to see his error, that he may reform. But you are not to judge or to condemn. Make no attempt at self-justification. Let all your effort be for his recovery. In treating the wounds of the soul, there is need of the most delicate touch, the finest sensibility. Only the love that flows from the Suffering One of Calvary can avail here. With pitying tenderness, let brother deal with brother, knowing that if you succeed, you will "save a soul from death," and "hide a multitude of sins." James 5:20.

But even this effort may be unavailing. Then, said Jesus, "take with thee one or two more." It may be that their united influence will prevail where that of the first was unsuccessful. Not being parties to the trouble, they will be more likely to act impartially, and this fact will give their counsel greater weight with the erring one.

If he will not hear them, then, and not till then, the matter is to be brought before the whole body of believers. Let the members of the church, as the representatives of Christ, unite in prayer and loving entreaty that the offender may be restored. The Holy Spirit will speak through His servants, pleading with the wanderer to return to God. Paul the apostle, speaking by inspiration, says, "As though God did beseech you by us: we pray you in Christ's stead, be ye reconciled to God." 2 Cor. 5:20. He who rejects this united overture has broken the tie that binds him to Christ, and thus has severed himself from the fellowship of the church. Henceforth, said Jesus, "let him be unto thee as an heathen man and a publican." But he is not to be regarded as cut off from the mercy of God. Let him not be despised or neglected by his former brethren, but be treated with tenderness and compassion, as one of the lost sheep that Christ is still seeking to bring to His fold.

Christ's instruction as to the treatment of the erring repeats in more specific form the teaching given to Israel through Moses: "Thou shalt not hate thy brother in thine heart: thou shalt in anywise rebuke thy neighbor, that thou bear not sin for him." Lev. 19:17, margin. That is, if one neglects the duty Christ has enjoined, of trying to restore those who are in error and sin, he becomes a partaker in the sin. For evils that we might have checked, we are just as responsible as if we were guilty of the acts ourselves.

But it is to the wrongdoer himself that we are to present the wrong. We are not to make it a matter of comment and criticism among ourselves; nor even after it is told to the church, are we at liberty to repeat it to others. A knowledge of the faults of Christians will be only a cause of stumbling to the unbelieving world; and by dwelling upon these things, we ourselves can receive only harm; for it is by beholding that we become changed. While we seek to correct the errors of a brother, the Spirit of Christ will lead us to shield him, as far as possible, from the criticism of even his own brethren, and how much more from the censure of the unbelieving world. We ourselves are erring, and need Christ's pity and forgiveness, and just as we wish Him to deal with us, He bids us deal with one another.

"Whatsoever ye shall bind on earth shall be bound in heaven: and whatsoever ye shall loose on earth shall be loosed in heaven." You are acting as the ambassadors of heaven, and the issues of your work are for eternity.

But we are not to bear this great responsibility alone. Wherever His word is obeyed with a sincere heart, there Christ abides. Not only is He present in the assemblies of the church, but wherever disciples, however few, meet in His name, there also He will be. And He says, "If two of you shall agree on earth as touching anything that they shall ask, it shall be done for them of My Father which is in heaven."

Jesus says, *"My* Father which is in heaven," as reminding His disciples that while by His humanity He is linked with them, a sharer in their trials, and sympathizing with them in their sufferings, by His divinity He is connected with the throne of the Infinite. Wonderful assurance! The heavenly intelligences unite with men in sympathy and labor for the saving of that which was lost. And all the power of heaven is brought to combine with human ability in drawing souls to Christ.

Chapter 23

MAN IN THE CENTER

THREE TIMES a year the Jews were required to assemble at Jerusalem for religious purposes. Enshrouded in the pillar of cloud, Israel's invisible Leader had given the directions in regard to these gatherings. During the captivity of the Jews, they could not be observed; but when the people were restored to their own land, the observance of these memorials was once more begun. It was God's design that these anniversaries should call Him to the minds of the people. But with few exceptions, the priests and leaders of the nation had lost sight of this purpose. He who had ordained these national assemblies and understood their significance witnessed their perversion.

The Feast of Tabernacles was the closing gathering of the year. It was God's design that at this time the people should reflect on His goodness and mercy. The whole land had been under His guidance, receiving His blessing. Day and night His watchcare had continued. The sun and rain had caused the earth to produce her fruits. From the valleys and plains of Palestine the harvest had been gathered. The olive berries had been picked, and the precious oil stored in bottles. The palm had yielded her store. The purple clusters of the vine had been trodden in the wine press.

The feast continued for seven days, and for its celebration the inhabitants of Palestine, with many from other lands, left their homes, and came to Jerusalem. From far and near the people came, bringing in their hands a token of rejoicing. Old and young, rich and poor, all brought some gift as a tribute of thanksgiving to Him who had crowned the year with His goodness, and made His paths drop fatness. Everything that could please the eye, and

This chapter is based on John 7:1-15, 37-39.

give expression to the universal joy, was brought from the woods; the city bore the appearance of a beautiful forest.

This feast was not only the harvest thanksgiving, but the memorial of God's protecting care over Israel in the wilderness. In commemoration of their tent life, the Israelites during the feast dwelt in booths or tabernacles of green boughs. These were erected in the streets, in the courts of the temple, or on the housetops. The hills and valleys surrounding Jerusalem were also dotted with these leafy dwellings, and seemed to be alive with people.

With sacred song and thanksgiving the worshipers celebrated this occasion. A little before the feast was the Day of Atonement, when, after confession of their sins, the people were declared to be at peace with Heaven. Thus the way was prepared for the rejoicing of the feast. "O give thanks unto the Lord; for He is good: for His mercy endureth forever" (Ps. 106:1) rose triumphantly, while all kinds of music, mingled with shouts of hosanna, accompanied the united singing. The temple was the center of the universal joy. Here was the pomp of the sacrificial ceremonies. Here, ranged on either side of the white marble steps of the sacred building, the choir of Levites led the service of song. The multitude of worshipers, waving their branches of palm and myrtle, took up the strain, and echoed the chorus; and again the melody was caught up by voices near and afar off, till the encircling hills were vocal with praise.

At night the temple and its court blazed with artificial light. The music, the waving of palm branches, the glad hosannas, the great concourse of people, over whom the light streamed from the hanging lamps, the array of the priests, and the majesty of the ceremonies, combined to make a scene that deeply impressed the beholders. But the most impressive ceremony of the feast, one that called forth greatest rejoicing, was one commemorating an event in the wilderness sojourn.

At the first dawn of day, the priests sounded a long, shrill blast upon their silver trumpets, and the answering trumpets, and the glad shouts of the people from their booths, echoing over hill and valley, welcomed the festal day. Then the priest dipped from the flowing waters of the Kedron a flagon of water, and, lifting it on high, while the trumpets were sounding, he ascended the broad steps of the temple, keeping time with the music with slow and measured tread, chanting meanwhile, "Our feet shall stand within thy gates, O Jerusalem." Ps. 122:2.

He bore the flagon to the altar, which occupied a central position in the court of the priests. Here were two silver basins, with a priest standing at each one. The flagon of water was poured onto one, and a flagon of wine into the other; and the contents of both flowed into a pipe which communicated with the Kedron, and was conducted to the Dead Sea. This display of the consecrated water represented the fountain that at the command of God had gushed from the rock to quench the thirst of the children of Israel. Then the jubilant strains rang forth, "The Lord Jehovah is my strength and my song;" "therefore with joy shall ye draw water out of the wells of salvation." Isa. 12:2, 3.

As the sons of Joseph made preparation to attend the Feast of Tabernacles, they saw that Christ made no movement signifying His intention of attending. They watched Him with anxiety. Since the healing at Bethesda He had not attended the national gatherings. To avoid useless conflict with the leaders at Jerusalem, He had restricted His labors to Galilee. His apparent neglect of the great religious assemblies, and the enmity manifested toward Him by the priests and rabbis, were a cause of perplexity to the people about Him, and even to His own disciples and His kindred. In His teachings He had dwelt upon the blessings of obedience to the law of God, and yet He Himself seemed to be indifferent to the service which had been divinely established. His mingling with publicans and others of ill repute, His disregard of the rabbinical observances, and the freedom with which He set aside the traditional requirements concerning the Sabbath, all seeming to place Him in antagonism to the religious authorities, excited much questioning. His brothers thought it a mistake for Him to alienate the great and learned men of the nation. They felt that these men must be in the right, and that Jesus was at fault in placing Himself in antagonism to them. But they had witnessed His blameless life, and though they did not rank themselves with His disciples, they had been deeply impressed by His works. His popularity in Galilee was gratifying to their ambition; they still hoped that He would give an evidence of His power which would lead the Pharisees to see that He was what He claimed to be. What if He were the Messiah, the Prince of Israel! They cherished this thought with proud satisfaction.

So anxious were they about this that they urged Christ to go to Jerusalem. "Depart hence," they said, "and go into Judea, that Thy disciples also may see the works that Thou doest. For there is no man that doeth anything in secret, and he himself seeketh to be known openly. If Thou do these things, show Thyself to the world." The "if" expressed doubt and unbelief. They attributed cowardice and weakness to Him. If He knew that He was the Messiah, why this strange reserve and inaction? If He really possessed such power, why not go boldly to Jerusalem, and assert His claims? Why not perform in Jerusalem the wonderful works reported of Him in Galilee? Do not hide in secluded provinces, they said, and perform your mighty works for the benefit of ignorant peasants and fishermen. Present yourself at the capital, win the support of the priests and rulers and unite the nation in establishing the new kingdom.

These brothers of Jesus reasoned from the selfish motive so often found in the hearts of those ambitious for display. This spirit was the ruling spirit of the world. They were offended because, instead of seeking a temporal throne, Christ had declared Himself to be the bread of life. They were greatly disappointed when so many of His disciples forsook Him. They themselves turned from Him to escape the cross of acknowledging what His works revealed—that He was the Sent of God.

"Then Jesus said unto them, My time is not yet come: but your time is alway ready. The world cannot hate you; but Me it hateth, because I testify of it, that the works thereof are evil. Go ye up unto this feast: I go not up yet unto this feast; for My time is not yet full come. When He had said these words unto them, He abode still in Galilee." His brothers had spoken to Him in a tone of authority, prescribing the course He should pursue. He cast their rebuke back to them, classing them not with His self-denying disciples, but with the world. "The world cannot hate you," He said, "but Me it hateth, because I testify of it, that the works thereof are evil." The world does not hate those who are like it in spirit; it loves them as if its own.

The world for Christ was not a place of ease and self-aggrandizement. He was not watching for an opportunity to seize its power and its glory. It held out no such prize for Him. It was the place into which His Father had sent Him. He had been given for the life of the world, to work out the great plan of redemption. He was accomplishing His work for the fallen race. But He was not to be presumptuous, not to rush into danger, not to hasten a crisis. Each event in His work had its appointed hour. He must wait patiently. He knew that He was to receive the world's hatred; He knew that His work would result in His death; but to prematurely expose Himself would not be the will of His Father.

From Jerusalem the report of Christ's miracles had spread wherever the Jews were dispersed; and although for many months He had been absent from the feasts, the interest in Him had not abated. Many from all parts of the world had come up to the Feast of Tabernacles in the hope of seeing Him. At the beginning of the feast many inquiries were made for Him. The Pharisees and rulers looked for Him to come, hoping for an opportunity to condemn Him. They anxiously inquired, "Where is He?" but no one knew. The thought of Him was uppermost in all minds. Through fear of the priests and rulers, none dared acknowledge Him as the Messiah, but everywhere there was quiet yet earnest discussion concerning Him. Many defended Him as one sent from God, while others denounced Him as a deceiver of the people.

Meanwhile Jesus had quietly arrived at Jerusalem. He had chosen an unfrequented route by which to go, in order to avoid the travelers who were making their way to the city from all quarters. Had He joined any of the caravans that went up to the feast, public attention would have been attracted to Him on His entrance into the city, and a popular demonstration in His favor would have aroused the authorities against Him. It was to avoid this that He chose to make the journey alone.

In the midst of the feast, when the excitement concerning Him was at its height, He entered the court of the temple in the presence of the multitude. Because of His absence from the feast, it had been urged that He dared not place Himself in the power of the priests and rulers. All were surprised at His presence. Every voice was hushed. All wondered at the dignity and courage of His bearing in the midst of powerful enemies who were thirsting for His life.

Standing thus, the center of attraction to that vast throng, Jesus addressed them as no man had ever done. His words showed a knowledge of the laws and institutions of Israel, of the sacrificial service and the teachings of the prophets, far exceeding that of the priests and rabbis. He broke through the barriers of formalism and tradition. The scenes of the future life seemed outspread before Him. As one who beheld the Unseen, He spoke of the earthly and the heavenly, the human and the divine, with positive authority. His words were most clear and convincing; and again, as at Capernaum, the people were astonished at His teaching; "for His word was with power." Luke 4:32. Under a variety of representations He warned His hearers of the calamity that would follow all who rejected the blessings He came to bring them. He had given them every possible proof that He came forth from God, and made every possible effort to bring them to repentance. He would not be rejected and murdered by His own nation if He could save them from the guilt of such a deed.

All wondered at His knowledge of the law and the prophecies; and the question passed from one to another, "How knoweth this Man letters, having never learned?" No one was regarded as qualified to be a religious teacher unless he had studied in the rabbinical schools, and both Jesus and John the Baptist had been represented as ignorant because they had not received this training. Those who heard them were astonished at their knowledge of the Scriptures, "having never learned." Of men they had not, truly; but the God of heaven was their teacher, and from Him they had received the highest kind of wisdom.

As Jesus spoke in the temple court, the people were held spellbound. The very men who were the most violent against Him felt themselves powerless to do Him harm. For the time, all other interests were forgotten.

Day after day He taught the people, until the last, "that great day of the feast." The morning of this day found the people wearied from the long season of festivity. Suddenly Jesus lifted up His voice, in tones that rang through the courts of the temple:

"If any man thirst, let him come unto Me, and drink. He that believeth on Me, as the scripture hath said, out of his belly shall flow rivers of living water." The condition of the people made this appeal very forcible. They had been engaged in a continued scene of pomp and festivity, their eyes had been dazzled with light and color, and their ears regaled with the richest music; but there had been nothing in all this round of ceremonies to meet the wants of the spirit, nothing to satisfy the thirst of the soul for that which perishes not. Jesus invited them to come and drink of the fountain of life, of that which would be in them a well of water, springing up unto everlasting life.

The priest had that morning performed the ceremony which commemorated the smiting of the rock in the wilderness. That rock was a symbol of Him who by His death would cause living streams of salvation to flow to all who are athirst. Christ's words were the water of life. There in the presence of the assembled multitude He set Himself apart to be smitten, that the water of life might flow to the world. In smiting Christ, Satan thought to destroy the Prince of life; but from the smitten rock there flowed living water. As Jesus thus spoke to the people, their hearts thrilled with a strange awe, and many were ready to exclaim, with the woman of Samaria, "Give me this water, that I thirst not." John 4:15.

Jesus knew the wants of the soul. Pomp, riches, and honor cannot satisfy the heart. "If any man thirst, let him come unto Me." The rich, the poor, the high, the low, are alike welcome. He promises to relieve the burdened mind, to comfort the sorrowing, and to give hope to the despondent. Many of those who heard Jesus were mourners over disappointed hopes, many were nourishing a secret grief, many were seeking to satisfy their restless longing with the things of the world and the praise of men; but when all was gained, they found that they had toiled only to reach a broken cistern, from which they could not quench their thirst. Amid the glitter of the joyous scene they stood, dissatisfied and sad. That sudden cry, "If any man thirst," startled them from their sorrowful meditation, and as they listened to the words that followed, their minds kindled with a new hope. The Holy Spirit presented the symbol before them until they saw in it the offer of the priceless gift of salvation.

The cry of Christ to the thirsty soul is still going forth, and it appeals to us with even greater power than to those who heard it in the temple on that last day of the feast. The fountain is open for all. The weary and exhausted ones are offered the refreshing draught of eternal life. Jesus is still crying, "If any man thirst, let him come unto Me, and drink." "Let him that is athirst come. And whosoever will, let him take the water of life freely." "Whosoever drinketh of the water that I shall give him shall never thirst; but the water that I shall give him shall be in him a well of water springing up into everlasting life." Rev. 22:17; John 4:14.

Chapter 24

THE GOOD SHEPHERD

"I AM THE Good Shepherd: the good shepherd giveth his life for the sheep." "I am the Good Shepherd, and know My sheep, and am known of Mine. As the Father knoweth Me, even so know I the Father: and I lay down My life for the sheep."

Again Jesus found access to the minds of His hearers by the pathway of their familiar associations. He had likened the Spirit's influence to the cool, refreshing water. He had represented Himself as the light, the source of life and gladness to nature and to man. Now in a beautiful pastoral picture He represents His relation to those that believe on Him. No picture was more familiar to His hearers than this, and Christ's words linked it forever with Himself. Never could the disciples look on the shepherds tending their flocks without recalling the Saviour's lesson. They would see Christ in each faithful shepherd. They would see themselves in each helpless and dependent flock.

This figure the prophet Isaiah had applied to the Messiah's mission, in the comforting words, "O Zion, that bringest good tidings, get thee up into the high mountain; O Jerusalem, that bringest good tidings, lift up thy voice with strength; lift it up, be not afraid; say unto the cities of Judah, Behold your God! . . . He shall feed His flock like a shepherd: He shall gather the lambs with His arm, and carry them in His bosom." Isa. 40:9-11. David had sung, "The Lord is my shepherd; I shall not want." Ps. 23:1. And the Holy Spirit through Ezekiel had declared: "I will set up one Shepherd over them, and He shall feed them." "I will seek that which was lost, and bring again that which was driven away, and will bind up that which was broken, and will strengthen that which was sick." "And I

This chapter is based on John 10:1-30.

188

will make with them a covenant of peace." "And they shall no more be a prey to the heathen; . . . but they shall dwell safely, and none shall make them afraid." Ezek. 34:23, 16, 25, 28.

Christ applied these prophecies to Himself, and He showed the contrast between His own character and that of the leaders in Israel. The Pharisees had just driven one from the fold, because he dared to bear witness to the power of Christ. They had cut off a soul whom the True Shepherd was drawing to Himself. In this they had shown themselves ignorant of the work committed to them, and unworthy of their trust as shepherds of the flock. Jesus now set before them the contrast between them and the Good Shepherd, and He pointed to Himself as the real keeper of the Lord's flock. Before doing this, however, He speaks of Himself under another figure.

He said, "He that entereth not by the door into the sheepfold, but climbeth up some other way, the same is a thief and a robber. But he that entereth in by the door is the shepherd of the sheep." The Pharisees did not discern that these words were spoken against them. When they reasoned in their hearts as to the meaning, Jesus told them plainly, "I am the door: by Me if any man enter in, he shall be saved, and shall go in and out, and find pasture. The thief cometh not, but for to steal, and to kill, and to destroy: I am come that they might have life, and that they might have it more abundantly."

Christ is the door to the fold of God. Through this door all His children, from the earliest times, have found entrance. In Jesus, as shown in types, as shadowed in symbols, as manifested in the revelation of the prophets, as unveiled in the lessons given to His disciples, and in the miracles wrought for the sons of men, they have beheld "the Lamb of God, which taketh away the sin of the world" (John 1:29), and through Him they are brought within the fold of His grace. Many have come presenting other objects for the faith of the world; ceremonies and systems have been devised by which men hope to receive justification and peace with God, and thus find entrance to His fold. But the only door is Christ, and all who have interposed something to take the place of Christ, all who have tried to enter the fold in some other way, are thieves and robbers.

The Pharisees had not entered by the door. They had climbed into the fold by another way than Christ, and they were not fulfilling the work of the true shepherd. The priests and rulers, the scribes and Pharisees, destroyed the living pastures, and defiled the wellsprings of the water of life. Faithfully do the words of inspiration describe those false shepherds: "The diseased have ye not strengthened, neither have ye healed that which was sick, neither have ye bound up that which was broken, neither have ye brought again that which was driven away; . . . but with force and with cruelty have ye ruled them." Ezek. 34:4.

In all ages, philosophers and teachers have been presenting to the world theories by which to satisfy the soul's need. Every heathen nation has had its great teachers and religious systems offering some other means of redemption than Christ, turning the eyes of men away from the Father's face, and filling their hearts with fear of Him who has given them only blessing. The trend of their work is to rob God of that which is His own, both by creation and by redemption. And these false teachers rob man as well. Millions of human beings are bound down under false religions, in the bondage of slavish fear, of stolid indifference, toiling like beasts of burden, bereft of hope or joy or aspiration here, and with only a dull fear of the hereafter. It is the gospel of the grace of God alone that can uplift the soul. The contemplation of the love of God manifested in His Son will stir the heart and arouse the powers of the soul as nothing else can. Christ came that He might recreate the image of God in man; and whoever turns men away from Christ is turning them away from the source of true development; he is defrauding them of the hope and purpose and glory of life. He is a thief and a robber.

"He that entereth in by the door is the shepherd of the sheep." Christ is both the door and the shepherd. He enters in by Himself. It is through His own sacrifice that He becomes the shepherd of the sheep. "To Him the porter openeth; and the sheep hear His voice: and He calleth His own sheep by name, and leadeth them out. And when He putteth forth His own sheep, He goeth before them, and the sheep follow Him: for they know His voice."

Of all creatures the sheep is one of the most timid and helpless, and in the East the shepherd's care for his flock is untiring and incessant. Anciently as now there was little security outside of the walled towns. Marauders from the roving border tribes, or beasts of prey from their hiding places in the rocks, lay in wait to plunder the flocks. The shepherd watched his charge, knowing that it was at the peril of his own life. Jacob, who kept the flocks of Laban in the pasture grounds of Haran, describing his own unwearied labor, said, "In the day the drought consumed me, and the frost by night; and my sleep departed from mine eyes." Gen. 31:40. And it was while guarding his father's sheep that the boy David, single-handed, encountered the lion and the bear, and rescued from their teeth the stolen lamb.

As the shepherd leads his flock over the rocky hills, through forest and wild ravines, to grassy nooks by the riverside; as he watches them on the mountains through the lonely night, shielding from robbers, caring tenderly for the sickly and feeble, his life comes to be one with theirs. A strong and tender attachment unites him to the objects of his care. However large the flock, the shepherd knows every sheep. Every one has its name, and responds to the name at the shepherd's call.

As an earthly shepherd knows his sheep, so does the divine Shepherd know His flock that are scattered throughout the world. "Ye My flock, the flock of My pasture, are men, and I am your God, saith the Lord God." Jesus says, "I have called thee by thy name; thou art Mine." "I have graven thee upon the palms of My hands." Ezek. 34:31; Isa. 43:1; 49:16.

Jesus knows us individually, and is touched with the feeling of our infirmities. He knows us all by name. He knows the very house in which we live, the name of each occupant. He has at times given directions to His servants to go to a certain street in a certain city, to such a house, to find one of His sheep.

Every soul is as fully known to Jesus as if he were the only one for whom the Saviour died. The distress of every one touches His heart. The cry for aid reaches His ear. He came to draw all men unto Himself. He bids them, "Follow Me," and His Spirit moves upon their hearts to draw them to come to Him. Many refuse to be drawn. Jesus knows who they are. He also knows who gladly hear His call, and are ready to come under His pastoral care. He says, "My sheep hear My voice, and I know them, and they follow Me." He cares for each one as if there were not another on the face of the earth.

"He calleth His own sheep by name, and leadeth them out. . . . And the sheep follow Him: for they know His voice." The Eastern shepherd does not drive his sheep. He depends not upon force or fear; but going before, he calls them. They know his voice, and obey the call. So does the Saviour-Shepherd with His sheep. The Scripture says, "Thou leddest Thy people like a flock by the hand of Moses and Aaron." Through the prophet, Jesus declares, "I have loved thee with an everlasting love: therefore with loving-kindness have I drawn thee." He compels none to follow Him. "I drew them," He says, "with cords of a man, with bands of love." Ps. 77:20; Jer. 31:3; Hosea 11:4.

It is not the fear of punishment, or the hope of everlasting reward, that leads the disciples of Christ to follow Him. They behold the Saviour's matchless love, revealed throughout His pilgrimage on earth, from the manger of Bethlehem to Calvary's cross, and the sight of Him attracts, it softens and subdues the soul. Love awakens in the heart of the beholders. They hear His voice, and they follow Him.

As the shepherd goes before his sheep, himself first encountering the perils of the way, so does Jesus with His people. "When He putteth forth His own sheep, He goeth before them." The way to heaven is consecrated by the Saviour's footprints. The path may be steep and rugged, but Jesus has traveled that way; His feet have pressed down the cruel thorns, to make the pathway easier for us. Every burden that we are called to bear He Himself has borne.

Though now He has ascended to the presence of God, and shares the throne of the universe, Jesus has lost none of His compassionate nature. Today the same tender, sympathizing heart is open to all the woes of humanity. Today the hand that was pierced is reached forth to bless more abundantly His people that are in the world. "And they shall never perish, neither shall any man pluck them out of My hand." The soul that has given himself to Christ is more precious in His sight than the whole world. The Saviour would have passed through the agony of Calvary that one might be saved in His kingdom. He will never abandon one for whom He has died. Unless His followers choose to leave Him, He will hold them fast.

Through all our trials we have a never-failing Helper. He does not leave us alone to struggle with temptation, to battle with evil, and be finally crushed with burdens and sorrow. Though now He is hidden from mortal sight, the ear of faith can hear His voice saying, Fear not; I am with you. "I am He that liveth, and was dead; and, behold, I am alive forevermore." Rev. 1:18. I have endured your sorrows, experienced your struggles, encountered your temptations. I know your tears; I also have wept. The griefs that lie too deep to be breathed into any human ear, I know. Think not that you are desolate and forsaken. Though your pain touch no responsive chord in any heart on earth, look unto Me, and live. "The mountains shall depart, and the hills be removed; but My kindness shall not depart from thee, neither shall the covenant of My peace be removed, saith the Lord that hath mercy on thee." Isa. 54:10.

However much a shepherd may love his sheep, he loves his sons and daughters more. Jesus is not only our shepherd; He is our "everlasting Father." And He says, "I know Mine own, and Mine own know Me, even as the Father knoweth Me, and I know the Father." R. V. What a statement is this!—the only-begotten Son, He who is in the bosom of the Father, He whom God has declared to be "the Man that is My fellow" (Zech. 13:7),—the communion between Him and the eternal God is taken to represent the communion between Christ and His children on the earth!

Because we are the gift of His Father, and the reward of His work, Jesus loves us. He loves us as His children. Reader, He loves you. Heaven itself can bestow nothing greater, nothing better. Therefore trust.

Jesus thought upon the souls all over the earth who were misled by false shepherds. Those whom He longed to gather as the sheep of His pasture were scattered among wolves, and He said, "Other sheep I have, which are not of this fold: them also I must bring, and they shall hear My voice; and they shall become one flock, one shepherd." R. V.

"Therefore doth My Father love Me, because I lay down My life, that I might take it again." That is, My Father has so loved you, that He even loves Me more for giving My life to redeem you. In becoming your substitute and surety, by surrendering My life, by taking your liabilities, your transgressions, I am endeared to My Father.

"I lay down My life, that I might take it again. No man taketh it from Me, but I lay it down of Myself. I have power to lay it down, and I have power to take it again." While as a member of the human family He was mortal, as God He was the fountain of life for the world. He could have withstood the avances of death, and refused to come under its dominion; but voluntarily He laid down His life, that He might bring life and immortality to light.

He bore the sin of the world, endured its curse, yielded up His life as a sacrifice, that men might not eternally die. "Surely He hath borne our griefs, and carried our sorrows. . . . He was wounded for our transgressions, He was bruised for our iniquities: the chastisement of our peace was upon Him; and with His stripes we are healed. All we like sheep have gone astray; we have turned every one to his own way; and the Lord hath laid on Him the iniquity of us all." Isa. 53:4-6.

Chapter 25

THE GOOD SAMARITAN

IN THE STORY of the good Samaritan, Christ illustrates the nature of true religion. He shows that it consists not in systems, creeds, or rites, but in the performance of loving deeds, in bringing the greatest good to others, in genuine goodness.

As Christ was teaching the people, "a certain lawyer stood up, and tempted Him, saying, Master, what shall I do to inherit eternal life?" With breathless attention the large congregation awaited the answer. The priests and rabbis had thought to entangle Christ by having the lawyer ask this question. But the Saviour entered into no controversy. He required the answer from the questioner himself. "What is written in the law?" He said; "how readest thou?" The Jews still accused Jesus of lightly regarding the law given from Sinai; but He turned the question of salvation upon the keeping of God's commandments.

The lawyer said, "Thou shalt love the Lord thy God with all thy heart, and with all thy soul, and with all thy strength, and with all thy mind; and thy neighbor as thyself." Jesus said, "Thou hast answered right: this do, and thou shalt live."

The lawyer was not satisfied with the position and works of the Pharisees. He had been studying the Scriptures with a desire to learn their real meaning. He had a vital interest in the matter, and had asked in sincerity, "What shall I do?" In his answer as to the requirements of the law, he passed by all the mass of ceremonial and ritualistic precepts. For these he claimed no value, but presented the two great principles on which hang all the law and the prophets. This answer, being commended by Christ, placed the Saviour on vantage ground with the rabbis.

This chapter is based on Luke 10:25-37.

195

They could not condemn Him for sanctioning that which had been advanced by an expositor of the law.

"This do, and thou shalt live," Jesus said. He presented the law as a divine unity, and in this lesson taught that it is not possible to keep one precept, and break another; for the same principle runs through them all. Man's destiny will be determined by his obedience to the whole law. Supreme love to God and impartial love to man are the principles to be wrought out in the life.

The lawyer found himself a lawbreaker. He was convicted under Christ's searching words. The righteousness of the law, which he claimed to understand, he had not practiced. He had not manifested love toward his fellow man. Repentance was demanded; but instead of repenting, he tried to justify himself. Rather than acknowledge the truth, he sought to show how difficult of fulfillment the commandment is. Thus he hoped both to parry conviction and to vindicate himself in the eyes of the people. The Saviour's words had shown that his question was needless, since he had been able to answer it himself. Yet he put another question, saying, "Who is my neighbor?"

Among the Jews this question caused endless dispute. They had no doubt as to the heathen and the Samaritans; these were strangers and enemies. But where should the distinction be made among the people of their own nation, and among the different classes of society? Whom should the priest, the rabbi, the elder, regard as neighbor? They spent their lives in a round of ceremonies to make themselves pure. Contact with the ignorant and careless multitude, they taught, would cause defilement that would require wearisome effort to remove. Were they to regard the "unclean" as neighbors?

Again Jesus refused to be drawn into controversy. He did not denounce the bigotry of those who were watching to condemn Him. But by a simple story He held up before His hearers such a picture of the outflowing of heaven-born love as touched all hearts, and drew from the lawyer a confession of the truth.

The way to dispel darkness is to admit light. The best way to deal with error is to present truth. It is the revelation of God's love that makes manifest the deformity and sin of the heart centered in self.

"A certain man," said Jesus, "was going down from Jerusalem to Jericho; and he fell among robbers, which both stripped him and beat him, and departed, leaving him half dead. And by chance a certain priest was going down that way: and when he saw him, he passed by on the other side. And in like manner a Levite also, when he came to the place, and saw him, passed by on the other side." R. V. This was no imaginary scene, but an actual occurrence, which was known to be exactly as represented. The priest and the Levite who had passed by on the other side were in the company that listened to Christ's words.

In journeying from Jerusalem to Jericho, the traveler had to pass through a portion of the wilderness of Judea. The road led down a wild, rocky ravine, which was infested by robbers, and was often the scene of violence. It was here that the traveler was attacked, stripped of all that was valuable, wounded and bruised, and left half dead by the wayside. As he lay thus, the priest came that way; but he merely glanced toward the wounded man. Then the Levite appeared. Curious to know what had happened, he stopped and looked at the sufferer. He was convicted of what he ought to do; but it was not an agreeable duty. He wished that he had not come that way, so that he need not have seen the wounded man. He persuaded himself that the case was no concern of his.

Both these men were in sacred office, and professed to expound the Scriptures. They were of the class specially chosen to be representatives of God to the people. They were to "have compassion on the ignorant, and on them that are out of the way" (Heb. 5:2), that they might lead men to understand God's great love toward humanity. The work they were called to do was the same that Jesus had described as His own when He said, "The Spirit of the Lord is upon Me, because He hath anointed Me to preach the gospel to the poor; He hath sent Me to heal the brokenhearted, to preach deliverance to the captives, and recovering of sight to the blind, to set at liberty them that are bruised." Luke 4:18.

The angels of heaven look upon the distress of God's family upon the earth, and they are prepared to co-operate with men in relieving oppression and suffering. God in His providence had brought the priest and the Levite along the road where the wounded sufferer lay, that they might see his need of mercy and help. All heaven watched to see if the hearts of these men would be touched with pity for human woe. The Saviour was the One who had instructed the Hebrews in the wilderness; from the pillar of cloud and of fire He had taught a very different lesson from that which the people were now receiving from their priests and teachers. The merciful provisions of the law extended even to the lower animals, which cannot express in words their want and suffering. Directions had been given to Moses for the children of Israel to this effect: "If thou meet thine enemy's ox or his ass going astray, thou shalt surely bring it back to him again. If thou see the ass of him that hateth thee lying under his burden, and wouldest forbear to help him, thou shalt surely help with him." Ex. 23:4, 5. But in the man wounded by robbers, Jesus presented the case of a brother in suffering. How much more should their hearts have been moved with pity for him than for a beast of burden! The message had been given them through Moses that the Lord their God, "a great God, a mighty, and a terrible," "doth execute the judgment of the fatherless and widow, and loveth the stranger." Wherefore He commanded, "Love ye therefore the stranger." "Thou shalt love him as thyself." Deut. 10:17-19; Lev. 19:34.

Job had said, "The stranger did not lodge in the street: but I opened my doors to the traveler." And when the two angels in the guise of men came to Sodom, Lot bowed himself with his face toward the ground, and said, "Behold now, my lords, turn in, I pray you, into your servant's house, and tarry all night." Job 31:32; Gen. 19:2. With all these lessons the priest and the Levite were familiar, but they had not brought them into practical life. Trained in the school of national bigotry, they had become selfish, narrow, and exclusive. When they looked upon the wounded man, they could not tell whether he was of their nation or not. They thought he might be of the Samaritans, and they turned away.

In their action, as Christ had described it, the lawyer saw nothing contrary to what he had been taught concerning the requirements of the law. But now another scene was presented:

A certain Samaritan, in his journey, came where the sufferer was, and when he saw him, he had compassion on him. He did not question whether the stranger was a Jew or a Gentile. If a Jew, the Samaritan well knew that, were their condition reversed, the man would spit in his face, and pass him by with contempt. But he did not hesitate on account of this. He did not consider that he himself might be in danger of violence by tarrying in the place. It was enough that there was before him a human being in need and suffering. He took off his own garment with which to cover him. The oil and wine provided for his own journey he used to heal and refresh the wounded man. He lifted him on his own beast, and moved slowly along with even pace, so that the stranger might not be jarred, and made to suffer increased pain. He brought him to an inn, and cared for him through the night, watching him tenderly. In the morning, as the sick man had improved, the Samaritan ventured to go on his way. But before doing this, he placed him in the care of the innkeeper, paid the charges, and left a deposit for his benefit; and not satisfied even with this, he made provision for any further need, saying to the host, "Take care of him; and whatsoever thou spendest more, when I come again, I will repay thee."

The story ended, Jesus fixed His eyes upon the lawyer, in a glance that seemed to read his soul, and said, "Which of these three, thinkest *thou*, proved neighbor unto him that fell among the robbers?"

The lawyer would not, even now, take the name Samaritan upon his lips, and he made answer, "He that showed mercy on him." Jesus said, "Go, and do *thou* likewise."

Thus the question, "Who is my neighbor?" is forever answered. Christ has shown that our neighbor does not mean merely one of the church or faith to which we belong. It has no reference to race, color, or class distinction. Our neighbor is every person who needs our help. Our neighbor is every soul who is wounded and bruised by the adversary. Our neighbor is everyone who is the property of God.

In the story of the good Samaritan, Jesus gave a picture of Himself and His mission. Man had been deceived, bruised, robbed, and ruined by Satan, and left to perish; but the Saviour had compassion on our helpless condition. He left His glory, to come to our rescue. He found us ready to die, and He undertook our case. He healed our wounds. He covered us with His robe of righteousness. He opened to us a refuge of safety, and made complete provision for us at His own charges. He died to redeem us. Pointing to His own example, He says to His followers, "These things I command you, that ye love one another." "As I have loved you, that ye also love one another." John 15:17; 13:34.

The lawyer's question to Jesus had been, "What shall I do?" And Jesus, recognizing love to God and man as the sum of righteousness, had said, "This do, and thou shalt live." The Samaritan had obeyed the dictates of a kind and loving heart, and in this had proved himself a doer of the law. Christ bade the lawyer, "Go, and do thou likewise." Doing, and not saying merely, is expected of the children of God. "He that saith he abideth in Him ought himself also so to walk, even as He walked." 1 John 2:6.

The lesson is no less needed in the world today than when it fell from the lips of Jesus. Selfishness and cold formality have well-nigh extinguished the fire of love, and dispelled the graces that should make fragrant the character. Many who profess His name have lost sight of the fact that Christians are to represent Christ. Unless there is practical self-sacrifice for the good of others, in the family circle, in the neighborhood, in the church, and wherever we may be, then whatever our profession, we are not Christians.

Christ has linked His interest with that of humanity, and He asks us to become one with Him for the saving of humanity. "Freely ye have received," He says, "freely give." Matt. 10:8. Sin is the greatest of all evils, and it is ours to pity and help the sinner. There are many who err, and who feel their shame and their folly. They are hungry for words of encouragement. Thy look upon their mistakes and errors, until they are driven almost to desperation. These souls we are not to neglect. If we are Christians, we shall not pass by on the other side, keeping as far as possible from the very ones who most need our help. When we see human beings in distress, whether through affliction or through sin, we shall never say, This does not concern me.

"Ye which are spiritual, restore such an one in the spirit of meekness." Gal. 6:1. By faith and prayer press back the power of the enemy. Speak words of faith and courage that will be as a healing balsam to the bruised and wounded one. Many, many, have fainted and become discouraged in the great struggle of life, when one word of kindly cheer would have strengthened them to overcome. Never should we pass by one suffering soul without seeking to impart to him of the comfort wherewith we are comforted of God.

All this is but a fulfillment of the principle of the law,— the principle that is illustrated in the story of the good Samaritan, and made manifest in the life of Jesus. His character reveals the true significance of the law, and shows what is meant by loving our neighbor as ourselves. And when the children of God manifest mercy, kindness, and love toward all men, they also are witnessing to the character of the statutes of heaven. They are bearing testimony to the fact that "the law of the Lord is perfect, converting the soul." Ps. 19:7. And whoever fails to manifest this love is breaking the law which he professes to revere. For the spirit we manifest toward our brethren declares what is our spirit toward God. The love of God in the heart is the only spring of love toward our neighbor. "If a man say, I love God, and hateth his brother, he is a liar: for he that loveth not his brother whom he hath seen, how can he love God whom he hath not seen?" Beloved, "if we love one another, God dwelleth in us, and His love is perfected in us." 1 John 4:20, 12.

Chapter 26

POOR, RICH MAN

"AND WHEN HE was gone forth into the way, there came one running, and kneeled to Him, and asked Him, Good Master, what shall I do that I may inherit eternal life?"

The young man who asked this question was a ruler. He had great possessions, and occupied a position of responsibility. He saw the love that Christ manifested toward the children brought to Him; he saw how tenderly He received them, and took them up in His arms, and his heart kindled with love for the Saviour. He felt a desire to be His disciple. He was so deeply moved that as Christ was going on His way, he ran after Him, and kneeling at His feet, asked with sincerity and earnestness the question so important to his soul and to the soul of every human being, "Good Master, what shall I do that I may inherit eternal life?"

"Why callest thou Me good?" said Christ, "there is none good but One, that is, God." Jesus desired to test the ruler's sincerity, and to draw from him the way in which he regarded Him as good. Did he realize that the One to whom he was speaking was the Son of God? What was the true sentiment of his heart?

This ruler had a high estimate of his own righteousness. He did not really suppose that he was defective in anything, yet he was not altogether satisfied. He felt the want of something that he did not possess. Could not Jesus bless him as He blessed the little children, and satisfy his soul want?

In reply to this question Jesus told him that obedience to the commandments of God was necessary if he would obtain eternal life; and He quoted several of the commandments which show man's duty to his fellow men. The

This chapter is based on Matt. 19:16-22; Mark 10:17-22; Luke 18:18-23.

ruler's answer was positive: "All these things have I kept from my youth up: what lack I yet?"

Christ looked into the face of the young man, as if reading his life and searching his character. He loved him, and He hungered to give him that peace and grace and joy which would materially change his character. "One thing thou lackest," He said; "go thy way, sell whatsoever thou hast, and give to the poor, and thou shalt have treasure in heaven: and come, take up the cross, and follow Me."

Christ was drawn to this young man. He knew him to be sincere in his assertion, "All these things have I kept from my youth." The Redeemer longed to create in him that discernment which would enable him to see the necessity of heart devotion and Christian goodness. He longed to see in him a humble and contrite heart, conscious of the supreme love to be given to God, and hiding its lack in the perfection of Christ.

Jesus saw in this ruler just the help He needed if the young man would become a colaborer with Him in the work of salvation. If he would place himself under Christ's guidance, he would be a power for good. In a marked degree the ruler could have represented Christ; for he possessed qualifications, which, if he were united with the Saviour, would enable him to become a divine force among men. Christ, seeing into his character, loved him. Love for Christ was awakening in the ruler's heart; for love begets love. Jesus longed to see him a coworker with Him. He longed to make him like Himself, a mirror in which the likeness of God would be reflected. He longed to develop the excellence of his character, and sanctify it to the Master's use. If the ruler had then given himself to Christ, he would have grown in the atmosphere of His presence. If he had made this choice, how different would have been his future!

"One thing thou lackest," Jesus said. "If thou wilt be perfect, go and sell that thou hast, and give to the poor, and thou shalt have treasure in heaven: and come and follow Me." Christ read the ruler's heart. Only one thing he lacked, but that was a vital principle. He needed the love of God in the soul. This lack, unless supplied, would prove fatal to him; his whole nature would become corrupted. By indulgence, selfishness would strengthen. That he might receive the love of God, his supreme love of self must be surrendered.

Christ gave this man a test. He called upon him to

choose between the heavenly treasure and worldly greatness. The heavenly treasure was assured him if he would follow Christ. But self must yield; his will must be given into Christ's control. The very holiness of God was offered to the young ruler. He had the privilege of becoming a son of God, and a coheir with Christ to the heavenly treasure. But he must take up the cross, and follow the Saviour in the path of self-denial.

Christ's words were verily to the ruler the invitation, "Choose you this day whom ye will serve." Joshua 24:15. The choice was left with him. Jesus was yearning for his conversion. He had shown him the plague spot in his character, and with what deep interest He watched the issue as the young man weighed the question! If he decided to follow Christ, he must obey His words in everything. He must turn from his ambitious projects. With what earnest, anxious longing, what soul hunger, did the Saviour look at the young man, hoping that he would yield to the invitation of the Spirit of God!

Christ made the only terms which could place the ruler where he would perfect a Christian character. His words were words of wisdom, though they appeared severe and exacting. In accepting and obeying them was the ruler's only hope of salvation. His exalted position and his possessions were exerting a subtle influence for evil upon his character. If cherished, they would supplant God in his affections. To keep back little or much from God was to retain that which would lessen his moral strength and efficiency; for if the things of this world are cherished, however uncertain and unworthy they may be, they will become all-absorbing.

The ruler was quick to discern all that Christ's words involved, and he became sad. If he had realized the value of the offered gift, quickly would he have enrolled himself as one of Christ's followers. He was a member of the honored council of the Jews, and Satan was tempting him with flattering prospects of the future. He wanted the heavenly treasure, but he wanted also the temporal advantages his riches would bring him. He was sorry that such conditions existed; he desired eternal life, but he was not willing to make the sacrifice. The cost of eternal life seemed too great, and he went away sorrowful; "for he had great possessions."

His claim that he had kept the law of God was a deception. He showed that riches were his idol. He could not keep the commandments of God while the world was first in his affections. He loved the gifts of God more than he loved the Giver. Christ had offered the young man fellowship with Himself. "Follow Me," He said. But the Saviour was not so much to him as his own name among men or his possessions. To give up his earthly treasure, that was seen, for the heavenly treasure, that was unseen, was too great a risk. He refused the offer of eternal life, and went away, and ever after the world was to receive his worship. Thousands are passing through this ordeal, weighing Christ against the world; and many choose the world. Like the young ruler, they turn from the Saviour, saying in their hearts, I will not have this Man as my leader.

Christ's dealing with the young man is presented as an object lesson. God has given us the rule of conduct which every one of His servants must follow. It is obedience to His law, not merely a legal obedience, but an obedience which enters into the life, and is exemplified in the character. God has set His own standard of character for all who would become subjects of His kingdom. Only those who will become coworkers with Christ, only those who will say, Lord, all I have and all I am is Thine, will be acknowledged as sons and daughters of God. All should consider what it means to desire heaven, and yet to turn away because of the conditions laid down. Think of what it means to say "No" to Christ. The ruler said, No, I cannot give You all. Do we say the same? The Saviour offers to share with us the work God has given us to do. He offers to use the means God has given us, to carry forward His work in the world. Only in this way can He save us.

The ruler's possessions were entrusted to him that he might prove himself a faithful steward; he was to dispense these goods for the blessing of those in need. So God now entrusts men with means, with talents and opportunities, that they may be His agents in helping the poor and the suffering. He who uses his entrusted gifts as God designs becomes a coworker with the Saviour. He wins souls to Christ, because he is a representative of His character.

To those who, like the young ruler, are in high positions of trust and have great possessions, it may seem too great a sacrifice to give up all in order to follow Christ. But this is the rule of conduct for all who would become His disciples. Nothing short of. obedience can be accepted. Self-surrender is the substance of the teachings of Christ. Often it is presented and enjoined in language that seems authoritative, because there is no other way to save man than to cut away those things which, if entertained, will demoralize the whole being.

When Christ's followers give back to the Lord His own, they are accumulating treasure which will be given to them when they shall hear the words, "Well done, good and faithful servant; . . . enter thou into the joy of thy Lord." "Who for the joy that was set before Him endured the cross, despising the shame, and is set down at the right hand of the throne of God." Matt. 25:23; Heb. 12:2. The joy of seeing souls redeemed, souls eternally saved, is the reward of all that put their feet in the footprints of Him who said, "Follow Me."

Chapter 27

"WHY DIDN'T YOU COME?"

AMONG THE most steadfast of Christ's disciples was Lazarus of Bethany. From their first meeting his faith in Christ had been strong; his love for Him was deep, and he was greatly beloved by the Saviour. It was for Lazarus that the greatest of Christ's miracles was performed. The Saviour blessed all who sought His help; He loves all the human family, but to some He is bound by peculiarly tender associations. His heart was knit by a strong bond of affection to the family at Bethany, and for one of them His most wonderful work was wrought.

At the home of Lazarus, Jesus had often found rest. The Saviour had no home of His own; He was dependent on the hospitality of His friends and disciples, and often, when weary, thirsting for human fellowship, He had been glad to escape to this peaceful household, away from the suspicion and jealousy of the angry Pharisees. Here He found a sincere welcome, and pure, holy friendship. Here He could speak with simplicity and perfect freedom, knowing that His words would be understood and treasured.

Our Saviour appreciated a quiet home and interested listeners. He longed for human tenderness, courtesy, and affection. Those who received the heavenly instruction He was always ready to impart were greatly blessed. As the multitudes followed Christ through the open fields, He unfolded to them the beauties of the natural world. He sought to open the eyes of their understanding, that they might see how the hand of God upholds the world. In order to call out an appreciation of God's goodness and benevolence, He called the attention of His hearers to the gently falling dew, to the soft showers of rain and the bright sunshine, given alike to good and evil. He desired

This chapter is based on Luke 10:38-42; John 11:1-44.

207

men to realize more fully the regard that God bestows on the human instrumentalities He has created. But the multitudes were slow of hearing, and in the home at Bethany Christ found rest from the weary conflict of public life. Here He opened to an appreciative audience the volume of Providence. In these private interviews He unfolded to His hearers that which He did not attempt to tell to the mixed multitude. He needed not to speak to His friends in parables.

As Christ gave His wonderful lessons, Mary sat at His feet, a reverent and devoted listener. On one occasion, Martha, perplexed with the care of preparing the meal, went to Christ, saying, "Lord, dost Thou not care that my sister hath left me to serve alone? bid her therefore that she help me." This was the time of Christ's first visit to Bethany. The Saviour and His disciples had just made the toilsome journey on foot from Jericho. Martha was anxious to provide for their comfort, and in her anxiety she forgot the courtesy due to her Guest. Jesus answered her with mild and patient words, "Martha, Martha, thou art careful and troubled about many things: but one thing is needful: and Mary hath chosen that good part, which shall not be taken away from her." Mary was storing her mind with the precious words falling from the Saviour's lips, words that were more precious to her than earth's most costly jewels.

The "one thing" that Martha needed was a calm, devotional spirit, a deeper anxiety for knowledge concerning the future, immortal life, and the graces necessary for spiritual advancement. She needed less anxiety for the things which pass away, and more for those things which endure forever. Jesus would teach His children to seize every opportunity of gaining that knowledge which will make them wise unto salvation. The cause of Christ needs careful, energetic workers. There is a wide field for the Marthas, with their zeal in active religious work. But let them first sit with Mary at the feet of Jesus. Let diligence, promptness, and energy be sanctified by the grace of Christ; then the life will be an unconquerable power for good.

Sorrow entered the peaceful home where Jesus had rested. Lazarus was stricken with sudden illness, and his sisters sent to the Saviour, saying, "Lord, behold, he whom Thou lovest is sick." They saw the violence of the disease that had seized their brother, but they knew that Christ had shown Himself able to heal all manner of diseases. They believed that He would sympathize with them in their distress; therefore they made no urgent demand for His immediate presence, but sent only the confiding message, "He whom Thou lovest is sick." They thought that He would immediately respond to their message, and be with them as soon as He could reach Bethany.

Anxiously they waited for a word from Jesus. As long as the spark of life was yet alive in their brother, they prayed and watched for Jesus to come. But the messenger returned without Him. Yet he brought the message, "This sickness is not unto death," and they clung to the hope that Lazarus would live. Tenderly they tried to speak words of hope and encouragement to the almost unconscious sufferer. When Lazarus died, they were bitterly disappointed; but they felt the sustaining grace of Christ, and this kept them from reflecting any blame on the Saviour.

When Christ heard the message, the disciples thought He received it coldly. He did not manifest the sorrow they expected Him to show. Looking up to them, He said, "This sickness is not unto death, but for the glory of God, that the Son of God might be glorified thereby." For two days He remained in the place where He was. This delay was a mystery to the disciples. What a comfort His presence would be to the afflicted household! they thought. His strong affection for the family at Bethany was well known to the disciples, and they were surprised that He did not respond to the sad message, "He whom Thou lovest is sick."

During the two days Christ seemed to have dismissed the message from His mind; for He did not speak of Lazarus. The disciples thought of John the Baptist, the forerunner of Jesus. They had wondered why Jesus, with the power to perform wonderful miracles, had permitted John to languish in prison, and to die a violent death. Possessing such power, why did not Christ save John's life? This question had often been asked by the Pharisees, who presented it as an unanswerable argument against Christ's claim to be the Son of God. The Saviour had warned His disciples of trials, losses, and persecution. Would He forsake them in trial? Some questioned if they had mistaken His mission. All were deeply troubled.

After waiting for two days, Jesus said to the disciples, "Let us go into Judea again." The disciples questioned why, if Jesus were going to Judea, He had waited two days. But anxiety for Christ and for themselves was now uppermost in their minds. They could see nothing but danger in the course He was about to pursue. "Master," they said, "the Jews of late sought to stone Thee; and goest Thou thither again? Jesus answered, Are there not twelve hours in the day?" I am under the guidance of My Father; as long as I do His will, My life is safe. My twelve hours of day are not yet ended. I have entered upon the last remnant of My day; but while any of this remains, I am safe.

"If any man walk in the day," He continued, "he stumbleth not, because he seeth the light of this world." He who does the will of God, who walks in the path that God has marked out, cannot stumble and fall. The light of God's guiding Spirit gives him a clear perception of his duty, and leads him aright till the close of his work. "But if a man walk in the night, he stumbleth, because there is no light in him." He who walks in a path of his own choosing, where God has not called him, will stumble. For him day is turned into night, and wherever he may be, he is not secure.

"These things said He: and after that He saith unto them, Our friend Lazarus sleepeth; but I go, that I may awake him out of sleep." "Our friend Lazarus sleepeth." How touching the words! how full of sympathy! In the thought of the peril their Master was about to incur by going to Jerusalem, the disciples had almost forgotten the bereaved family at Bethany. But not so Christ. The disciples felt rebuked. They had been disappointed because Christ did not respond more promptly to the message. They had been tempted to think that He had not the tender love for Lazarus and his sisters that they had thought He had, or He would have hastened back with the messenger. But the words, "Our friend Lazarus sleepeth," awakened right feelings in their minds. They were convinced that Christ had not forgotten His suffering friends.

"Then said His disciples, Lord, if he sleep, he shall do well. Howbeit Jesus spake of his death: but they thought that He had spoken of taking of rest in sleep." Christ represents death as a sleep to His believing children. Their life is hid with Christ in God, and until the last trump shall sound those who die will sleep in Him.

"Then said Jesus unto them plainly, Lazarus is dead. And I am glad for your sakes that I was not there, to the intent ye may believe; nevertheless let us go unto him." Thomas could see nothing but death in store for his Master if he went to Judea; but he girded up his spirit, and said to the other disciples, "Let us also go, that we may die with Him." He knew the hatred of the Jews toward Christ. It was their purpose to compass His death, but this purpose had not succeeded, because some of His allotted time still remained. During this time Jesus had the guardianship of heavenly angels; and even in the regions of Judea, where the rabbis were plotting how they might take Him and put Him to death, no harm could come to Him.

The disciples marveled at Christ's words when He said, "Lazarus is dead. And I am glad . . . that I was not there." Did the Saviour by His own choice avoid the home of His suffering friends? Apparently Mary and Martha and the dying Lazarus were left alone. But they were not alone. Christ beheld the whole scene, and after the death of Lazarus the bereaved sisters were upheld by His grace. Jesus witnessed the sorrow of their rent hearts, as their brother wrestled with his strong foe, death. He felt every pang of anguish, as He said to His disciples, "Lazarus is dead." But Christ had not only the loved ones at Bethany to think of; He had the training of His disciples to consider. They were to be His representatives to the world, that the Father's blessing might embrace all. For their sake He permitted Lazarus to die. Had He restored him from illness to health, the miracle that is the most positive evidence of His divine character would not have been performed.

Had Christ been in the sickroom, Lazarus would not have died; for Satan would have had no power over him. Death could not have aimed his dart at Lazarus in the presence of the Life-giver. Therefore Christ remained away. He suffered the enemy to exercise his power, that He might drive him back, a conquered foe. He permitted Lazarus to pass under the dominion of death; and the suffering sisters saw their brother laid in the grave. Christ knew that as they looked on the dead face of their brother their faith in their Redeemer would be severely tried. But He knew that because of the struggle through which they were now passing their faith would shine forth with far greater power. He suffered every pang of sorrow that they endured. He loved them no less because He tarried; but He knew that for them, for Lazarus, for Himself, and for His disciples, a victory was to be gained.

"For your sakes," "to the intent ye may believe." To all who are reaching out to feel the guiding hand of God, the moment of greatest discouragement is the time when divine help is nearest. They will look back with thankfulness upon the darkest part of their way. "The Lord knoweth how to deliver the godly." 2 Peter 2:9. From every temptation and every trial He will bring them forth with firmer faith and a richer experience.

In delaying to come to Lazarus, Christ had a purpose of mercy toward those who had not received Him. He tarried, that by raising Lazarus from the dead He might give to His stubborn, unbelieving people another evidence that He was indeed "the resurrection, and the life." He was loath to give up all hope of the people, the poor, wandering sheep of the house of Israel. His heart was breaking because of their impenitence. In His mercy He purposed to give them one more evidence that He was the Restorer, the One who alone could bring life and immortality to light. This was to be an evidence that the priests could not misinterpret. This was the reason of His delay in going to Bethany. This crowning miracle, the raising of Lazarus, was to set the seal of God on His work and on His claim to divinity.

On His journey to Bethany, Jesus, according to His custom, ministered to the sick and the needy. Upon reaching the town He sent a messenger to the sisters with the tidings of His arrival. Christ did not at once enter the house, but remained in a quiet place by the wayside. The great outward display observed by the Jews at the death of friends or relatives was not in harmony with the spirit of Christ. He heard the sound of wailing from the hired mourners, and He did not wish to meet the sisters in the scene of confusion. Among the mourning friends were relatives of the family, some of whom held high positions of responsibility in Jerusalem. Among these were some of Christ's bitterest enemies. Christ knew their purposes, and therefore He did not at once make Himself known.

The message was given to Martha so quietly that others in the room did not hear. Absorbed in her grief, Mary did not hear the words. Rising at once, Martha went out to meet her Lord, but thinking that she had gone to the place where Lazarus was buried, Mary sat still in her sorrow, making no outcry.

Martha hastened to meet Jesus, her heart agitated by conflicting emotions. In His expressive face she read the same tenderness and love that had always been there. Her confidence in Him was unbroken, but she thought of her dearly loved brother, whom Jesus also had loved. With grief surging in her heart because Christ had not come before, yet with hope that even now He would do something to comfort them, she said, "Lord, if Thou hadst been here, my brother had not died." Over and over again, amid the tumult made by the mourners, the sisters had repeated these words.

With human and divine pity Jesus looked into her sorrowful, careworn face. Martha had no inclination to recount the past; all was expressed by the pathetic words, "Lord, if Thou hadst been here, my brother had not died." But looking into that face of love, she added, "I know, that even now, whatsoever Thou wilt ask of God, God will give it Thee."

Jesus encouraged her faith, saying, "Thy brother shall rise again." His answer was not intended to inspire hope of an immediate change. He carried Martha's thoughts beyond the present restoration of her brother, and fixed them upon the resurrection of the just. This He did that she might see in the resurrection of Lazarus a pledge of the resurrection of all the righteous dead, and an assurance that it would be accomplished by the Saviour's power.

Martha answered, "I know that he shall rise again in the resurrection at the last day."

Still seeking to give a true direction to her faith, Jesus declared, "I am the resurrection, and the life." In Christ is life, original, unborrowed, underived. "He that hath the Son hath life." 1 John 5:12. The divinity of Christ is the believer's assurance of eternal life. "He that believeth in Me," said Jesus, "though he were dead, yet shall he live: and whosoever liveth and believeth in Me shall never die. Believest thou this?" Christ here looks forward to the time of His second coming. Then the righteous dead shall be raised incorruptible, and the living righteous shall be translated to heaven without seeing death. The miracle which Christ was about to perform, in raising Lazarus from the dead, would represent the resurrection of all the righteous dead. By His word and His works He declared Himself the Author of the resurrection. He who Himself was soon to die upon the cross stood with the keys of death, a conqueror of the grave, and asserted His right and power to give eternal life.

To the Saviour's words, "Believest thou?" Martha responded, "Yea, Lord: I believe that Thou art the Christ, the Son of God, which should come into the world." She did not comprehend in all their significance the words spoken by Christ, but she confessed her faith in His divinity, and her confidence that He was able to perform whatever it pleased Him to do.

"And when she had so said, she went her way, and called Mary her sister secretly, saying, The Master is come, and calleth for thee." She delivered her message as quietly as possible; for the priests and rulers were prepared to arrest Jesus when opportunity offered. The cries of the mourners prevented her words from being heard.

On hearing the message, Mary rose hastily, and with an eager look on her face left the room. Thinking that she had gone to the grave to weep, the mourners followed her. When she reached the place where Jesus was waiting, she knelt at His feet, and said with quivering lips, "Lord, if Thou hadst been here, my brother had not died." The cries of the mourners were painful to her; for she longed for a few quiet words alone with Jesus. But she knew of the envy and jealousy cherished in the hearts of some present against Christ, and she was restrained from fully expressing her grief.

"When Jesus therefore saw her weeping, and the Jews also weeping which came with her, He groaned in the spirit, and was troubled." He read the hearts of all assembled. He saw that with many, what passed as a demonstration of grief was only pretense. He knew that some in the company, now manifesting hypocritical sorrow, would erelong be planning the death, not only of the mighty miracle worker, but of the one to be raised from the dead. Christ could have stripped from them their robe of pretended sorrow. But He restrained His righteous indignation. The words He could in all truth have spoken, He did not speak, because of the loved one kneeling at His feet in sorrow, who truly believed in Him.

"Where have ye laid him?" He asked. "They said unto Him, Lord, come and see." Together they proceeded to the grave. It was a mournful scene. Lazarus had been much beloved, and his sisters wept for him with breaking hearts, while those who had been his friends mingled their tears with those of the bereaved sisters. In view of this human distress, and of the fact that the afflicted friends could mourn over the dead while the Saviour of the world stood by,—"Jesus wept." Though He was the Son of God, yet He had taken human nature upon Him, and He was moved by human sorrow. His tender, pitying heart is ever awakened to sympathy by suffering. He weeps with those that weep, and rejoices with those that rejoice.

But it was not only because of His human sympathy with Mary and Martha that Jesus wept. In His tears there was a sorrow as high above human sorrow as the heavens are higher than the earth. Christ did not weep for Lazarus; for He was about to call him from the grave. He wept because many of those now mourning for Lazarus would soon plan the death of Him who was the resurrection and the life. But how unable were the unbelieving Jews rightly to interpret His tears! Some, who could see nothing more than the outward circumstances of the scene before Him as a cause for His grief, said softly, "Behold how He loved him!" Others, seeking to drop the seed of unbelief into the hearts of those present, said derisively, "Could not this Man, which opened the eyes of the blind, have caused that even this man should not have died?" If it were in Christ's power to save Lazarus, why then did He suffer him to die?

With prophetic eye Christ saw the enmity of the Pharisees and the Sadducees. He knew that they were premeditating His death. He knew that some of those now apparently so sympathetic would soon close against themselves the door of hope and the gates of the city of God. A scene was about to take place, in His humiliation and crucifixion, that would result in the destruction of Jerusalem, and at that time none would make lamentation for the dead. The retribution that was coming upon Jerusalem was plainly portrayed before Him. He saw Jerusalem compassed by the Roman legions. He knew that many now weeping for Lazarus would die in the siege of the city, and in their death there would be no hope.

It was not only because of the scene before Him that Christ wept. The weight of the grief of ages was upon Him. He saw the terrible effects of the transgression of God's law. He saw that in the history of the world, beginning with the death of Abel, the conflict between good and evil had been unceasing. Looking down the years to come, He saw the suffering and sorrow, tears and death, that were to be the lot of men. His heart was pierced with the pain of the human family of all ages and in all lands. The woes of the sinful race were heavy upon His soul, and the fountain of His tears was broken up as He longed to relieve all their distress.

"Jesus therefore again groaning in Himself cometh to the grave." Lazarus had been laid in a cave in a rock, and a massive stone had been placed before the entrance. "Take ye away the stone," Christ said. Thinking that He only wished to look upon the dead, Martha objected, saying that the body had been buried four days, and corruption had already begun its work. This statement, made before the raising of Lazarus, left no room for Christ's enemies to say that a deception had been practiced. In the past the Pharisees had circulated false statements regarding the most wonderful manifestations of the power of God. When Christ raised to life the daughter of Jairus, He had said, "The damsel is not dead, but sleepeth." Mark 5:39. As she had been sick only a short time, and was raised immediately after death, the Pharisees declared that the child had not been dead; that Christ Himself had said she was only asleep. They had tried to make it appear that Christ could not cure disease, that there was foul play about His miracles. But in this case, none could deny that Lazarus was dead.

When the Lord is about to do a work, Satan moves upon someone to object. "Take ye away the stone," Christ said. As far as possible, prepare the way for My work. But Martha's positive and ambitious nature asserted itself. She was unwilling that the decomposing body should be brought to view. The human heart is slow to understand Christ's words, and Martha's faith had not grasped the true meaning of His promise.

Christ reproved Martha, but His words were spoken with the utmost gentleness. "Said I not unto thee, that, if thou wouldest believe, thou shouldest see the glory of God?" Why should you doubt in regard to My power? Why reason in opposition to My requirements? You have My word. If you will believe, you shall see the glory of God. Natural impossibilities cannot prevent the work of the Omnipotent One. Skepticism and unbelief are not humility. Implicit belief in Christ's word is true humility, true self-surrender.

"Take ye away the stone." Christ could have commanded the stone to remove, and it would have obeyed His voice. He could have bidden the angels who were close by His side to do this. At His bidding, invisible hands would have removed the stone. But it was to be taken away by human hands. Thus Christ would show that humanity is to co-operate with divinity. What human power can do divine power is not summoned to do. God does not dispense with man's aid. He strengthens him, co-operating with him as he uses the powers and capabilities given him.

The command is obeyed. The stone is rolled away. Everything is done openly and deliberately. All are given a chance to see that no deception is practiced. There lies the body of Lazarus in its rocky grave, cold and silent in death. The cries of the mourners are hushed. Surprised and expectant, the company stand around the sepulcher, waiting to see what is to follow.

Calmly Christ stands before the tomb. A sacred solemnity rests upon all present. Christ steps closer to the sepulcher. Lifting His eyes to heaven, He says, "Father, I thank Thee that Thou has heard Me." Not long before this, Christ's enemies had accused Him of blasphemy, and had taken up stones to cast at Him because He claimed to be the Son of God. They accused Him of performing miracles by the power of Satan. But here Christ claims God as His Father, and with perfect confidence declares that He is the Son of God.

In all that He did, Christ was co-operating with His Father. Ever He had been careful to make it evident that He did not work independently; it was by faith and prayer that He wrought His miracles. Christ desired all to know His relationship with His Father. "Father," He said, "I thank Thee that Thou hast heard Me. And I knew that Thou hearest Me always: but because of the people which stand by I said it, that they may believe that Thou hast sent Me." Here the disciples and the people were to be given the most convincing evidence in regard to the relationship existing between Christ and God. They were to be shown that Christ's claim was not a deception.

"And when He thus had spoken, He cried with a loud voice, Lazarus, come forth." His voice, clear and penetrating, pierces the ear of the dead. As He speaks, divinity flashes through humanity. In His face, which is lighted up by the glory of God, the people see the assurance of His power. Every eye is fastened on the entrance to the cave. Every ear is bent to catch the slightest sound. With intense and painful interest all wait for the test of Christ's divinity, the evidence that is to substantiate His claim to be the Son of God, or to extinguish the hope forever.

There is a stir in the silent tomb, and he who was dead stands at the door of the sepulcher. His movements are impeded by the graveclothes in which he was laid away, and Christ says to the astonished spectators, "Loose him, and let him go." Again they are shown that the human worker is to co-operate with God. Humanity is to work for humanity. Lazarus is set free, and stands before the company, not as one emaciated from disease, and with feeble, tottering limbs, but as a man in the prime of life, and in the vigor of a noble manhood. His eyes beam with intelligence and with love for his Saviour. He casts himself in adoration at the feet of Jesus.

The beholders are at first speechless with amazement. Then there follows an inexpressible scene of rejoicing and thanksgiving. The sisters receive their brother back to life as the gift of God, and with joyful tears they brokenly express their thanks to the Saviour. But while brother, sisters, and friends are rejoicing in this reunion, Jesus withdraws from the scene. When they look for the Life-giver, He is not to be found.

Chapter 28

A TRAP

BETHANY WAS so near Jerusalem that the news of the raising of Lazarus was soon carried to the city. Through spies
who had witnessed the miracle the Jewish rulers were
speedily in possession of the facts. A meeting of the Sanhedrin was at once called to decide as to what should be
done. Christ had now fully made manifest His control of
death and the grave. That mighty miracle was the crowning evidence offered by God to men that He had sent His
Son into the world for their salvation. It was a demonstration of divine power sufficient to convince every mind
that was under control of reason and enlightened conscience. Many who witnessed the resurrection of Lazarus
were led to believe on Jesus. But the hatred of the priests
against Him was intensified. They had rejected all lesser
evidence of His divinity, and they were only enraged at
this new miracle. The dead had been raised in the full light
of day, and before a crowd of witnesses. No artifice could
explain away such evidence. For this very reason the enmity of the priests grew deadlier. They were more than ever
determined to put a stop to Christ's work.

The Sadducees, though not favorable to Christ, had not
been so full of malignity toward Him as were the Pharisees. Their hatred had not been so bitter. But they were
now thoroughly alarmed. They did not believe in a resurrection of the dead. Producing so-called science, they had
reasoned that it would be an impossibility for a dead body
to be brought to life. But by a few words from Christ their
theory had been overthrown. They were shown to be ignorant both of the Scriptures and of the power of God. They
could see no possibility of removing the impression made
on the people by the miracle. How could men be turned

This chapter is based on John 11:47-54.

away from Him who had prevailed to rob the grave of its dead? Lying reports were put in circulation, but the miracle could not be denied, and how to counteract its effect they knew not. Thus far the Sadducees had not encouraged the plan of putting Christ to death. But after the resurrection of Lazarus they decided that only by His death could His fearless denunciations against them be stopped.

The Pharisees believed in the resurrection, and they could not but see that this miracle was an evidence that the Messiah was among them. But they had ever opposed Christ's work. From the first they had hated Him because He had exposed their hypocritical pretensions. He had torn aside the cloak of rigorous rites under which their moral deformity was hidden. The pure religion that He taught had condemned their hollow professions of piety. They thirsted to be revenged upon Him for His pointed rebukes. They had tried to provoke Him to say or do something that would give them occasion to condemn Him. Several times they had attempted to stone Him, but He had quietly withdrawn, and they had lost sight of Him.

The miracles He performed on the Sabbath were all for the relief of the afflicted, but the Pharisees had sought to condemn Him as a Sabbathbreaker. They had tried to arouse the Herodians against Him. They represented that He was seeking to set up a rival kingdom, and consulted with them how to destroy Him. To excite the Romans against Him, they had represented Him as trying to subvert their authority. They had tried every pretext to cut Him off from influencing the people. But so far their attempts had been foiled. The multitudes who witnessed His works of mercy and heard His pure and holy teachings knew that these were not the deeds and words of a Sabbathbreaker or blasphemer. Even the officers sent by the Pharisees had been so influenced by His words that they could not lay hands on Him. In desperation the Jews had finally passed an edict that any man who professed faith in Jesus should be cast out of the synagogue.

So, as the priests, the rulers, and the elders gathered for consultation, it was their fixed determination to silence Him who did such marvelous works that all men wondered. Pharisees and Sadducees were more nearly united than ever before. Divided hitherto, they became one in their opposition to Christ. Nicodemus and Joseph had, in former councils, prevented the condemnation of Jesus and for this reason they were not now summoned. There were present at the council other influential men who believed on Jesus, but their influence prevailed nothing against that of the malignant Pharisees.

Yet the members of the council were not all agreed. The Sanhedrin was not at this time a legal assembly. It existed only by tolerance. Some of its number questioned the wisdom of putting Christ to death. They feared that this would excite an insurrection among the people, causing the Romans to withhold further favors from the priesthood, and to take from them the power they still held. The Sadducees were united in their hatred of Christ, yet they were inclined to be cautious in their movements, fearing that the Romans would deprive them of their high standing.

In this council, assembled to plan the death of Christ, the Witness was present who heard the boastful words of Nebuchadnezzar, who witnessed the idolatrous feast of Belshazzar, who was present when Christ in Nazareth announced Himself the Anointed One. This Witness was now impressing the rulers with the work they were doing. Events in the life of Christ rose up before them with a distinctness that alarmed them. They remembered the scene in the temple, when Jesus, then a child of twelve, stood before the learned doctors of the law, asking them questions at which they wondered. The miracle just performed bore witness that Jesus was none other than the Son of God. In their true significance, the Old Testament Scriptures regarding Christ flashed before their minds. Perplexed and troubled, the rulers asked, "What do we?" There was a division in the council. Under the impression of the Holy Spirit, the priests and rulers could not banish the conviction that they were fighting against God.

While the council was at the height of its perplexity, Caiaphas the high priest arose. Caiaphas was a proud and cruel man, overbearing and intolerant. Among his family connections were Sadducees, proud, bold, reckless, full of ambition and cruelty, which they hid under a cloak of pretended righteousness. Caiaphas had studied the prophecies, and although ignorant of their true meaning, he spoke with great authority and assurance: "Ye know nothing at all, nor consider that it is expedient for us, that one man should die for the people, and that the whole nation perish not." Even if Jesus were innocent, urged the high priest, He must be put out of the way. He was troublesome, drawing the people to Himself, and lessening the authority of the rulers. He was only one; it was better that He should die than that the authority of the rulers should be weakened. If the people were to lose confidence in their rulers, the national power would be destroyed. Caiaphas urged that after this miracle the followers of Jesus would likely rise in revolt. The Romans will then come, he said, and will close our temple, and abolish our laws, destroying us as a nation. What is the life of this Galilean worth in comparison with the life of the nation? If He stands in the way of Israel's well-being, is it not doing God a service to remove Him? Better that one man perish than that the whole nation be destroyed.

In declaring that one man should die for the nation, Caiaphas indicated that he had some knowledge of the prophecies, although it was very limited. But John, in his account of this scene, takes up the prophecy, and shows its broad and deep significance. He says, "And not for that nation only, but that also He should gather together in one the children of God that were scattered abroad." How blindly did the haughty Caiaphas acknowledge the Saviour's mission!

On the lips of Caiaphas this most precious truth was turned into a lie. The policy he advocated was based on a principle borrowed from heathenism. Among the heathen, the dim consciousness that one was to die for the human race had led to the offering of human sacrifices. So Caiaphas proposed by the sacrifice of Jesus to save the guilty nation, not from transgression, but in transgression, that they might continue in sin. And by his reasoning he thought to silence the remonstrances of those who might dare to say that as yet nothing worthy of death had been found in Jesus.

At this council Christ's enemies had been deeply convicted. The Holy Spirit had impressed their minds. But Satan strove to gain control of them. He urged upon their notice the grievances they had suffered on account of Christ. How little He had honored their righteousness. He presented a righteousness far greater, which all who would be children of God must possess. Taking no notice of their forms and ceremonies, He had encouraged sinners to go directly to God as a merciful Father, and make known their wants. Thus, in their opinion, He had set aside the priesthood. He had refused to acknowledge the theology of the rabbinical schools. He had exposed the evil practices of the priests, and had irreparably hurt their influence. He had injured the effect of their maxims and traditions, declaring that though they strictly enforced the ritual law, they made void the law of God. All this Satan now brought to their minds.

Satan told them that in order to maintain their authority, they must put Jesus to death. This counsel they followed. The fact that they might lose the power they then exercised, was, they thought, sufficient reason for coming to some decision. With the exception of a few who dared not speak their minds, the Sanhedrin received the words of Caiaphas as the words of God. Relief came to the council; the discord ceased. They resolved to put Christ to death at the first favorable opportunity. In rejecting the proof of the divinity of Jesus, these priests and rulers had locked themselves in impenetrable darkness. They had come wholly under the sway of Satan, to be hurried by him over the brink of eternal ruin. Yet such was their deception that they were well pleased with themselves. They regarded themselves as patriots, who were seeking the nation's salvation.

The Sanhedrin feared, however, to take rash measures against Jesus, lest the people should become incensed, and the violence meditated toward Him should fall upon themselves. On this account the council delayed to execute the sentence they had pronounced. The Saviour understood the plotting of the priests. He knew that they longed to remove Him, and that their purpose would soon be accomplished. But it was not His place to hasten the crisis, and He withdrew from that region, taking the disciples with Him. Thus by His own example Jesus again enforced the instruction He had given to the disciples, "When they persecute you in this city, flee ye into another." Matt. 10:23. There was a wide field in which to work for the salvation of souls; and unless loyalty to Him required it, the Lord's servants were not to imperil their lives.

Jesus had now given three years of public labor to the world. His example of self-denial and disinterested benevolence was before them. His life of purity, of suffering and devotion, was known to all. Yet this short period of three years was as long as the world could endure the presence of its Redeemer.

His life had been one of persecution and insult. Driven from Bethlehem by a jealous king, rejected by His own people at Nazareth, condemned to death without a cause at Jerusalem, Jesus, with His few faithful followers, found a temporary asylum in a strange city. He who was ever touched by human woe, who healed the sick, restored sight to the blind, hearing to the deaf, and speech to the dumb, who fed the hungry and comforted the sorrowful, was driven from the people He had labored to save. He who walked upon the heaving billows, and by a word silenced their angry roaring, who cast out devils that in departing acknowledged Him to be the Son of God, who broke the slumbers of the dead, who held thousands entranced by His words of wisdom, was unable to reach the hearts of those who were blinded by prejudice and hatred, and who stubbornly rejected the light.

Chapter 29

SHORT MAN — TALL SURPRIZE!

ON THE WAY to Jerusalem "Jesus entered and passed through Jericho." A few miles from the Jordan, on the western edge of the valley that here spread out into a plain, the city lay in the midst of tropic verdure and luxuriance of beauty. With its palm trees and rich gardens watered by living springs, it gleamed like an emerald in the setting of limestone hills and desolate ravines that interposed between Jerusalem and the city of the plain.

Many caravans on their way to the feast passed through Jericho. Their arrival was always a festive season, but now a deeper interest stirred the people. It was known that the Galilean Rabbi who had so lately brought Lazarus to life was in the throng; and though whispers were rife as to the plottings of the priests, the multitudes were eager to do Him homage.

Jericho was one of the cities anciently set apart for the priests, and at this time large numbers of priests had their residence there. But the city had also a population of a widely different character. It was a great center of traffic, and Roman officials and soldiers, with strangers from different quarters, were found there, while the collection of customs made it the home of many publicans.

"The chief among the publicans," Zacchaeus, was a Jew, and detested by his countrymen. His rank and wealth were the reward of a calling they abhorred, and which was regarded as another name for injustice and extortion. Yet the wealthy customs officer was not altogether the hardened man of the world that he seemed. Beneath the appearance of worldliness and pride was a heart susceptible to divine influences. Zacchaeus had heard of Jesus. The report of One who had borne Himself with kindness and

This chapter is based on Luke 19:1-10.

courtesy toward the proscribed classes had spread far and wide. In this chief of the publicans was awakened a longing for a better life. Only a few miles from Jericho, John the Baptist had preached at the Jordan, and Zacchaeus had heard of the call to repentance. The instruction to the publicans, "Exact no more than that which is appointed you" (Luke 3:13), though outwardly disregarded, had impressed his mind. He knew the Scriptures, and was convicted that his practice was wrong. Now, hearing the words reported to have come from the Great Teacher, he felt that he was a sinner in the sight of God. Yet what he had heard of Jesus kindled hope in his heart. Repentance, reformation of life, was possible, even to him; was not one of the new Teacher's most trusted disciples a publican? Zacchaeus began at once to follow the conviction that had taken hold upon him, and to make restitution to those whom he had wronged.

Already he had begun thus to retrace his steps, when the news sounded through Jericho that Jesus was entering the town. Zacchaeus determined to see Him. He was beginning to realize how bitter are the fruits of sin, and how difficult the path of him who tries to return from a course of wrong. To be misunderstood, to be met with suspicion and distrust in the effort to correct his errors, was hard to bear. The chief publican longed to look upon the face of Him whose words had brought hope to his heart.

The streets were crowded, and Zacchaeus, who was small of stature, could see nothing over the heads of the people. None would give way for him; so, running a little in advance of the multitude, to where a wide-branching fig tree hung over the way, the rich tax collector climbed to a seat among the boughs, whence he could survey the procession as it passed below. The crowd comes near, it is going by, and Zacchaeus scans with eager eyes to discern the one figure he longs to see.

Above the clamor of priests and rabbis and the shouts of welcome from the multitude, that unuttered desire of the chief publican spoke to the heart of Jesus. Suddenly, just beneath the fig tree, a group halts, the company before and behind come to a standstill, and One looks upward whose glance seems to read the soul. Almost doubting his senses, the man in the tree hears the words, "Zacchaeus, make haste, and come down; for today I must abide at thy house."

The multitude give way, and Zacchaeus, walking as in a

dream, leads the way toward his own home. But the rabbis look on with scowling faces, and murmur in discontent and scorn, "that He was gone to be guest with a man that is a sinner."

Zacchaeus had been overwhelmed, amazed, and silenced at the love and condescension of Christ in stooping to him, so unworthy. Now love and loyalty to his new-found Master unseal his lips. He will make public his confession and his repentance.

In the presence of the multitude, "Zacchaeus stood, and said unto the Lord; Behold, Lord, the half of my goods I give to the poor; and if I have taken anything from any man by false accusation, I restore him fourfold.

"And Jesus said unto him, This day is salvation come to this house, forsomuch as he also is a son of Abraham."

When the rich young ruler had turned away from Jesus, the disciples had marveled at their Master's saying, "How hard it is for them that trust in riches to enter into the kingdom of God!" They had exclaimed one to another, "Who then can be saved?" Now they had a demonstration of the truth of Christ's words, "The things which are impossible with men are possible with God." Mark 10:24, 26; Luke 18:27. They saw how, through the grace of God, a rich man could enter into the kingdom.

Before Zacchaeus had looked upon the face of Christ, he had begun the work that made him manifest as a true penitent. Before being accused by man, he had confessed his sin. He had yielded to the conviction of the Holy Spirit, and had begun to carry out the teaching of the words written for ancient Israel as well as for ourselves. The Lord had said long before, "If thy brother be waxen poor, and fallen in decay with thee; then thou shalt relieve him: yea, though he be a stranger, or a sojourner; that he may live with thee. Take thou no usury of him, or increase: but fear thy God; that thy brother may live with thee. Thou shalt not give him thy money upon usury, nor lend him thy victuals for increase." "Ye shall not therefore oppress one another; but thou shalt fear thy God." Lev. 25:35-37, 17. These words had been spoken by Christ Himself when He was enshrouded in the pillar of cloud, and the very first response of Zacchaeus to the love of Christ was in manifesting compassion toward the poor and suffering.

Among the publicans there was a confederacy, so that they could oppress the people, and sustain one another in their fraudulent practices. In their extortion they were but carrying out what had become an almost universal custom. Even the priests and rabbis who despised them were guilty of enriching themselves by dishonest practices under cover of their sacred calling. But no sooner did Zacchaeus yield to the influence of the Holy Spirit than he cast aside every practice contrary to integrity.

No repentance is genuine that does not work reformation. The righteousness of Christ is not a cloak to cover unconfessed and unforsaken sin; it is a principle of life that transforms the character and controls the conduct. Holiness is wholeness for God; it is the entire surrender of heart and life to the indwelling of the principles of heaven.

The Christian in his business life is to represent to the world the manner in which our Lord would conduct business enterprises. In every transaction he is to make it manifest that God is his teacher. "Holiness unto the Lord" is to be written upon daybooks and ledgers, on deeds, receipts, and bills of exchange. Those who profess to be followers of Christ, and who deal in an unrighteous manner, are bearing false witness against the character of a holy, just, and merciful God. Every converted soul will, like Zacchaeus, signalize the entrance of Christ into his heart by an abandonment of the unrighteous practices that have marked his life. Like the chief publican, he will give proof of his sincerity by making restitution. The Lord says, "If the wicked restore the pledge, give again that he had robbed, walk in the statutes of life, without committing iniquity; . . . none of his sins that he hath committed shall be mentioned unto him: . . . He shall surely live." Ezek. 33:15, 16.

If we have injured others through any unjust business transaction, if we have overreached in trade, or defrauded any man, even though it be within the pale of the law, we should confess our wrong, and make restitution as far as lies in our power. It is right for us to restore not only that which we have taken, but all that it would have accumulated if put to a right and wise use during the time it has been in our possession.

To Zacchaeus the Saviour said, "This day is salvation come to this house." Not only was Zacchaeus himself blessed, but all his household with him. Christ went to his home to give him lessons of truth, and to instruct his household in the things of the kingdom. They had been shut out from the synagogues by the contempt of rabbis and worshipers; but now, the most favored household in all Jericho, they gathered in their own home about the divine Teacher, and heard for themselves the words of life.

It is when Christ is received as a personal Saviour that salvation comes to the soul. Zacchaeus had received Jesus, not merely as a passing guest in his home, but as One to abide in the soul temple. The scribes and Pharisees accused him as a sinner, they murmured against Christ for becoming his guest, but the Lord recognized him as a son of Abraham. For "they which are of faith, the same are the children of Abraham." Gal. 3:7.

Chapter 30

THE ALABASTER BOX

SIMON OF Bethany was accounted a disciple of Jesus. He was one of the few Pharisees who had openly joined Christ's followers. He acknowledged Jesus as a teacher, and hoped that He might be the Messiah, but he had not accepted Him as a Saviour. His character was not transformed; his principles were unchanged.

Simon had been healed of the leprosy, and it was this that had drawn him to Jesus. He desired to show his gratitude, and at Christ's last visit to Bethany he made a feast for the Saviour and His disciples. This feast brought together many of the Jews. There was at this time much excitement at Jerusalem. Christ and His mission were attracting greater attention than ever before. Those who had come to the feast closely watched His movements, and some of them with unfriendly eyes.

The Saviour had reached Bethany only six days before the Passover, and according to His custom had sought rest at the home of Lazarus. The crowds of travelers who passed on to the city spread the tidings that He was on His way to Jerusalem, and that He would rest over the Sabbath at Bethany. Among the people there was great enthusiasm. Many flocked to Bethany, some out of sympathy with Jesus, and others from curiosity to see one who had been raised from the dead.

Many expected to hear from Lazarus a wonderful account of scenes witnessed after death. They were surprised that he told them nothing. He had nothing of this kind to tell. Inspiration declares, "The dead know not anything. . . . Their love, and their hatred, and their envy, is now perished." Eccl. 9:5, 6. But Lazarus did have a wonderful

This chapter is based on Matt. 26:6-13; Mark 14:3-11; Luke 7:36-50; John 11:55-57; 12:1-11.

testimony to bear in regard to the work of Christ. He had been raised from the dead for this purpose. With assurance and power he declared that Jesus was the Son of God.

The reports carried back to Jerusalem by the visitors to Bethany increased the excitement. The people were eager to see and hear Jesus. There was a general inquiry as to whether Lazarus would accompany Him to Jerusalem, and if the prophet would be crowned king at the Passover. The priests and rulers saw that their hold upon the people was still weakening, and their rage against Jesus grew more bitter. They could hardly wait for the opportunity of removing Him forever from their way. As time passed, they began to fear that after all He might not come to Jerusalem. They remembered how often He had baffled their murderous designs, and they were fearful that He had now read their purposes against Him, and would remain away. They could ill conceal their anxiety, and questioned among themselves, "What think ye, that He will not come to the feast?"

A council of the priests and Pharisees was called. Since the raising of Lazarus the sympathies of the people were so fully with Christ that it would be dangerous to seize upon Him openly. So the authorities determined to take Him secretly, and carry on the trial as quietly as possible. They hoped that when His condemnation became known, the fickle tide of public opinion would set in their favor.

Thus they proposed to destroy Jesus. But so long as Lazarus lived, the priests and rabbis knew that they were not secure. The very existence of a man who had been four days in the grave, and who had been restored by a word from Jesus, would sooner or later cause a reaction. The people would be avenged on their leaders for taking the life of One who could perform such a miracle. The Sanhedrin therefore decided that Lazarus also must die. To such lengths do envy and prejudice lead their slaves. The hatred and unbelief of the Jewish leaders had increased until they would even take the life of one whom infinite power had rescued from the grave.

While this plotting was going on at Jerusalem, Jesus and His friends were invited to Simon's feast. At the table the Saviour sat with Simon, whom He had cured of a loathsome disease, on one side, and Lazarus, whom He had raised from the dead, on the other. Martha served at the table, but Mary was earnestly listening to every word from the lips of Jesus. In His mercy, Jesus had pardoned her sins, He had called forth her beloved brother from the grave, and Mary's heart was filled with gratitude. She had heard Jesus speak of His approaching death, and in her deep love and sorrow she had longed to show Him honor. At great personal sacrifice she had purchased an alabaster box of "ointment of spikenard, very costly," with which to anoint His body. But now many were declaring that He was about to be crowned king. Her grief was turned to joy, and she was eager to be first in honoring her Lord. Breaking her box of ointment, she poured its contents upon the head and feet of Jesus; then, as she knelt weeping, moistening them with her tears, she wiped His feet with her long, flowing hair.

She had sought to avoid observation, and her movements might have passed unnoticed, but the ointment filled the room with its fragrance, and published her act to all present. Judas looked upon this act with great displeasure. Instead of waiting to hear what Christ would say of the matter, he began to whisper his complaints to those near him, throwing reproach upon Christ for suffering such waste. Craftily he made suggestions that would be likely to cause disaffection.

Judas was treasurer for the disciples, and from their little store he had secretly drawn for his own use, thus narrowing down their resources to a meager pittance. He was eager to put into the bag all that he could obtain. The treasure in the bag was often drawn upon to relieve the poor; and when something that Judas did not think essential was bought, he would say, Why is this waste? why was not the cost of this put into the bag that I carry for the poor? Now the act of Mary was in such marked contrast to his selfishness that he was put to shame; and according to his custom, he sought to assign a worthy motive for his objection to her gift. Turning to the disciples, he asked, "Why was not this ointment sold for three hundred pence, and given to the poor? This he said, not that he cared for the poor; but because he was a thief, and had the bag, and bare what was put therein." Judas had no heart for the poor. Had Mary's ointment been sold, and the proceeds fallen into his possession, the poor would have received no benefit.

Judas had a high opinion of his own executive ability. As a financier he thought himself greatly superior to his fellow disciples, and he had led them to regard him in the same light. He had gained their confidence, and had a strong influence over them. His professed sympathy for the poor deceived them, and his artful insinuation caused them to look distrustfully upon Mary's devotion. The murmur passed round the table, "To what purpose is this waste? For this ointment might have been sold for much, and given to the poor."

Mary heard the words of criticism. Her heart trembled within her. She feared that her sister would reproach her for extravagance. The Master, too, might think her improvident. Without apology or excuse she was about to shrink away, when the voice of her Lord was heard, "Let her alone; why trouble ye her?" He saw that she was embarrassed and distressed. He knew that in this act of service she had expressed her gratitude for the forgiveness of her sins, and He brought relief to her mind. Lifting His voice above the murmur of criticism, He said, "She hath wrought a good work on Me. For ye have the poor with you always, and whensoever ye will ye may do them good: but Me ye have not always. She hath done what she could: she is come aforehand to anoint My body to the burying."

The fragrant gift which Mary had thought to lavish upon the dead body of the Saviour she poured upon His living form. At the burial its sweetness could only have pervaded the tomb; now it gladdened His heart with the assurance of her faith and love. Joseph of Arimathaea and Nicodemus offered not their gift of love to Jesus in His life. With bitter tears they brought their costly spices for His cold, unconscious form. The women who bore spices to the tomb found their errand in vain, for He had risen. But Mary, pouring out her love upon the Saviour while He was conscious of her devotion, was anointing Him for the burial. And as He went down into the darkness of His great trial, He carried with Him the memory of that deed, an earnest of the love that would be His from His redeemed ones forever.

Many there are who bring their precious gifts for the dead. As they stand about the cold, silent form, words of love are freely spoken. Tenderness, appreciation, devotion, all are lavished upon one who sees not nor hears. Had these words been spoken when the weary spirit needed them so much, when the ear could hear and the heart could feel, how precious would have been their fragrance!

Mary knew not the full significance of her deed of love. She could not answer her accusers. She could not explain why she had chosen that occasion for anointing Jesus. The Holy Spirit had planned for her, and she had obeyed His promptings. Inspiration stoops to give no reason. An unseen presence, it speaks to mind and soul, and moves the heart to action. It is its own justification.

Christ told Mary the meaning of her act, and in this He gave her more than He had received. "In that she hath poured this ointment on My body," He said, "she did it for My burial." As the alabaster box was broken, and filled the whole house with its fragrance, so Christ was to die, His body was to be broken; but He was to rise from the tomb, and the fragrance of His life was to fill the earth. Christ "hath loved us, and hath given Himself for us an offering and a sacrifice to God for a sweet-smelling savor." Eph. 5:2.

"Verily I say unto you," Christ declared, "Wheresoever this gospel shall be preached throughout the whole world, this also that she hath done shall be spoken of for a memorial of her." Looking into the future, the Saviour spoke with certainty concerning His gospel. It was to be preached throughout the world. And as far as the gospel extended, Mary's gift would shed its fragrance, and hearts would be blessed through her unstudied act. Kingdoms would rise and fall; the names of monarchs and conquerors would be forgotten; but this woman's deed would be immortalized upon the pages of sacred history. Until time should be no more, that broken alabaster box would tell the story of the abundant love of God for a fallen race.

Mary's act was in marked contrast with that which Judas was about to do. What a sharp lesson Christ might have given him who had dropped the seed of criticism and evil thinking into the minds of the disciples! How justly the accuser might have been accused! He who reads the motives of every heart, and understands every action, might have opened before those at the feast dark chapters in the experience of Judas. The hollow pretense on which the traitor based his words might have been laid bare; for, instead of sympathizing with the poor, he was robbing them of the money intended for their relief. Indignation might have been excited against him for his oppression of the widow, the orphan, and the hireling. But had Christ unmasked Judas, this would have been urged as a reason for the betrayal. And though charged with being a thief, Judas would have gained sympathy, even among the disciples. The Saviour reproached him not, and thus avoided giving him an excuse for his treachery.

But the look which Jesus cast upon Judas convinced him that the Saviour penetrated his hypocrisy, and read his base, contemptible character. And in commending Mary's action, which had been so severely condemned, Christ had rebuked Judas. Prior to this, the Saviour had never given him a direct rebuke. Now the reproof rankled in his heart. He determined to be revenged. From the supper he went directly to the palace of the high priest, where he found the council assembled, and he offered to betray Jesus into their hands.

The priests were greatly rejoiced. These leaders of Israel had been given the privilege of receiving Christ as their Saviour, without money and without price. But they refused the precious gift offered them in the most tender spirit of constraining love. They refused to accept that salvation which is of more value than gold, and bought their Lord for thirty pieces of silver.

Judas had indulged avarice until it overpowered every good trait of his character. He grudged the offering made to Jesus. His heart burned with envy that the Saviour should be the recipient of a gift suitable for the monarchs of the earth. For a sum far less than the box of ointment cost, he betrayed his Lord.

The disciples were not like Judas. They loved the Saviour. But they did not rightly appreciate His exalted character. Had they realized what He had done for them, they would have felt that nothing bestowed upon Him was wasted. The wise men from the East, who knew so little of Jesus, had shown a truer appreciation of the honor due Him. They brought precious gifts to the Saviour, and bowed in homage before Him when He was but a babe, and cradled in a manger.

Christ values acts of heartfelt courtesy. When anyone did Him a favor, with heavenly politeness He blessed the actor. He did not refuse the simplest flower plucked by the hand of a child, and offered to Him in love. He accepted the offerings of children, and blessed the givers, inscribing their names in the book of life. In the Scriptures, Mary's anointing of Jesus is mentioned as distinguishing her from the other Marys. Acts of love and reverence for Jesus are an evidence of faith in Him as the Son of God. And the Holy Spirit mentions, as evidences of woman's loyalty to Christ: "If she have washed the saints' feet, if she have relieved the afflicted, if she have diligently followed every good work." 1 Tim. 5:10.

Christ delighted in the earnest desire of Mary to do the will of her Lord. He accepted the wealth of pure affection which His disciples did not, would not, understand. The desire that Mary had to do this service for her Lord was of more value to Christ than all the precious ointment in the world, because it expressed her appreciation of the world's Redeemer. It was the love of Christ that constrained her. The matchless excellence of the character of Christ filled her soul. That ointment was a symbol of the heart of the giver. It was the outward demonstration of a love fed by heavenly streams until it overflowed.

The work of Mary was just the lesson the disciples needed to show them that the expression of their love for Him would be pleasing to Christ. He had been everything to them, and they did not realize that soon they would be deprived of His presence, that soon they could offer Him no token of their gratitude for His great love. The loneliness of Christ, separated from the heavenly courts, living the life of humanity, was never understood or appreciated by the disciples as it should have been. He was often grieved because His disciples did not give Him that which He should have received from them. He knew that if they were under the influence of the heavenly angels that accompanied Him, they too would think no offering of sufficient value to declare the heart's spiritual affection.

Their afterknowledge gave them a true sense of the many things they might have done for Jesus expressive of the love and gratitude of their hearts, while they were near Him. When Jesus was no longer with them, and they felt indeed as sheep without a shepherd, they began to see how they might have shown Him attentions that would have brought gladness to His heart. They no longer cast blame upon Mary, but upon themselves. Oh, if they could have taken back their censuring, their presenting the poor as more worthy of the gift than was Christ! They felt the reproof keenly as they took from the cross the bruised body of their Lord.

The same want is evident in our world today. But few appreciate all that Christ is to them. If they did, the great love of Mary would be expressed, the anointing would be freely bestowed. The expensive ointment would not be called a waste. Nothing would be thought too costly to give for Christ, no self-denial or self-sacrifice too great to be endured for His sake.

The words spoken in indignation, "To what purpose is this waste?" brought vividly before Christ the greatest sacrifice ever made,—the gift of Himself as the propitiation for a lost world. The Lord would be so bountiful to His human family that it could not be said of Him that He could do more. In the gift of Jesus, God gave all heaven. From a human point of view, such a sacrifice was a wanton waste. To human reasoning the whole plan of salvation is a waste of mercies and resources. Self-denial and whole-hearted sacrifice meet us everywhere. Well may the heavenly host look with amazement upon the human family who refuse to be uplifted and enriched with the boundless love expressed in Christ. Well may they exclaim, Why this great waste?

But the atonement for a lost world was to be full, abundant, and complete. Christ's offering was exceedingly abundant to reach every soul that God had created. It could not be restricted so as not to exceed the number who would accept the great Gift. All men are not saved; yet the plan of redemption is not a waste because it does not accomplish all that its liberality has provided for. There must be enough and to spare.

Simon the host had been influenced by the criticism of Judas upon Mary's gift, and he was surprised at the conduct of Jesus. His Pharisaic pride was offended. He knew that many of his guests were looking upon Christ with distrust and displeasure. Simon said in his heart, "This Man, if He were a prophet, would have known who and what manner of woman this is that toucheth Him: for she is a sinner."

By curing Simon of leprosy, Christ had saved him from a living death. But now Simon questioned whether the Saviour were a prophet. Because Christ allowed this woman to approach Him, because He did not indignantly spurn her as one whose sins were too great to be forgiven, because He did not show that He realized she had fallen, Simon was tempted to think that He was not a prophet. Jesus knows nothing of this woman who is so free in her demonstrations, he thought, or He would not allow her to touch Him.

But it was Simon's ignorance of God and of Christ that led him to think as he did. He did not realize that God's Son must act in God's way, with compassion, tenderness, and mercy. Simon's way was to take no notice of Mary's penitent service. Her act of kissing Christ's feet and anointing them with ointment was exasperating to his hardheartedness. He thought that if Christ were a prophet, He would recognize sinners and rebuke them.

To this unspoken thought the Saviour answered:
"Simon, I have somewhat to say unto thee. . . . There was
a certain creditor which had two debtors: the one owed
five hundred pence, and the other fifty. And when they
had nothing to pay, he frankly forgave them both. Tell Me
therefore, which of them will love him most? Simon answered and said, I suppose that he, to whom he forgave
most. And He said unto him, Thou hast rightly judged."

As did Nathan with David, Christ concealed His home
thrust under the veil of a parable. He threw upon His host
the burden of pronouncing sentence upon himself. Simon
had led into sin the woman he now despised. She had been
deeply wronged by him. By the two debtors of the parable,
Simon and the woman were represented. Jesus did not design to teach that different degrees of obligation should
be felt by the two persons, for each owed a debt of gratitude
that never could be repaid. But Simon felt himself more
righteous than Mary, and Jesus desired him to see how
great his guilt really was. He would show him that his sin
was greater than hers, as much greater as a debt of five
hundred pence exceeds a debt of fifty pence.

Simon now began to see himself in a new light. He saw
how Mary was regarded by One who was more than a
prophet. He saw that with keen prophetic eye Christ read
her heart of love and devotion. Shame seized upon him,
and he realized that he was in the presence of One superi-
or to himself.

"I entered into thine house," Christ continued, "thou
gavest Me no water for My feet;" but with tears of repentance, prompted by love, Mary hath washed My feet, and
wiped them with the hair of her head. "Thou gavest Me no
kiss: but this woman," whom you despise, "since the time I
came in hath not ceased to kiss My feet." Christ recounted
the opportunities Simon had had to show his love for his
Lord, and his appreciation of what had been done for him.
Plainly, yet with delicate politeness, the Saviour assured
His disciples that His heart is grieved when His children
neglect to show their gratitude to Him by words and deeds
of love.

The Heart Searcher read the motive that led to Mary's
action, and He saw also the spirit that prompted Simon's
words. "Seest thou this woman?" He said to him. She is a
sinner. "I say unto thee, Her sins, which are many, are
forgiven; for she loved much: but to whom little is forgiven, the same loveth little."

Simon's coldness and neglect toward the Saviour showed how little he appreciated the mercy he had received. He had thought he honored Jesus by inviting Him to his house. But he now saw himself as he really was. While he thought himself reading his Guest, his Guest had been reading him. He saw how true Christ's judgment of him was. His religion had been a robe of Pharisaism. He had despised the compassion of Jesus. He had not recognized Him as the representative of God. While Mary was a sinner pardoned, he was a sinner unpardoned. The rigid rule of justice he had desired to enforce against her condemned him.

Simon was touched by the kindness of Jesus in not openly rebuking him before the guests. He had not been treated as he desired Mary to be treated. He saw that Jesus did not wish to expose his guilt to others, but sought by a true statement of the case to convince his mind, and by pitying kindness to subdue his heart. Stern denunciation would have hardened Simon against repentance, but patient admonition convinced him of his error. He saw the magnitude of the debt which he owed his Lord. His pride was humbled, he repented, and the proud Pharisee became a lowly, self-sacrificing disciple.

Mary had been looked upon as a great sinner, but Christ knew the circumstances that had shaped her life. He might have extinguished every spark of hope in her soul, but He did not. It was He who had lifted her from despair and ruin. Seven times she had heard His rebuke of the demons that controlled her heart and mind. She had heard His strong cries to the Father in her behalf. She knew how offensive is sin to His unsullied purity, and in His strength she had overcome.

When to human eyes her case appeared hopeless, Christ saw in Mary capabilities for good. He saw the better traits of her character. The plan of redemption has invested humanity with great possibilities, and in Mary these possibilities were to be realized. Through His grace she became a partaker of the divine nature. The one who had fallen, and whose mind had been a habitation of demons, was brought very near to the Saviour in fellowship and ministry. It was Mary who sat at His feet and learned of Him. It was Mary who poured upon His head the precious anointing oil, and bathed His feet with her tears. Mary stood beside the cross, and followed Him to the sepulcher. Mary was first at the tomb after His resurrection. It was Mary who first proclaimed a risen Saviour.

Jesus knows the circumstances of every soul. You may say, I am sinful, very sinful. You may be; but the worse you are, the more you need Jesus. He turns no weeping, contrite one away. He does not tell to any all that He might reveal, but He bids every trembling soul take courage. Freely will He pardon all who come to Him for forgiveness and restoration.

Christ might commission the angels of heaven to pour out the vials of His wrath on our world, to destroy those who are filled with hatred of God. He might wipe this dark spot from His universe. But He does not do this. He is today standing at the altar of incense, presenting before God the prayers of those who desire His help.

The souls that turn to Him for refuge, Jesus lifts above the accusing and the strife of tongues. No man or evil angel can impeach these souls. Christ unites them to His own divine-human nature. They stand beside the great Sin Bearer, in the light proceeding from the throne of God. "Who shall lay anything to the charge of God's elect? It is God that justifieth. Who is he that condemneth? It is Christ that died, yea rather, that is risen again, who is even at the right hand of God, who also maketh intercession for us." Rom. 8:33, 34.

Chapter 31

CRYING STONES — CRYING KING

"Rejoice greatly, O daughter of Zion; shout, O daughter of Jerusalem: behold, thy King cometh unto thee: He is just, and having salvation; lowly, and riding upon an ass, and upon a colt the foal of an ass." Zech. 9:9.

Five hundred years before the birth of Christ, the prophet Zechariah thus foretold the coming of the King to Israel. This prophecy is now to be fulfilled. He who has so long refused royal honors now comes to Jerusalem as the promised heir to David's throne.

It was on the first day of the week that Christ made His triumphal entry into Jerusalem. Multitudes who had flocked to see Him at Bethany now accompanied Him, eager to witness His reception. Many people were on their way to the city to keep the Passover, and these joined the multitude attending Jesus. All nature seemed to rejoice. The trees were clothed with verdure, and their blossoms shed a delicate fragrance on the air. A new life and joy animated the people. The hope of the new kingdom was again springing up.

Purposing to ride into Jerusalem. Jesus had sent two of His disciples to bring to Him an ass and its colt. At His birth the Saviour was dependent upon the hospitality of strangers. The manger in which He lay was a borrowed resting place. Now, although the cattle on a thousand hills are His, He is dependent on a stranger's kindness for an animal on which to enter Jerusalem as its King. But again His divinity is revealed, even in the minute directions given His disciples for this errand. As He foretold, the plea, "The Lord hath need of them," was readily granted. Jesus chose for His use the colt on which never man had

This chapter is based on Matt. 21:1-11; Mark 11:1-10; Luke 19:29-44; John 12:12-19.

sat. The disciples, with glad enthusiasm, spread their garments on the beast, and seated their Master upon it. Heretofore Jesus had always traveled on foot, and the disciples had at first wondered that He should now choose to ride. But hope brightened in their hearts with the joyous thought that He was about to enter the capital, proclaim Himself King, and assert His royal power. While on their errand they communicated their glowing expectations to the friends of Jesus, and the excitement spread far and near, raising the expectations of the people to the highest pitch.

Christ was following the Jewish custom for a royal entry. The animal on which He rode was that ridden by the kings of Israel, and prophecy had foretold that thus the Messiah should come to His kingdom. No sooner was He seated upon the colt than a loud shout of triumph rent the air. The multitude hailed Him as Messiah, their King. Jesus now accepted the homage which He had never before permitted, and the disciples received this as proof that their glad hopes were to be realized by seeing Him established on the throne. The multitude were convinced that the hour of their emancipation was at hand. In imagination they saw the Roman armies driven from Jerusalem, and Israel once more an independent nation. All were happy and excited; the people vied with one another in paying Him homage. They could not display outward pomp and splendor, but they gave Him the worship of happy hearts. They were unable to present Him with costly gifts, but they spread their outer garments as a carpet in His path, and they also strewed the leafy branches of the olive and the palm in the way. They could lead the triumphal procession with no royal standards, but they cut down the spreading palm boughs, Nature's emblem of victory, and waved them aloft with loud acclamations and hosannas.

As they proceeded, the multitude was continually increased by those who had heard of the coming of Jesus and hastened to join the procession. Spectators were constantly mingling with the throng, and asking, Who is this? What does all this commotion signify? They had all heard of Jesus, and expected Him to go to Jerusalem; but they knew that He had heretofore discouraged all effort to place Him on the throne, and they were greatly astonished to learn that this was He. They wondered what could have wrought this change in Him who had declared that His kingdom was not of this world.

Their questionings are silenced by a shout of triumph. Again and again it is repeated by the eager throng; it is taken up by the people afar off, and echoed from the surrounding hills and valleys. And now the procession is joined by crowds from Jerusalem. From the multitudes gathered to attend the Passover, thousands go forth to welcome Jesus. They greet Him with the waving of palm branches and a burst of sacred song. The priests at the temple sound the trumpet for evening service, but there are few to respond, and the rulers say to one another in alarm, "The world is gone after Him."

Never before in His earthly life had Jesus permitted such a demonstration. He clearly foresaw the result. It would bring Him to the cross. But it was His purpose thus publicly to present Himself as the Redeemer. He desired to call attention to the sacrifice that was to crown His mission to a fallen world. While the people were assembling at Jerusalem to celebrate the Passover, He, the antitypical Lamb, by a voluntary act set Himself apart as an oblation. It would be needful for His church in all succeeding ages to make His death for the sins of the world a subject of deep thought and study. Every fact connected with it should be verified beyond a doubt. It was necessary, then, that the eyes of all people should now be directed to Him; the events which preceded His great sacrifice must be such as to call attention to the sacrifice itself. After such a demonstration as that attending His entry into Jerusalem, all eyes would follow His rapid progress to the final scene.

The events connected with this triumphal ride would be the talk of every tongue, and would bring Jesus before every mind. After His crucifixion, many would recall these events in their connection with His trial and death. They would be led to search the prophecies, and would be convinced that Jesus was the Messiah; and in all lands converts to the faith would be multiplied.

In this one triumphant scene of His earthly life, the Saviour might have appeared escorted by heavenly angels, and heralded by the trump of God; but such a demonstration would have been contrary to the purpose of His mission, contrary to the law which had governed His life. He remained true to the humble lot He had accepted. The burden of humanity He must bear until His life was given for the life of the world.

This day, which seemed to the disciples the crowning day of their lives, would have been shadowed with gloomy clouds had they known that this scene of rejoicing was but a prelude to the suffering and death of their Master. Although He had repeatedly told them of His certain sacrifice, yet in the glad triumph of the present they forgot His sorrowful words, and looked forward to His prosperous reign on David's throne.

New accessions were made continually to the procession, and, with few exceptions, all who joined it caught the inspiration of the hour, and helped to swell the hosannas that echoed and re-echoed from hill to hill and from valley to valley. The shouts went up continually, "Hosanna to the Son of David: Blessed is He that cometh in the name of the Lord; Hosanna in the highest."

Never before had the world seen such a triumphal procession. It was not like that of the earth's famous conquerors. No train of mourning captives, as trophies of kingly valor, made a feature of that scene. But about the Saviour were the glorious trophies of His labors of love for sinful man. There were the captives whom He had rescued from Satan's power, praising God for their deliverance. The blind whom He had restored to sight were leading the way. The dumb whose tongues He had loosed shouted the loudest hosannas. The cripples whom He had healed bounded with joy, and were the most active in breaking the palm branches and waving them before the Saviour. Widows and orphans were exalting the name of Jesus for His works of mercy to them. The lepers whom He had cleansed spread their untainted garments in His path, and hailed Him as the King of glory. Those whom His voice had awakened from the sleep of death were in that throng. Lazarus, whose body had seen corruption in the grave, but who now rejoiced in the strength of glorious manhood, led the beast on which the Saviour rode.

Many Pharisees witnessed the scene, and, burning with envy and malice, sought to turn the current of popular feeling. With all their authority they tried to silence the people; but their appeals and threats only increased the enthusiasm. They feared that this multitude, in the strength of their numbers, would make Jesus king. As a last resort they pressed through the crowd to where the Saviour was, and accosted Him with reproving and threatening words: "Master, rebuke Thy disciples." They declared that such noisy demonstrations were unlawful, and would not be permitted by the authorities. But they were silenced by the reply of Jesus, "I tell you that, if these should hold their peace, the stones would immediately cry out." That scene of triumph was of God's own appointing. It had been foretold by the prophet, and man was powerless to turn aside God's purpose. Had men failed to carry out His plan, He would have given a voice to the inanimate stones, and they would have hailed His Son with acclamations of praise. As the silenced Pharisees drew back, the words of Zechariah were taken up by hundreds of voices: "Rejoice greatly, O daughter of Zion; shout, O daughter of Jerusalem: behold, thy King cometh unto thee: He is just, and having salvation; lowly, and riding upon an ass, and upon a colt the foal of an ass."

When the procession reached the brow of the hill, and was about to descend into the city, Jesus halted, and all the multitude with Him. Before them lay Jerusalem in its glory, now bathed in the light of the declining sun. The temple attracted all eyes. In stately grandeur it towered above all else, seeming to point toward heaven as if directing the people to the only true and living God. The temple had long been the pride and glory of the Jewish nation. The Romans also prided themselves in its magnificence. A king appointed by the Romans had united with the Jews to rebuild and embellish it, and the emperor of Rome had enriched it with his gifts. Its strength, richness, and magnificence had made it one of the wonders of the world.

While the westering sun was tinting and gilding the heavens, its resplendent glory lighted up the pure white marble of the temple walls, and sparkled on its goldcapped pillars. From the crest of the hill where Jesus and His followers stood, it had the appearance of a massive structure of snow, set with golden pinnacles. At the entrance to the temple was a vine of gold and silver, with green leaves and massive clusters of grapes executed by the most skillful artists. This design represented Israel as a prosperous vine. The gold, silver, and living green were combined with rare taste and exquisite workmanship; as it twined gracefully about the white and glistening pillars, clinging with shining tendrils to their golden ornaments, it caught the splendor of the setting sun, shining as if with a glory borrowed from heaven.

Jesus gazes upon the scene, and the vast multitude hush their shouts, spellbound by the sudden vision of beauty. All eyes turn upon the Saviour, expecting to see in His countenance the admiration they themselves feel. But instead of this they behold a cloud of sorrow. They are surprised and disappointed to see His eyes fill with tears, and His body rock to and fro like a tree before the tempest, while a wail of anguish bursts from His quivering lips, as if from the depths of a broken heart. What a sight was this for angels to behold! their loved Commander in an agony of tears! What a sight was this for the glad throng that with shouts of triumph and the waving of palm branches were escorting Him to the glorious city, where they fondly hoped He was about to reign! Jesus had wept at the grave of Lazarus, but it was in a godlike grief in sympathy with human woe. But this sudden sorrow was like a note of wailing in a grand triumphal chorus. In the midst of a scene of rejoicing, where all were paying Him homage, Israel's King was in tears; not silent tears of gladness, but tears and groans of insuppressible agony. The multitude were struck with a sudden gloom. Their acclamations were silenced. Many wept in sympathy with a grief they could not comprehend.

The tears of Jesus were not in anticipation of His own suffering. Just before Him was Gethsemane, where soon the horror of a great darkness would overshadow Him. The sheepgate also was in sight, through which for centuries the beasts for sacrificial offerings had been led. This gate was soon to open for Him, the great Antitype, toward whose sacrifice for the sins of the world all these offerings had pointed. Near by was Calvary, the scene of His approaching agony. Yet it was not because of these reminders of His cruel death that the Redeemer wept and groaned in anguish of spirit. His was no selfish sorrow. The thought of His own agony did not intimidate that noble, self-sacrificing soul. It was the sight of Jerusalem that pierced the heart of Jesus—Jerusalem that had rejected the Son of God and scorned His love, that refused to be convinced by His mighty miracles, and was about to take His life. He saw what she was in her guilt of rejecting her Redeemer, and what she might have been had she accepted Him who alone could heal her wound. He had come to save her; how could He give her up?

Israel had been a favored people; God had made their temple His habitation; it was "beautiful for situation, the joy of the whole earth." Ps. 48:2. The record of more than a thousand years of Christ's guardian care and tender love, such as a father bears his only child, was there. In that temple the prophets had uttered their solemn warnings. There had the burning censers waved, while incense, mingled with the prayers of the worshipers, had ascended to God. There the blood of beasts had flowed, typical of the blood of Christ. There Jehovah had manifested His glory above the mercy seat. There the priests had officiated, and the pomp of symbol and ceremony had gone on for ages. But all this must have an end.

Jesus raised His hand,—that had so often blessed the sick and suffering,—and waving it toward the doomed city, in broken utterances of grief exclaimed: "If thou hadst known, even thou, at least in this thy day, the things which belong unto thy peace!—" Here the Saviour paused, and left unsaid what might have been the condition of Jerusalem had she accepted the help that God desired to give her,—the gift of His beloved Son. If Jerusalem had known what it was her privilege to know, and had heeded the light which Heaven had sent her, she might have stood forth in the pride of prosperity, the queen of kingdoms, free in the strength of her God-given power. There would have been no armed soldiers standing at her gates, no Roman banners waving from her walls. The glorious destiny that might have blessed Jerusalem had she accepted her Redeemer rose before the Son of God. He saw that she might through Him have been healed of her grievous malady, liberated from bondage, and established as the mighty metropolis of the earth. From her walls the dove of peace would have gone forth to all nations. She would have been the world's diadem of glory.

But the bright picture of what Jerusalem might have been fades from the Saviour's sight. He realizes what she now is under the Roman yoke, bearing the frown of God, doomed to His retributive judgment. He takes up the broken thread of His lamentation: "But now they are hid from thine eyes. For the days shall come upon thee, that thine enemies shall cast a trench about thee, and compass thee round, and keep thee in on every side, and shall lay thee even with the ground, and thy children within thee; and they shall not leave in thee one stone upon another; because thou knewest not the time of thy visitation."

Christ came to save Jerusalem with her children; but Pharisaical pride, hypocrisy, jealousy, and malice had prevented Him from accomplishing His purpose. Jesus knew the terrible retribution which would be visited upon the doomed city. He saw Jerusalem encompassed with armies, the besieged inhabitants driven to starvation and death, mothers feeding upon the dead bodies of their own children, and both parents and children snatching the last morsel of food from one another, natural affection being destroyed by the gnawing pangs of hunger. He saw that the stubbornness of the Jews, as evinced in their rejection of His salvation, would also lead them to refuse submission to the invading armies. He beheld Calvary, on which He was to be lifted up, set with crosses as thickly as forest trees. He saw the wretched inhabitants suffering torture on the rack and by crucifixion, the beautiful palaces destroyed, the temple in ruins, and of its massive walls not one stone left upon another, while the city was plowed like a field. Well might the Saviour weep in agony in view of that fearful scene.

Jerusalem had been the child of His care, and as a tender father mourns over a wayward son, so Jesus wept over the beloved city. How can I give thee up? How can I see thee devoted to destruction? Must I let thee go to fill up the cup of thine iniquity? One soul is of such value that, in comparison with it, worlds sink into insignificance; but here was a whole nation to be lost. When the fast westering sun should pass from sight in the heavens, Jerusalem's day of grace would be ended. While the procession was halting on the brow of Olivet, it was not yet too late for Jerusalem to repent. The angel of mercy was then folding her wings to step down from the golden throne to give place to justice and swift-coming judgment. But Christ's great heart of love still pleaded for Jerusalem, that had scorned His mercies, despised His warnings, and was about to imbrue her hands in His blood. If Jerusalem would but repent, it was not yet too late. While the last rays of the setting sun were lingering on temple, tower, and pinnacle, would not some good angel lead her to the Saviour's love, and avert her doom? Beautiful and unholy city that had stoned the prophets, that had rejected the Son of God, that was locking herself by her impenitence in fetters of bondage,—her day of mercy was almost spent!

Yet again the Spirit of God speaks to Jerusalem. Before the day is done, another testimony is borne to Christ. The voice of witness is lifted up, responding to the call from a prophetic past. If Jerusalem will hear the call, if she will receive the Saviour who is entering her gates, she may yet be saved.

Reports have reached the rulers in Jerusalem that Jesus

is approaching the city with a great concourse of people. But they have no welcome for the Son of God. In fear they go out to meet Him, hoping to disperse the throng. As the procession is about to descend the Mount of Olives, it is intercepted by the rulers. They inquire the cause of the tumultuous rejoicing. As they question, "Who is this?" the disciples, filled with the spirit of inspiration, answer this question. In eloquent strains they repeat the prophecies concerning Christ:

Adam will tell you, It is the seed of the woman that shall bruise the serpent's head.

Ask Abraham, he will tell you, It is "Melchizedek King of Salem," King of Peace. Gen. 14:18.

Jacob will tell you, He is Shiloh of the tribe of Judah.

Isaiah will tell you, "Immanuel," "Wonderful, Counselor, The mighty God, The everlasting Father, The Prince of Peace." Isa. 7:14; 9:6.

Jeremiah will tell you, The Branch of David, ' the Lord our Righteousness." Jer. 23:6.

Daniel will tell you, He is the Messiah.

Hosea will tell you, He is "the Lord God of hosts; the Lord is His memorial." Hosea 12:5.

John the Baptist will tell you, He is "the Lamb of God, which taketh away the sin of the world." John 1:29

The great Jehovah has proclaimed from His throne, "This is My beloved Son." Matt. 3:17.

We, His disciples, declare, This is Jesus, the Messiah, the Prince of life, the Redeemer of the world.

And the prince of the powers of darkness acknowledges Him, saying, "I know Thee who Thou art, the Holy One of God." Mark 1:24.

Chapter 32

SIGNS OF THE END

CHRIST'S WORDS to the priests and rulers, "Behold, your house is left unto you desolate" (Matt. 23:38), had struck terror to their hearts. They affected indifference, but the question kept rising in their minds as to the import of these words. An unseen danger seemed to threaten them. Could it be that the magnificent temple, which was the nation's glory, was soon to be a heap of ruins? The foreboding of evil was shared by the disciples, and they anxiously waited for some more definite statement from Jesus. As they passed with Him out of the temple, they called His attention to its strength and beauty. The stones of the temple were of the purest marble, of perfect whiteness, and some of them of almost fabulous size. A portion of the wall had withstood the siege by Nebuchadnezzar's army. In its perfect masonry it appeared like one solid stone dug entire from the quarry. How those mighty walls could be overthrown the disciples could not comprehend.

As Christ's attention was attracted to the magnificence of the temple, what must have been the unuttered thoughts of that Rejected One! The view before Him was indeed beautiful, but He said with sadness, I see it all. The buildings are indeed wonderful. You point to these walls as apparently indestructible; but listen to My words: The day will come when "there shall not be left one stone upon another, that shall not be thrown down."

Christ's words had been spoken in the hearing of a large number of people; but when He was alone, Peter, John, James, and Andrew came to Him as He sat upon the Mount of Olives. "Tell us," they said, "when shall these things be? and what shall be the sign of Thy coming, and of the end of the world?" Jesus did not answer His disci-

This chapter is based on Matt. 24; Mark 13; Luke 21:5-38.

ples by taking up separately the destruction of Jerusalem and the great day of His coming. He mingled the description of these two events. Had He opened to His disciples future events as He beheld them, they would have been unable to endure the sight. In mercy to them He blended the description of the two great crises, leaving the disciples to study out the meaning for themselves. When He referred to the destruction of Jerusalem, His prophetic words reached beyond that event to the final conflagration in that day when the Lord shall rise out of His place to punish the world for their iniquity, when the earth shall disclose her blood, and shall no more cover her slain. This entire discourse was given, not for the disciples only, but for those who should live in the last scenes of this earth's history.

Turning to the disciples, Christ said, "Take heed that no man deceive you. For many shall come in My name, saying, I am Christ; and shall deceive many." Many false messiahs will appear, claiming to work miracles, and declaring that the time of the deliverance of the Jewish nation has come. These will mislead many. Christ's words were fulfilled. Between His death and the siege of Jerusalem many false messiahs appeared. But this warning was given also to those who live in this age of the world. The same deceptions practiced prior to the destruction of Jerusalem have been practiced through the ages, and will be practiced again.

"And ye shall hear of wars and rumors of wars: see that ye be not troubled: for all these things must come to pass, but the end is not yet." Prior to the destruction of Jerusalem, men wrestled for the supremacy. Emperors were murdered. Those supposed to be standing next the throne were slain. There were wars and rumors of wars. "All these things must come to pass," said Christ, "but the end [of the Jewish nation as a nation] is not yet. For nation shall rise against nation, and kingdom against kingdom: and there shall be famines, and pestilences, and earthquakes, in divers places. All these are the beginning of sorrows." Christ said, As the rabbis see these signs, they will declare them to be God's judgments upon the nations for holding in bondage His chosen people. They will declare that these signs are the token of the advent of the Messiah. Be not deceived; they are the beginning of His judgments. The people have looked to themselves. They have not repented and been converted that I should heal them. The signs that they represent as tokens of their release from bondage are signs of their destruction.

"Then shall they deliver you up to be afflicted, and shall kill you: and ye shall be hated of all nations for 'My name's sake. And then shall many be offended, and shall betray one another, and shall hate one another." All this the Christians suffered. Fathers and mothers betrayed their children. Children betrayed their parents. Friends delivered their friends up to the Sanhedrin. The persecutors wrought out their purpose by killing Stephen, James, and other Christians.

Through His servants, God gave the Jewish people a last opportunity to repent. He manifested Himself through His witnesses in their arrest, in their trial, and in their imprisonment. Yet their judges pronounced on them the death sentence. They were men of whom the world was not worthy, and by killing them the Jews crucified afresh the Son of God. So it will be again. The authorities will make laws to restrict religious liberty. They will assume the right that is God's alone. They will think they can force the conscience, which God alone should control. Even now they are making a beginning; this work they will continue to carry forward till they reach a boundary over which they cannot step. God will interpose in behalf of His loyal, commandment-keeping people.

On every occasion when persecution takes place, those who witness it make decisions either for Christ or against Him. Those who manifest sympathy for the ones wrongly condemned show their attachment for Christ. Others are offended because the principles of truth cut directly across their practice. Many stumble and fall, apostatizing from the faith they once advocated. Those who apostatize in time of trial will, to secure their own safety, bear false witness, and betray their brethren. Christ has warned us of this, that we may not be surprised at the unnatural, cruel course of those who reject the light.

Christ gave His disciples a sign of the ruin to come on Jerusalem, and He told them how to escape: "When ye shall see Jerusalem compassed with armies, then know that the desolation thereof is nigh. Then let them which are in Judea flee to the mountains; and let them which are in the midst of it depart out; and let not them that are in the countries enter thereinto. For these be the days of vengeance, that all things which are written may be fulfilled." This warning was given to be heeded forty years after, at the destruction of Jerusalem. The Christians obeyed the warning, and not a Christian perished in the fall of the city.

"Pray ye that your flight be not in the winter, neither on the Sabbath day," Christ said. He who made the Sabbath did not abolish it, nailing it to His cross. The Sabbath was not rendered null and void by His death. Forty years after His crucifixion it was still to be held sacred. For forty years the disciples were to pray that their flight might not be on the Sabbath day.

From the destruction of Jerusalem, Christ passed on rapidly to the greater event, the last link in the chain of this earth's history,—the coming of the Son of God in majesty and glory. Between these two events, there lay open to Christ's view long centuries of darkness, centuries for His church marked with blood and tears and agony. Upon these scenes His disciples could not then endure to look, and Jesus passed them by with a brief mention. "Then shall be great tribulation," He said, "such as was not since the beginning of the world to this time, no, nor ever shall be. And except those days should be shortened, there should no flesh be saved: but for the elect's sake those days shall be shortened." For more than a thousand years such persecution as the world had never before known was to come upon Christ's followers. Millions upon millions of His faithful witnesses were to be slain. Had not God's hand been stretched out to preserve His people, all would have perished. "But for the elect's sake," He said, "those days shall be shortened."

Now, in unmistakable language, our Lord speaks of His second coming, and He gives warning of dangers to precede His advent to the world. "If any man shall say unto you, Lo, here is Christ, or there; believe it not. For there shall arise false christs, and false prophets, and shall show great signs and wonders; insomuch that, if it were possible, they shall deceive the very elect. Behold, I have told you before. Wherefore if they shall say unto you, Behold, He is in the desert; go not forth: behold, He is in the secret chambers; believe it not. For as the lightning cometh out of the east, and shineth even unto the west; so shall also the coming of the Son of man be." As one of the signs of Jerusalem's destruction, Christ had said, "Many false prophets shall rise, and shall deceive many." False prophets did rise, deceiving the people, and leading great numbers into the desert. Magicians and sorcerers, claiming miraculous power, drew the people after them into the mountain solitudes. But this prophecy was spoken also for the last days. This sign is given as a sign of the second advent. Even now false christs and false prophets are showing signs and wonders to seduce His disciples. Do we not hear the cry, "Behold, He is in the desert"? Have not thousands gone forth into the desert, hoping to find Christ? And from thousands of gatherings where men profess to hold communion with departed spirits is not the call now heard, "Behold, He is in the secret chambers"? This is the very claim that spiritism puts forth. But what says Christ? "Believe it not. For as the lightning cometh out of the east, and shineth even unto the west; so shall also the coming of the Son of man be."

The Saviour gives signs of His coming, and more than this, He fixes the time when the first of these signs shall appear: "Immediately after the tribulation of those days shall the sun be darkened, and the moon shall not give her light, and the stars shall fall from heaven, and the powers of the heavens shall be shaken: and then shall appear the sign of the Son of man in heaven: and then shall all the tribes of the earth mourn, and they shall see the Son of man coming in the clouds of heaven with power and great glory. And He shall send His angels with a great sound of a trumpet, and they shall gather together His elect from the four winds, from one end of heaven to the other."

At the close of the great papal persecution, Christ declared, the sun should be darkened, and the moon should not give her light. Next, the stars should fall from heaven. And He says, "Learn a parable of the fig tree; When his branch is yet tender, and putteth forth leaves, ye know that summer is nigh: so likewise ye, when ye shall see all these things, know that He is near, even at the doors." margin.

Christ has given signs of His coming. He declares that we may know when He is near, even at the doors. He says of those who see these signs, "This generation shall not pass, till all these things be fulfilled." These signs have appeared. Now we know of a surety that the Lord's coming is at hand. "Heaven and earth shall pass away," He says, "but My words shall not pass away."

Christ is coming with clouds and with great glory. A multitude of shining angels will attend Him. He will come to raise the dead, and to change the living saints from glory to glory. He will come to honor those who have

loved Him, and kept His commandments, and to take
them to Himself. He has not forgotten them nor His
promise. There will be a relinking of the family chain.
When we look upon our dead, we may think of the morning when the trump of God shall sound, when "the dead
shall be raised incorruptible, and we shall be changed."
1 Cor. 15:52. A little longer, and we shall see the King in
His beauty. A little longer, and He will wipe all tears from
our eyes. A little longer, and He will present us "faultless
before the presence of His glory with exceeding joy." Jude
24. Wherefore, when He gave the signs of His coming He
said, "When these things begin to come to pass, then look
up, and lift up your heads; for your redemption draweth
nigh."

But the day and the hour of His coming Christ has not
revealed. He stated plainly to His disciples that He Himself could not make known the day or the hour of His second appearing. Had He been at liberty to reveal this, why
need He have exhorted them to maintain an attitude of
constant expectancy? There are those who claim to know
the very day and hour of our Lord's appearing. Very earnest are they in mapping out the future. But the Lord has
warned them off the ground they occupy. The exact time
of the second coming of the Son of man is God's mystery.

Christ continues, pointing out the condition of the
world at His coming: "As the days of Noah were, so shall
also the coming of the Son of man be. For as in the days
that were before the Flood they were eating and drinking,
marrying and giving in marriage, until the day that Noah
entered into the ark, and knew not until the Flood came,
and took them all away; so shall also the coming of the
Son of man be." Christ does not here bring to view a temporal millennium, a thousand years in which all are to prepare for eternity. He tells us that as it was in Noah's day,
so will it be when the Son of man comes again.

How was it in Noah's day? "God saw that the wickedness of man was great in the earth, and that every imagination of the thoughts of his heart was only evil continually." Gen. 6:5. The inhabitants of the antediluvian world
turned from Jehovah, refusing to do His holy will. They
followed their own unholy imagination and perverted
ideas. It was because of their wickedness that they were
destroyed; and today the world is following the same way.
It presents no flattering signs of millennial glory. The
transgressors of God's law are filling the earth with wick-

edness. Their betting, their horse racing, their gambling, their dissipation, their lustful practices, their untamable passions, are fast filling the world with violence.

In the prophecy of Jerusalem's destruction Christ said, "Because iniquity shall abound, the love of many shall wax cold. But he that shall endure unto the end, the same shall be saved. And this gospel of the kingdom shall be preached in all the world for a witness unto all nations; and then shall the end come." This prophecy will again be fulfilled. The abounding iniquity of that day finds its counterpart in this generation. So with the prediction in regard to the preaching of the gospel. Before the fall of Jerusalem, Paul, writing by the Holy Spirit, declared that the gospel was preached to "every creature which is under heaven." Col. 1:23. So now, before the coming of the Son of man, the everlasting gospel is to be preached "to every nation, and kindred, and tongue, and people." Rev. 14:6, 14. God "hath appointed a day, in the which He will judge the world." Acts 17:31. Christ tells us when that day shall be ushered in. He does not say that all the world will be converted, but that "this gospel of the kingdom shall be preached in all the world for a witness unto all nations; and then shall the end come." By giving the gospel to the world it is in our power to hasten our Lord's return. We are not only to look for but to hasten the coming of the day of God. 2 Peter 3:12, margin. Had the church of Christ done her appointed work as the Lord ordained, the whole world would before this have been warned, and the Lord Jesus would have come to our earth in power and great glory.

After He had given the signs of His coming, Christ said, "When ye see these things come to pass, know ye that the kingdom of God is nigh at hand." "Take ye heed, watch and pray." God has always given men warning of coming judgments. Those who had faith in His message for their time, and who acted out their faith, in obedience to His commandments, escaped the judgments that fell upon the disobedient and unbelieving. The word came to Noah, "Come thou and all thy house into the ark; for thee have I seen righteous before Me." Noah obeyed and was saved. The message came to Lot, "Up, get you out of this place; for the Lord will destroy this city." Gen. 7:1; 19:14. Lot placed himself under the guardianship of the heavenly messengers, and was saved. So Christ's disciples were given warning of the destruction of Jerusalem. Those who watched for the sign of the coming ruin, and fled from the city, escaped the destruction. So now we are given warning of Christ's second coming and of the destruction to fall upon the world. Those who heed the warning will be saved.

Because we know not the exact time of His coming, we are commanded to watch. "Blessed are those servants, whom the Lord when He cometh shall find watching." Luke 12:37. Those who watch for the Lord's coming are not waiting in idle expectancy. The expectation of Christ's coming is to make men fear the Lord, and fear His judgments upon transgression. It is to awaken them to the great sin of rejecting His offers of mercy. Those who are watching for the Lord are purifying their souls by obedience to the truth. With vigilant watching they combine earnest working. Because they know that the Lord is at the door, their zeal is quickened to co-operate with the divine intelligences in working for the salvation of souls. These are the faithful and wise servants who give to the Lord's household "their portion of meat in due season." Luke 12:42. They are declaring the truth that is now specially applicable. As Enoch, Noah, Abraham, and Moses each declared the truth for his time, so will Christ's servants now give the special warning for their generation.

But Christ brings to view another class: "If that evil servant shall say in his heart, My lord delayeth his coming; and shall begin to smite his fellow servants, and to eat and drink with the drunken; the lord of that servant shall come in a day when he looketh not for him."

The evil servant says in his heart, "My lord delayeth his coming." He does not say that Christ will not come. He does not scoff at the idea of His second coming. But in his heart and by his actions and words he declares that the Lord's coming is delayed. He banishes from the minds of others the conviction that the Lord is coming quickly. His influence leads men to presumptuous, careless delay. They are confirmed in their worldliness and stupor. Earthly passions, corrupt thoughts, take possession of the mind. The evil servant eats and drinks with the drunken, unites with the world in pleasure seeking. He smites his fellow servants, accusing and condemning those who are faithful to their Master. He mingles with the world. Like grows with like in transgression. It is a fearful assimilation. With the world he is taken in the snare. "The lord of that servant shall come . . . in an hour that he is not aware of, and shall cut him asunder, and appoint him his portion with the hypocrites."

"If therefore thou shalt not watch, I will come on thee as a thief, and thou shalt not know what hour I will come upon thee." Rev. 3:3. The advent of Christ will surprise the false teachers. They are saying, "Peace and safety." Like the priests and teachers before the fall of Jerusalem, they look for the church to enjoy earthly prosperity and glory. The signs of the times they interpret as foreshadowing this. But what saith the word of Inspiration? "Sudden destruction cometh upon them." 1 Thess. 5:3. Upon all who dwell on the face of the whole earth, upon all who make this world their home, the day of God will come as a snare. It comes to them as a prowling thief.

The world, full of rioting, full of godless pleasure, is asleep, asleep in carnal security. Men are putting afar off the coming of the Lord. They laugh at warnings. The proud boast is made, "All things continue as they were from the beginning." "Tomorrow shall be as this day, and much more abundant." 2 Peter 3:4; Isa. 56:12. We will go deeper into pleasure loving. But Christ says, "Behold, I come as a thief." Rev. 16:15. At the very time when the world is asking in scorn, "Where is the promise of His coming?" the signs are fulfilling. While they cry, "Peace and safety," sudden destruction is coming. When the scorner, the rejecter of truth, has become presumptuous; when the routine of work in the various money-making lines is carried on without regard to principle; when the student is eagerly seeking knowledge of everything but his Bible, Christ comes as a thief.

Everything in the world is in agitation. The signs of the times are ominous. Coming events cast their shadows before. The Spirit of God is withdrawing from the earth, and calamity follows calamity by sea and by land. There are tempests, earthquakes, fires, floods, murders of every grade. Who can read the future? Where is security? There is assurance in nothing that is human or earthly. Rapidly are men ranging themselves under the banner they have chosen. Restlessly are they waiting and watching the movements of their leaders. There are those who are waiting and watching and working for our Lord's appearing. Another class are falling into line under the generalship of the first great apostate. Few believe with heart and soul that we have a hell to shun and a heaven to win.

The crisis is stealing gradually upon us. The sun shines

in the heavens, passing over its usual round, and the heavens still declare the glory of God. Men are still eating and drinking, planting and building, marrying, and giving in marriage. Merchants are still buying and selling. Men are jostling one against another, contending for the highest place. Pleasure lovers are still crowding to theaters, horse races, gambling hells. The highest excitement prevails, yet probation's hour is fast closing, and every case is about to be eternally decided. Satan sees that his time is short. He has set all his agencies at work that men may be deceived, deluded, occupied and entranced, until the day of probation shall be ended, and the door of mercy be forever shut.

Solemnly there come to us down through the centuries the warning words of our Lord from the Mount of Olives: "Take heed to yourselves, lest at any time your hearts be overcharged with surfeiting, and drunkenness, and cares of this life, and so that day come upon you unawares." "Watch ye therefore, and pray always, that ye may be accounted worthy to escape all these things that shall come to pass, and to stand before the Son of man."

Chapter 33

THE SERVANT

IN THE upper chamber of a dwelling at Jerusalem, Christ was sitting at table with His disciples. They had gathered to celebrate the Passover. The Saviour desired to keep this feast alone with the twelve. He knew that His hour was come; He Himself was the true paschal lamb, and on the day the Passover was eaten He was to be sacrificed. He was about to drink the cup of wrath; He must soon receive the final baptism of suffering. But a few quiet hours yet remained to Him, and these were to be spent for the benefit of His beloved disciples.

The whole life of Christ had been a life of unselfish service. "Not to be ministered unto, but to minister" (Matt. 20:28), had been the lesson of His every act. But not yet had the disciples learned the lesson. At this last Passover supper, Jesus repeated His teaching by an illustration that impressed it forever on their minds and hearts.

The interviews between Jesus and His disciples were usually seasons of calm joy, highly prized by them all. The Passover suppers had been scenes of special interest; but upon this occasion Jesus was troubled. His heart was burdened, and a shadow rested upon His countenance. As He met the disciples in the upper chamber, they perceived that something weighed heavily upon His mind, and although they knew not its cause, they sympathized with His grief.

As they were gathered about the table, He said in tones of touching sadness, "With desire I have desired to eat this Passover with you before I suffer: for I say unto you, I will not any more eat thereof, until it be fulfilled in the kingdom of God. And He took the cup, and gave thanks, and said, Take this, and divide it among yourselves: for I

This chapter is based on Luke 22:7-18, 24; John 13:1-17.

say unto you, I will not drink of the fruit of the vine, until the kingdom of God shall come."

Christ knew that the time had come for Him to depart out of the world, and go to His Father. And having loved His own that were in the world, He loved them unto the end. He was now in the shadow of the cross, and the pain was torturing His heart. He knew that He would be deserted in the hour of His betrayal. He knew that by the most humiliating process to which criminals were subjected He would be put to death. He knew the ingratitude and cruelty of those He had come to save. He knew how great the sacrifice that He must make, and for how many it would be in vain. Knowing all that was before Him, He might naturally have been overwhelmed with the thought of His own humiliation and suffering. But He looked upon the twelve, who had been with Him as His own, and who, after His shame and sorrow and painful usage were over, would be left to struggle in the world. His thoughts of what He Himself must suffer were ever connected with His disciples. He did not think of Himself. His care for them was uppermost in His mind.

On this last evening with His disciples, Jesus had much to tell them. If they had been prepared to receive what He longed to impart, they would have been saved from heart-breaking anguish, from disappointment and unbelief. But Jesus saw that they could not bear what He had to say. As He looked into their faces, the words of warning and comfort were stayed upon His lips. Moments passed in silence. Jesus appeared to be waiting. The disciples were ill at ease. The sympathy and tenderness awakened by Christ's grief seemed to have passed away. His sorrowful words, pointing to His own suffering, had made little impression. The glances they cast upon each other told of jealousy and contention.

There was "a strife among them, which of them should be accounted the greatest." This contention, carried on in the presence of Christ, grieved and wounded Him. The disciples clung to their favorite idea that Christ would assert His power, and take His position on the throne of David. And in heart each still longed for the highest place in the kingdom. They had placed their own estimate upon themselves and upon one another, and, instead of regarding their brethren as more worthy, they had placed themselves first. The request of James and John to sit on the right and left of Christ's throne had excited the indignation of the others. That the two brothers should presume to ask for the highest position so stirred the ten that alienation threatened. They felt that they were misjudged, that their fidelity and talents were not appreciated. Judas was the most severe upon James and John.

When the disciples entered the supper room, their hearts were full of resentful feelings. Judas pressed next to Christ on the left side; John was on the right. If there was a highest place, Judas was determined to have it, and that place was thought to be next to Christ. And Judas was a traitor.

Another cause of dissension had arisen. At a feast it was customary for a servant to wash the feet of the guests, and on this occasion preparation had been made for the service. The pitcher, the basin, and the towel were there, in readiness for the feet washing; but no servant was present, and it was the disciples' part to perform it. But each of the disciples, yielding to wounded pride, determined not to act the part of a servant. All manifested a stoical unconcern, seeming unconscious that there was anything for them to do. By their silence they refused to humble themselves.

How was Christ to bring these poor souls where Satan would not gain over them a decided victory? How could He show that a mere profession of discipleship did not make them disciples, or insure them a place in His kingdom? How could He show that it is loving service, true humility, which constitutes real greatness? How was He to kindle love in their hearts, and enable them to comprehend what He longed to tell them?

The disciples made no move toward serving one another. Jesus waited for a time to see what they would do. Then He, the divine Teacher, rose from the table. Laying aside the outer garment that would have impeded His movements, He took a towel, and girded himself. With surprised interest the disciples looked on, and in silence waited to see what was to follow. "After that He poureth water into a basin, and began to wash the disciples' feet, and to wipe them with the towel wherewith He was girded." This action opened the eyes of the disciples. Bitter shame and humiliation filled their hearts. They understood the unspoken rebuke, and saw themselves in altogether a new light.

So Christ expressed His love for His disciples. Their selfish spirit filled Him with sorrow, but He entered into no controversy with them regarding their difficulty. Instead He gave them an example they would never forget. His love for them was not easily disturbed or quenched. He knew that the Father had given all things into His hands, and that He came from God, and went to God. He had a full consciousness of His divinity; but He had laid aside His royal crown and kingly robes, and had taken the form of a servant. One of the last acts of His life on earth was to gird Himself as a servant, and perform a servant's part.

Before the Passover Judas had met a second time with the priests and scribes, and had closed the contract to deliver Jesus into their hands. Yet he afterward mingled with the disciples as though innocent of any wrong, and interested in the work of preparing for the feast. The disciples knew nothing of the purpose of Judas. Jesus alone could read his secret. Yet He did not expose him. Jesus hungered for his soul. He felt for him such a burden as for Jerusalem when He wept over the doomed city. His heart was crying, How can I give thee up? The constraining power of that love was felt by Judas. When the Saviour's hands were bathing those soiled feet, and wiping them with the towel, the heart of Judas thrilled through and through with the impulse then and there to confess his sin. But he would not humble himself. He hardened his heart against repentance; and the old impulses, for the moment put aside, again controlled him. Judas was now offended at Christ's act in washing the feet of His disciples. If Jesus could so humble Himself, he thought, He could not be Israel's king. All hope of worldly honor in a temporal kingdom was destroyed. Judas was satisfied that there was nothing to be gained by following Christ. After seeing Him degrade Himself, as he thought, he was confirmed in his purpose to disown Him, and confess himself deceived. He was possessed by a demon, and he resolved to complete the work he had agreed to do in betraying his Lord.

Judas, in choosing his position at table, had tried to place himself first, and Christ as a servant served him first. John, toward whom Judas had felt so much bitterness, was left till the last. But John did not take this as a rebuke or slight. As the disciples watched Christ's action, they were greatly moved. When Peter's turn came, he exclaimed with astonishment, "Lord, dost Thou wash my feet?" Christ's condescension broke his heart. He was filled with shame to think that one of the disciples was not performing this service. "What I do," Christ said, "thou knowest not now: but thou shalt know hereafter." Peter could not bear to see his Lord, whom he believed to be the Son of God, acting the part of a servant. His whole soul rose up against this humiliation. He did not realize that for this Christ came into the world. With great emphasis he exclaimed, "Thou shalt never wash my feet."

Solemnly Christ said to Peter, "If I wash thee not, thou hast no part with Me." The service which Peter refused was the type of a higher cleansing. Christ had come to wash the heart from the stain of sin. In refusing to allow Christ to wash his feet, Peter was refusing the higher cleansing included in the lower. He was really rejecting his Lord. It is not humiliating to the Master to allow Him to work for our purification. The truest humility is to receive with thankful heart any provision made in our behalf, and with earnestness do service for Christ.

At the words, "If I wash thee not, thou hast no part with Me," Peter surrendered his pride and self-will. He could not endure the thought of separation from Christ; that would have been death to him. "Not my feet only," he said, "but also my hands and my head. Jesus saith to him, He that is washed needeth not save to wash his feet, but is clean every whit."

These words mean more than bodily cleanliness. Christ is still speaking of the higher cleansing as illustrated by the lower. He who came from the bath was clean, but the sandaled feet soon became dusty, and again needed to be washed. So Peter and his brethren had been washed in the great fountain opened for sin and uncleanness. Christ acknowledged them as His. But temptation had led them into evil, and they still needed His cleansing grace. When Jesus girded Himself with a towel to wash the dust from their feet, He desired by that very act to wash the alienation, jealousy, and pride from their hearts. This was of far more consequence than the washing of their dusty feet. With the spirit they then had, not one of them was prepared for communion with Christ. Until brought into a state of humility and love, they were not prepared to partake of the paschal supper, or to share in the memorial service which Christ was about to institute. Their hearts must be cleansed. Pride and self-seeking create dissension and hatred, but all this Jesus washed away in washing their feet. A change of feeling was brought about. Looking upon them, Jesus could say, "Ye are clean." Now there was union of heart, love for one another. They had become humble and teachable. Except Judas, each was ready to concede to another the highest place. Now with subdued and grateful hearts they could receive Christ's words.

Like Peter and his brethren, we too have been washed in the blood of Christ, yet often through contact with evil the heart's purity is soiled. We must come to Christ for His cleansing grace. Peter shrank from bringing his soiled feet in contact with the hands of his Lord and Master; but how often we bring our sinful, polluted hearts in contact with the heart of Christ! How grievous to Him is our evil temper, our vanity and pride! Yet all our infirmity and defilement we must bring to Him. He alone can wash us clean. We are not prepared for communion with Him unless cleansed by His efficacy.

Jesus said to the disciples, "Ye are clean, but not all." He had washed the feet of Judas, but the heart had not been yielded to Him. It was not purified. Judas had not submitted himself to Christ.

After Christ had washed the disciples' feet, and had taken His garments and sat down again, He said to them, "Know ye what I have done to you? Ye call Me Master and Lord: and ye say well; for so I am. If I then, your Lord and Master, have washed your feet; ye also ought to wash one another's feet. For I have given you an example, that ye should do as I have done to you. Verily, verily, I say unto you, The servant is not greater than his lord; neither he that is sent greater than he that sent him."

Christ would have His disciples understand that although He had washed their feet, this did not in the least detract from His dignity. "Ye call Me Master and Lord: and ye say well; for so I am." And being so infinitely superior, He imparted grace and significance to the service. No one was so exalted as Christ, and yet He stooped to the humblest duty. That His people might not be misled by the selfishness which dwells in the natural heart, and which strengthens by self-serving, Christ Himself set the example of humility. He would not leave this great subject in man's charge. Of so much consequence did He regard it, that He Himself, One equal with God, acted as servant to His disciples. While they were contending for the highest place, He to whom every knee shall bow, He whom the angels of glory count it honor to serve, bowed down to wash the feet of those who called Him Lord. He washed the feet of His betrayer.

In His life and lessons, Christ has given a perfect exemplification of the unselfish ministry which has it origin in

God. God does not live for Himself. By creating the world, and by upholding all things, He is constantly ministering for others. "He maketh His sun to rise on the 'evil and on the good, and sendeth rain on the just and on²the unjust." Matt. 5:45. This ideal of ministry God has committed to His Son. Jesus was given to stand at the head of humanity, that by His example He might teach what it means to minister. His whole life was under a law of service. He served all, ministered to all. Thus He lived the law of God, and by His example showed how we are to obey it.

Again and again Jesus has tried to establish this principle among His disciples. When James and John made their request for pre-eminence, He had said, "Whosoever will be great among you, let him be your minister." Matt. 20:26. In My kingdom the principle of preference and supremacy has no place. The only greatness is the greatness of humility. The only distinction is found in devotion to the service of others.

Now, having washed the disciples' feet, He said, "I have given you an example, that ye should do as I have done to you." In these words Christ was not merely enjoining the practice of hospitality. More was meant than the washing of the feet of guests to remove the dust of travel. Christ was here instituting a religious service. By the act of our Lord this humiliating ceremony was made a consecrated ordinance. It was to be observed by the disciples, that they might ever keep in mind His lessons of humility and service.

This ordinance is Christ's appointed preparation for the sacramental service. While pride, variance, and strife for supremacy are cherished, the heart cannot enter into fellowship with Christ. We are not prepared to receive the communion of His body and His blood. Therefore it was that Jesus appointed the memorial of His humiliation to be first observed.

As they come to this ordinance, the children of God should bring to remembrance the words of the Lord of life and glory: "Know ye what I have done to you? Ye call Me Master and Lord: and ye say well; for so I am. If I then, your Lord and Master, have washed your feet; ye also ought to wash one another's feet. For I have given you an example, that ye should do as I have done to you. Verily, verily, I say unto you, The servant is not greater than his lord; neither he that is sent greater than he that sent him. If ye know these things, happy are ye if ye do them."

There is in man a disposition to esteem himself more highly than his brother, to work for self, to seek the highest place; and often this results in evil surmisings and bitterness of spirit. The ordinance preceding the Lord's Supper is to clear away these misunderstandings, to bring man out of his selfishness, down from his stilts of self-exaltation, to the humility of heart that will lead him to serve his brother.

The holy Watcher from heaven is present at this season to make it one of soul searching, of conviction of sin, and of the blessed assurance of sins forgiven. Christ in the fullness of His grace is there to change the current of the thoughts that have been running in selfish channels. The Holy Spirit quickens the sensibilities of those who follow the example of their Lord. As the Saviour's humiliation for us is remembered, thought links with thought; a chain of memories is called up, memories of God's great goodness and of the favor and tenderness of earthly friends. Blessings forgotten, mercies abused, kindnesses slighted, are called to mind. Roots of bitterness that have crowded out the precious plant of love are made manifest. Defects of character, neglect of duties, ingratitude to God, coldness toward our brethren, are called to remembrance. Sin is seen in the light in which God views it. Our thoughts are not thoughts of self-complacency, but of severe self-censure and humiliation. The mind is energized to break down every barrier that has caused alienation. Evil thinking and evil speaking are put away. Sins are confessed, they are forgiven. The subduing grace of Christ comes into the soul, and the love of Christ draws hearts together in a blessed unity.

As the lesson of the preparatory service is thus learned, the desire is kindled for a higher spiritual life. To this desire the divine Witness will respond. The soul will be uplifted. We can partake of the Communion with a consciousness of sins forgiven. The sunshine of Christ's righteousness will fill the chambers of the mind and the soul temple. We "behold the Lamb of God, which taketh away the sin of the world." John 1:29.

To those who receive the spirit of this service, it can never become a mere ceremonial. Its constant lesson will be, "By love serve one another." Gal. 5:13. In washing the feet of His disciples, Christ gave evidence that He would do any service, however humble, that would make them heirs with Him of the eternal wealth of heaven's treasure. His disciples, in performing the same rite, pledge themselves in like manner to serve their brethren. Whenever this ordinance is rightly celebrated, the children of God are brought into a holy relationship, to help and bless each other. They covenant that the life shall be given to unselfish ministry. And this, not only for one another. Their field of labor is as wide as their Master's was. The world is full of those who need our ministry. The poor, the helpless, the ignorant, are on every hand. Those who have communed with Christ in the upper chamber will go forth to minister as He did.

Jesus, the served of all, came to be the servant of all. And because He ministered to all, He will again be served and honored by all. And those who would partake of His divine attributes, and share with Him the joy of seeing souls redeemed, must follow His example of unselfish ministry.

All this was comprehended in the words of Jesus, "I have given you an example, that ye should do as I have done to you." This was the intent of the service He established. And He says, "If ye know these things," if you know the purpose of His lessons, "happy are ye if ye do them."

Chapter 34

"DO NOT FORGET"

"THE LORD Jesus the same night in which He was betrayed took bread: and when He had given thanks, He brake it, and said, Take, eat: this is My body, which is broken for you: this do in remembrance of Me. After the same manner also He took the cup, when He had supped, saying, This cup is the new testament in My blood: this do ye, as oft as ye drink it, in remembrance of Me. For as often as ye eat this bread, and drink this cup, ye do show the Lord's death till He come." 1 Cor. 11:23-26.

Christ was standing at the point of transition between two economies and their two great festivals. He, the spotless Lamb of God, was about to present Himself as a sin offering, that He would thus bring to an end the system of types and ceremonies that for four thousand years had pointed to His death. As He ate the Passover with His disciples, He instituted in its place the service that was to be the memorial of His great sacrifice. The national festival of the Jews was to pass away forever. The service which Christ established was to be observed by His followers in all lands and through all ages.

The Passover was ordained as a commemoration of the deliverance of Israel from Egyptian bondage. God had directed that, year by year, as the children should ask the meaning of this ordinance, the history should be repeated. Thus the wonderful deliverance was to be kept fresh in the minds of all. The ordinance of the Lord's Supper was given to commemorate the great deliverance wrought out as the result of the death of Christ. Till He shall come the second time in power and glory, this ordinance is to be

This chapter is based on Matt. 26:20-29; Mark 14:17-25; Luke 22:14-23; John 13:18-30.

celebrated. It is the means by which His great work for us is to be kept fresh in our minds.

At the time of their deliverance from Egypt, the children of Israel ate the Passover supper standing, with their loins girded, and with their staves in their hands, ready for their journey. The manner in which they celebrated this ordinance harmonized with their condition; for they were about to be thrust out of the land of Egypt, and were to begin a painful and difficult journey through the wilderness. But in Christ's time the condition of things had changed. They were not now about to be thrust out of a strange country, but were dwellers in their own land. In harmony with the rest that had been given them, the people then partook of the Passover supper in a reclining position. Couches were placed about the table, and the guests lay upon them, resting upon the left arm, and having the right hand free for use in eating. In this position a guest could lay his head upon the breast of the one who sat next above him. And the feet, being at the outer edge of the couch, could be washed by one passing around the outside of the circle.

Christ is still at the table on which the paschal supper has been spread. The unleavened cakes used at the Passover season are before Him. The Passover wine, untouched by fermentation, is on the table. These emblems Christ employs to represent His own unblemished sacrifice. Nothing corrupted by fermentation, the symbol of sin and death, could represent the "Lamb without blemish and without spot." 1 Peter 1:19.

"And as they were eating, Jesus took bread, and blessed it, and brake it, and gave it to the disciples, and said, Take, eat; this is My body. And He took the cup, and gave thanks, and gave it to them, saying, Drink ye all of it; for this is My blood of the new testament, which is shed for many for the remission of sins. But I say unto you, I will not drink henceforth of this fruit of the vine, until that day when I drink it new with you in My Father's kingdom."

Judas the betrayer was present at the sacramental service. He received from Jesus the emblems of His broken body and His spilled blood. He heard the words, "This do in remembrance of Me." And sitting there in the very presence of the Lamb of God, the betrayer brooded upon his own dark purposes, and cherished his sullen, revengeful thoughts.

At the feet washing, Christ had given convincing proof that He understood the character of Judas. "Ye are not all clean" (John 13:11), He said. These words convinced the false disciple that Christ read his secret purpose. Now Christ spoke out more plainly. As they were seated at the table He said, looking upon His disciples, "I speak not of you all: I know whom I have chosen: but that the scripture may be fulfilled, He that eateth bread with Me hath lifted up his heel against Me."

Even now the disciples did not suspect Judas. But they saw that Christ appeared greatly troubled. A cloud settled over them all, a premonition of some dreadful calamity, the nature of which they did not understand. As they ate in silence, Jesus said, "Verily I say unto you, that one of you shall betray Me." At these words amazement and consternation seized them. They could not comprehend how any one of them could deal treacherously with their divine Teacher. For what cause could they betray Him? and to whom? Whose heart could give birth to such a design? Surely not one of the favored twelve, who had been privileged above all others to hear His teachings, who had shared His wonderful love, and for whom He had shown such great regard by bringing them into close communion with Himself!

As they realized the import of His words, and remembered how true His sayings were, fear and self-distrust seized them. They began to search their own hearts to see if one thought against their Master were harbored there. With the most painful emotion, one after another inquired, "Lord, is it I?" But Judas sat silent. John in deep distress at last inquired, "Lord, who is it?" And Jesus answered, "He that dippeth his hand with Me in the dish, the same shall betray Me. The Son of man goeth as it is written of Him: but woe unto that man by whom the Son of man is betrayed! it had been good for that man if he had not been born." The disciples had searched one another's faces closely as they asked, "Lord, is it I?" And now the silence of Judas drew all eyes to him. Amid the confusion of questions and expressions of astonishment, Judas had not heard the words of Jesus in answer to John's question. But now, to escape the scrutiny of the disciples, he asked as they had done, "Master, is it I?" Jesus solemnly replied, "Thou hast said."

In surprise and confusion at the exposure of his purpose, Judas rose hastily to leave the room. "Then said

Jesus unto him, That thou doest, do quickly. . . . He then having received the sop went immediately out: and it was night." Night it was to the traitor as he turned away from Christ into the outer darkness.

Until this step was taken, Judas had not passed beyond the possibility of repentance. But when he left the presence of his Lord and his fellow disciples, the final decision had been made. He had passed the boundary line.

Wonderful had been the long-suffering of Jesus in His dealing with this tempted soul. Nothing that could be done to save Judas had been left undone. After he had twice covenanted to betray his Lord, Jesus still gave him opportunity for repentance. By reading the secret purpose of the traitor's heart, Christ gave to Judas the final, convincing evidence of His divinity. This was to the false disciple that last call to repentance. No appeal that the divine-human heart of Christ could make had been spared. The waves of mercy, beaten back by stubborn pride, returned in a stronger tide of subduing love. But although surprised and alarmed at the discovery of his guilt, Judas became only the more determined. From the sacramental supper he went out to complete the work of betrayal.

In pronouncing the woe upon Judas, Christ also had a purpose of mercy toward His disciples. He thus gave them the crowning evidence of His Messiahship. "I tell you before it come," He said, that, when it is come to pass, ye may believe that I AM." Had Jesus remained silent, in apparent ignorance of what was to come upon Him, the disciples might have thought that their Master had not divine foresight, and had been surprised and betrayed into the hands of the murderous mob. A year before, Jesus had told the disciples that He had chosen twelve, and that one was a devil. Now His words to Judas, showing that his treachery was fully known to his Master, would strengthen the faith of Christ's true followers during His humiliation. And when Judas should have come to his dreadful end, they would remember the woe that Jesus had pronounced upon the betrayer.

And the Saviour had still another purpose. He had not withheld His ministry from him whom He knew to be a traitor. The disciples did not understand His words when He said at the feet washing, "Ye are not all clean," nor yet when at the table He declared, "He that eateth bread with Me hath lifted up his heel against Me." John 13:11, 18. But afterward, when His meaning was made plain, they had something to consider as to the patience and mercy of God toward the most grievously erring.

Though Jesus knew Judas from the beginning, He washed his feet. And the betrayer was privileged to unite with Christ in partaking of the sacrament. A long-suffering Saviour held out every inducement for the sinner to receive Him, to repent, and to be cleansed from the defilement of sin. This example is for us. When we suppose one to be in error and sin, we are not to divorce ourselves from him. By no careless separation are we to leave him a prey to temptation, or drive him upon Satan's battleground. This is not Christ's method. It was because the disciples were erring and faulty that He washed their feet, and all but one of the twelve were thus brought to repentance.

Christ's example forbids exclusiveness at the Lord's Supper. It is true that open sin excludes the guilty. This the Holy Spirit plainly teaches. 1 Cor. 5:11. But beyond this none are to pass judgment. God has not left it with men to say who shall present themselves on these occasions. For who can read the heart? Who can distinguish the tares from the wheat? "Let a man examine himself, and so let him eat of that bread, and drink of that cup." For "whosoever shall eat this bread, and drink this cup of the Lord, unworthily, shall be guilty of the body and blood of the Lord." "He that eateth and drinketh unworthily, eateth and drinketh damnation to himself, not discerning the Lord's body." 1 Cor. 11:28, 27, 29.

When believers assemble to celebrate the ordinances, there are present messengers unseen by human eyes. There may be a Judas in the company, and if so, messengers from the prince of darkness are there, for they attend all who refuse to be controlled by the Holy Spirit. Heavenly angels also are present. These unseen visitants are present on every such occasion. There may come into the company persons who are not in heart servants of truth and holiness, but who may wish to take part in the service. They should not be forbidden. There are witnesses present who were present when Jesus washed the feet of the disciples and of Judas. More than human eyes beheld the scene.

Christ by the Holy Spirit is there to set the seal to His own ordinance. He is there to convict and soften the heart. Not a look, not a thought of contrition, escapes His notice. For the repentant, brokenhearted one He is waiting. All things are ready for that soul's reception. He who washed the feet of Judas longs to wash every heart from the stain of sin.

None should exclude themselves from the Communion because some who are unworthy may be present. Every disciple is called upon to participate publicly, and thus bear witness that he accepts Christ as a personal Saviour. It is at these, His own appointments, that Christ meets His people, and energizes them by His presence. Hearts and hands that are unworthy may even administer the ordinance, yet Christ is there to minister to His children. All who come with their faith fixed upon Him will be greatly blessed. All who neglect these seasons of divine privilege will suffer loss. Of them it may appropriately be said, "Ye are not all clean."

In partaking with His disciples of the bread and wine, Christ pledged Himself to them as their Redeemer. He committed to them the new covenant, by which all who receive Him become children of God, and joint heirs with Christ. By this covenant every blessing that heaven could bestow for this life and the life to come was theirs. This covenant deed was to be ratified with the blood of Christ. And the administration of the Sacrament was to keep before the disciples the infinite sacrifice made for each of them individually as a part of the great whole of fallen humanity.

But the Communion service was not to be a season of sorrowing. This was not its purpose. As the Lord's disciples gather about His table, they are not to remember and lament their shortcomings. They are not to dwell upon their past religious experience, whether that experience has been elevating or depressing. They are not to recall the differences between them and their brethren. The preparatory service has embraced all this. The self-examination, the confession of sin, the reconciling of differences, has all been done. Now they come to meet with Christ. They are not to stand in the shadow of the cross, but in its saving light. They are to open the soul to the bright beams of the Sun of Righteousness. With hearts cleansed by Christ's most precious blood, in full consciousness of His presence, although unseen, they are to hear His words, "Peace I leave with you, My peace I give unto you: not as the world giveth, give I unto you." John 14:27.

Our Lord says, Under conviction of sin, remember that I died for you. When oppressed and persecuted and afflicted for My sake and the gospel's, remember My love, so great that for you I gave My life. When your duties appear stern and severe, and your burdens too heavy to bear, remember that for your sake I endured the cross, despising the shame. When your heart shrinks from the trying ordeal, remember that your Redeemer liveth to make intercession for you.

The Communion service points to Christ's second coming. It was designed to keep this hope vivid in the minds of the disciples. Whenever they met together to commemorate His death, they recounted how "He took the cup, and gave thanks, and gave it to them, saying, Drink ye all of it; for this is My blood of the new testament, which is shed for many for the remission of sins. But I say unto you, I will not drink henceforth of this fruit of the vine, until that day when I drink it new with you in My Father's kingdom." In their tribulation they found comfort in the hope of their Lord's return. Unspeakably precious to them was the thought, "As often as ye eat this bread, and drink this cup, ye do show the Lord's death till He come." 1 Cor. 11:26.

These are the things we are never to forget. The love of Jesus, with its constraining power, is to be kept fresh in our memory. Christ has instituted this service that it may speak to our senses of the love of God that has been expressed in our behalf. There can be no union between our souls and God except through Christ. The union and love between brother and brother must be cemented and rendered eternal by the love of Jesus. And nothing less than the death of Christ could make His love efficacious for us. It is only because of His death that we can look with joy to His second coming. His sacrifice is the center of our hope. Upon this we must fix our faith.

The ordinances that point to our Lord's humiliation and suffering are regarded too much as a form. They were instituted for a purpose. Our senses need to be quickened to lay hold of the mystery of godliness. It is the privilege of all to comprehend, far more than we do, the expiatory sufferings of Christ. "As Moses lifted up the serpent in the wilderness," even so has the Son of man been lifted up, "that whosoever believeth in Him should not perish, but have eternal life." John 3:14, 15. To the cross of Calvary, bearing a dying Saviour, we must look. Our eternal interests demand that we show faith in Christ.

Our Lord has said, "Except ye eat the flesh of the Son

of man, and drink His blood, ye have no life in you. . . .
For My flesh is meat indeed, and My blood is drink indeed." John 6:53-55. This is true of our physical nature.
To the death of Christ we owe even this earthly life. The
bread we eat is the purchase of His broken body. The
water we drink is bought by His spilled blood. Never one,
saint or sinner, eats his daily food, but he is nourished by
the body and the blood of Christ. The cross of Calvary is
stamped on every loaf. It is reflected in every water spring.
All this Christ has taught in appointing the emblems of
His great sacrifice. The light shining from that Communion service in the upper chamber makes sacred the provisions for our daily life. The family board becomes as the
table of the Lord, and every meal a sacrament.

And how much more are Christ's words true of our
spiritual nature. He declares, "Whoso eateth My flesh, and
drinketh My blood, hath eternal life." It is by receiving the
life for us poured out on Calvary's cross, that we can live
the life of holiness. And this life we receive by receiving
His word, by doing those things which He has commanded. Thus we become one with Him. "He that eateth My
flesh," He says, "and drinketh My blood, dwelleth in Me,
and I in him. As the living Father hath sent Me, and I live
by the Father: so he that eateth Me, even he shall live by
Me." John 6:54, 56, 57. To the holy Communion this
scripture in a special sense applies. As faith contemplates
our Lord's great sacrifice, the soul assimilates the spiritual
life of Christ. That soul will receive spiritual strength from
every Communion. The service forms a living connection
by which the believer is bound up with Christ, and thus
bound up with the Father. In a special sense it forms a
connection between dependent human beings and God.

As we receive the bread and wine symbolizing Christ's
broken body and spilled blood, we in imagination join in
the scene of Communion in the upper chamber. We seem
to be passing through the garden consecrated by the agony
of Him who bore the sins of the world. We witness the
struggle by which our reconciliation with God was obtained. Christ is set forth crucified among us.

Looking upon the crucified Redeemer, we more fully
comprehend the magnitude and meaning of the sacrifice
made by the Majesty of heaven. The plan of salvation is
glorified before us, and the thought of Calvary awakens
living and sacred emotions in our hearts. Praise to God
and the Lamb will be in our hearts and on our lips; for

pride and self-worship cannot flourish in the soul that keeps fresh in memory the scenes of Calvary.

He who beholds the Saviour's matchless love will be elevated in thought, purified in heart, transformed in character. He will go forth to be a light to the world, to reflect in some degree this mysterious love. The more we contemplate the cross of Christ, the more fully shall we adopt the language of the apostle when he said, "God forbid that I should glory, save in the cross of our Lord Jesus Christ, by whom the world is crucified unto me, and I unto the world." Gal. 6:14.

Chapter 35

NO OTHER WAY

Looking upon His disciples with divine love and with the tenderest sympathy, Christ said, "Now is the Son of man glorified, and God is glorified in Him." Judas had left the upper chamber, and Christ was alone with the eleven. He was about to speak of His approaching separation from them; but before doing this He pointed to the great object of His mission. It was this that He kept ever before Him. It was His joy that all His humiliation and suffering would glorify the Father's name. To this He first directs the thoughts of His disciples.

Then addressing them by the endearing term, "Little children," He said, "yet a little while I am with you. Ye shall seek Me: and as I said unto the Jews, Whither I go, ye cannot come; so now I say to you."

The disciples could not rejoice when they heard this. Fear fell upon them. They pressed close about the Saviour. Their Master and Lord, their beloved Teacher and Friend, He was dearer to them than life. To Him they had looked for help in all their difficulties, for comfort in their sorrows and disappointments. Now He was to leave them, a lonely, dependent company. Dark were the forebodings that filled their hearts.

But the Saviour's words to them were full of hope. He knew that they were to be assailed by the enemy, and that Satan's craft is most successful against those who are depressed by difficulties. Therefore He pointed them away from "the things which are seen," to "the things which are not seen." 2 Cor. 4:18. From earthly exile He turned their thoughts to the heavenly home.

"Let not your heart be troubled," He said; "ye believe in God, believe also in Me. In My Father's house are many

This chapter is based on John 13:31-38; 14-17.

278

mansions: if it were not so, I would have told you. I go to prepare a place for you. And if I go and prepare a place for you, I will come again, and receive you unto Myself; that where I am, there ye may be also. And whither I go ye know, and the way ye know." For your sake I came into the world. I am working in your behalf. When I go away, I shall still work earnestly for you. I came into the world to reveal Myself to you, that you might believe. I go to the Father to co-operate with Him in your behalf. The object of Christ's departure was the opposite of what the disciples feared. It did not mean a final separation. He was going to prepare a place for them, that He might come again, and receive them unto Himself. While He was building mansions for them, they were to build characters after the divine similitude.

Still the disciples were perplexed. Thomas, always troubled by doubts, said, "Lord, we know not whither Thou goest; and how can we know the way? Jesus saith unto him, I am the way, the truth, and the life: no man cometh unto the Father, but by Me. If ye had known Me, ye should have known My Father also: and from henceforth ye know Him, and have seen Him."

There are not many ways to heaven. Each one may not choose his own way. Christ says, "I am the way: . . . no man cometh unto the Father, but by Me." Since the first gospel sermon was preached, when in Eden it was declared that the seed of the woman should bruise the serpent's head, Christ had been uplifted as the way, the truth, and the life. He was the way when Adam lived, when Abel presented to God the blood of the slain lamb, representing the blood of the Redeemer. Christ was the way by which patriarchs and prophets were saved. He is the way by which alone we can have access to God.

"If ye had known Me," Christ said, "ye should have known My Father also: and from henceforth ye know Him, and have seen Him." But not yet did the disciples understand. "Lord, show us the Father," exclaimed Philip, "and it sufficeth us."

Amazed at his dullness of comprehension, Christ asked with pained surprise, "Have I been so long time with you, and yet hast thou not known Me, Philip?" Is it possible that you do not see the Father in the works He does through Me? Do you not believe that I came to testify of the Father? "How sayest thou then, Show us the Father?" "He that hath seen Me hath seen the Father." Christ had not ceased to be God when He became man. Though He had humbled Himself to humanity, the Godhead was still His own. Christ alone could represent the Father to humanity, and this representation the disciples had been privileged to behold for over three years.

"Believe Me that I am in the Father, and the Father in Me: or else believe Me for the very works' sake." Their faith might safely rest on the evidence given in Christ's works, works that no man, of himself, ever had done, or ever could do. Christ's work testified to His divinity. Through Him the Father had been revealed.

If the disciples believed this vital connection between the Father and the Son, their faith would not forsake them when they saw Christ's suffering and death to save a perishing world. Christ was seeking to lead them from their low condition of faith to the experience they might receive if they truly realized what He was—God in human flesh. He desired them to see that their faith must lead up to God, and be anchored there. How earnestly and perseveringly our compassionate Saviour sought to prepare His disciples for the storm of temptation that was soon to beat upon them. He would have them hid with Him in God.

As Christ was speaking these words, the glory of God was shining from His countenance, and all present felt a sacred awe as they listened with rapt attention to His words. Their hearts were more decidedly drawn to Him; and as they were drawn to Christ in greater love, they were drawn to one another. They felt that heaven was very near, and that the words to which they listened were a message to them from their heavenly Father.

"Verily, verily, I say unto you," Christ continued, "He that believeth on Me, the works that I do shall he do also." The Saviour was deeply anxious for His disciples to understand for what purpose His divinity was united to humanity. He came to the world to display the glory of God, that man might be uplifted by its restoring power. God was manifested in Him that He might be manifested in them. Jesus revealed no qualities, and exercised no powers, that men may not have through faith in Him. His perfect humanity is that which all His followers may possess, if they will be in subjection to God as He was.

"And greater works than these shall he do; because I go unto My Father." By this Christ did not mean that the disciples' work would be of a more exalted character than His, but that it would have greater extent. He did not refer merely to miracle working, but to all that would take place under the working of the Holy Spirit.

After the Lord's ascension, the disciples realized the fulfillment of His promise. The scenes of the crucifixion, resurrection, and ascension of Christ were a living reality to them. They saw that the prophecies had been literally fulfilled. They searched the Scriptures, and accepted their teaching with a faith and assurance unknown before. They knew that the divine Teacher was all that He had claimed to be. As they told their experience, and exalted the love of God, men's hearts were melted and subdued, and multitudes believed on Jesus.

The Saviour's promise to His disciples is a promise to His church to the end of time. God did not design that His wonderful plan to redeem men should achieve only insignificant results. All who will go to work, trusting not in what they themselves can do, but in what God can do for and through them, will certainly realize the fulfillment of His promise. "Greater works than these shall he do," He declares; "because I go unto My Father."

As yet the disciples were unacquainted with the Saviour's unlimited resources and power. He said to them, "Hitherto have ye asked nothing in My name." John 16:24. He explained that the secret of their success would be in asking for strength and grace in His name. He would be present before the Father to make request for them. The prayer of the humble suppliant He presents as His own desire in that soul's behalf. Every sincere prayer is heard in heaven. It may not be fluently expressed; but if the heart is in it, it will ascend to the sanctuary where Jesus ministers, and He will present it to the Father without one awkward, stammering word, beautiful and fragrant with the incense of His own perfection.

The path of sincerity and integrity is not a path free from obstruction, but in every difficulty we are to see a call to prayer. There is no one living who has any power that he has not received from God, and the source whence it comes is open to the weakest human being. "Whatsoever ye shall ask in My name," said Jesus, "that will I do, that the Father may be glorified in the Son. If ye shall ask anything in My name, I will do it."

"In My name," Christ bade His disciples pray. In Christ's name His followers are to stand before God. Through the value of the sacrifice made for them, they are of value in the Lord's sight. Because of the imputed righteousness of Christ they are accounted precious. For Christ's sake the Lord pardons those that fear Him. He does not see in them the vileness of the sinner. He recognizes in them the likeness of His Son, in whom they believe.

The Lord is disappointed when His people place a low estimate upon themselves. He desires His chosen heritage to value themselves according to the price He has placed upon them. God wanted them, else He would not have sent His Son on such an expensive errand to redeem them. He has a use for them, and He is well pleased when they make the very highest demands upon Him, that they may glorify His name. They may expect large things if they have faith in His promises.

But to pray in Christ's name means much. It means that we are to accept His character, manifest His spirit, and work His works. The Saviour's promise is given on condition. "If ye love Me," He says, "keep My commandments." He saves men, not in sin, but from sin; and those who love Him will show their love by obedience.

All true obedience comes from the heart. It was heart work with Christ. And if we consent, He will so identify Himself with our thoughts and aims, so blend our hearts and minds into conformity to His will, that when obeying Him we shall be but carrying out our own impulses. The will, refined and santified, will find its highest delight in doing His service. When we know God as it is our privilege to know Him, our life will be a life of continual obedience. Through an appreciation of the character of Christ, through communion with God, sin will become hateful to us.

As Christ lived the law in humanity, so we may do if we will take hold of the Strong for strength. But we are not to place the responsibility of our duty upon others, and wait for them to tell us what to do. We cannot depend for counsel upon humanity. The Lord will teach us our duty just as willingly as He will teach somebody else. If we come to Him in faith, He will speak His mysteries to us personally. Our hearts will often burn within us as One draws nigh to commune with us as He did with Enoch. Those who decide to do nothing in any line that will displease God, will know, after presenting their case before Him, just what course to pursue. And they will receive not only wisdom, but strength. Power for obedience, for service, will be imparted to them, as Christ has promised.

Whatever was given to Christ—the "all things" to supply the need of fallen men—was given to Him as the head and representative of humanity. And "whatsoever we ask, we receive of Him, because we keep His commandments, and do those things that are pleasing in His sight." 1 John 3:22.

Before offering Himself as the sacrificial victim, Christ sought for the most essential and complete gift to bestow upon His followers, a gift that would bring within their reach the boundless resources of grace. "I will pray the Father," He said, "and He shall give you another Comforter, that He may abide with you forever; even the Spirit of truth; whom the world cannot receive, because it seeth Him not, neither knoweth Him: but ye know Him; for He dwelleth with you, and shall be in you. I will not leave you orphans: I will come to you." margin.

Before this the Spirit had been in the world; from the very beginning of the work of redemption He had been moving upon men's hearts. But while Christ was on earth, the disciples had desired no other helper. Not until they were deprived of His presence would they feel their need of the Spirit, and then He would come.

The Holy Spirit is Christ's representative, but divested of the personality of humanity, and independent thereof. Cumbered with humanity, Christ could not be in every place personally. Therefore it was for their interest that He should go to the Father, and send the Spirit to be His successor on earth. No one could then have any advantage because of his location or his personal contact with Christ. By the Spirit the Saviour would be accessible to all. In this sense He would be nearer to them than if He had not ascended on high.

"He that loveth Me shall be loved of My Father, and I will love him, and will manifest Myself to him." Jesus read the future of His disciples. He saw one brought to the scaffold, one to the cross, one to exile among the lonely rocks of the sea, others to persecution and death. He encouraged them with the promise that in every trial He would be with them. That promise has lost none of its force. The Lord knows all about His faithful servants who for His sake are lying in prison or who are banished to lonely islands. He comforts them with His own presence. When for the truth's sake the believer stands at the bar of unrighteous tribunals, Christ stands by his side. All the reproaches that fall upon him, fall upon Christ. Christ is condemned over again in the person of His disciple. When one is incarcerated in prison walls, Christ ravishes the heart with His love. When one suffers death for His sake, Christ says, "I am He that liveth, and was dead; and, behold, I am alive forevermore, . . . and have the keys of hell and of death." Rev. 1:18. The life that is sacrificed for Me is preserved unto eternal glory.

At all times and in all places, in all sorrows and in all afflictions, when the outlook seems dark and the future perplexing, and we feel helpless and alone, the Comforter will be sent in answer to the prayer of faith. Circumstances may separate us from every earthly friend; but no circumstance, no distance, can separate us from the heavenly Comforter. Wherever we are, wherever we may go, He is always at our right hand to support, sustain, uphold, and cheer.

The disciples still failed to understand Christ's words in their spiritual sense, and again He explained His meaning. By the Spirit, He said, He would manifest Himself to them. "The Comforter, which is the Holy Ghost, whom the Father will send in My name, He shall teach you all things." No more will you say, I cannot comprehend. No longer will you see through a glass, darkly. You shall "be able to comprehend with all saints what is the breadth, and length, and depth, and height; and to know the love of Christ, which passeth knowledge." Eph. 3:18, 19.

The disciples were to bear witness to the life and work of Christ. Through their word He was to speak to all the people on the face of the earth. But in the humiliation and death of Christ they were to suffer great trial and disappointment. That after this experience their word might be accurate, Jesus promised that the Comforter should "bring all things to your remembrance, whatsoever I have said unto you."

"I have yet many things to say unto you," He continued, "but ye cannot bear them now. Howbeit when He, the Spirit of truth, is come, He will guide you into all truth: for He shall not speak of Himself; but whatsoever He shall hear, that shall He speak: and He will show you things to come. He shall glorify Me: for He shall receive of Mine, and shall show it unto you." Jesus had opened before His disciples a vast tract of truth. But it was most difficult for them to keep His lessons distinct from the traditions and maxims of the scribes and Pharisees. They had been educated to accept the teaching of the rabbis as the voice of God, and it still held a power over their minds, and molded their sentiments. Earthly ideas, temporal things, still had a large place in their thoughts. They did not understand the spiritual nature of Christ's kingdom, though He had so often explained it to them. Their minds had become confused. They did not comprehend the value of the scriptures Christ presented. Many of His lessons seemed almost lost upon them. Jesus saw that they did not lay hold of the real meaning of His words. He compassionately promised that the Holy Spirit should recall these sayings to their minds. And He had left unsaid many things that could not be comprehended by the disciples. These also would be opened to them by the Spirit. The Spirit was to quicken their understanding, that they might have an appreciation of heavenly things. "When He, the Spirit of truth, is come," said Jesus, "He will guide you into all truth."

The Comforter is called "the Spirit of truth." His work is to define and maintain the truth. He first dwells in the heart as the Spirit of truth, and thus He becomes the Comforter. There is comfort and peace in the truth, but no real peace or comfort can be found in falsehood. It is through false theories and traditions that Satan gains his power over the mind. By directing men to false standards, he misshapes the character. Through the Scriptures the Holy Spirit speaks to the mind, and impresses truth upon the heart. Thus He exposes error, and expels it from the soul. It is by the Spirit of truth, working through the word of God, that Christ subdues His chosen people to Himself.

In describing to His disciples the office work of the Holy Spirit, Jesus sought to inspire them with the joy and hope that inspired His own heart. He rejoiced because of the abundant help He had provided for His church. The Holy Spirit was the highest of all gifts that He could solicit from His Father for the exaltation of His people. The Spirit was to be given as a regenerating agent, and without this the sacrifice of Christ would have been of no avail. The power of evil had been strengthening for centuries, and the submission of men to this satanic captivity was amazing. Sin could be resisted and overcome only through the mighty agency of the Third Person of the Godhead, who would come with no modified energy, but in the fullness of divine power. It is the Spirit that makes effectual what has been wrought out by the world's Redeemer. It is by the Spirit that the heart is made pure. Through the Spirit the believer becomes a partaker of the divine nature. Christ has given His Spirit as a divine power to overcome all hereditary and cultivated tendencies to evil, and to impress His own character upon His church.

Of the Spirit Jesus said, "He shall glorify Me." The Saviour came to glorify the Father by the demonstration of His love; so the Spirit was to glorify Christ by revealing His grace to the world. The very image of God is to be reproduced in humanity. The honor of God, the honor of Christ, is involved in the perfection of the character of His people.

"When He [the Spirit of truth] is come, He will reprove the world of sin, and of righteousness, and of judgment." The preaching of the word will be of no avail without the continual presence and aid of the Holy Spirit. This is the only effectual teacher of divine truth. Only when the truth is accompanied to the heart by the Spirit will it quicken the conscience or transform the life. One might be able to present the letter of the word of God, he might be familiar with all its commands and promises; but unless the Holy Spirit sets home the truth, no souls will fall on the Rock and be broken. No amount of education, no advantages, however great, can make one a channel of light without the co-operation of the Spirit of God. The sowing of the gospel seed will not be a success unless the seed is quickened into life by the dew of heaven. Before one book of the New Testament was written, before one gospel sermon had been preached after Christ's ascension, the Holy Spirit came upon the praying apostles. Then the testimony of their enemies was, "Ye have filled Jerusalem with your doctrine." Acts 5:28.

Christ has promised the gift of the Holy Spirit to His church, and the promise belongs to us as much as to the first disciples. But like every other promise, it is given on conditions. There are many who believe and profess to claim the Lord's promise; they talk *about* Christ and *about* the Holy Spirit, yet receive no benefit. They do not surrender the soul to be guided and controlled by the divine agencies. We cannot use the Holy Spirit. The Spirit is to use us. Through the Spirit God works in His people "to will and to do of His good pleasure." Phil. 2:13. But many will not submit to this. They want to manage themselves. This is why they do not not receive the heavenly gift. Only to those who wait humbly upon God, who watch for His guidance and grace, is the Spirit given. The power of God awaits their demand and reception. This promised blessing, claimed by faith, brings all other blessings in its train. It is given according to the riches of the grace of Christ, and He is ready to supply every soul according to the capacity to receive.

In His discourse to the disciples, Jesus made no mournful allusion to His own sufferings and death. His last legacy to them was a legacy of peace. He said, "Peace I leave with you, My peace I give unto you: not as the world giveth, give I unto you. Let not your heart be troubled, neither let it be afraid."

Before leaving the upper chamber, the Saviour led His disciples in a song of praise. His voice was heard, not in the strains of some mournful lament, but in the joyful notes of the Passover hallel:

> "O praise the Lord, all ye nations:
> Praise Him, all ye people.
> For His merciful kindness is great toward us.
> And the truth of the Lord endureth forever.
> Praise ye the Lord." Psalm 117.

After the hymn, they went out. Through the crowded streets they made their way, passing out of the city gate toward the Mount of Olives. Slowly they proceeded, each busy with his own thoughts. As they began to descend toward the mount, Jesus said, in a tone of deepest sadness, "All ye shall be offended because of Me this night: for it is written, I will smite the shepherd, and the sheep of the flock shall be scattered abroad." Matt. 26:31. The disciples listened in sorrow and amazement. They remembered how in the synagogue at Capernaum, when Christ spoke of Himself as the bread of life, many had been offended, and had turned away from Him. But the twelve had not shown themselves unfaithful. Peter, speaking for his brethren, had then declared his loyalty to Christ. Then the Saviour had said, "Have not I chosen you twelve, and one of you is a devil?" John 6:70. In the upper chamber Jesus said that one of the twelve would betray Him, and that Peter would deny Him. But now His words include them all.

Now Peter's voice is heard vehemently protesting, "Although all shall be offended, yet will not I." In the upper chamber he had declared, "I will lay down my life for Thy sake." Jesus had warned him that he would that very night deny his Saviour. Now Christ repeats the warning: "Verily

I say unto thee, That this day, even in this night, before the cock crow twice, thou shalt deny Me thrice." But Peter only "spake the more vehemently, If I should die with Thee, I will not deny Thee in anywise. Likewise also said they all." Mark 14:29, 30, 31. In their self-confidence they denied the repeated statement of Him who knew. They were unprepared for the test; when temptation should overtake them, they would understand their own weakness.

When Peter said he would follow his Lord to prison and to death, he meant it, every word of it; but he did not know himself. Hidden in his heart were elements of evil that circumstances would fan into life. Unless he was made conscious of his danger, these would prove his eternal ruin. The Saviour saw in him a self-love and assurance that would overbear even his love for Christ. Much of infirmity, of unmortified sin, carelessness of spirit, unsanctified temper, heedlessness in entering into temptation, had been revealed in his experience. Christ's solemn warning was a call to heart searching. Peter needed to distrust himself, and to have a deeper faith in Christ. Had he in humility received the warning, he would have appealed to the Shepherd of the flock to keep His sheep. When on the Sea of Galilee he was about to sink, he cried, "Lord, save me." Matt. 14:30. Then the hand of Christ was outstretched to grasp his hand. So now if he had cried to Jesus, Save me from myself, he would have been kept. But Peter felt that he was distrusted, and he thought it cruel. He was already offended, and he became more persistent in his self-confidence.

Jesus looks with compassion on His disciples. He cannot save them from the trial, but He does not leave them comfortless. He assures them that He is to break the fetters of the tomb, and that His love for them will not fail. "After I am risen again," He says, "I will go before you into Galilee." Matt. 26:32. Before the denial, they have the assurance of forgiveness. After His death and resurrection, they knew that they were forgiven, and were dear to the heart of Christ.

Jesus and the disciples were on the way to Gethsemane, at the foot of Mount Olivet, a retired spot which He had often visited for meditation and prayer. The Saviour had been explaining to His disciples His mission to the world, and the spiritual relation to Him which they were to sustain. Now He illustrates the lesson. The moon is shining bright, and reveals to Him a flourishing grapevine. Drawing the attention of the disciples to it, He employs it as a symbol.

"I am the true Vine," He says. Instead of choosing the graceful palm, the lofty cedar, or the strong oak, Jesus takes the vine with its clinging tendrils to represent Himself. The palm tree, the cedar, and the oak stand alone. They require no support. But the vine entwines about the trellis, and thus climbs heavenward. So Christ in His humanity was dependent upon divine power. "I can of Mine own self do nothing," He declared. John 5:30.

"I am the true Vine." The Jews had always regarded the vine as the most noble of plants, and a type of all that was powerful, excellent, and fruitful. Israel had been represented as a vine which God had planted in the Promised Land. The Jews based their hope of salvation on the fact of their connection with Israel. But Jesus says, I am the real Vine. Think not that through a connection with Israel you may become partakers of the life of God, and inheritors of His promise. Through Me alone is spiritual life received.

"I am the true Vine, and My Father is the husbandman." On the hills of Palestine our heavenly Father had planted this goodly Vine, and He Himself was the husbandman. Many were attracted by the beauty of this Vine, and declared its heavenly origin. But to the leaders in Israel it appeared as a root out of a dry ground. They took the plant, and bruised it, and trampled it under their unholy feet. Their thought was to destroy it forever. But the heavenly Husbandman never lost sight of His plant. After men thought they had killed it, He took it, and replanted it on the other side of the wall. The vine stock was to be no longer visible. It was hidden from the rude assaults of men. But the branches of the Vine hung over the wall. They were to represent the Vine. Through them grafts might still be united to the Vine. From them fruit has been obtained. There has been a harvest which the passers-by have plucked.

"I am the Vine, ye are the branches," Christ said to His disciples. Though He was about to be removed from them, their spiritual union with Him was to be unchanged. The connection of the branch with the vine, He said, represents the relation you are to sustain to Me. The scion is engrafted into the living vine, and fiber by fiber, vein by vein, it grows into the vine stock. The life of the vine becomes the life of the branch. So the soul dead in trespasses and sins receives life through connection with Christ. By faith in

Him as a personal Saviour the union is formed. The sinner unites his weakness to Christ's strength, his emptiness to Christ's fullness, his frailty to Christ's enduring might. Then he has the mind of Christ. The humanity of Christ has touched our humanity, and our humanity has touched divinity. Thus through the agency of the Holy Spirit man becomes a partaker of the divine nature. He is accepted in the Beloved.

This union with Christ, once formed, must be maintained. Christ said, "Abide in Me, and I in you. As the branch cannot bear fruit of itself, except it abide in the vine; no more can ye, except ye abide in Me." This is no casual touch, no off-and-on connection. The branch becomes a part of the living vine. The communication of life, strength, and fruitfulness from the root to the branches is unobstructed and constant. Separated from the vine, the branch cannot live. No more, said Jesus, can you live apart from Me. The life you have received from Me can be preserved only by continual communion. Without Me you cannot overcome one sin, or resist one temptation.

"Abide in Me, and I in you." Abiding in Christ means a constant receiving of His Spirit, a life of unreserved surrender to His service. The channel of communication must be open continually between man and his God. As the vine branch constantly draws the sap from the living vine, so are we to cling to Jesus, and receive from Him by faith the strength and perfection of His own character.

The root sends its nourishment through the branch to the outermost twig. So Christ communicates the current of spiritual strength to every believer. So long as the soul is united to Christ, there is no danger that it will wither or decay.

The life of the vine will be manifest in fragrant fruit on the branches. "He that abideth in Me," said Jesus, "and I in him, the same bringeth forth much fruit: for without Me ye can do nothing." When we live by faith on the Son of God, the fruits of the Spirit will be seen in our life; not one will be missing.

"My Father is the husbandman. Every branch in Me that beareth not fruit He taketh away." While the graft is outwardly united with the vine, there may be no vital connection. Then there will be no growth or fruitfulness. So there may be an apparent connection with Christ without a real union with Him by faith. A profession of religion places men in the church, but the character and conduct show whether they are in connection with Christ. If they bear no fruit, they are false branches. Their separation from Christ involves a ruin as complete as that represented by the dead branch. "If a man abide not in Me," said Christ, "he is cast forth as a branch, and is withered; and men gather them, and cast them into the fire, and they are burned."

"And every branch that beareth fruit, He purgeth [pruneth] it, that it may bring forth more fruit." From the chosen twelve who had followed Jesus, one as a withered branch was about to be taken away; the rest were to pass under the pruning knife of bitter trial. Jesus with solemn tenderness explained the purpose of the husbandman. The pruning will cause pain, but it is the Father who applies the knife. He works with no wanton hand or indifferent heart. There are branches trailing upon the ground; these must be cut loose from the earthly supports to which their tendrils are fastening. They are to reach heavenward, and find their support in God. The excessive foliage that draws away the life current from the fruit must be pruned off. The overgrowth must be cut out, to give room for the healing beams of the Sun of Righteousness. The husbandman prunes away the harmful growth, that the fruit may be richer and more abundant.

"Herein is My Father glorified," said Jesus, "that ye bear much fruit." God desires to manifest through you the holiness, the benevolence, the compassion, of His own character. Yet the Saviour does not bid the disciples labor to bear fruit. He tells them to abide in Him. "If ye abide in Me," He says, "and My words abide in you, ye shall ask what ye will, and it shall be done unto you." It is through the word that Christ abides in His followers. This is the same vital union that is represented by eating His flesh and drinking His blood. The words of Christ are spirit and life. Receiving them, you receive the life of the Vine. You live "by every word that proceedeth out of the mouth of God." Matt. 4:4. The life of Christ in you produces the same fruits as in Him. Living in Christ, adhering to Christ, supported by Christ, drawing nourishment from Christ, you bear fruit after the similitude of Christ.

In this last meeting with His disciples, the great desire which Christ expressed for them was that they might love one another as He had loved them. Again and again He spoke of this. "These things I command you," He said repeatedly, "that ye love one another." His very first injunction when alone with them in the upper chamber was, "A new commandment I give unto you, That ye love one another; as I have loved you, that ye also love one another." To the disciples this commandment was new; for they had not loved one another as Christ had loved them. He saw that new ideas and impulses must control them; that new principles must be practiced by them; through His life and death they were to receive a new conception of love. The command to love one another had a new meaning in the light of His self-sacrifice. The whole work of grace is one continual service of love, of self-denying, self-sacrificing effort. During every hour of Christ's sojourn upon the earth, the love of God was flowing from Him in irrepressible streams. All who are imbued with His Spirit will love as He loved. The very principle that actuated Christ will actuate them in all their dealing one with another.

This love is the evidence of their discipleship. "By this shall all men know that ye are My disciples," said Jesus, "if ye have love one to another." When men are bound together, not by force or self-interest, but by love, they show the working of an influence that is above every human influence. Where this oneness exists, it is evidence that the image of God is being restored in humanity, that a new principle of life has been implanted. It shows that there is power in the divine nature to withstand the supernatural agencies of evil, and that the grace of God subdues the selfishness inherent in the natural heart.

This love, manifested in the church, will surely stir the wrath of Satan. Christ did not mark out for His disciples an easy path. "If the world hate you," He said, "ye know that it hated Me before it hated you. If ye were of the world, the world would love his own: but because ye are not of the world, but I have chosen you out of the world, therefore the world hateth you. Remember the word that I said unto you, The servant is not greater than his lord. If they have persecuted Me, they will also persecute you; if they have kept My saying, they will keep yours also. But all these things will they do unto you for My name's sake, because they know not Him that sent Me." The gospel is to be carried forward by aggressive warfare, in the midst of opposition, peril, loss, and suffering. But those who do this work are only following in their Master's steps.

As the world's Redeemer, Christ was constantly confronted with apparent failure. He, the messenger of mercy to our world, seemed to do little of the work He longed to do in uplifting and saving. Satanic influences were constantly working to oppose His way. But He would not be discouraged. Through the prophecy of Isaiah He declares, "I have labored in vain, I have spent My strength for nought, and in vain: yet surely My judgment is with the Lord, and My work with My God. . . . Though Israel be not gathered, yet shall I be glorious in the eyes of the Lord, and My God shall be My strength." It is to Christ that the promise is given, "Thus saith the Lord, the Redeemer of Israel, and His Holy One, to Him whom man despiseth, to Him whom the nation abhorreth; . . . thus saith the Lord: . . . I will preserve Thee, and give Thee for a covenant of the people, to establish the earth, to cause to inherit the desolate heritages; that Thou mayest say to the prisoners, Go forth; to them that are in darkness, Show yourselves. . . . They shall not hunger nor thirst; neither shall the heat nor sun smite them: for He that hath mercy on them shall lead them, even by the springs of water shall He guide them." Isa. 49:4, 5, 7-10.

Upon this word Jesus rested, and He gave Satan no advantage. When the last steps of Christ's humiliation were to be taken, when the deepest sorrow was closing about His soul, He said to His disciples, "The prince of this world cometh, and hath nothing in Me." "The prince of this world is judged." Now shall he be cast out. John 14:30; 16:11; 12:31. With prophetic eye Christ traced the scenes to take place in His last great conflict. He knew that when He should exclaim, "It is finished," all heaven would triumph. His ear caught the distant music and the shouts of victory in the heavenly courts. He knew that the knell of Satan's empire would then be sounded, and the name of Christ would be heralded from world to world throughout the universe.

Christ rejoiced that He could do more for His followers than they could ask or think. He spoke with assurance, knowing that an almighty decree had been given before the world was made. He knew that truth, armed with the omnipotence of the Holy Spirit, would conquer in the contest with evil; and that the bloodstained banner would wave triumphantly over His followers. He knew that the life of His trusting disciples would be like His, a series of uninterrupted victories, not seen to be such here, but recognized as such in the great hereafter.

"These things I have spoken unto you," He said, "that

in Me ye might have peace. In the world ye shall have tribulation: but be of good cheer; I have overcome the world." Christ did not fail, neither was He discouraged, and His followers are to manifest a faith of the same enduring nature. They are to live as He lived, and work as He worked, because they depend on Him as the great Master Worker. Courage, energy, and perseverance they must possess. Though apparent impossibilities obstruct their way, by His grace they are to go forward. Instead of deploring difficulties, they are called upon to surmount them. They are to despair of nothing, and to hope for everything. With the golden chain of His matchless love Christ has bound them to the throne of God. It is His purpose that the highest influence in the universe, emanating from the source of all power, shall be theirs. They are to have power to resist evil, power that neither earth, nor death, nor hell can master, power that will enable them to overcome as Christ overcame.

Christ designs that heaven's order, heaven's plan of government, heaven's divine harmony, shall be represented in His church on earth. Thus in His people He is glorified. Through them the Sun of Righteousness will shine in undimmed luster to the world. Christ has given to His church ample facilities, that He may receive a large revenue of glory from His redeemed, purchased possession. He has bestowed upon His people capabilities and blessings that they may represent His own sufficiency. The church, endowed with the righteousness of Christ, is His depositary, in which the riches of His mercy, His grace, and His love, are to appear in full and final display. Christ looks upon His people in their purity and perfection, as the reward of His humiliation, and the supplement of His glory, —Christ, the great Center, from whom radiates all glory.

With strong, hopeful words the Saviour ended His instruction. Then He poured out the burden of His soul in prayer for His disciples. Lifting His eyes to heaven, He said, "Father, the hour is come; glorify Thy Son, that Thy Son also may glorify Thee: as Thou hast given Him power over all flesh, that He should give eternal life to as many as Thou hast given Him. And this is life eternal, that they might know Thee the only true God, and Jesus Christ, whom Thou hast sent."

Christ had finished the work that was given Him to do. He had glorified God on the earth. He had manifested the Father's name. He had gathered out those who were to continue His work among men. And He said, "I am glorified in them. And now I am no more in the world, but these are in the world, and I come to Thee. Holy Father, keep through Thine own name those whom Thou hast given Me, that they may be one, as We are." "Neither pray I for these alone, but for them also which shall believe on Me through their word; that they all may be one; . . . I in them, and Thou in Me, that they may be made perfect in one; and that the world may know that Thou hast sent Me, and hast loved them, as Thou hast loved Me."

Thus in the language of one who has divine authority, Christ gives His elect church into the Father's arms. As a consecrated high priest He intercedes for His people. As a faithful shepherd He gathers His flock under the shadow of the Almighty, in the strong and sure refuge. For Him there waits the last battle with Satan, and He goes forth to meet it.

Chapter 36

GETHSEMANE

IN COMPANY with His disciples, the Saviour slowly made His way to the garden of Gethsemane. The Passover moon, broad and full, shone from a cloudless sky. The city of pilgrims' tents was hushed into silence.

Jesus had been earnestly conversing with His disciples and instructing them; but as He neared Gethsemane, He became strangely silent. He had often visited this spot for meditation and prayer; but never with a heart so full of sorrow as upon this night of His last agony. Throughout His life on earth He had walked in the light of God's presence. When in conflict with men who were inspired by the very spirit of Satan, He could say, "He that sent Me is with Me: the Father hath not left Me alone; for I do always those things that please Him." John 8:29. But now He seemed to be shut out from the light of God's sustaining presence. Now He was numbered with the transgressors. The guilt of fallen humanity He must bear. Upon Him who knew no sin must be laid the iniquity of us all. So dreadful does sin appear to Him, so great is the weight of guilt which He must bear, that He is tempted to fear it will shut Him out forever from His Father's love. Feeling how terrible is the wrath of God against transgression, He exclaims, "My soul is exceeding sorrowful, even unto death."

As they approached the garden, the disciples had marked the change that came over their Master. Never before had they seen Him so utterly sad and silent. As He proceeded, this strange sadness deepened; yet they dared not question Him as to the cause. His form swayed as if He were about to fall. Upon reaching the garden, the dis-

This chapter is based on Matt. 26:36-56; Mark 14:32-50; Luke 22:39-53; John 18:1-12.

ciples looked anxiously for His usual place of retirement, that their Master might rest. Every step that He now took was with labored effort. He groaned aloud, as if suffering under the pressure of a terrible burden. Twice His companions supported Him, or He would have fallen to the earth.

Near the entrance to the garden, Jesus left all but three of the disciples, bidding them pray for themselves and for Him. With Peter, James, and John, He entered its secluded recesses. These three disciples were Christ's closest companions. They had beheld His glory on the mount of transfiguration; they had seen Moses and Elijah talking with Him; they had heard the voice from heaven; now in His great struggle, Christ desired their presence near Him. Often they had passed the night with Him in this retreat. On these occasions, after a season of watching and prayer, they would sleep undisturbed at a little distance from their Master, until He awoke them in the morning to go forth anew to labor. But now He desired them to spend the night with Him in prayer. Yet He could not bear that even they should witness the agony He was to endure.

"Tarry ye here," He said, "and watch with Me."

He went a little distance from them—not so far but that they could both see and hear Him—and fell prostrate upon the ground. He felt that by sin He was being separated from His Father. The gulf was so broad, so black, so deep, that His spirit shuddered before it. This agony He must not exert His divine power to escape. As man He must suffer the consequences of man's sin. As man He must endure the wrath of God against transgression.

Christ was now standing in a different attitude from that in which He had ever stood before. His suffering can best be described in the words of the prophet, "Awake, O sword, against My shepherd, and against the man that is My fellow, saith the Lord of hosts." Zech. 13:7. As the substitute and surety for sinful man, Christ was suffering under divine justice. He saw what justice meant. Hitherto He had been as an intercessor for others; now He longed to have an intercessor for Himself.

As Christ felt His unity with the Father broken up, He feared that in His human nature He would be unable to endure the coming conflict with the powers of darkness. In the wilderness of temptation the destiny of the human race had been at stake. Christ was then conqueror. Now the tempter had come for the last fearful struggle. For this he had been preparing during the three years of Christ's ministry. Everything was at stake with him. If he failed here, his hope of mastery was lost; the kingdoms of the world would finally become Christ's; he himself would be overthrown and cast out. But if Christ could be overcome, the earth would become Satan's kingdom, and the human race would be forever in his power. With the issues of the conflict before Him, Christ's soul was filled with dread of separation from God. Satan told Him that if He became the surety for a sinful world, the separation would be eternal. He would be identified with Satan's kingdom, and would nevermore be one with God.

And what was to be gained by this sacrifice? How hopeless appeared the guilt and ingratitude of men! In its hardest features Satan pressed the situation upon the Redeemer: The people who claim to be above all others in temporal and spiritual advantages have rejected You. They are seeking to destroy You, the foundation, the center and seal of the promises made to them as a peculiar people. One of Your own disciples, who has listened to Your instruction, and has been among the foremost in church activities, will betray You. One of Your most zealous followers will deny You. All will forsake You. Christ's whole being abhorred the thought. That those whom He had undertaken to save, those whom He loved so much, should unite in the plots of Satan, this pierced His soul. The conflict was terrible. Its measure was the guilt of His nation, of His accusers and betrayer, the guilt of a world lying in wickedness. The sins of men weighed heavily upon Christ, and the sense of God's wrath against sin was crushing out His life.

Behold Him contemplating the price to be paid for the human soul. In His agony He clings to the cold ground, as if to prevent Himself from being drawn farther from God. The chilling dew of night falls upon His prostrate form, but He heeds it not. From His pale lips comes the bitter cry, "O My Father, if it be possible, let this cup pass from Me." Yet even now He adds, "Nevertheless not as I will, but as Thou wilt."

The human heart longs for sympathy in suffering. This longing Christ felt to the very depths of His being. In the supreme agony of His soul He came to His disciples with a yearning desire to hear some words of comfort from those whom He had so often blessed and comforted, and shielded in sorrow and distress. The One who had always had words of sympathy for them was now suffering superhuman agony, and He longed to know that they were praying for Him and for themselves. How dark seemed the malignity of sin! Terrible was the temptation to let the human race bear the consequences of its own guilt, while He stood innocent before God. If He could only know that His disciples understood and appreciated this, He would be strengthened.

Rising with painful effort, He staggered to the place where He had left His companions. But He "findeth them asleep." Had He found them praying, He would have been relieved. Had they been seeking refuge in God, that satanic agencies might not prevail over them, He would have been comforted by their steadfast faith. But they had not heeded the repeated warning, "Watch and pray." At first they had been much troubled to see their Master, usually so calm and dignified, wrestling with a sorrow that was beyond comprehension. They had prayed as they heard the strong cries of the sufferer. They did not intend to forsake their Lord, but they seemed paralyzed by a stupor which they might have shaken off if they had continued pleading with God. They did not realize the necessity of watchfulness and earnest prayer in order to withstand temptation.

Just before He bent His footsteps to the garden, Jesus had said to the disciples, "All ye shall be offended because of Me this night." They had given Him the strongest assurance that they would go with Him to prison and to death. And poor, self-sufficient Peter had added, "Although all shall be offended, yet will not I." Mark 14:27, 29. But the disciples trusted to themselves. They did not look to the mighty Helper as Christ had counseled them to do. Thus when the Saviour was most in need of their sympathy and prayers, they were found asleep. Even Peter was sleeping.

And John, the loving disciple who had leaned upon the breast of Jesus, was asleep. Surely, the love of John for his Master should have kept him awake. His earnest prayers should have mingled with those of his loved Saviour in the time of His supreme sorrow. The Redeemer had spent entire nights praying for His disciples, that their faith might not fail. Should Jesus now put to James and John the question He had once asked them, "Are ye able to drink of the cup that I shall drink of, and to be baptized with the baptism that I am baptized with?" they would not have ventured to answer, "We are able." Matt. 20:22.

The disciples awakened at the voice of Jesus, but they hardly knew Him, His face was so changed by anguish.

Addressing Peter, Jesus said, "Simon, sleepest thou? couldest not thou watch one hour? Watch ye and pray, lest ye enter into temptation. The spirit truly is ready, but the flesh is weak." The weakness of His disciples awakened the sympathy of Jesus. He feared that they would not be able to endure the test which would come upon them in His betrayal and death. He did not reprove them, but said, "Watch ye and pray, lest ye enter into temptation." Even in His great agony, He was seeking to excuse their weakness. "The spirit truly is ready," He said, "but the flesh is weak."

Again the Son of God was seized with superhuman agony, and fainting and exhausted, He staggered back to the place of His former struggle. His suffering was even greater than before. As the agony of soul came upon Him, "His sweat was as it were great drops of blood falling down to the ground." The cypress and palm trees were the silent witnesses of His anguish. From their leafy branches dropped heavy dew upon His stricken form, as if nature wept over its Author wrestling alone with the powers of darkness.

A short time before, Jesus had stood like a mighty cedar, withstanding the storm of opposition that spent its fury upon Him. Stubborn wills, and hearts filled with malice and subtlety, had striven in vain to confuse and overpower Him. He stood forth in divine majesty as the Son of God. Now He was like a reed beaten and bent by the angry storm. He had approached the consummation of His work a conqueror, having at each step gained the victory over the powers of darkness. As one already glorified, He had claimed oneness with God. In unfaltering accents He had poured out His songs of praise. He had spoken to His disciples in words of courage and tenderness. Now had come the hour of the power of darkness. Now His voice was heard on the still evening air, not in tones of triumph, but full of human anguish. The words of the Saviour were borne to the ears of the drowsy disciples, "O My Father, if this cup may not pass away from Me, except I drink it, Thy will be done."

The first impulse of the disciples was to go to Him; but He had bidden them tarry there, watching unto prayer. When Jesus came to them, He found them still sleeping. Again He had felt a longing for companionship, for some words from His disciples which would bring relief, and break the spell of darkness that well-nigh overpowered

Him. But their eyes were heavy; "neither wist they what to answer Him." His presence aroused them. They saw His face marked with the bloody sweat of agony, and they were filled with fear. His anguish of mind they could not understand. "His visage was so marred more than any man, and His form more than the sons of men." Isa. 52:14.

Turning away, Jesus sought again His retreat, and fell prostrate, overcome by the horror of a great darkness. The humanity of the Son of God trembled in that trying hour. He prayed not now for His disciples that their faith might not fail, but for His own tempted, agonized soul. The awful moment had come—that moment which was to decide the destiny of the world. The fate of humanity trembled in the balance. Christ might even now refuse to drink the cup apportioned to guilty man. It was not yet too late. He might wipe the bloody sweat from His brow, and leave man to perish in his iniquity. He might say, Let the transgressor receive the penalty of his sin, and I will go back to My Father. Will the Son of God drink the bitter cup of humiliation and agony? Will the innocent suffer the consequences of the curse of sin, to save the guilty? The words fall tremblingly from the pale lips of Jesus, "O My Father, if this cup may not pass away from Me, except I drink it, Thy will be done."

Three times has He uttered that prayer. Three times has humanity shrunk from the last, crowning sacrifice. But now the history of the human race comes up before the world's Redeemer. He sees that the transgressors of the law, if left to themselves, must perish. He sees the helplessness of man. He sees the power of sin. The woes and lamentations of a doomed world rise before Him. He beholds its impending fate, and His decision is made. He will save man at any cost to Himself. He accepts His baptism of blood, that through Him perishing millions may gain everlasting life. He has left the courts of heaven, where all is purity, happiness, and glory, to save the one lost sheep; the one world that has fallen by transgression. And He will not turn from His mission. He will become the propitiation of a race that has willed to sin. His prayer now breathes only submission: "If this cup may not pass away from Me, except I drink it, Thy will be done."

Having made the decision, He fell dying to the ground from which He had partially risen. Where now were His disciples, to place their hands tenderly beneath the head of their fainting Master, and bathe that brow, marred indeed more than the sons of men? The Saviour trod the wine press alone, and of the people there was none with Him.

But God suffered with His Son. Angels beheld the Saviour's agony. They saw their Lord enclosed by legions of satanic forces, His nature weighed down with a shuddering, mysterious dread. There was silence in heaven. No harp was touched. Could mortals have viewed the amazement of the angelic host as in silent grief they watched the Father separating His beams of light, love, and glory from His beloved Son, they would better understand how offensive in His sight is sin.

The worlds unfallen and the heavenly angels had watched with intense interest as the conflict drew to its close. Satan and his confederacy of evil, the legions of apostasy, watched intently this great crisis in the work of redemption. The powers of good and evil waited to see what answer would come to Christ's thrice-repeated prayer. Angels had longed to bring relief to the divine sufferer, but this might not be. No way of escape was found for the Son of God. In this awful crisis, when everything was at stake, when the mysterious cup trembled in the hand of the sufferer, the heavens opened, a light shone forth amid the stormy darkness of the crisis hour, and the mighty angel who stands in God's presence, occupying the position from which Satan fell, came to the side of Christ. The angel came not to take the cup from Christ's hand, but to strengthen Him to drink it, with the assurance of the Father's love. He came to give power to the divine-human suppliant. He pointed Him to the open heavens, telling Him of the souls that would be saved as the result of His sufferings. He assured Him that His Father is greater and more powerful than Satan, that His death would result in the utter discomfiture of Satan, and that the kingdom of this world would be given to the saints of the Most High. He told Him that He would see of the travail of His soul, and be satisfied, for He would see a multitude of the human race saved, eternally saved.

Christ's agony did not cease, but His depression and discouragement left Him. The storm had in nowise abated, but He who was its object was strengthened to meet its fury. He came forth calm and serene. A heavenly peace rested upon His bloodstained face. He had borne that which no human being could ever bear; for He had tasted the sufferings of death for every man.

The sleeping disciples had been suddenly awakened by

the light surrounding the Saviour. They saw the angel bending over their prostrate Master. They saw him lift the Saviour's head upon his bosom, and point toward heaven. They heard his voice, like sweetest music, speaking words of comfort and hope. The disciples recalled the scene upon the mount of transfiguration. They remembered the glory that in the temple had encircled Jesus, and the voice of God that spoke from the cloud. Now that same glory was again revealed, and they had no further fear for their Master. He was under the care of God; a mighty angel had been sent to protect Him. Again the disciples in their weariness yield to the strange stupor that overpowers them. Again Jesus finds them sleeping.

Looking sorrowfully upon them He says, "Sleep on now, and take your rest: behold, the hour is at hand, and the Son of man is betrayed into the hands of sinners."

Even as He spoke these words, He heard the footsteps of the mob in search of Him, and said, "Rise, let us be going: behold, he is at hand that doth betray Me."

No traces of His recent agony were visible as Jesus stepped forth to meet His betrayer. Standing in advance of His disciples He said, "Whom seek ye?" They answered, "Jesus of Nazareth." Jesus replied, "I am He." As these words were spoken, the angel who had lately ministered to Jesus moved between Him and the mob. A divine light illuminated the Saviour's face, and a dovelike form overshadowed Him. In the presence of this divine glory, the murderous throng could not stand for a moment. They staggered back. Priests, elders, soldiers, and even Judas, fell as dead men to the ground.

The angel withdrew, and the light faded away. Jesus had opportunity to escape, but He remained, calm and self-possessed. As one glorified He stood in the midst of that hardened band, now prostrate and helpless at His feet. The disciples looked on, silent with wonder and awe.

But quickly the scene changed. The mob started up. The Roman soldiers, the priests and Judas, gathered about Christ. They seemed ashamed of their weakness, and fearful that He would yet escape. Again the question was asked by the Redeemer, "Whom seek ye?" They had had evidence that He who stood before them was the Son of God, but they would not be convinced. To the question, "Whom seek ye?" again they answered, "Jesus of Nazareth." The Saviour then said, "I have told you that I am He: if therefore ye seek Me, let these go their way"—

pointing to the disciples. He knew how weak was their faith, and He sought to shield them from temptation and trial. For them He was ready to sacrifice Himself.

Judas the betrayer did not forget the part he was to act. When the mob entered the garden, he had led the way, closely followed by the high priest. To the pursuers of Jesus he had given a sign, saying, "Whomsoever I shall kiss, that same is He: hold Him fast." Matt. 26:48. Now he pretends to have no part with them. Coming close to Jesus, he takes His hand as a familiar friend. With the words, "Hail, Master," he kisses Him repeatedly, and appears to weep as if in sympathy with Him in His peril.

Jesus said to him, "Friend, wherefore art thou come?" His voice trembled with sorrow as He added, "Judas, betrayest thou the Son of man with a kiss?" This appeal should have aroused the conscience of the betrayer, and touched his stubborn heart; but honor, fidelity, and human tenderness had forsaken him. He stood bold and defiant, showing no disposition to relent. He had given himself up to Satan, and he had no power to resist him. Jesus did not refuse the traitor's kiss.

The mob grew bold as they saw Judas touch the person of Him who had so recently been glorified before their eyes. They now laid hold of Jesus, and proceeded to bind those precious hands that had ever been employed in doing good.

The disciples had thought that their Master would not suffer Himself to be taken. For the same power that had caused the mob to fall as dead men could keep them helpless, until Jesus and His companions should escape. They were disappointed and indignant as they saw the cords brought forward to bind the hands of Him whom they loved. Peter in his anger rashly drew his sword and tried to defend his Master, but he only cut off an ear of the high priest's servant. When Jesus saw what was done, He released His hands, though held firmly by the Roman soldiers, and saying, "Suffer ye thus far," He touched the wounded ear, and it was instantly made whole. He then said to Peter, "Put up again thy sword into his place: for all they that take the sword shall perish with the sword. Thinkest thou that I cannot now pray to My Father, and He shall presently give Me more than twelve legions of angels?"—a legion in place of each one of the disciples. Oh, why, the disciples thought, does He not save Himself and us? Answering their unspoken thought, He added,

"But how then shall the scriptures be fulfilled, that thus it must be?" "The cup which My Father hath given Me, shall I not drink it?"

The official dignity of the Jewish leaders had not prevented them from joining in the pursuit of Jesus. His arrest was too important a matter to be trusted to subordinates; the wily priests and elders had joined the temple police and the rabble in following Judas to Gethsemane. What a company for those dignitaries to unite with—a mob that was eager for excitement, and armed with all kinds of implements, as if in pursuit of a wild beast!

Turning to the priests and elders, Christ fixed upon them His searching glance. The words He spoke they would never forget as long as life should last. They were as the sharp arrows of the Almighty. With dignity He said: You come out against Me with swords and staves as you would against a thief or a robber. Day by day I sat teaching in the temple. You had every opportunity of laying hands upon Me, and you did nothing. The night is better suited to your work. "This is your hour, and the power of darkness."

The disciples were terrified as they saw Jesus permit Himself to be taken and bound. They were offended that He should suffer this humiliation to Himself and them. They could not understand His conduct, and they blamed Him for submitting to the mob. In their indignation and fear, Peter proposed that they save themselves. Following this suggestion, "they all forsook Him, and fled." But Christ had foretold this desertion. "Behold," He had said, "the hour cometh, yea, is now come, that ye shall be scattered, every man to his own, and shall leave Me alone: and yet I am not alone, because the Father is with Me." John 16:32.

Chapter 37

NIGHT OF TRIALS

OVER THE brook Kedron, past gardens and olive groves, and through the hushed streets of the sleeping city, they hurried Jesus. It was past midnight, and the cries of the hooting mob that followed Him broke sharply upon the still air. The Saviour was bound and closely guarded, and He moved painfully. But in eager haste His captors made their way with Him to the palace of Annas, the ex-high priest.

Annas was the head of the officiating priestly family, and in deference to his age he was recognized by the people as high priest. His counsel was sought and carried out as the voice of God. He must first see Jesus a captive to priestly power. He must be present at the examination of the prisoner, for fear that the less-experienced Caiaphas might fail of securing the object for which they were working. His artifice, cunning, and subtlety must be used on this occasion; for, at all events, Christ's condemnation must be secured.

Christ was to be tried formally before the Sanhedrin; but before Annas He was subjected to a preliminary trial. Under the Roman rule the Sanhedrin could not execute the sentence of death. They could only examine a prisoner, and pass judgment, to be ratified by the Roman authorities. It was therefore necessary to bring against Christ charges that would be regarded as criminal by the Romans. An accusation must also be found which would condemn Him in the eyes of the Jews. Not a few among the priests and rulers had been convicted by Christ's teaching, and only fear of excommunication prevented them from confessing Him. The priests well remembered the question

This chapter is based on Matt. 26:57-75; 27:1; Mark 14:53-72; 15:1; Luke 22:54-71; John 18:13-27.

of Nicodemus, "Doth our law judge any man, before it hear him, and know what he doeth?" John 7:51. This question had for the time broken up the council, and thwarted their plans. Joseph of Arimathaea and Nicodemus were not now to be summoned, but there were others who might dare to speak in favor of justice. The trial must be so conducted as to unite the members of the Sanhedrin against Christ. There were two charges which the 'priests desired to maintain. If Jesus could be proved a blasphemer, He would be condemned by the Jews. If convicted of sedition, it would secure His condemnation by the Romans. The second charge Annas tried first to establish. He questioned Jesus concerning His disciples and His doctrines, hoping the prisoner would say something that would give him material upon which to work. He thought to draw out some statement to prove that He was seeking to establish a secret society, with the purpose of setting up a new kingdom. Then the priests could deliver Him to the Romans as a disturber of the peace and a creator of insurrection.

Christ read the priest's purpose as an open book. As if reading the inmost soul of His questioner, He denied that there was between Him and His followers any secret bond of union, or that He gathered them secretly and in the darkness to conceal His designs. He had no secrets in regard to His purposes or doctrines. "I spake openly to the world," He answered; "I ever taught in the synagogue, and in the temple, whither the Jews always resort; and in secret have I said nothing."

The Saviour contrasted His own manner of work with the methods of His accusers. For months they had hunted Him, striving to entrap Him and bring Him before a secret tribunal, where they might obtain by perjury what it was impossible to gain by fair means. Now they were carrying out their purpose. The midnight seizure by a mob, the mockery and abuse before He was condemned, or even accused, was their manner of work, not His. Their action was in violation of the law. Their own rules declared that every man should be treated as innocent until proved guilty. By their own rules the priests stood condemned.

Turning upon His questioner, Jesus said, "Why askest thou Me?" Had not the priests and rulers sent spies to watch His movements, and report His every word? Had not these been present at every gathering of the people, and carried to the priests information of all His sayings and doings? "Ask them which heard Me, what I have said unto them," replied Jesus; "behold, they know what I said."

Annas was silenced by the decision of the answer. Fearing that Christ would say something regarding his course of action that he would prefer to keep covered up, he said nothing more to Him at this time. One of his officers, filled with wrath as he saw Annas silenced, struck Jesus on the face, saying, "Answerest Thou the high priest so?"

Christ calmly replied, "If I have spoken evil, bear witness of the evil: but if well, why smitest thou Me?" He spoke no burning words of retaliation. His calm answer came from a heart sinless, patient, and gentle, that would not be provoked.

Christ suffered keenly under abuse and insult. At the hands of the beings whom He had created, and for whom He was making an infinite sacrifice, He received every indignity. And He suffered in proportion to the perfection of His holiness and His hatred of sin. His trial by men who acted as fiends was to Him a perpetual sacrifice. To be surrounded by human beings under the control of Satan was revolting to Him. And He knew that in a moment, by the flashing forth of His divine power, He could lay His cruel tormentors in the dust. This made the trial the harder to bear.

The Jews were looking for a Messiah to be revealed in outward show. They expected Him, by one flash of overmastering will, to change the current of men's thoughts, and force from them an acknowledgment of His supremacy. Thus, they believed, He was to secure His own exaltation, and gratify their ambitious hopes. Thus when Christ was treated with contempt, there came to Him a strong temptation to manifest His divine character. By a word, by a look, He could compel His persecutors to confess that He was Lord above kings and rulers, priests and temple. But it was His difficult task to keep to the position He had chosen as one with humanity.

The angels of heaven witnessed every movement made against their loved Commander. They longed to deliver Christ. Under God the angels are all-powerful. On one occasion, in obedience to the command of Christ, they slew of the Assyrian army in one night one hundred and eighty-five thousand men. How easily could the angels, beholding the shameful scene of the trial of Christ, have testified their indignation by consuming the adversaries of God!

But they were not commanded to do this. He who could have doomed His enemies to death bore with their cruelty. His love for His Father, and His pledge, made from the foundation of the world, to become the Sin Bearer, led Him to endure uncomplainingly the coarse treatment of those He came to save. It was a part of His mission to bear, in His humanity, all the taunts and abuse that men could heap upon Him. The only hope of humanity was in this submission of Christ to all that He could endure from the hands and hearts of men.

Christ had said nothing that could give His accusers an advantage; yet He was bound, to signify that He was condemned. There must, however, be a pretense of justice. It was necessary that there should be the form of a legal trial. This the authorities were determined to hasten. They knew the regard in which Jesus was held by the people, and feared that if the arrest were noised abroad, a rescue would be attempted. Again, if the trial and execution were not brought about at once, there would be a week's delay on account of the celebration of the Passover. This might defeat their plans. In securing the condemnation of Jesus they depended largely upon the clamor of the mob, many of them the rabble of Jerusalem. Should there be a week's delay, the excitement would abate, and a reaction would be likely to set in. The better part of the people would be aroused in Christ's favor; many would come forward with testimony in His vindication, bringing to light the mighty works He had done. This would excite popular indignation against the Sanhedrin. Their proceedings would be condemned, and Jesus would be set free, to receive new homage from the multitudes. The priests and rulers therefore determined that before their purpose could become known, Jesus should be delivered into the hands of the Romans.

But first of all, an accusation was to be found. They had gained nothing as yet. Annas ordered Jesus to be taken to Caiaphas. Caiaphas belonged to the Sadducees, some of whom were now the most desperate enemies of Jesus. He himself, though wanting in force of character, was fully as severe, heartless, and unscrupulous as was Annas. He would leave no means untried to destroy Jesus. It was now early morning, and very dark; by the light of torches and lanterns the armed band with their prisoner proceeded to the high priest's palace. Here, while the members of the

Sanhedrin were coming together, Annas and Caiaphas again questioned Jesus, but without success.

When the council had assembled in the judgment hall, Caiaphas took his seat as presiding officer. On either side were the judges, and those specially interested in the trial. The Roman soldiers were stationed on the platform below the throne. At the foot of the throne stood Jesus. Upon Him the gaze of the whole multitude was fixed. The excitement was intense. Of all the throng He alone was calm and serene. The very atmosphere surrounding Him seemed pervaded by a holy influence.

Caiaphas had regarded Jesus as his rival. The eagerness of the people to hear the Saviour, and their apparent readiness to accept His teachings, had aroused the bitter jealousy of the high priest. But as Caiaphas now looked upon the prisoner, he was struck with admiration for His noble and dignified bearing. A conviction came over him that this Man was akin to God. The next instant he scornfully banished the thought. Immediately his voice was heard in sneering, haughty tones demanding that Jesus work one of His mighty miracles before them. But his words fell upon the Saviour's ears as though He heard them not. The people compared the excited and malignant deportment of Annas and Caiaphas with the calm, majestic bearing of Jesus. Even in the minds of that hardened multitude arose the question, Is this man of godlike presence to be condemned as a criminal?

Caiaphas, perceiving the influence that was obtaining, hastened the trial. The enemies of Jesus were in great perplexity. They were bent on securing His condemnation, but how to accomplish this they knew not. The members of the council were divided between the Pharisees and the Sadducees. There was bitter animosity and controversy between them; certain disputed points they dared not approach for fear of a quarrel. With a few words Jesus could have excited their prejudices against each other, and thus have averted their wrath from Himself. Caiaphas knew this, and he wished to avoid stirring up a contention. There were plenty of witnesses to prove that Christ had denounced the priests and scribes, that He had called them hypocrites and murderers; but this testimony it was not expedient to bring forward. The Sadducees in their sharp contentions with the Pharisees had used to them similar language. And such testimony would have no weight with the Romans, who were themselves disgusted with the pretensions of the Pharisees. There was abundant evidence that Jesus had disregarded the traditions of the Jews, and had spoken irreverently of many of their ordinances; but in regard to tradition the Pharisees and Sadducees were at swords' points; and this evidence also would have no weight with the Romans. Christ's enemies dared not accuse Him of Sabbathbreaking, lest an examination should reveal the character of His work. If His miracles of healing were brought to light, the very object of the priests would be defeated.

False witnesses had been bribed to accuse Jesus of inciting rebellion and seeking to establish a separate government. But their testimony proved to be vague and contradictory. Under examination they falsified their own statements.

Early in His ministry Christ had said, "Destroy this temple, and in three days I will raise it up." In the figurative language of prophecy, He had thus foretold His own death and resurrection. "He spake of the temple of His body." John 2:19, 21. These words the Jews had understood in a literal sense, as referring to the temple at Jerusalem. Of all that Christ had said, the priests could find nothing to use against Him save this. By misstating these words they hoped to gain an advantage. The Romans had engaged in rebuilding and embellishing the temple, and they took great pride in it; any contempt shown to it would be sure to excite their indignation. Here Romans and Jews, Pharisees and Sadducees, could meet; for all held the temple in great veneration. On this point two witnesses were found whose testimony was not so contradictory as that of the others had been. One of them, who had been bribed to accuse Jesus, declared, "This fellow said, I am able to destroy the temple of God, and to build it in three days." Thus Christ's words were misstated. If they had been reported exactly as He spoke them, they would not have secured His condemnation even by the Sanhedrin. Had Jesus been a mere man, as the Jews claimed, His declaration would only have indicated an unreasonable, boastful spirit, but could not have been construed into blasphemy. Even as misrepresented by the false witnesses, His words contained nothing which would be regarded by the Romans as a crime worthy of death.

Patiently Jesus listened to the conflicting testimonies. No word did He utter in self-defense. At last His accusers were entangled, confused, and maddened. The trial was making no headway; it seemed that their plottings were to fail. Caiaphas was desperate. One last resort remained; Christ must be forced to condemn Himself. The high priest started from the judgment seat, his face contorted with passion, his voice and demeanor plainly indicating that were it in his power he would strike down the prisoner before him. "Answerest Thou nothing?" he exclaimed; "what is it which these witness against Thee?"

Jesus held His peace. "He was oppressed, and He was afflicted, yet He opened not His mouth: He is brought as a lamb to the slaughter, and as a sheep before her shearers is dumb, so He openeth not His mouth." Isaiah 53:7.

At last, Caiaphas, raising his right hand toward heaven, addressed Jesus in the form of a solemn oath: "I adjure Thee by the living God, that Thou tell us whether Thou be the Christ, the Son of God."

To this appeal Christ could not remain silent. There was a time to be silent, and a time to speak. He had not spoken until directly questioned. He knew that to answer now would make His death certain. But the appeal was made by the highest acknowledged authority of the nation, and in the name of the Most High. Christ would not fail to show proper respect for the law. More than this, His own relation to the Father was called in question. He must plainly declare His character and mission. Jesus had said to His disciples, "Whosoever therefore shall confess Me before men, him will I confess also before My Father which is in heaven." Matt. 10:32. Now by His own example He repeated the lesson.

Every ear was bent to listen, and every eye was fixed on His face as He answered, "Thou hast said." A heavenly light seemed to illuminate His pale countenance as He added, "Nevertheless I say unto you, Hereafter shall ye see the Son of man sitting on the right hand of power, and coming in the clouds of heaven."

For a moment the divinity of Christ flashed through His guise of humanity. The high priest quailed before the penetrating eyes of the Saviour. That look seemed to read his hidden thoughts, and burn into his heart. Never in afterlife did he forget that searching glance of the persecuted Son of God.

"Hereafter," said Jesus, "shall ye see the Son of man sitting on the right hand of power, and coming in the clouds of heaven." In these words Christ presented the reverse of the scene then taking place. He, the Lord of life and glory, would be seated at God's right hand. He would be the judge of all the earth, and from His decision there could be no appeal. Then every secret thing would be set in the light of God's countenance, and judgment be passed upon every man according to his deeds.

The words of Christ startled the high priest. The thought that there was to be a resurrection of the dead, when all would stand at the bar of God, to be rewarded according to their works, was a thought of terror to Caiaphas. He did not wish to believe that in future he would receive sentence according to his works. There rushed before his mind as a panorama the scenes of the final judgment. For a moment he saw the fearful spectacle of the graves giving up their dead, with the secrets he had hoped were forever hidden. For a moment he felt as if standing before the eternal Judge, whose eye, which sees all things, was reading his soul, bringing to light mysteries supposed to be hidden with the dead.

The scene passed from the priest's vision. Christ's words cut him, the Sadducee, to the quick. Caiaphas had denied the doctrine of the resurrection, the judgment, and a future life. Now he was maddened by satanic fury. Was this man, a prisoner before him, to assail his most cherished theories? Rending his robe, that the people might see his pretended horror, he demanded that without further preliminaries the prisoner be condemned for blasphemy. "What further need have we of witnesses?" he said; "behold, now ye have heard His blasphemy. What think ye?" And they all condemned Him.

Conviction mingled with passion led Caiaphas to do as he did. He was furious with himself for believing Christ's words, and instead of rending his heart under a deep sense of truth, and confessing that Jesus was the Messiah, he rent his priestly robes in determined resistance. This act was deeply significant. Little did Caiaphas realize its meaning. In this act, done to influence the judges and secure Christ's condemnation, the high priest had condemned himself. By the law of God he was disqualified for the priesthood. He had pronounced upon himself the death sentence.

A high priest was not to rend his garments. By the Levitical law, this was prohibited under sentence of death. Under no circumstances, on no occasion, was the priest to rend his robe. It was the custom among the Jews for the garments to be rent at the death of friends, but this custom the priests were not to observe. Express command had been given by Christ to Moses concerning this. Lev. 10:6.

Everything worn by the priest was to be whole and without blemish. By those beautiful official garments was represented the character of the great antitype, Jesus Christ. Nothing but perfection, in dress and attitude, in word and spirit, could be acceptable to God. He is holy, and His glory and perfection must be represented by the earthly service. Nothing but perfection could properly represent the sacredness of the heavenly service. Finite man might rend his own heart by showing a contrite and humble spirit. This God would discern. But no rent must be made in the priestly robes, for this would mar the representation of heavenly things. The high priest who dared to appear in holy office, and engage in the service of the sanctuary, with a rent robe, was looked upon as having severed himself from God. By rending his garment he cut himself off from being a representative character. He was no longer accepted by God as an officiating priest. This course of action, as exhibited by Caiaphas, showed human passion, human imperfection.

By rending his garments, Caiaphas made of no effect the law of God, to follow the tradition of men. A manmade law provided that in case of blasphemy a priest might rend his garments in horror at the sin, and be guiltless. Thus the law of God was made void by the laws of men.

Each action of the high priest was watched with interest by the people; and Caiaphas thought for effect to display his piety. But in this act, designed as an accusation against Christ, he was reviling the One of whom God had said, "My name is in Him." Ex. 23:21. He himself was committing blasphemy. Standing under the condemnation of God, he pronounced sentence upon Christ as a blasphemer.

When Caiaphas rent his garment, his act was significant of the place that the Jewish nation as a nation would thereafter occupy toward God. The once favored people of God were separating themselves from Him, and were fast becoming a people disowned by Jehovah. When Christ upon the cross cried out, "It is finished" (John 19:30), and the veil of the temple was rent in twain, the Holy Watcher declared that the Jewish people had rejected Him who was the antitype of all their types, the substance of all their shadows. Israel was divorced from God. Well might Caiaphas then rend his official robes, which signified that he claimed to be a representative of the great High Priest; for no longer had they any meaning for him or for the people. Well might the high priest rend his robes in horror for himself and for the nation.

The Sanhedrin had pronounced Jesus worthy of death; but it was contrary to the Jewish law to try a prisoner by night. In legal condemnation nothing could be done except in the light of day and before a full session of the council. Notwithstanding this, the Saviour was now treated as a condemned criminal, and given up to be abused by the lowest and vilest of humankind. The palace of the high priest surrounded an open court in which the soldiers and the multitude had gathered. Through this court, Jesus was taken to the guardroom, on every side meeting with mockery of His claim to be the Son of God. His own words, "sitting on the right hand of power," and, "coming in the clouds of heaven," were jeeringly repeated. While in the guardroom, awaiting His legal trial, He was not protected. The ignorant rabble had seen the cruelty with which He was treated before the council, and from this they took license to manifest all the satanic elements of their nature. Christ's very nobility and godlike bearing goaded them to madness. His meekness, His innocence, His majestic patience, filled them with hatred born of Satan. Mercy and justice were trampled upon. Never was criminal treated in so inhuman a manner as was the Son of God.

But a keener anguish rent the heart of Jesus; the blow that inflicted the deepest pain no enemy's hand could have dealt. While He was undergoing the mockery of an examination before Caiaphas, Christ had been denied by one of His own disciples.

After deserting their Master in the garden, two of the disciples had ventured to follow, at a distance, the mob that had Jesus in charge. These disciples were Peter and John. The priests recognized John as a well-known disciple of Jesus, and admitted him to the hall, hoping that as he witnessed the humiliation of his Leader, he would scorn the idea of such a one being the Son of God. John spoke in favor of Peter, and gained an entrance for him also.

In the court a fire had been kindled; for it was the coldest hour of the night, being just before the dawn. A company drew about the fire, and Peter presumptuously took his place with them. He did not wish to be recognized as a disciple of Jesus. By mingling carelessly with the crowd, he hoped to be taken for one of those who had brought Jesus to the hall.

But as the light flashed upon Peter's face, the woman who kept the door cast a searching glance upon him. She had noticed that he came in with John, she marked the look of dejection on his face, and thought that he might be a disciple of Jesus. She was one of the servants of Caiaphas' household, and was curious to know. She said to Peter, "Art not thou also one of this Man's disciples?" Peter was startled and confused; the eyes of the company instantly fastened upon him. He pretended not to understand her; but she was persistent, and said to those around her that this man was with Jesus. Peter felt compelled to answer, and said angrily, "Woman, I know Him not." This was the first denial, and immediately the cock crew. O Peter, so soon ashamed of thy Master! so soon to deny thy Lord!

The disciple John, upon entering the judgment hall, did not try to conceal the fact that he was a follower of Jesus. He did not mingle with the rough company who were reviling his Master. He was not questioned, for he did not assume a false character, and thus lay himself liable to suspicion. He sought a retired corner secure from the notice of the mob, but as near Jesus as it was possible for him to be. Here he could see and hear all that took place at the trial of his Lord.

Peter had not designed that his real character should be known. In assuming an air of indifference he had placed himself on the enemy's ground, and he became an easy prey to temptation. If he had been called to fight for his Master, he would have been a courageous soldier; but when the finger of scorn was pointed at him, he proved himself a coward. Many who do not shrink from active warfare for their Lord are driven by ridicule to deny their faith. By associating with those whom they should avoid, they place themselves in the way of temptation. They invite the enemy to tempt them, and are led to say and do that of which under other circumstances they would never have been guilty. The disciple of Christ who in our day disguises his faith through dread of suffering or reproach denies his Lord as really as did Peter in the judgment hall.

Peter tried to show no interest in the trial of his Master, but his heart was wrung with sorrow as he heard the cruel taunts, and saw the abuse He was suffering. More than this, he was surprised and angry that Jesus should humiliate Himself and His followers by submitting to such treatment. In order to conceal his true feelings, he endeavored to join with the persecutors of Jesus in their untimely jests. But his appearance was unnatural. He was acting a lie, and while seeking to talk unconcernedly he could not restrain expressions of indignation at the abuse heaped upon his Master.

Attention was called to him the second time, and he was again charged with being a follower of Jesus. He now declared with an oath, "I do not know the Man." Still another opportunity was given him. An hour had passed, when one of the servants of the high priest, being a near kinsman of the man whose ear Peter had cut off, asked him, "Did not I see thee in the garden with Him?" "Surely thou art one of them: for thou art a Galilean, and thy speech agreeth thereto." At this Peter flew into a rage. The disciples of Jesus were noted for the purity of their language, and in order fully to deceive his questioners, and justify his assumed character, Peter now denied his Master with cursing and swearing. Again the cock crew. Peter heard it then, and he remembered the words of Jesus, "Before the cock crow twice, thou shalt deny Me thrice." Mark 14:30.

While the degrading oaths were fresh upon Peter's lips, and the shrill crowing of the cock was still ringing in his ears, the Saviour turned from the frowning judges, and looked full upon His poor disciple. At the same time Peter's eyes were drawn to his Master. In that gentle countenance he read deep pity and sorrow, but there was no anger there.

The sight of that pale, suffering face, those quivering lips, that look of compassion and forgiveness, pierced his heart like an arrow. Conscience was aroused. Memory was active. Peter called to mind his promise of a few short hours before that he would go with his Lord to prison and to death. He remembered his grief when the Saviour told him in the upper chamber that he would deny his Lord thrice that same night. Peter had just declared that he knew not Jesus, but he now realized with bitter grief how well his Lord knew him, and how accurately He had read his heart, the falseness of which was unknown even to himself.

A tide of memories rushed over him. The Saviour's tender mercy, His kindness and long-suffering, His gentleness and patience toward His erring disciples,—all was remembered. He recalled the caution, "Simon, behold, Satan hath desired to have you, that he may sift you as wheat:

but I have prayed for thee, that thy faith fail not." Luke 22:31, 32. He reflected with horror upon his own ingratitude, his falsehood, his perjury. Once more he looked at his Master, and saw a sacrilegious hand raised to smite Him in the face. Unable longer to endure the scene, he rushed, heartbroken, from the hall.

He pressed on in solitude and darkness, he knew not and cared not whither. At last he found himself in Gethsemane. The scene of a few hours before came vividly to his mind. The suffering face of his Lord, stained with bloody sweat and convulsed with anguish, rose before him. He remembered with bitter remorse that Jesus had wept and agonized in prayer alone, while those who should have united with Him in that trying hour were sleeping. He remembered His solemn charge, "Watch and pray, that ye enter not into temptation." Matt. 26:41. He witnessed again the scene in the judgment hall. It was torture to his bleeding heart to know that he had added the heaviest burden to the Saviour's humiliation and grief. On the very spot where Jesus had poured out His soul in agony to His Father, Peter fell upon his face, and wished that he might die.

It was in sleeping when Jesus bade him watch and pray that Peter had prepared the way for his great sin. All the disciples, by sleeping in that critical hour, sustained a great loss. Christ knew the fiery ordeal through which they were to pass. He knew how Satan would work to paralyze their senses that they might be unready for the trial. Therefore it was that He gave them warning. Had those hours in the garden been spent in watching and prayer, Peter would not have been left to depend upon his own feeble strength. He would not have denied his Lord. Had the disciples watched with Christ in His agony, they would have been prepared to behold His suffering upon the cross. They would have understood in some degree the nature of His overpowering anguish. They would have been able to recall His words that foretold His sufferings, His death, and His resurrection. Amid the gloom of the most trying hour, some rays of hope would have lighted up the darkness and sustained their faith.

As soon as it was day, the Sanhedrin again assembled, and again Jesus was brought into the council room. He had declared Himself the Son of God, and they had construed His words into a charge against Him. But they could not condemn Him on this, for many of them had

not been present at the night session, and they had not
heard His words. And they knew that the Roman tribunal
would find in them nothing worthy of death. But if from
His own lips they could all hear those words repeated,
their object might be gained. His claim to the Messiahship
they might construe into a seditious political claim.

"Art Thou the Christ?" they said, "tell us." But Christ
remained silent. They continued to ply Him with questions. At last in tones of mournful pathos He answered, "If
I tell you, ye will not believe: and if I also ask you, ye will
not answer Me, nor let Me go." But that they might be left
without excuse He added the solemn warning, "Hereafter
shall the Son of man sit on the right hand of the power of
God."

"Art Thou then the Son of God?" they asked with one
voice. He said unto them, "Ye say that I am." They cried
out, "What need we any further witness? for we ourselves
have heard of His own mouth."

And so by the third condemnation of the Jewish authorities, Jesus was to die. All that was now necessary, they
thought, was for the Romans to ratify this condemnation,
and deliver Him into their hands.

Then came the third scene of abuse and mockery, worse
even than that received from the ignorant rabble. In the
very presence of the priests and rulers, and with their
sanction, this took place. Every feeling of sympathy or humanity had gone out of their hearts. If their arguments
were weak, and failed to silence His voice, they had other
weapons, such as in all ages have been used to silence
heretics,—suffering, and violence, and death.

When the condemnation of Jesus was pronounced by
the judges, a satanic fury took possession of the people.
The roar of voices was like that of wild beasts. The crowd
made a rush toward Jesus, crying, He is guilty, put Him to
death! Had it not been for the Roman soldiers, Jesus
would not have lived to be nailed to the cross of Calvary.
He would have been torn in pieces before His judges, had
not Roman authority interfered, and by force of arms restrained the violence of the mob.

Heathen men were angry at the brutal treatment of one
against whom nothing had been proved. The Roman officers declared that the Jews in pronouncing condemnation
upon Jesus were infringing upon the Roman power, and
that it was even against the Jewish law to condemn a man
to death upon his own testimony. This intervention

brought a momentary lull in the proceedings; but the Jewish leaders were dead alike to pity and to shame.

Priests and rulers forgot the dignity of their office, and abused the Son of God with foul epithets. They taunted Him with His parentage. They declared that His presumption in proclaiming Himself the Messiah made Him deserving of the most ignominious death. The most dissolute men engaged in infamous abuse of the Saviour. An old garment was thrown over His head, and His persecutors struck Him in the face, saying, "Prophesy unto us, Thou Christ, Who is he that smote Thee?" When the garment was removed, one poor wretch spat in His face.

The angels of God faithfully recorded every insulting look, word, and act against their beloved Commander. One day the base men who scorned and spat upon the calm, pale face of Christ will look upon it in its glory, shining brighter than the sun.

Chapter 38

KISS OF DEATH

THE HISTORY of Judas presents the sad ending of a life that might have been honored of God. Had Judas died before his last journey to Jerusalem he would have been regarded as a man worthy of a place among the twelve, and one who would be greatly missed. The abhorrence which has followed him through the centuries would not have existed but for the attributes revealed at the close of his history. But it was for a purpose that his character was laid open to the world. It was to be a warning to all who, like him, should betray sacred trusts.

A little before the Passover, Judas had renewed his contract with the priests to deliver Jesus into their hands. Then it was arranged that the Saviour should be taken at one of His resorts for meditation and prayer. Since the feast at the house of Simon, Judas had had opportunity to reflect upon the deed which he had covenanted to perform, but his purpose was unchanged. For thirty pieces of silver—the price of a slave—he sold the Lord of glory to ignominy and death.

Judas had naturally a strong love for money; but he had not always been corrupt enough to do such a deed as this. He had fostered the evil spirit of avarice until it had become the ruling motive of his life. The love of mammon overbalanced his love for Christ. Through becoming the slave of one vice he gave himself to Satan, to be driven to any lengths in sin.

Judas had joined the disciples when multitudes were following Christ. The Saviour's teaching moved their hearts as they hung entranced upon His words, spoken in the synagogue, by the seaside, upon the mount. Judas saw the sick, the lame, the blind, flock to Jesus from the towns and cities. He saw the dying laid at His feet. He witnessed the Saviour's mighty works in healing the sick, casting out devils, and raising the dead. He felt in his own person the evidence of Christ's power. He recognized the teaching of Christ as superior to all that he had ever heard. He loved the Great Teacher, and desired to be with Him. He felt a desire to be changed in character and life, and he hoped to experience this through connecting himself with Jesus. The Saviour did not repulse Judas. He gave him a place among the twelve. He trusted him to do the work of an evangelist. He endowed him with power to heal the sick and to cast out devils. But Judas did not come to the point of surrendering himself fully to Christ. He did not give up his worldly ambition or his love of money. While he accepted the position of a minister of Christ, he did not bring himself under the divine molding. He felt that he could retain his own judgment and opinions, and he cultivated a disposition to criticize and accuse.

Judas was highly regarded by the disciples, and had great influence over them. He himself had a high opinion of his own qualifications, and looked upon his brethren as greatly inferior to him in judgment and ability. They did not see their opportunities, he thought, and take advantage of circumstances. The church would never prosper with such shortsighted men as leaders. Peter was impetuous; he would move without consideration. John, who was treasuring up the truths that fell from Christ's lips, was looked upon by Judas as a poor financier. Matthew, whose training had taught him accuracy in all things, was very particular in regard to honesty, and he was ever contemplating the words of Christ, and became so absorbed in them that, as Judas thought, he could not be trusted to do sharp, far-seeing business. Thus Judas summed up all the disciples, and flattered himself that the church would often be brought into perplexity and embarrassment if it were not for his ability as a manager. Judas regarded himself as the capable one, who could not be overreached. In his own estimation he was an honor to the cause, and as such he always represented himself.

Judas was blinded to his own weakness of character, and Christ placed him where he would have an opportunity to see and correct this. As treasurer for the disciples, he was called upon to provide for the needs of the little company, and to relieve the necessities of the poor. When in the Passover chamber Jesus said to him, "That thou doest, do quickly" (John 13:27), the disciples thought He had bidden him buy what was needed for the feast, or give something to the poor. In ministering to others, Judas might have developed an unselfish spirit. But while listening daily to the lessons of Christ and witnessing His unselfish life, Judas indulged his covetous disposition. The small sums that came into his hands were a continual temptation. Often when he did a little service for Christ, or devoted time to religious purposes, he paid himself out of this meager fund. In his own eyes these pretexts served to excuse his action; but in God's sight he was a thief.

Christ's oft-repeated statement that His kingdom was not of this world offended Judas. He had marked out a line upon which he expected Christ to work. He had planned that John the Baptist should be delivered from prison. But lo, John was left to be beheaded. And Jesus, instead of asserting His royal right and avenging the death of John, retired with His disciples into a country place. Judas wanted more aggressive warfare. He thought that if Jesus would not prevent the disciples from carrying out their schemes, the work would be more successful. He marked the increasing enmity of the Jewish leaders, and saw their challenge unheeded when they demanded from Christ a sign from heaven. His heart was open to unbelief, and the enemy supplied thoughts of questioning and rebellion. Why did Jesus dwell so much upon that which was discouraging? Why did He predict trial and persecution for Himself and for His disciples? The prospect of having a high place in the new kingdom had led Judas to espouse the cause of Christ. Were his hopes to be disappointed? Judas had not decided that Jesus was not the Son of God; but he was questioning, and seeking to find some explanation of His mighty works.

Notwithstanding the Saviour's own teaching, Judas was continually advancing the idea that Christ would reign as king in Jerusalem. At the feeding of the five thousand he tried to bring this about. On this occasion Judas assisted in distributing the food to the hungry multitude. He had an opportunity to see the benefit which it was in his power to impart to others. He felt the satisfaction that always comes in service to God. He helped to bring the sick and suffering from among the multitude to Christ. He saw what relief, what joy and gladness, come to human hearts through the healing power of the restorer. He might have comprehended the methods of Christ. But he was blinded by his own selfish desires. Judas was first to take advantage of the enthusiasm excited by the miracle of the loaves. It was he who set on foot the project to take Christ by force and make Him king. His hopes were high. His disappointment was bitter.

Christ's discourse in the synagogue concerning the bread of life was the turning point in the history of Judas. He heard the words, "Except ye eat the flesh of the Son of man, and drink His blood, ye have no life in you." John 6:53. He saw that Christ was offering spiritual rather than worldly good. He regarded himself as farsighted, and thought he could see that Jesus would have no honor, and that He could bestow no high position upon His followers. He determined not to unite himself so closely to Christ but that he could draw away. He would watch. And he did watch.

From that time he expressed doubts that confused the disciples. He introduced controversies and misleading sentiments, repeating the arguments urged by the scribes and Pharisees against the claims of Christ. All the little and large troubles and crosses, the difficulties and the apparent hindrances to the advancement of the gospel, Judas interpreted as evidences against its truthfulness. He would introduce texts of Scripture that had no connection with the truths Christ was presenting. These texts, separated from their connection, perplexed the disciples, and increased the discouragement that was constantly pressing upon them. Yet all this was done by Judas in such a way as to make it appear that he was conscientious. And while the disciples were searching for evidence to confirm the words of the Great Teacher, Judas would lead them almost imperceptibly on another track. Thus in a very religious, and apparently wise, way he was presenting matters in a different light from that in which Jesus had given them, and attaching to His words a meaning that He had not conveyed. His suggestions were constantly exciting an ambitious desire for temporal preferment, and thus turning the disciples from the important things they should have considered. The dissension as to which of them should be greatest was generally excited by Judas.

When Jesus presented to the rich young ruler the condition of discipleship, Judas was displeased. He thought that a mistake had been made. If such men as this ruler could be connected with the believers, they would help sustain Christ's cause. If Judas were only received as a counselor, he thought, he could suggest many plans for the advantage of the little church. His principles and methods would differ somewhat from Christ's, but in these things he thought himself wiser than Christ.

In all that Christ said to His disciples, there was something with which, in heart, Judas disagreed. Under his influence the leaven of disaffection was fast doing its work. The disciples did not see the real agency in all this; but Jesus saw that Satan was communicating his attributes to Judas, and thus opening up a channel through which to influence the other disciples. This, a year before the betrayal, Christ declared. "Have not I chosen you twelve," He said, "and one of you is a devil?" John 6:70.

Yet Judas made no open opposition, nor seemed to question the Saviour's lessons. He made no outward murmur until the time of the feast in Simon's house. When Mary anointed the Saviour's feet, Judas manifested his covetous disposition. At the reproof from Jesus his very spirit seemed turned to gall. Wounded pride and desire for revenge broke down the barriers, and the greed so long indulged held him in control. This will be the experience of everyone who persists in tampering with sin. The elements of depravity that are not resisted and overcome respond to Satan's temptation, and the soul is led captive at his will.

But Judas was not yet wholly hardened. Even after he had twice pledged himself to betray the Saviour, there was opportunity for repentance. At the Passover supper Jesus proved His divinity by revealing the traitor's purpose. He tenderly included Judas in the ministry to the disciples. But the last appeal of love was unheeded. Then the case of Judas was decided, and the feet that Jesus had washed went forth to the betrayer's work.

Judas reasoned that if Jesus was to be crucified, the event must come to pass. His own act in betraying the Saviour would not change the result. If Jesus was not to die, it would only force Him to deliver Himself. At all events, Judas would gain something by his treachery. He counted that he had made a sharp bargain in betraying his Lord.

Judas did not, however, believe that Christ would permit Himself to be arrested. In betraying Him, it was his purpose to teach Him a lesson. He intended to play a part that would make the Saviour careful thenceforth to treat him with due respect. But Judas knew not that he was giving Christ up to death. How often, as the Saviour taught in parables, the scribes and Pharisees had been carried away with His striking illustrations! How often they had pronounced judgment against themselves! Often when the truth was brought home to their hearts, they had been filled with rage, and had taken up stones to cast at Him; but again and again He had made His escape. Since He had escaped so many snares, thought Judas, He certainly would not now allow Himself to be taken.

Judas decided to put the matter to the test. If Jesus really was the Messiah, the people, for whom He had done so much, would rally about Him, and would proclaim Him king. This would forever settle many minds that were now in uncertainty. Judas would have the credit of having placed the king on David's throne. And this act would secure to him the first position, next to Christ, in the new kingdom.

The false disciple acted his part in betraying Jesus. In the garden, when he said to the leaders of the mob, "Whomsoever I shall kiss, that same is He: hold Him fast" (Matt. 26:48), he fully believed that Christ would escape out of their hands. Then if they should blame him, he could say, Did I not tell you to hold Him fast?

Judas beheld the captors of Christ, acting upon his words, bind Him firmly. In amazement he saw that the Saviour suffered Himself to be led away. Anxiously he followed Him from the garden to the trial before the Jewish rulers. At every movement he looked for Him to surprise His enemies, by appearing before them as the Son of God, and setting at nought all their plots and power. But as hour after hour went by, and Jesus submitted to all the abuse heaped upon Him, a terrible fear came to the traitor that he had sold his Master to His death.

As the trial drew to a close, Judas could endure the torture of his guilty conscience no longer. Suddenly a hoarse voice rang through the hall, sending a thrill of terror to all hearts: He is innocent; spare Him, O Caiaphas!

The tall form of Judas was now seen pressing through the startled throng. His face was pale and haggard, and great drops of sweat stood on his forehead. Rushing to the throne of judgment, he threw down before the high priest the pieces of silver that had been the price of his Lord's betrayal. Eagerly grasping the robe of Caiaphas, he implored him to release Jesus, declaring that He had done nothing worthy of death. Caiaphas angrily shook him off, but was confused, and knew not what to say. The perfidy of the priests was revealed. It was evident that they had bribed the disciple to betray his Master.

"I have sinned," again cried Judas, "in that I have betrayed the innocent blood." But the high priest, regaining his self-possession, answered with scorn, "What is that to us? see thou to that." Matt. 27:4. The priests had been willing to make Judas their tool; but they despised his baseness. When he turned to them with confession, they spurned him.

Judas now cast himself at the feet of Jesus, acknowledging Him to be the Son of God, and entreating Him to deliver Himself. The Saviour did not reproach His betrayer. He knew that Judas did not repent; his confession was forced from his guilty soul by an awful sense of condemnation and a looking for of judgment, but he felt no deep, heartbreaking grief that he had betrayed the spotless Son of God, and denied the Holy One of Israel. Yet Jesus spoke no word of condemnation. He looked pityingly upon Judas, and said, For this hour came I into the world.

A murmur of surprise ran through the assembly. With amazement they beheld the forbearance of Christ toward His betrayer. Again there swept over them the conviction that this Man was more than mortal. But if He was the Son of God, they questioned, why did He not free Himself from His bonds and triumph over His accusers?

Judas saw that his entreaties were in vain, and he rushed from the hall exclaiming, It is too late! It is too late! He felt that he could not live to see Jesus crucified, and in despair went out and hanged himself.

Later that same day, on the road from Pilate's hall to Calvary, there came an interruption to the shouts and jeers of the wicked throng who were leading Jesus to the place of crucifixion. As they passed a retired spot, they saw at the foot of a lifeless tree, the body of Judas. It was a most revolting sight. His weight had broken the cord by which he had hanged himself to the tree. In falling, his body had been horribly mangled, and dogs were now devouring it. His remains were immediately buried out of sight; but there was less mockery among the throng, and many a pale face revealed the thoughts within. Retribution seemed already visiting those who were guilty of the blood of Jesus.

Chapter 39

CLEAN, BLOODY HANDS

In the judgment hall of Pilate, the Roman governor, Christ stands bound as a prisoner. About Him are the guard of soldiers, and the hall is fast filling with spectators. Just outside the entrance are the judges of the Sanhedrin, priests, rulers, elders, and the mob.

After condemning Jesus, the council of the Sanhedrin had come to Pilate to have the sentence confirmed and executed. But these Jewish officials would not enter the Roman judgment hall. According to their ceremonial law they would be defiled thereby, and thus prevented from taking part in the feast of the Passover. In their blindness they did not see that murderous hatred had defiled their hearts. They did not see that Christ was the real Passover lamb, and that, since they had rejected Him, the great feast had for them lost its significance.

When the Saviour was brought into the judgment hall, Pilate looked upon Him with no friendly eyes. The Roman governor had been called from his bedchamber in haste, and he determined to do his work as quickly as possible. He was prepared to deal with the prisoner with magisterial severity. Assuming his severest expression, he turned to see what kind of man he had to examine, that he had been called from his repose at so early an hour. He knew that it must be someone whom the Jewish authorities were anxious to have tried and punished with haste.

Pilate looked at the men who had Jesus in charge, and then his gaze rested searchingly on Jesus. He had had to deal with all kinds of criminals; but never before had a man bearing marks of such goodness and nobility been brought before him. On His face he saw no sign of guilt,

This chapter is based on Matt. 27:2, 11-31; Mark 15:1-20; Luke 23:1-25; John 18:28-40; 19:1-16.

no expression of fear, no boldness or defiance. He saw a man of calm and dignified bearing, whose countenance bore not the marks of a criminal, but the signature of heaven.

Christ's appearance made a favorable impression upon Pilate. His better nature was roused. He had heard of Jesus and His works. His wife had told him something of the wonderful deeds performed by the Galilean prophet, who cured the sick and raised the dead. Now this revived as a dream in Pilate's mind. He recalled rumors that he had heard from several sources. He resolved to demand of the Jews their charges against the prisoner.

Who is this Man, and wherefore have ye brought Him? he said. What accusation bring ye against Him? The Jews were disconcerted. Knowing that they could not substantiate their charges against Christ, they did not desire a public examination. They answered that He was a deceiver called Jesus of Nazareth.

Again Pilate asked, "What accusation bring ye against this Man?" The priests did not answer his question, but in words that showed their irritation, they said, "If He were not a malefactor, we would not have delivered Him up unto thee." When those composing the Sanhedrin, the first men of the nation, bring to you a man they deem worthy of death, is there need to ask for an accusation against him? They hoped to impress Pilate with a sense of their importance, and thus lead him to accede to their request without going through many preliminaries. They were eager to have their sentence ratified; for they knew that the people who had witnessed Christ's marvelous works could tell a story very different from the fabrication they themselves were now rehearsing.

The priests thought that with the weak and vacillating Pilate they could carry through their plans without trouble Before this he had signed the death warrant hastily, condemning to death men they knew were not worthy of death. In his estimation the life of a prisoner was of little account; whether he were innocent or guilty was of no special consequence. The priests hoped that Pilate would now inflict the death penalty on Jesus without giving Him a hearing. This they besought as a favor on the occasion of their great national festival.

But there was something in the prisoner that held Pilate back from this. He dared not do it. He read the purposes of the priests. He remembered how, not long before, Jesus had raised Lazarus, a man that had been dead four days; and he determined to know, before signing the sentence of condemnation, what were the charges against Him, and whether they could be proved.

If your judgment is sufficient, he said, why bring the prisoner to me? "Take ye Him, and judge Him according to your law." Thus pressed, the priests said that they had already passed sentence upon Him, but that they must have Pilate's sentence to render their condemnation valid. What is your sentence? Pilate asked. The death sentence, they answered; but it is not lawful for us to put any man to death. They asked Pilate to take their word as to Christ's guilt, and enforce their sentence. They would take the responsibility of the result.

Pilate was not a just or a conscientious judge; but weak though he was in moral power, he refused to grant this request. He would not condemn Jesus until a charge had been brought against Him.

The priests were in a dilemma. They saw that they must cloak their hypocrisy under the thickest concealment. They must not allow it to appear that Christ had been arrested on religious grounds. Were this put forward as a reason, their proceedings would have no weight with Pilate. They must make it appear that Jesus was working against the common law; then He could be punished as a political offender. Tumults and insurrection against the Roman government were constantly arising among the Jews. With these revolts the Romans had dealt very rigorously, and they were constantly on the watch to repress everything that could lead to an outbreak.

Only a few days before this the Pharisees had tried to entrap Christ with the question, "Is it lawful for us to give tribute unto Caesar?" But Christ had unveiled their hypocrisy. The Romans who were present had seen the utter failure of the plotters, and their discomfiture at His answer, "Render therefore unto Caesar the things which be Caesar's." Luke 20:22-25.

Now the priests thought to make it appear that on this occasion Christ had taught what they hoped He would teach. In their extremity they called false witnesses to their aid, "and they began to accuse Him, saying, We found this fellow perverting the nation, and forbidding to give tribute to Caesar, saying that He Himself is Christ a King." Three charges, each without foundation. The priests knew this, but they were willing to commit perjury could they but secure their end.

Pilate saw through their purpose. He did not believe that the prisoner had plotted against the government. His meek and humble appearance was altogether out of harmony with the charge. Pilate was convinced that a deep plot had been laid to destroy an innocent man who stood in the way of the Jewish dignitaries. Turning to Jesus he asked, "Art Thou the King of the Jews?" The Saviour answered, "Thou sayest it." And as He spoke, His countenance lighted up as if a sunbeam were shining upon it.

When they heard His answer, Caiaphas and those that were with him called Pilate to witness that Jesus had admitted the crime with which He was charged. With noisy cries, priests, scribes, and rulers demanded that He be sentenced to death. The cries were taken up by the mob, and the uproar was deafening. Pilate was confused. Seeing that Jesus made no answer to His accusers, Pilate said to Him, "Answerest Thou nothing? behold how many things they witness against Thee. But Jesus yet answered nothing."

Standing behind Pilate, in view of all in the court, Christ heard the abuse; but to all the false charges against Him He answered not a word. His whole bearing gave evidence of conscious innocence. He stood unmoved by the fury of the waves that beat about Him. It was as if the heavy surges of wrath, rising higher and higher, like the waves of the boisterous ocean, broke about Him, but did not touch Him. He stood silent, but His silence was eloquence. It was as a light shining from the inner to the outer man.

Pilate was astonished at His bearing. Does this Man disregard the proceedings because He does not care to save His life? he asked himself. As he looked at Jesus, bearing insult and mockery without retaliation, he felt that He could not be as unrighteous and unjust as were the clamoring priests. Hoping to gain the truth from Him and to escape the tumult of the crowd, Pilate took Jesus aside with him, and again questioned, "Art Thou the King of the Jews?"

Jesus did not directly answer this question. He knew that the Holy Spirit was striving with Pilate, and He gave him opportunity to acknowledge his conviction. "Sayest thou this thing of thyself," He asked, "or did others tell it thee of Me?" That is, was it the accusations of the priests, or a desire to receive light from Christ, that prompted Pilate's question? Pilate understood Christ's meaning; but pride arose in his heart. He would not acknowledge the conviction that pressed upon him. "Am I a Jew?" he said. "Thine own nation and the chief priests have delivered Thee unto me: what hast Thou done?"

Pilate's golden opportunity had passed. Yet Jesus did not leave him without further light. While He did not directly answer Pilate's question, He plainly stated His own mission. He gave Pilate to understand that He was not seeking an earthly throne.

"My kingdom is not of this world," He said; "if My kingdom were of this world, then would My servants fight, that I should not be delivered to the Jews: but now is My kingdom not from hence. Pilate therefore said unto Him, Art Thou a king then? Jesus answered, Thou sayest that I am a king. To this end was I born, and for this cause came I into the world, that I should bear witness unto the truth. Everyone that is of the truth heareth My voice."

Christ affirmed that His word was in itself a key which would unlock the mystery to those who were prepared to receive it. It had a self-commending power, and this was the secret of the spread of His kingdom of truth. He desired Pilate to understand that only by receiving and appropriating truth could his ruined nature be reconstructed.

Pilate had a desire to know the truth. His mind was confused. He eagerly grasped the words of the Saviour, and his heart was stirred with a great longing to know what it really was, and how he could obtain it. "What is truth?" he inquired. But he did not wait for an answer. The tumult outside recalled him to the interests of the hour; for the priests were clamorous for immediate action. Going out to the Jews, he declared emphatically, "I find in Him no fault at all."

These words from a heathen judge were a scathing rebuke to the perfidy and falsehood of the rulers of Israel who were accusing the Saviour. As the priests and elders heard this from Pilate, their disappointment and rage knew no bounds. They had long plotted and waited for this opportunity. As they saw the prospect of the release of Jesus, they seemed ready to tear Him in pieces. They loudly denounced Pilate, and threatened him with the censure of the Roman government. They accused him of refusing to condemn Jesus, who, they affirmed, had set Himself up against Caesar.

Angry voices were now heard, declaring that the seditious influence of Jesus was well known throughout the country. The priests said, "He stirreth up the people, teaching throughout all Jewry, beginning from Galilee to this place."

Pilate at this time had no thought of condemning Jesus. He knew that the Jews had accused Him through hatred and prejudice. He knew what his duty was. Justice demanded that Christ should be immediately released. But Pilate dreaded the ill will of the people. Should he refuse to give Jesus into their hands, a tumult would be raised, and this he feared to meet. When he heard that Christ was from Galilee, he decided to send Him to Herod, the ruler of that province, who was then in Jerusalem. By this course, Pilate thought to shift the responsibility of the trial from himself to Herod. He also thought this a good opportunity to heal an old quarrel between himself and Herod. And so it proved. The two magistrates made friends over the trial of the Saviour.

Pilate delivered Jesus again to the soldiers, and amid the jeers and insults of the mob He was hurried to the judgment hall of Herod. "When Herod saw Jesus, he was exceeding glad." He had never before met the Saviour, but "he was desirous to see Him of a long season, because he had heard many things of Him; and he hoped to have seen some miracle done by Him." This Herod was he whose hands were stained with the blood of John the Baptist. When Herod-first heard of Jesus, he was terror-stricken, and said, "It is John, whom I beheaded: he is risen from the dead;" "therefore mighty works do show forth themselves in him." Mark 6:16; Matt. 14:2. Yet Herod desired to see Jesus. Now there was opportunity to save the life of this prophet, and the king hoped to banish forever from his mind the memory of that bloody head brought to him in a charger. He also desired to have his curiosity gratified, and thought that if Christ were given any prospect of release, He would do anything that was asked of Him.

A large company of the priests and elders had accompanied Christ to Herod. And when the Saviour was brought in, these dignitaries, all speaking excitedly, urged their accusations against Him. But Herod paid little regard to their charges. He commanded silence, desiring an opportunity to question Christ. He ordered that the fetters of Christ should be unloosed, at the same time charging His enemies with roughly treating Him. Looking with compassion into the serene face of the world's Redeemer, he read in it only wisdom and purity. He as well as Pilate was satisfied that Christ had been accused through malice and envy.

Herod questioned Christ in many words, but throughout the Saviour maintained a profound silence. At the command of the king the decrepit and maimed were then called in, and Christ was ordered to prove His claims by working a miracle. Men say that Thou canst heal the sick, said Herod. I am anxious to see that Thy widespread fame has not been belied. Jesus did not respond, and Herod still continued to urge: If Thou canst work miracles for others, work them now for Thine own good, and it will serve Thee a good purpose. Again he commanded, Show us a sign that Thou hast the power with which rumor had accredited Thee. But Christ was as one who heard and saw not. The Son of God had taken upon Himself man's nature. He must do as man must do in like circumstances. Therefore He would not work a miracle to save Himself the pain and humiliation that man must endure when placed in a similar position.

Herod promised that if Christ would perform some miracle in his presence, He should be released. Christ's accusers had seen with their own eyes the mighty works wrought by His power. They had heard Him command the grave to give up its dead. They had seen the dead come forth obedient to His voice. Fear seized them lest He should now work a miracle. Of all things they most dreaded an exhibition of His power. Such a manifestation would prove a deathblow to their plans, and would perhaps cost them their lives. Again the priests and rulers, in great anxiety, urged their accusations against Him. Raising their voices, they declared, He is a traitor, ·a blasphemer. He works His miracles through the power given Him by Beelzebub, the prince of the devils. The hall became a scene of confusion, some crying one thing and some another.

Herod's conscience was now far less sensitive than when he had trembled with horror at the request of Herodias for the head of John the Baptist. For a time he had felt the keen stings of remorse for his terrible act; but his moral perceptions had become more and more degraded by his licentious life. Now his heart had become so hardened that he could even boast of the punishment he had inflicted upon John for daring to reprove him. And he now threatened Jesus, declaring repeatedly that he had power to release or to condemn Him. But no sign from Jesus gave evidence that He heard a word.

Herod was irritated by this silence. It seemed to indicate utter indifference to his authority. To the vain and pompous king, open rebuke would have been less offensive than to be thus ignored. Again he angrily threatened Jesus, who still remained unmoved and silent.

The mission of Christ in this world was not to gratify idle curiosity. He came to heal the brokenhearted. Could He have spoken any word to heal the bruises of sin-sick souls, He would not have kept silent. But He had no words for those who would but trample the truth under their unholy feet.

Christ might have spoken words to Herod that would have pierced the ears of the hardened king. He might have stricken him with fear and trembling by laying before him the full iniquity of his life, and the horror of his approaching doom. But Christ's silence was the severest rebuke that He could have given. Herod had rejected the truth spoken to him by the greatest of the prophets, and no other message was he to receive. Not a word had the Majesty of heaven for him. That ear that had ever been open to human woe, had no room for Herod's commands. Those eyes that had ever rested upon the penitent sinner in pitying, forgiving love had no look to bestow upon Herod. Those lips that had uttered the most impressive truth, that in tones of tenderest entreaty had pleaded with the most sinful and the most degraded, were closed to the haughty king who felt no need of a Saviour.

Herod's face grew dark with passion. Turning to the multitude, he angrily denounced Jesus as an impostor. Then to Christ he said, If You will give no evidence of Your claim, I will deliver You up to the soldiers and the people. They may succeed in making You speak. If You are an impostor, death at their hands is only what You merit; if You are the Son of God, save Yourself by working a miracle.

No sooner were these words spoken than a rush was made for Christ. Like wild beasts, the crowd darted upon their prey. Jesus was dragged this way and that, Herod joining the mob in seeking to humiliate the Son of God. Had not the Roman soldiers interposed, and forced back the maddened throng, the Saviour would have been torn in pieces.

"Herod with his men of war set Him at nought, and

mocked Him, and arrayed Him in a gorgeous robe." The Roman soldiers joined in this abuse. All that these wicked, corrupt soldiers, helped on by Herod and the Jewish dignitaries, could instigate was heaped upon the Saviour. Yet His divine patience failed not.

Christ's persecutors had tried to measure His character by their own; they had represented Him as vile as themselves. But back of all the present appearance another scene intruded itself,—a scene which they will one day see in all its glory. There were some who trembled in Christ's presence. While the rude throng were bowing in mockery before Him, some who came forward for that purpose turned back, afraid and silenced. Herod was convicted. The last rays of merciful light were shining upon his sin-hardened heart. He felt that this was no common man; for divinity had flashed through humanity. At the very time when Christ was encompassed by mockers, adulterers, and murderers, Herod felt that he was beholding a God upon His throne.

Hardened as he was, Herod dared not ratify the condemnation of Christ. He wished to relieve himself of the terrible responsibility, and he sent Jesus back to the Roman judgment hall.

Pilate was disappointed and much displeased. When the Jews returned with their prisoner, he asked impatiently what they would have him do. He reminded them that he had already examined Jesus, and found no fault in Him; he told them that they had brought complaints against Him, but they had not been able to prove a single charge. He had sent Jesus to Herod, the tetrarch of Galilee, and one of their own nation, but he also had found in Him nothing worthy of death. "I will therefore chastise Him," Pilate said, "and release Him."

Here Pilate showed his weakness. He had declared that Jesus was innocent, yet he was willing for Him to be scourged to pacify His accusers. He would sacrifice justice and principle in order to compromise with the mob. This placed him at a disadvantage. The crowd presumed upon his indecision, and clamored the more for the life of the prisoner. If at the first Pilate had stood firm, refusing to condemn a man whom he found guiltless, he would have broken the fatal chain that was to bind him in remorse and guilt as long as he lived. Had he carried out his convictions of right, the Jews would not have presumed to dictate to him. Christ would have been put to death, but the guilt would not have rested upon Pilate. But Pilate had taken step after step in the violation of his conscience. He had excused himself from judging with justice and equity, and he now found himself almost helpless in the hands of the priests and rulers. His wavering and indecision proved his ruin.

Even now Pilate was not left to act blindly. A message from God warned him from the deed he was about to commit. In answer to Christ's prayer, the wife of Pilate had been visited by an angel from heaven, and in a dream she had beheld the Saviour and conversed with Him. Pilate's wife was not a Jew, but as she looked upon Jesus in her dream, she had no doubt of His character or mission. She knew Him to be the Prince of God. She saw Him on trial in the judgment hall. She saw the hands tightly bound as the hands of a criminal. She saw Herod and his soldiers doing their dreadful work. She heard the priests and rulers, filled with envy and malice, madly accusing. She heard the words, "We have a law, and by our law He ought to die." She saw Pilate give Jesus to the scourging, after he had declared, "I find no fault in Him." She heard the condemnation pronounced by Pilate, and saw him give Christ up to His murderers. She saw the cross uplifted on Calvary. She saw the earth wrapped in darkness, and heard the mysterious cry, "It is finished." Still another scene met her gaze. She saw Christ seated upon the great white cloud, while the earth reeled in space, and His murderers fled from the presence of His glory. With a cry of horror she awoke, and at once wrote to Pilate words of warning.

While Pilate was hesitating as to what he should do, a messenger pressed through the crowd, and handed him the letter from his wife, which read:

"Have thou nothing to do with that just Man: for I have suffered many things this day in a dream because of Him."

Pilate's face grew pale. He was confused by his own conflicting emotions. But while he had been delaying to act, the priests and rulers were still further inflaming the minds of the people. Pilate was forced to action. He now bethought himself of a custom which might serve to secure Christ's release. It was customary at this feast to release some one prisoner whom the people might choose. This custom was of pagan invention; there was not a shadow of justice in it, but it was greatly prized by the Jews. The

Roman authorities at this time held a prisoner named Barabbas, who was under sentence of death. This man had claimed to be the Messiah. He claimed authority to establish a different order of things, to set the world right. Under satanic delusion he claimed that whatever he could obtain by theft and robbery was his own. He had done wonderful things through satanic agencies, he had gained a following among the people, and had excited sedition against the Roman government. Under cover of religious enthusiasm he was a hardened and desperate villain, bent on rebellion and cruelty. By giving the people a choice between this man and the innocent Saviour, Pilate thought to arouse them to a sense of justice. He hoped to gain their sympathy for Jesus in opposition to the priests and rulers. So, turning to the crowd, he said with great earnestness, "Whom will ye that I release unto you? Barabbas, or Jesus which is called Christ?"

Like the bellowing of wild beasts came the answer of the mob, "Release unto us Barabbas!" Louder and louder swelled the cry, Barabbas! Barabbas! Thinking that the people had not understood his question, Pilate asked, "Will ye that I release unto you the King of the Jews?" But they cried out again, "Away with this Man, and release unto us Barabbas"! "What shall I do then with Jesus which is called Christ?" Pilate asked. Again the surging multitude roared like demons. Demons themselves, in human form, were in the crowd, and what could be expected but the answer, "Let Him be crucified"?

Pilate was troubled. He had not thought it would come to that. He shrank from delivering an innocent man to the most ignominious and cruel death that could be inflicted. After the roar of voices had ceased, he turned to the people, saying, "Why, what evil hath He done?" But the case had gone too far for argument. It was not evidence of Christ's innocence that they wanted, but His condemnation.

Still Pilate endeavored to save Him. "He said unto them the third time, Why, what evil hath He done? I have found no cause of death in Him: I will therefore chastise Him, and let Him go." But the very mention of His release stirred the people to a tenfold frenzy. "Crucify Him, crucify Him," they cried. Louder and louder swelled the storm that Pilate's indecision had called forth.

Jesus was taken, faint with weariness and covered with wounds, and scourged in the sight of the multitude. "And the soldiers led Him away into the hall, called Praetorium; and they call together the whole band. And they clothed Him with purple, and platted a crown of thorns, and put it about His head, and began to salute Him, Hail, King of the Jews! And they . . . did spit upon Him, and bowing their knees worshiped Him." Occasionally some wicked hand snatched the reed that had been placed in His hand, and struck the crown upon His brow, forcing the thorns into His temples, and sending the blood-trickling down His face and beard.

Wonder, O heavens! and be astonished, O earth! Behold the oppressor and the oppressed. A maddened throng enclose the Saviour of the world. Mocking and jeering are mingled with the coarse oaths of blasphemy. His lowly birth and humble life are commented upon by the unfeeling mob. His claim to be the Son of God is ridiculed, and the vulgar jest and insulting sneer are passed from lip to lip.

Satan led the cruel mob in its abuse of the Saviour. It was his purpose to provoke Him to retaliation if possible, or to drive Him to perform a miracle to release Himself, and thus break up the plan of salvation. One stain upon His human life, one failure of His humanity to endure the terrible test, and the Lamb of God would have been an imperfect offering, and the redemption of man a failure. But He who by a command could bring the heavenly host to His aid—He who could have driven that mob in terror from His sight by the flashing forth of His divine majesty —submitted with perfect calmness to the coarsest insult and outrage.

Christ's enemies had demanded a miracle as evidence of His divinity. They had evidence far greater than any they had sought. As their cruelty degraded His torturers below humanity into the likeness of Satan, so did His meekness and patience exalt Jesus above humanity, and prove His kinship to God. His abasement was the pledge of His exaltation. The blood drops of agony that from His wounded temples flowed down His face and beard were the pledge of His anointing with "the oil of gladness" (Heb. 1:9) as our great high priest.

Satan's rage was great as he saw that all the abuse inflicted upon the Saviour had not forced the least murmur from His lips. Although He had taken upon Him the nature of man, He was sustained by a godlike fortitude, and departed in no particular from the will of His Father.

When Pilate gave Jesus up to be scourged and mocked, he thought to excite the pity of the multitude. He hoped they would decide that this was sufficient punishment. Even the malice of the priests, he thought, would now be satisfied. But with keen perception the Jews saw the weakness of thus punishing a man who had been declared innocent. They knew that Pilate was trying to save the life of the prisoner, and they were determined that Jesus should not be released. To please and satisfy us, Pilate has scourged Him, they thought, and if we press the matter to a decided issue, we shall surely gain our end.

Pilate now sent for Barabbas to be brought into the court. He then presented the two prisoners side by side, and pointing to the Saviour he said in a voice of solemn entreaty, "Behold the Man!" "I bring Him forth to you, that ye may know that I find no fault in Him."

There stood the Son of God, wearing the robe of mockery and the crown of thorns. Stripped to the waist, His back showed the long, cruel stripes, from which the blood flowed freely. His face was stained with blood, and bore the marks of exhaustion and pain; but never had it appeared more beautiful than now. The Saviour's visage was not marred before His enemies. Every feature expressed gentleness and resignation and the tenderest pity for His cruel foes. In His manner there was no cowardly weakness, but the strength and dignity of long-suffering. In striking contrast was the prisoner at His side. Every line of the countenance of Barabbas proclaimed him the hardened ruffian that he was. The contrast spoke to every beholder. Some of the spectators were weeping. As they looked upon Jesus, their hearts were full of sympathy. Even the priests and rulers were convicted that He was all that He claimed to be.

The Roman soldiers that surrounded Christ were not all hardened; some were looking earnestly into His face for one evidence that He was a criminal or dangerous character. From time to time they would turn and cast a look of contempt upon Barabbas. It needed no deep insight to read him through and through. Again they would turn to the One upon trial. They looked at the divine sufferer with feelings of deep pity. The silent submission of Christ stamped upon their minds the scene, never to be effaced until they either acknowledged Him as the Christ, or by rejecting Him decided their own destiny.

Pilate was filled with amazement at the uncomplaining

patience of the Saviour. He did not doubt that the sight of this Man, in contrast with Barabbas, would move the Jews to sympathy. But he did not understand the fanatical hatred of the priests for Him, who, as the Light of the world, had made manifest their darkness and error. They had moved the mob to a mad fury, and again priests, rulers, and people raised that awful cry, "Crucify Him, crucify Him." At last, losing all patience with their unreasoning cruelty, Pilate cried out despairingly, "Take ye Him, and crucify Him: for I find no fault in Him."

The Roman governor, though familiar with cruel scenes, was moved with sympathy for the suffering prisoner, who, condemned and scourged, with bleeding brow and lacerated back, still had the bearing of a king upon his throne. But the priests declared, "We have a law, and by our law He ought to die, because He made Himself the Son of God."

Pilate was startled. He had no correct idea of Christ and His mission; but he had an indistinct faith in God and in beings superior to humanity. A thought that had once before passed through his mind now took more definite shape. He questioned whether it might not be a divine being that stood before him, clad in the purple robe of mockery, and crowned with thorns.

Again he went into the judgment hall, and said to Jesus, "Whence art Thou?" But Jesus gave him no answer. The Saviour had spoken freely to Pilate, explaining His own mission as a witness to the truth. Pilate had disregarded the light. He had abused the high office of judge by yielding his principles and authority to the demands of the mob. Jesus had no further light for him. Vexed at His silence, Pilate said haughtily:

"Speakest Thou not unto me? knowest Thou not that I have power to crucify Thee, and have power to release Thee?"

Jesus answered, "Thou couldest have no power at all against Me, except it were given thee from above: therefore he that delivered Me unto thee hath the greater sin."

Thus the pitying Saviour, in the midst of His intense suffering and grief, excused as far as possible the act of the Roman governor who gave Him up to be crucified. What a scene was this to hand down to the world for all time! What a light it sheds upon the character of Him who is the Judge of all the earth!

"He that delivered Me unto thee," said Jesus, "hath the

greater sin." By this Christ meant Caiaphas, who, as high priest, represented the Jewish nation. They knew the principles that controlled the Roman authorities. They had had light in the prophecies that testified of Christ, and in His own teachings and miracles. The Jewish judges had received unmistakable evidence of the divinity of Him whom they condemned to death. And according to their light would they be judged.

The greatest guilt and heaviest responsibility belonged to those who stood in the highest places in the nation, the depositaries of sacred trusts that they were basely betraying. Pilate, Herod, and the Roman soldiers were comparatively ignorant of Jesus. They thought to please the priests and rulers by abusing Him. They had not the light which the Jewish nation had so abundantly received. Had the light been given to the soldiers, they would not have treated Christ as cruelly as they did.

Again Pilate proposed to release the Saviour. "But the Jews cried out, saying, If thou let this man go, thou art not Caesar's friend." Thus these hypocrites pretended to be jealous for the authority of Caesar. Of all the opponents of the Roman rule, the Jews were most bitter. When it was safe for them to do so, they were most tyrannical in enforcing their own national and religious requirements; but when they desired to bring about some purpose of cruelty, they exalted the power of Caesar. To accomplish the destruction of Christ, they would profess loyalty to the foreign rule which they hated.

"Whosoever maketh himself a king," they continued, "speaketh against Caesar." This was touching Pilate in a weak point. He was under suspicion by the Roman government, and he knew that such a report would be ruin to him. He knew that if the Jews were thwarted, their rage would be turned against him. They would leave nothing undone to accomplish their revenge. He had before him an example of the persistence with which they sought the life of One whom they hated without reason.

Pilate then took his place on the judgment seat, and again presented Jesus to the people, saying, "Behold, your King!" Again the mad cry was heard, "Away with Him, crucify Him." In a voice that was heard far and near, Pilate asked, "Shall I crucify your King?" But from profane, blasphemous lips went forth the words, "We have no king but Caesar."

Thus by choosing a heathen ruler, the Jewish nation had

withdrawn from the theocracy. They had rejected God as their king. Henceforth they had no deliverer. They had no king but Caesar. To this the priests and teachers had led the people. For this, with the fearful results that followed, they were responsible. A nation's sin and a nation's ruin were due to the religious leaders.

"When Pilate saw that he could prevail nothing, but that rather a tumult was made, he took water, and washed his hands before the multitude, saying, I am innocent of the blood of this just Person: see ye to it." In fear and self-condemnation Pilate looked upon the Saviour. In the vast sea of upturned faces, His alone was peaceful. About His head a soft light seemed to shine. Pilate said in his heart, He is a God. Turning to the multitude he declared, I am clear of His blood. Take ye Him, and crucify Him. But mark ye, priests and rulers, I pronounce Him a just man. May He whom He claims as His Father judge you and not me for this day's work. Then to Jesus he said, Forgive me for this act; I cannot save You. And when he had again scourged Jesus, he delivered Him to be crucified.

Pilate longed to deliver Jesus. But he saw that he could not do this, and yet retain his own position and honor. Rather than lose his worldly power, he chose to sacrifice an innocent life. How many, to escape loss or suffering, in like manner sacrifice principle. Conscience and duty point one way, and self-interest points another. The current sets strongly in the wrong direction, and he who compromises with evil is swept away into the thick darkness of guilt.

Pilate yielded to the demands of the mob. Rather than risk losing his position, he delivered Jesus up to be crucified. But in spite of his precautions, the very thing he dreaded afterward came upon him. His honors were stripped from him, he was cast down from his high office, and, stung by remorse and wounded pride, not long after the crucifixion he ended his own life. So all who compromise with sin will gain only sorrow and ruin. "There is a way which seemeth right unto a man, but the end thereof are the ways of death." Prov. 14:12.

When Pilate declared himself innocent of the blood of Christ, Caiaphas answered defiantly, "His blood be on us, and on our children." The awful words were taken up by the priests and rulers, and echoed by the crowd in an inhuman roar of voices. The whole multitude answered and said, "His blood be on us, and on our children."

The people of Israel had made their choice. Pointing to

Jesus they had said, "Not this man, but Barabbas." Barabbas, the robber and murderer, was the representative of Satan. Christ was the representative of God. Christ had been rejected; Barabbas had been chosen. Barabbas they were to have. In making this choice they accepted him who from the beginning was a liar and a murderer. Satan was their leader. As a nation they would act out his dictation. His works they would do. His rule they must endure. That people who chose Barabbas in the place of Christ were to feel the cruelty of Barabbas as long as time should last.

Looking upon the smitten Lamb of God, the Jews had cried, "His blood be on us, and on our children." That awful cry ascended to the throne of God. That sentence, pronounced upon themselves, was written in heaven. That prayer was heard. The blood of the Son of God was upon their children and their children's children, a perpetual curse.

Terribly was it realized in the destruction of Jerusalem. Terribly has it been manifested in the condition of the Jewish nation for eighteen hundred years,—a branch severed from the vine, a dead, fruitless branch, to be gathered up and burned. From land to land throughout the world, from century to century, dead, dead in trespasses and sins!

Terribly will that prayer be fulfilled in the great judgment day. When Christ shall come to the earth again, not as a prisoner surrounded by a rabble will men see Him. They will see Him then as heaven's King. Christ will come in His own glory, in the glory of His Father, and the glory of the holy angels. Ten thousand times ten thousand, and thousands of thousands of angels, the beautiful and triumphant sons of God, possessing surpassing loveliness and glory, will escort Him on His way. Then shall He sit upon the throne of His glory, and before Him shall be gathered all nations. Then every eye shall see Him, and they also that pierced Him. In the place of a crown of thorns, He will wear a crown of glory,—a crown within a crown. In place of that old purple kingly robe, He will be clothed in raiment of whitest white, "so as no fuller on earth can white them." Mark 9:3. And on His vesture and on His thigh a name will be written, "King of kings, and Lord of lords." Rev. 19:16. Those who mocked and smote Him will be there. The priests and rulers will behold again the scene in the judgment hall. Every circumstance will appear before them, as if written in letters of fire. Then those who prayed, "His blood be on us, and on our children," will receive the answer to their prayer. Then the whole world will know and understand. They will realize who and what they, poor, feeble, finite beings, have been warring against. In awful agony and horror they will cry to the mountains and rocks, "Fall on us, and hide us from the face of Him that sitteth on the throne, and from the wrath of the Lamb: for the great day of His wrath is come; and who shall be able to stand?" Rev. 6:16, 17.

Chapter 40

PLACE OF THE SKULL

"AND WHEN they were come to the place, which is called Calvary, there they crucified Him."

"That He might sanctify the people with His own blood," Christ "suffered without the gate." Heb. 13:12. For transgression of the law of God, Adam and Eve were banished from Eden. Christ, our substitute, was to suffer without the boundaries of Jerusalem. He died outside the gate, where felons and murderers were executed. Full of significance are the words, "Christ hath redeemed us from the curse of the law, being made a curse for us." Gal. 3:13.

A vast multitude followed Jesus from the judgment hall to Calvary. The news of His condemnation had spread throughout Jerusalem, and people of all classes and all ranks flocked toward the place of crucifixion. The priests and rulers had been bound by a promise not to molest Christ's followers if He Himself were delivered to them, and the disciples and believers from the city and the surrounding region joined the throng that followed the Saviour.

As Jesus passed the gate of Pilate's court, the cross which had been prepared for Barabbas was laid upon His bruised and bleeding shoulders. Two companions of Barabbas were to suffer death at the same time with Jesus, and upon them also crosses were placed. The Saviour's burden was too heavy for Him in His weak and suffering condition. Since the Passover supper with His disciples, He had taken neither food nor drink. He had agonized in the garden of Gethsemane in conflict with satanic agencies. He had endured the anguish of the betrayal, and had seen His disciples forsake Him and flee. He had been taken to

This chapter is based on Matt. 27:31-53; Mark 15:20-38; Luke 23:26-46; John 19:16-30.

346

Annas, then to Caiaphas, and then to Pilate. From Pilate
He had been sent to Herod, then sent again to Pilate.
From insult to renewed insult, from mockery to mockery,
twice tortured by the scourge,—all that night there had
been scene after scene of a character to try the soul of
man to the uttermost. Christ had not failed. He had spoken no word but that tended to glorify God. All through
the disgraceful farce of a trial He had borne Himself with
firmness and dignity. But when after the second scourging
the cross was laid upon Him, human nature could bear no
more. He fell fainting beneath the burden.

The crowd that followed the Saviour saw His weak and
staggering steps, but they manifested no compassion. They
taunted and reviled Him because He could not carry the
heavy cross. Again the burden was laid upon Him, and
again He fell fainting to the ground. His persecutors saw
that it was impossible for Him to carry His burden farther.
They were puzzled to find anyone who would bear the humiliating load. The Jews themselves could not do this, because the defilement would prevent them from keeping the
Passover. None even of the mob that followed Him would
stoop to bear the cross.

At this time a stranger, Simon a Cyrenian, coming in
from the country, meets the throng. He hears the taunts
and ribaldry of the crowd; he hears the words contemptu-
ously repeated, Make way for the King of the Jews! He
stops in astonishment at the scene; and as he expresses his
compassion, they seize him and place the cross upon his
shoulders.

Simon had heard of Jesus. His sons were believers in the
Saviour, but he himself was not a disciple. The bearing of
the cross to Calvary was a blessing to Simon, and he was
ever after grateful for this providence. It led him to take
upon himself the cross of Christ from choice, and ever
cheerfully stand beneath its burden.

Not a few women are in the crowd that follow the Un-
condemned to His cruel death. Their attention is fixed
upon Jesus. Some of them have seen Him before. Some
have carried to Him their sick and suffering ones.
Some have themselves been healed. The story of the scenes
that have taken place is related. They wonder at the hatred of
the crowd toward Him for whom their own hearts are
melting and ready to break. And notwithstanding the action of the maddened throng, and the angry words of the
priests and rulers, these women give expression to their

sympathy. As Jesus falls fainting beneath the cross, they break forth into mournful wailing.

This was the only thing that attracted Christ's attention. Although full of suffering, while bearing the sins of the world, He was not indifferent to the expression of grief. He looked upon these women wtih tender compassion. They were not believers in Him; He knew that they were not lamenting Him as one sent from God, but were moved by feelings of human pity. He did not despise their sympathy, but it awakened in His heart a deeper sympathy for them. "Daughters of Jerusalem," He said, "weep not for Me, but weep for yourselves, and for your children." From the scene before Him, Christ looked forward to the time of Jerusalem's destruction. In that terrible scene, many of those who were now weeping for Him were to perish with their children.

From the fall of Jerusalem the thoughts of Jesus passed to a wider judgment. In the destruction of the impenitent city He saw a symbol of the final destruction to come upon the world. He said, "Then shall they begin to say to the mountains, Fall on us; and to the hills, Cover us. For if they do these things in a green tree, what shall be done in the dry?" By the green tree, Jesus represented Himself, the innocent Redeemer. God suffered His wrath against transgression to fall on His beloved Son. Jesus was to be crucified for the sins of men. What suffering, then, would the sinner bear who continued in sin? All the impenitent and unbelieving would know a sorrow and misery that language would fail to express.

Of the multitude that followed the Saviour to Calvary, many had attended Him with joyful hosannas and the waving of palm branches as He rode triumphantly into Jerusalem. But not a few who had then shouted His praise, because it was popular to do so, now swelled the cry of "Crucify Him, crucify Him." When Christ rode into Jerusalem, the hopes of the disciples had been raised to the highest pitch. They had pressed close about their Master, feeling that it was a high honor to be connected with Him. Now in His humiliation they followed Him at a distance. They were filled with grief, and bowed down with disappointed hopes. How were the words of Jesus verified: "All ye shall be offended because of Me this night: for it is written, I will smite the shepherd, and the sheep of the flock shall be scattered abroad." Matt. 26:31.

Arriving at the place of execution, the prisoners were

bound to the instruments of torture. The two thieves wrestled in the hands of those who placed them on the cross; but Jesus made no resistance. The mother of Jesus, supported by John the beloved disciple, had followed the steps of her Son to Calvary. She had seen Him fainting under the burden of the cross, and had longed to place a supporting hand beneath His wounded head, and to bathe that brow which had once been pillowed upon her bosom. But she was not permitted this mournful privilege. With the disciples she still cherished the hope that Jesus would manifest His power, and deliver Himself from His enemies. Again her heart would sink as she recalled the words in which He had foretold the very scenes that were then taking place. As the thieves were bound to the cross, she looked on with agonizing suspense. Would He who had given life to the dead suffer Himself to be crucified? Would the Son of God suffer Himself to be thus cruelly slain? Must she give up her faith that Jesus was the Messiah? Must she witness His shame and sorrow, without even the privilege of ministering to Him in His distress? She saw His hands stretched upon the cross; the hammer and the nails were brought, and as the spikes were driven through the tender flesh, the heart-stricken disciples bore away from the cruel scene the fainting form of the mother of Jesus.

The Saviour made no murmur of complaint. His face remained calm and serene, but great drops of sweat stood upon His brow. There was no pitying hand to wipe the death dew from His face, nor words of sympathy and unchanging fidelity to stay His human heart. While the soldiers were doing their fearful work, Jesus prayed for His enemies, "Father, forgive them; for they know not what they do." His mind passed from His own suffering to the sin of His persecutors, and the terrible retribution that would be theirs. No curses were called down upon the soldiers who were handling Him so roughly. No vengeance was invoked upon the priests and rulers, who were gloating over the accomplishment of their purpose. Christ pitied them in their ignorance and guilt. He breathed only a plea for their forgiveness,—"for they know not what they do."

Had they known that they were putting to torture One who had come to save the sinful race from eternal ruin, they would have been seized with remorse and horror. But their ignorance did not remove their guilt; for it was their privilege to know and accept Jesus as their Saviour. Some of them would yet see their sin, and repent, and be converted. Some by their impenitence would make it an impossibility for the prayer of Christ to be answered for them. Yet, just the same, God's purpose was reaching its fulfillment. Jesus was earning the right to become the advocate of men in the Father's presence.

That prayer of Christ for His enemies embraced the world. It took in every sinner that had lived or should live, from the beginning of the world to the end of time. Upon all rests the guilt of crucifying the Son of God. To all, forgiveness is freely offered. "Whosoever will" may have peace with God, and inherit eternal life.

As soon as Jesus was nailed to the cross, it was lifted by strong men, and with great violence thrust into the place prepared for it. This caused the most intense agony to the Son of God. Pilate then wrote an inscription in Hebrew, Greek, and Latin, and placed it upon the cross, above the head of Jesus. It read, "Jesus of Nazareth the King of the Jews." This inscription irritated the Jews. In Pilate's court they had cried, "Crucify Him." "We have no king but Caesar." John 19:15. They had declared that whoever should acknowledge any other king was a traitor. Pilate wrote out the sentiment they had expressed. No offense was mentioned, except that Jesus was the King of the Jews. The inscription was a virtual acknowledgment of the allegiance of the Jews to the Roman power. It declared that whoever might claim to be the King of Israel would be judged by them worthy of death. The priests had overreached themselves. When they were plotting the death of Christ, Caiaphas had declared it expedient that one man should die to save the nation. Now their hypocrisy was revealed. In order to destroy Christ, they had been ready to sacrifice even their national existence.

The priests saw what they had done, and asked Pilate to change the inscription. They said "Write not, The King of the Jews; but that He said, I am King of the Jews." But Pilate was angry with himself because of his former weakness, and he thoroughly despised the jealous and artful priests and rulers. He replied coldly, "What I have written I have written."

A higher power than Pilate or the Jews had directed the placing of that inscription above the head of Jesus. In the providence of God it was to awaken thought, and investigation of the Scriptures. The place where Christ was crucified was near to the city. Thousands of people from all lands were then at Jerusalem, and the inscription declaring Jesus of Nazareth the Messiah would come to their notice. It was a living truth, transcribed by a hand that God had guided.

In the sufferings of Christ upon the cross prophecy was fulfilled. Centuries before the crucifixion, the Saviour had foretold the treatment He was to receive. He said, "Dogs have compassed Me: the assembly of the wicked have enclosed Me: they pierced My hands and My feet. I may tell all My bones: they look and stare upon Me. They part My garments among them, and cast lots upon My vesture." Ps. 22:16-18. The prophecy concerning His garments was carried out without counsel or interference from the friends or the enemies of the Crucified One. To the soldiers who had placed Him upon the cross, His clothing was given. Christ heard the men's contention as they parted the garments among them. His tunic was woven throughout without seam, and they said, "Let us not rend it, but cast lots for it, whose it shall be."

In another prophecy the Saviour declared, "Reproach hath broken My heart; and I am full of heaviness: and I looked for some to take pity, but there was none; and for comforters, but I found none. They gave Me also gall for My meat; and in My thirst they gave Me vinegar to drink." Ps. 69:20, 21. To those who suffered death by the cross, it was permitted to give a stupefying potion, to deaden the sense of pain. This was offered to Jesus; but when He had tasted it, He refused it. He would receive nothing that could becloud His mind. His faith must keep fast hold upon God. This was His only strength. To becloud His senses would give Satan an advantage.

The enemies of Jesus vented their rage upon Him as He hung upon the cross. Priests, rulers, and scribes joined with the mob in mocking the dying Saviour. At the baptism and at the transfiguration the voice of God had been heard proclaiming Christ as His Son. Again, just before Christ's betrayal, the Father had spoken, witnessing to His divinity. But now the voice from heaven was silent. No testimony in Christ's favor was heard. Alone He suffered abuse and mockery from wicked men.

"If Thou be the Son of God," they said, "come down from the cross." "Let Him save Himself, if He be Christ, the chosen of God." In the wilderness of temptation Satan had declared, "If Thou be the Son of God, command that these stones be made bread." "If Thou be the Son of God, cast Thyself down" from the pinnacle of the temple. Matt. 4:3,6. And Satan with his angels, in human form, was present at the cross. The archfiend and his hosts were cooperating with the priests and rulers. The teachers of the people had stimulated the ignorant mob to pronounce judgment against One upon whom many of them had never looked, until urged to bear testimony against Him. Priests, rulers, Pharisees, and the hardened rabble were confederated together in a satanic frenzy. Religious rulers united with Satan and his angels. They were doing his bidding.

Jesus, suffering and dying, heard every word as the priests declared, "He saved others; Himself He cannot save. Let Christ the King of Israel descend now from the cross, that we may see and believe." Christ could have come down from the cross. But it is because He would not save Himself that the sinner has hope of pardon and favor with God.

In their mockery of the Saviour, the men who professed to be the expounders of prophecy were repeating the very words which Inspiration had foretold they would utter upon this occasion. Yet in their blindness they did not see that they were fulfilling the prophecy. Those who in derision uttered the words, "He trusted in God; let Him deliver Him now, if He will have Him: for He said, I am the Son of God," little thought that their testimony would sound down the ages. But although spoken in mockery, these words led men to search the Scriptures as they had never done before. Wise men heard, searched, pondered, and prayed. There were those who never rested until, by comparing scripture with scripture, they saw the meaning of Christ's mission. Never before was there such a general knowledge of Jesus as when He hung upon the cross. Into the hearts of many who beheld the crucifixion scene, and who heard Christ's words, the light of truth was shining.

To Jesus in His agony on the cross there came one gleam of comfort. It was the prayer of the penitent thief. Both the men who were crucified with Jesus had at first railed upon Him; and one under his suffering only became more desperate and defiant. But not so with his companion. This man was not a hardened criminal; he had been led astray by evil associations, but he was less guilty than many of those who stood beside the cross reviling the

Saviour He had seen and heard Jesus, and had been convicted by His teaching, but he had been turned away from Him by the priests and rulers. Seeking to stifle conviction, he had plunged deeper and deeper into sin, until he was arrested, tried as a criminal, and condemned to die on the cross. In the judgment hall and on the way to Calvary he had been in company with Jesus. He had heard Pilate declare, "I find no fault in Him." John 19:4. He had marked His godlike bearing, and His pitying forgiveness of His tormentors. On the cross he sees the many great religionists shoot out the tongue with scorn, and ridicule the Lord Jesus. He sees the wagging heads. He hears the upbraiding speeches taken up by his companion in guilt: "If Thou be Christ, save Thyself and us." Among the passers-by he hears many defending Jesus. He hears them repeat His words, and tell of His works. The conviction comes back to him that this is the Christ. Turning to his fellow criminal he says, "Dost not thou fear God, seeing thou art in the same condemnation?" The dying thieves have no longer anything to fear from man. But upon one of them presses the conviction that there is a God to fear, a future to cause him to tremble. And now, all sin-polluted as it is, his life history is about to close. "And we indeed justly," he moans; "for we receive the due reward of our deeds: but this Man hath done nothing amiss."

There is no question now. There are no doubts, no reproaches. When condemned for his crime, the thief had become hopeless and despairing; but strange, tender thoughts now spring up. He calls to mind all he has heard of Jesus, how He has healed the sick and pardoned sin. He has heard the words of those who believed in Jesus and followed Him weeping. He has seen and read the title about the Saviour's head. He has heard the passers-by repeat it, some with grieved, quivering lips, others with jesting and mockery. The Holy Spirit illuminates his mind, and little by little the chain of evidence is joined together. In Jesus, bruised, mocked, and hanging upon the cross, he sees the Lamb of God, that taketh away the sin of the world. Hope is mingled with anguish in his voice as the helpless, dying soul casts himself upon a dying Saviour. "Lord, remember me," he cries, "when Thou comest into Thy kingdom."

Quickly the answer came. Soft and melodious the tone, full of love, compassion, and power the words: Verily I say unto thee today, Thou shalt be with Me in Paradise.

For long hours of agony, reviling and mockery have fallen upon the ears of Jesus. As He hangs upon the cross, there floats up to Him still the sound of jeers and curses. With longing heart He has listened for some expression of faith from His disciples. He has heard only the mournful words, "We trusted that it had been He which should have redeemed Israel." How grateful then to the Saviour was the utterance of faith and love from the dying thief! While the leading Jews deny Him, and even the disciples doubt His divinity, the poor thief, upon the brink of eternity, calls Jesus Lord. Many were ready to call Him Lord when He wrought miracles, and after He had risen from the grave; but none acknowledged Him as He hung dying upon the cross save the penitent thief who was saved at the eleventh hour.

The bystanders caught the words as the thief called Jesus Lord. The tone of the repentant man arrested their attention. Those who at the foot of the cross had been quarreling over Christ's garments, and casting lots upon His vesture, stopped to listen. Their angry tones were hushed. With bated breath they looked upon Christ, and waited for the response from those dying lips.

As He spoke the words of promise, the dark cloud that seemed to enshroud the cross was pierced by a bright and living light. To the penitent thief came the perfect peace of acceptance with God. Christ in His humiliation was glorified. He who in all other eyes appeared to be conquered was a Conqueror. He was acknowledged as the Sin Bearer. Men may exercise power over His human body. They may pierce the holy temples with the crown of thorns. They may strip from Him His raiment, and quarrel over its division. But they cannot rob Him of His power to forgive sins. In dying He bears testimony to His own divinity and to the glory of the Father. His ear is not heavy that it cannot hear, neither His arm shortened that it cannot save. It is His royal right to save unto the uttermost all who come unto God by Him.

I say unto thee today, Thou shalt be with Me in Paradise. Christ did not promise that the thief should be with Him in Paradise that day. He Himself did not go that day to Paradise. He slept in the tomb, and on the morning of the resurrection He said, "I am not yet ascended to My Father." John 20:17. But on the day of the crucifixion, the day of apparent defeat and darkness, the promise was given. "Today" while dying upon the cross as a malefactor,

Christ assures the poor sinner, Thou shalt be with Me in Paradise.

The thieves crucified with Jesus were placed "on either side one, and Jesus in the midst." This was done by the direction of the priests and rulers. Christ's position between the thieves was to indicate that He was the greatest criminal of the three. Thus was fulfilled the scripture, "He was numbered with the transgressors." Isa. 53:12. But the full meaning of their act the priests did not see. As Jesus, crucified with the thieves, was placed "in the midst," so His cross was placed in the midst of a world lying in sin. And the words of pardon spoken to the penitent thief kindled a light that will shine to the earth's remotest bounds.

With amazement the angels beheld the infinite love of Jesus, who, suffering the most intense agony of mind and body, thought only of others, and encouraged the penitent soul to believe. In His humiliation He as a prophet had addressed the daughters of Jerusalem; as priest and advocate He had pleaded with the Father to forgive His murderers; as a loving Saviour He had forgiven the sins of the penitent thief.

As the eyes of Jesus wandered over the multitude about Him, one figure arrested His attention. At the foot of the cross stood His mother, supported by the disciple John. She could not endure to remain away from her Son; and John, knowing that the end was near, had brought her again to the cross. In His dying hour, Christ remembered His mother. Looking into her grief-stricken face and then upon John, He said to her, "Woman, behold thy son!" then to John, "Behold thy mother!" John understood Christ's words, and accepted the trust. He at once took Mary to his home, and from that hour cared for her tenderly. O pitiful, loving Saviour; amid all His physical pain and mental anguish, He had a thoughtful care for His mother! He had no money with which to provide for her comfort; but He was enshrined in the heart of John, and He gave His mother to him as a precious legacy. Thus He provided for her that which she most needed,—the tender sympathy of one who loved her because she loved Jesus. And in receiving her as a sacred trust, John was receiving a great blessing. She was a constant reminder of his beloved Master.

The perfect example of Christ's filial love shines forth with undimmed luster from the mist of ages. For nearly thirty years Jesus by His daily toil had helped bear the burdens of the home. And now, even in His last agony, He remembers to provide for His sorrowing, widowed mother. The same spirit will be seen in every disciple of our Lord. Those who follow Christ will feel that it is a part of their religion to respect and provide for their parents. From the heart where His love is cherished, father and mother will never fail of receiving thoughtful care and tender sympathy.

And now the Lord of glory was dying, a ransom for the race. In yielding up His precious life, Christ was not upheld by triumphant joy. All was oppressive gloom. It was not the dread of death that weighed upon Him. It was not the pain and ignominy of the cross that caused His inexpressible agony. Christ was the prince of sufferers; but His suffering was from a sense of the malignity of sin, a knowledge that through familiarity with evil, man had become blinded to its enormity. Christ saw how deep is the hold of sin upon the human heart, how few would be willing·to break from its power. He knew that without help from God, humanity must perish, and He saw multitudes perishing within reach of abundant help.

Upon Christ as our substitute and surety was laid the iniquity of us all. He was counted a transgressor, that He might redeem us from the condemnation of the law. The guilt of every descendant of Adam was pressing upon His heart. The wrath of God against sin, the terrible manifestation of His displeasure because of iniquity, filled the soul of His Son with consternation. All His life Christ had been publishing to a fallen world the good news of the Father's mercy and pardoning love. Salvation for the chief of sinners was His theme. But now with the terrible weight of guilt He bears, He cannot see the Father's reconciling face. The withdrawal of the divine countenance from the Saviour in this hour of supreme anguish pierced His heart with a sorrow that can never be fully understood by man. So great was this agony that His physical pain was hardly felt.

Satan with his fierce temptations wrung the heart of Jesus. The Saviour could not see through the portals of the tomb. Hope did not present to Him His coming forth from the grave a conqueror, or tell Him of the Father's acceptance of the sacrifice. He feared that sin was so offensive to God that Their separation was to be eternal. Christ felt the anguish which the sinner will feel when mercy shall no longer plead for the guilty race. It was the sense of sin, bringing the Father's wrath upon Him as man's substitute, that made the cup He drank so bitter, and broke the heart of the Son of God.

With amazement angels witnessed the Saviour's despairing agony. The hosts of heaven veiled their faces from the fearful sight. Inanimate nature expressed sympathy with its insulted and dying Author. The sun refused to look upon the awful scene. Its full, bright rays were illuminating the earth at midday, when suddenly it seemed to be blotted out. Complete darkness, like a funeral pall, enveloped the cross. "There was darkness over all the land unto the ninth hour." There was no eclipse or other natural cause for this darkness, which was as deep as midnight without moon or stars. It was a miraculous testimony given by God that the faith of after generations might be confirmed.

In that thick darkness God's presence was hidden. He makes darkness His pavilion, and conceals His glory from human eyes. God and His holy angels were beside the cross. The Father was with His Son. Yet His presence was not revealed. Had His glory flashed forth from the cloud, every human beholder would have been destroyed. And in that dreadful hour Christ was not to be comforted with the Father's presence. He trod the wine press alone, and of the people there was none with Him.

In the thick darkness, God veiled the last human agony of His Son. All who had seen Christ in His suffering had been convicted of His divinity. That face, once beheld by humanity, was never forgotten. As the face of Cain expressed his guilt as a murderer, so the face of Christ revealed innocence, serenity, benevolence,—the image of God. But His accusers would not give heed to the signet of heaven. Through long hours of agony Christ had been gazed upon by the jeering multitude. Now He was mercifully hidden by the mantle of God.

The silence of the grave seemed to have fallen upon Calvary. A nameless terror held the throng that was gathered about the cross. The cursing and reviling ceased in the midst of half-uttered sentences. Men, women, and children fell prostrated upon the earth. Vivid lightnings occasionally flashed forth from the cloud, and revealed the cross and the crucified Redeemer. Priests, rulers, scribes, executioners, and the mob, all thought that their time of retribution had come. After a while some whispered that Jesus would now come down from the cross. Some attempted to grope their way back to the city, beating their breasts and wailing in fear.

At the ninth hour the darkness lifted from the people, but still enveloped the Saviour. It was a symbol of the agony and horror that weighed upon His heart. No eye could pierce the gloom that surrounded the cross, and none could penetrate the deeper gloom that enshrouded the suffering soul of Christ. The angry lightnings seemed to be hurled at Him as He hung upon the cross. Then "Jesus cried with a loud voice, saying, Eloi, Eloi, lama sabachthani?" "My God, My God, why hast Thou forsaken Me?" As the outer gloom settled about the Saviour, many voices exclaimed: The vengeance of heaven is upon Him. The bolts of God's wrath are hurled at Him, because He claimed to be the Son of God. Many who believed on Him heard His despairing cry. Hope left them. If God had forsaken Jesus, in what could His followers trust?

When the darkness lifted from the oppressed spirit of Christ, He revived to a sense of physical suffering, and said, "I thirst." One of the Roman soldiers, touched with pity as he looked at the parched lips, took a sponge on a stalk of hyssop, and dipping it in a vessel of vinegar, offered it to Jesus. But the priests mocked at His agony. When darkness covered the earth, they had been filled with fear; as their terror abated, the dread returned that Jesus would yet escape them. His words, "Eloi, Eloi, lama sabachthani?" they had misinterpreted. With bitter contempt and scorn they said, "This man calleth for Elias." The last opportunity to relieve His sufferings they refused. "Let be," they said, "let us see whether Elias will come to save Him."

The spotless Son of God hung upon the cross, His flesh lacerated with stripes; those hands so often reached out in blessing, nailed to the wooden bars; those feet so tireless on ministries of love, spiked to the tree; that royal head pierced by the crown of thorns; those quivering lips shaped to the cry of woe. And all that He endured—the blood drops that flowed from His head, His hands, His feet, the agony that racked His frame, and the unutterable anguish that filled His soul at the hiding of His Father's face—speaks to each child of humanity, declaring, It is for thee that the Son of God consents to bear this burden of guilt; for thee He spoils the domain of death, and opens the gates of Paradise. He who stilled the angry waves and walked the foam-capped billows, who made devils tremble and disease flee, who opened blind eyes and called forth the dead to life,—offers Himself upon the cross as a sacrifice, and this from love to thee. He, the Sin Bearer, endures the wrath of divine justice, and for thy sake becomes sin itself.

In silence the beholders watched for the end of the fearful scene. The sun shone forth; but the cross was still enveloped in darkness. Priests and rulers looked toward Jerusalem; and lo, the dense cloud had settled over the city and the plains of Judea. The Sun of Righteousness, the Light of the world, was withdrawing His beams from the once favored city of Jerusalem. The fierce lightnings of God's wrath were directed against the fated city.

Suddenly the gloom lifted from the cross, and in clear, trumpetlike tones, that seemed to resound throughout creation, Jesus cried, "It is finished." "Father, into Thy hands I commend My spirit." A light encircled the cross, and the face of the Saviour shone with a glory like the sun. He then bowed His head upon His breast, and died.

Amid the awful darkness, apparently forsaken of God, Christ had drained the last dregs in the cup of human woe. In those dreadful hours He had relied upon the evidence of His Father's acceptance heretofore given Him. He was acquainted with the character of His Father; He understood His justice, His mercy, and His great love. By faith He rested in Him whom it had ever been His joy to obey. And as in submission He committed Himself to God, the sense of the loss of His Father's favor was withdrawn. By faith, Christ was victor.

Never before had the earth witnessed such a scene. The multitude stood paralyzed, and with bated breath gazed upon the Saviour. Again darkness settled upon the earth, and a hoarse rumbling, like heavy thunder, was heard. There was a violent earthquake. The people were shaken together in heaps. The wildest confusion and consternation ensued. In the surrounding mountains, rocks were rent asunder, and went crashing down into the plains. Sepulchers were broken open, and the dead were cast out of their tombs. Creation seemed to be shivering to atoms. Priests, rulers, soldiers, executioners, and people, mute with terror, lay prostrate upon the ground.

When the loud cry, "It is finished," came from the lips of Christ, the priests were officiating in the temple. It was the hour of the evening sacrifice. The lamb representing Christ had been brought to be slain. Clothed in his significant and beautiful dress, the priest stood with lifted knife, as did Abraham when he was about to slay his son. With intense interest the people were looking on. But the earth trembles and quakes; for the Lord Himself draws near. With a rending noise the inner veil of the temple is torn from top to bottom by an unseen hand, throwing open to the gaze of the multitude a place once filled with the presence of God. In this place the Shekinah had dwelt. Here God had manifested His glory above the mercy seat. No one but the high priest ever lifted the veil separating this apartment from the rest of the temple. He entered in once a year to make an atonement for the sins of the people. But lo, this veil is rent in twain. The most holy place of the earthly sanctuary is no longer sacred.

All is terror and confusion. The priest is about to slay the victim; but the knife drops from his nerveless hand, and the lamb escapes. Type has met antitype in the death of God's Son. The great sacrifice has been made. The way into the holiest is laid open. A new and living way is prepared for all. No longer need sinful, sorrowing humanity await the coming of the high priest. Henceforth the Saviour was to officiate as priest and advocate in the heaven of heavens. It was as if a living voice had spoken to the worshipers: There is now an end to all sacrifices and offerings for sin. The Son of God is come according to His word, "Lo, I come (in the volume of the Book it is written of Me,) to do Thy will, O God." "By His own blood" He entereth "in once into the holy place, having obtained eternal redemption for us." Heb. 10:7; 9:12.

Chapter 41

TORN FLESH — TORN VEIL

CHRIST DID not yield up His life till He had accomplished the work which He came to do, and with His parting breath He exclaimed, "It is finished." John 19:30. The battle had been won. His right hand and His holy arm had gotten Him the victory. As a Conqueror He planted His banner on the eternal heights. Was there not joy among the angels? All heaven triumphed in the Saviour's victory. Satan was defeated, and knew that his kingdom was lost.

To the angels and the unfallen worlds the cry, "It is finished," had a deep significance. It was for them as well as for us that the great work of redemption had been accomplished. They with us share the fruits of Christ's victory.

Not until the death of Christ was the character of Satan clearly revealed to the angels or to the unfallen worlds. The archapostate had so clothed himself with deception that even holy beings had not understood his principles. They had not clearly seen the nature of his rebellion.

It was a being of wonderful power and glory that had set himself against God. Of Lucifer the Lord says, "Thou sealest up the sum, full of wisdom, and perfect in beauty." Ezek. 28:12. Lucifer had been the covering cherub. He had stood in the light of God's presence. He had been the highest of all created beings, and had been foremost in revealing God's purposes to the universe. After he had sinned, his power to deceive was the more deceptive, and the unveiling of his character was the more difficult, because of the exalted position he had held with the Father.

God could have destroyed Satan and his sympathizers as easily as one can cast a pebble to the earth; but He did not do this. Rebellion was not to be overcome by force. Compelling power is found only under Satan's government. The Lord's principles are not of this order. His authority rests upon goodness, mercy, and love; and the presentation

361

of these principles is the means to be used. God's government is moral, and truth and love are to be the prevailing power.

It was God's purpose to place things on an eternal basis of security, and in the councils of heaven it was decided that time must be given for Satan to develop the principles which were the foundation of his system of government. He had claimed that these were superior to God's principles. Time was given for the working of Satan's principles, that they might be seen by the heavenly universe.

Satan led men into sin, and the plan of redemption was put in operation. For four thousand years, Christ was working for man's uplifting, and Satan for his ruin and degradation. And the heavenly universe beheld it all.

When Jesus came into the world, Satan's power was turned against Him. From the time when He appeared as a babe in Bethlehem, the usurper worked to bring about His destruction. In every possible way he sought to prevent Jesus from developing a perfect childhood, a faultless manhood, a holy ministry, and an unblemished sacrifice. But he was defeated. He could not lead Jesus into sin. He could not discourage Him, or drive Him from a work He had come on earth to do. From the desert to Calvary, the storm of Satan's wrath beat upon Him, but the more mercilessly it fell, the more firmly did the Son of God cling to the hand of His Father and press on in the bloodstained path. All the efforts of Satan to oppress and overcome Him only brought out in a purer light His spotless character.

All heaven and the unfallen worlds had been witnesses to the controversy. With what intense interest did they follow the closing scenes of the conflict. They beheld the Saviour enter the garden of Gethsemane, His soul bowed down with the horror of a great darkness. They heard His bitter cry, "Father, if it be possible, let this cup pass from Me." Matt. 26:39. As the Father's presence was withdrawn, they saw Him sorrowful with a bitterness of sorrow exceeding that of the last great struggle with death. The bloody sweat was forced from His pores, and fell in drops upon the ground. Thrice the prayer for deliverance was wrung from His lips. Heaven could no longer endure the sight, and a messenger of comfort was sent to the Son of God.

Heaven beheld the Victim betrayed into the hands of the murderous mob, and with mockery and violence hurried from one tribunal to another. It heard the sneers of

His persecutors because of His lowly birth. It heard the denial with cursing and swearing by one of His best-loved disciples. It saw the frenzied work of Satan, and his power over the hearts of men. Oh, fearful scene! the Saviour seized at midnight in Gethsemane, dragged to and fro from palace to judgment hall, arraigned twice before the priests, twice before the Sanhedrin, twice before Pilate, and once before Herod, mocked, scourged, condemned, and led out to be crucified, bearing the heavy burden of the cross, amid the wailing of the daughters of Jerusalem and the jeering of the rabble.

Heaven viewed with grief and amazement Christ hanging upon the cross, blood flowing from His wounded temples, and sweat tinged with blood standing upon His brow. From His hands and feet the blood fell, drop by drop, upon the rock drilled for the foot of the cross. The wounds made by the nails gaped as the weight of His body dragged upon His hands. His labored breath grew quick and deep, as His soul panted under the burden of the sins of the world. All heaven was filled with wonder when the prayer of Christ was offered in the midst of His terrible suffering,—"Father, forgive them; for they know not what they do." Luke 23:34. Yet there stood men, formed in the image of God, joining to crush out the life of His only-begotten Son. What a sight for the heavenly universe!

The principalities and powers of darkness were assembled around the cross, casting the hellish shadow of unbelief into the hearts of men. When the Lord created these beings to stand before His throne, they were beautiful and glorious. Their loveliness and holiness were in accordance with their exalted station. They were enriched with the wisdom of God, and girded with the panoply of heaven. They were Jehovah's ministers. But who could recognize in the fallen angels the glorious seraphim that once ministered in the heavenly courts?

Satanic agencies confederated with evil men in leading the people to believe Christ the chief of sinners, and to make Him the object of detestation. Those who mocked Christ as He hung upon the cross were imbued with the spirit of the first great rebel. He filled them with vile and loathsome speeches. He inspired their taunts. But by all this he gained nothing.

Could one sin have been found in Christ, had He in one particular yielded to Satan to escape the terrible torture, the enemy of God and man would have triumphed. Christ bowed His head and died, but He held fast His faith and His submission to God. "And I heard a loud voice saying in heaven, Now is come salvation, and strength, and the kingdom of our God, and the power of His Christ: for the accuser of our brethren is cast down, which accused them before our God day and night." Rev. 12:10.

Satan saw that his disguise was torn away. His administration was laid open before the unfallen angels and before the heavenly universe. He had revealed himself as a murderer. By shedding the blood of the Son of God, he had uprooted himself from the sympathies of the heavenly beings. Henceforth his work was restricted. Whatever attitude he might assume, he could no longer await the angels as they came from the heavenly courts, and before them accuse Christ's brethren of being clothed with the garments of blackness and the defilement of sin. The last link of sympathy between Satan and the heavenly world was broken.

Yet Satan was not then destroyed. The angels did not even then understand all that was involved in the great controversy. The principles at stake were to be more fully revealed. And for the sake of man, Satan's existence must be continued. Man as well as angels must see the contrast between the Prince of light and the prince of darkness. He must choose whom he will serve.

In the opening of the great controversy, Satan had declared that the law of God could not be obeyed, that justice was inconsistent with mercy, and that, should the law be broken, it would be impossible for the sinner to be pardoned. Every sin must meet its punishment, urged Satan; and if God should remit the punishment of sin, He would not be a God of truth and justice. When men broke the law of God, and defied His will, Satan exulted. It was proved, he declared, that the law could not be obeyed; man could not be forgiven. Because he, after his rebellion, had been banished from heaven, Satan claimed that the human race must be forever shut out from God's favor. God could not be just, he urged, and yet show mercy to the sinner.

But even as a sinner, man was in a different position from that of Satan. Lucifer in heaven had sinned in the light of God's glory. To him as to no other created being was given a revelation of God's love. Understanding the character of God, knowing His goodness, Satan chose to follow his own selfish, independent will. This choice was final. There was no more that God could do to save him. But man was deceived; his mind was darkened by Satan's sophistry. The height and depth of the love of God he did not know. For him there was hope in a knowledge of God's love. By beholding His character he might be drawn back to God.

Through Jesus, God's mercy was manifested to men; but mercy does not set aside justice. The law reveals the attributes of God's character, and not a jot or tittle of it could be changed to meet man in his fallen condition. God did not change His law, but He sacrificed Himself, in Christ, for man's redemption. "God was in Christ, reconciling the world unto Himself." 2 Cor. 5:19.

The law requires righteousness,—a righteous life, a perfect character; and this man has not to give. He cannot meet the claims of God's holy law. But Christ, coming to the earth as man, lived a holy life, and developed a perfect character. These He offers as a free gift to all who will receive them. His life stands for the life of men. Thus they have remission of sins that are past, through the forbearance of God. More than this, Christ imbues men with the attributes of God. He builds up the human character after the similitude of the divine character, a goodly fabric of spiritual strength and beauty. Thus the very righteousness of the law is fulfilled in the believer in Christ. God can "be just, and the justifier of him which believeth in Jesus." Rom. 3:26.

God's love has been expressed in His justice no less than in His mercy. Justice is the foundation of His throne, and the fruit of His love. It had been Satan's purpose to divorce mercy from truth and justice. He sought to prove that the righteousness of God's law is an enemy to peace. But Christ shows that in God's plan they are indissolubly joined together; the one cannot exist without the other. "Mercy and truth are met together; righteousness and peace have kissed each other." Ps. 85:10.

By His life and His death, Christ proved that God's justice did not destroy His mercy, but that sin could be forgiven, and that the law is righteous, and can be perfectly obeyed. Satan's charges were refuted. God had given man unmistakable evidence of His love.

Another deception was now to be brought forward. Satan declared that mercy destroyed justice, that the death of Christ abrogated the Father's law. Had it been possible for the law to be changed or abrogated, then Christ need not have died. But to abrogate the law would be to immortalize transgression, and place the world under Satan's control. It was because the law was changeless, because man could be saved only through obedience to its precepts, that Jesus was lifted up on the cross. Yet the very means by which Christ established the law Satan represented as destroying it. Here will come the last conflict of the great controversy between Christ and Satan.

That the law which was spoken by God's own voice is faulty, that some specification has been set aside, is the claim which Satan now puts forward. It is the last great deception that he will bring upon the world. He needs not to assail the whole law; if he can lead men to disregard one precept, his purpose is gained. For "whosoever shall keep the whole law, and yet offend in one point, he is guilty of all." James 2:10. By consenting to break one precept, men are brought under Satan's power. By substituting human law for God's law, Satan will seek to control the world. This work is foretold in prophecy. Of the great apostate power which is the representative of Satan, it is declared, "He shall speak great words against the Most High, and shall wear out the saints of the Most High, and think to change times and laws: and they shall be given into his hand." Dan. 7:25.

Men will surely set up their laws to counterwork the laws of God. They will seek to compel the consciences of others, and in their zeal to enforce these laws they will oppress their fellow men.

The warfare against God's law, which was begun in heaven, will be continued until the end of time. Every man will be tested. Obedience or disobedience is the question to be decided by the whole world. All will be called to choose between the law of God and the laws of men. Here the dividing line will be drawn. There will be but two classes. Every character will be fully developed; and all will show whether they have chosen the side of loyalty or that of rebellion.

Then the end will come. God will vindicate His law and deliver His people. Satan and all who have joined him in rebellion will be cut off. Sin and sinners will perish, root and branch (Mal. 4:1),—Satan the root, and his followers the branches. The word will be fulfilled to the prince of evil, "Because thou hast set thine heart as the heart of God; . . . I will destroy thee, O covering cherub, from the midst of the stones of fire. . . . Thou shalt be a terror, and

never shalt thou be any more." Then "the wicked shall not
be: yea, thou shalt diligently consider his place, and it
shall not be;" "they shall be as though they had not been."
Ezek. 28:6-19; Ps. 37:10; Obadiah 16.

This is not an act of arbitrary power on the part of
God. The rejecters of His mercy reap that which they have
sown. God is the fountain of life; and when one chooses
the service of sin, he separates from God, and thus cuts
himself off from life. He is "alienated from the life of
God." Christ says, "All they that hate Me love death."
Eph. 4:18; Prov. 8:36. God gives them existence for a
time that they may develop their character and reveal their
principles. This accomplished, they receive the results of
their own choice. By a life of rebellion, Satan and all who
unite with him place themselves so out of harmony with
God that His very presence is to them a consuming fire.
The glory of Him who is love will destroy them.

At the beginning of the great controversy, the angels did
not understand this. Had Satan and his host then been left
to reap the full result of their sin, they would have
perished; but it would not have been apparent to heavenly
beings that this was the inevitable result of sin. A doubt of
God's goodness would have remained in their minds as
evil seed, to produce its deadly fruit of sin and woe.

But not so when the great controversy shall be ended.
Then, the plan of redemption having been completed, the
character of God is revealed to all created intelligences.
The precepts of His law are seen to be perfect and immutable. Then sin has made manifest its nature, Satan his
character. Then the extermination of sin will vindicate
God's love and establish His honor before a universe of
beings who delight to do His will, and in whose heart is
His law.

Well, then, might the angels rejoice as they looked upon
the Saviour's cross; for though they did not then understand all, they knew that the destruction of sin and Satan
was forever made certain, that the redemption of man was
assured, and that the universe was made eternally secure.
Christ Himself fully comprehended the results of the sacrifice made upon Calvary. To all these He looked forward
when upon the cross He cried out, "It is finished."

Chapter 42

THE TOMB

AT LAST Jesus was at rest. The long day of shame and torture was ended. As the last rays of the setting sun ushered in the Sabbath, the Son of God lay in quietude in Joseph's tomb. His work completed, His hands folded in peace, He rested through the sacred hours of the Sabbath day.

In the beginning the Father and the Son had rested upon the Sabbath after Their work of creation. When "the heavens and the earth were finished, and all the host of them" (Gen. 2:1), the Creator and all heavenly beings rejoiced in contemplation of the glorious scene. "The morning stars sang together, and all the sons of God shouted for joy." Job 38:7. Now Jesus rested from the work of redemption; and though there was grief among those who loved Him on earth, yet there was joy in heaven. Glorious to the eyes of heavenly beings was the promise of the future. A restored creation, a redeemed race, that having conquered sin could never fall,—this, the result to flow from Christ's completed work, God and angels saw. With this scene the day upon which Jesus rested is forever linked. For "His work is perfect;" and "whatsoever God doeth, it shall be forever." Deut. 32:4; Eccl. 3:14. When there shall be a "restitution of all things, which God hath spoken by the mouth of all His holy prophets since the world began" (Acts 3:21), the creation Sabbath, the day on which Jesus lay at rest in Joseph's tomb, will still be a day of rest and rejoicing. Heaven and earth will unite in praise, as "from one Sabbath to another" (Isa. 66:23) the nations of the saved shall bow in joyful worship to God and the Lamb.

In the closing events of the crucifixion day, fresh evidence was given of the fulfillment of prophecy, and new witness borne to Christ's divinity. When the darkness had lifted from the cross, and the Saviour's dying cry had been uttered, immediately another voice was heard, saying, "Truly this was the Son of God."

These words were said in no whispered tones. All eyes were turned to see whence they came. Who had spoken? It was the centurion, the Roman soldier. The divine patience of the Saviour, and His sudden death, with the cry of victory upon His lips, had impressed this heathen. In the bruised, broken body hanging upon the cross, the centurion recognized the form of the Son of God. He could not refrain from confessing his faith. Thus again evidence was given that our Redeemer was to see of the travail of His soul. Upon the very day of His death, three men, differing widely from one another, had declared their faith,—he who commanded the Roman guard, he who bore the cross of the Saviour and he who died upon the cross at His side.

As evening drew on, an unearthly stillness hung over Calvary. The crowd dispersed, and many returned to Jerusalem greatly changed in spirit from what they had been in the morning. Many had flocked to the crucifixion from curiosity, and not from hatred toward Christ. Still they believed the accusations of the priests, and looked upon Christ as a malefactor. Under an unnatural excitement they had united with the mob in railing against Him. But when the earth was wrapped in blackness, and they stood accused by their own consciences, they felt guilty of a great wrong. No jest or mocking laughter was heard in the midst of that fearful gloom; and when it was lifted, they made their way to their homes in solemn silence. They were convinced that the charges of the priests were false, that Jesus was no pretender; and a few weeks later, when Peter preached upon the day of Pentecost, they were among the thousands who became converts to Christ.

But the Jewish leaders were unchanged by the events they had witnessed. Their hatred of Jesus had not abated. The darkness that had mantled the earth at the crucifixion was not more dense than that which still enveloped the minds of the priests and rulers. At His birth the star had known Christ, and had guided the wise men to the manger where He lay. The heavenly hosts had known Him, and had sung His praise over the plains of Bethlehem. The sea had known His voice, and had obeyed His command. Disease and death had recognized His authority, and had yielded to Him their prey. The sun had known Him, and at the sight of His dying anguish, had hidden its face of light. The rocks had known Him, and had shivered into fragments at His cry. Inanimate nature had known Christ, and had borne witness to His divinity. But the priests and rulers of Israel knew not the Son of God.

Yet the priests and rulers were not at rest. They had carried out their purpose in putting Christ to death; but they did not feel the sense of victory they had expected. Even in the hour of their apparent triumph, they were harassed with doubts as to what would next take place. They had heard the cry, "It is finished." "Father, into Thy hands I commend My spirit." John 19:30; Luke 23:46. They had seen the rocks rent, and had felt the mighty earthquake, and they were restless and uneasy.

They had been jealous of Christ's influence with the people when living; they were jealous of Him even in death. They dreaded the dead Christ more, far more, than they had ever feared the living Christ. They dreaded to have the attention of the people directed any further to the events attending His crucifixion. They feared the results of that day's work. Not on any account would they have had His body remain on the cross during the Sabbath. The Sabbath was now drawing on, and it would be a violation of its sanctity for the bodies to hang upon the cross. So, using this as a pretext, the leading Jews requested Pilate that the death of the victims might be hastened, and their bodies be removed before the setting of the sun.

Pilate was as unwilling as they for the body of Jesus to remain upon the cross. His consent having been obtained, the legs of the two thieves were broken to hasten their death; but Jesus was found to be already dead. The rude soldiers had been softened by what they had heard and seen of Christ, and they were restrained from breaking His limbs. Thus in the offering of the Lamb of God was fulfilled the law of the Passover, "They shall leave none of it unto the morning, nor break any bone of it: according to all the ordinances of the Passover they shall keep it." Num. 9:12.

The priests and rulers were amazed to find that Christ was dead. Death by the cross was a lingering process; it was difficult to determine when life had ceased. It was an unheard-of thing for one to die within six hours of crucifixion. The priests wished to make sure of the death of Jesus, and at their suggestion a soldier thrust a spear into the Saviour's side. From the wound thus made, there flowed two copious and distinct streams, one of blood, the other of water. This was noted by all the beholders, and John states the occurrence very definitely. He says, "One of the soldiers with a spear pierced His side, and forthwith came there out blood and water. And he that saw it bare record, and his record is true: and he knoweth that he saith true, that ye might believe. For these things were done, that the scripture should be fulfilled, A bone of Him shall not be broken. And again another scripture saith, They shall look on Him whom they pierced." John 19:34-37.

After the resurrection the priests and rulers circulated the report that Christ did not die upon the cross, that He merely fainted, and was afterward revived. Another report affirmed that it was not a real body of flesh and bone, but the likeness of a body, that was laid in the tomb. The action of the Roman soldiers disproves these falsehoods. They broke not His legs, because He was already dead. To satisfy the priests, they pierced His side. Had not life been already extinct, this wound would have caused instant death.

But it was not the spear thrust, it was not the pain of the cross, that caused the death of Jesus. That cry, uttered "with a loud voice" (Matt. 27:50; Luke 23:46), at the moment of death, the stream of blood and water that flowed from His side, declared that He died of a broken heart. His heart was broken by mental anguish. He was slain by the sin of the world.

With the death of Christ the hopes of His disciples perished. They looked upon His closed eyelids and drooping head, His hair matted with blood, His pierced hands and feet, and their anguish was indescribable. Until the last they had not believed that He would die; they could hardly believe that He was really dead. Overwhelmed with sorrow, they did not recall His words foretelling this very scene. Nothing that He had said now gave them comfort. They saw only the cross and its bleeding Victim. The future seemed dark with despair. Their faith in Jesus had perished; but never had they loved their Lord as now. Never before had they so felt His worth, and their need of His presence.

Even in death, Christ's body was very precious to His disciples. They longed to give Him an honored burial, but knew not how to accomplish this. Treason against the Roman government was the crime for which Jesus was condemned, and persons put to death for this offense were consigned to a burial ground especially provided for such criminals. The disciple John with the women from Galilee had remained at the cross. They could not leave the body of their Lord to be handled by the unfeeling soldiers, and buried in a dishonored grave. Yet they could not prevent it. They could obtain no favors from the Jewish authorities, and they had no influence with Pilate.

In this emergency, Joseph of Arimathaea and Nicodemus came to the help of the disciples. Both these men were members of the Sanhedrin, and were acquainted with Pilate. Both were men of wealth and influence. They were determined that the body of Jesus should have an honorable burial.

Joseph went boldly to Pilate, and begged from him the body of Jesus. For the first time, Pilate learned that Jesus was really dead. Conflicting reports had reached him in regard to the events attending the crucifixion, but the knowledge of Christ's death had been purposely kept from him. Pilate had been warned by the priests and rulers against deception by Christ's disciples in regard to His body. Upon hearing Joseph's request, he therefore sent for the centurion who had charge at the cross, and learned for a certainty of the death of Jesus. He also drew from him an account of the scenes of Calvary, confirming the testimony of Joseph.

The request of Joseph was granted. While John was troubled about the burial of his Master, Joseph returned with Pilate's order for the body of Christ; and Nicodemus came bringing a costly mixture of myrrh and aloes, of about a hundred pounds' weight, for His embalming. The most honored in all Jerusalem could not have been shown more respect in death. The disciples were astonished to see these wealthy rulers as much interested as they themselves in the burial of their Lord.

Neither Joseph nor Nicodemus had openly accepted the Saviour while He was living. They knew that such a step would exclude them from the Sanhedrin, and they hoped to protect Him by their influence in its councils. For a time they had seemed to succeed; but the wily priests, seeing their favor to Christ, had thwarted their plans. In their absence Jesus had been condemned and delivered to be crucified. Now that He was dead, they no longer concealed their attachment to Him. While the disciples feared to show themselves openly as His followers, Joseph and Nicodemus came boldly to their aid. The help of these rich and honored men was greatly needed at this time. They could do for their dead Master what it was impossible for the poor disciples to do; and their wealth and influence protected them, in a great measure, from the malice of the priests and rulers.

Gently and reverently they removed with their own hands the body of Jesus from the cross. Their tears of sympathy fell fast as they looked upon His bruised and lacerated form. Joseph owned a new tomb, hewn in a rock. This he was reserving for himself; but it was near Calvary, and he now prepared it for Jesus. The body, together with the spices brought by Nicodemus, was carefully wrapped in a linen sheet, and the Redeemer was borne to the tomb. There the three disciples straightened the mangled limbs, and folded the bruised hands upon the pulseless breast. The Galilean women came to see that all had been done that could be done for the lifeless form of their beloved Teacher. Then they saw the heavy stone rolled against the entrance of the tomb, and the Saviour was left at rest. The women were last at the cross, and last at the tomb of Christ. While the evening shades were gathering, Mary Magdalene and the other Marys lingered about the resting place of their Lord, shedding tears of sorrow over the fate of Him whom they loved. "And they returned, . . . and rested the Sabbath day according to the commandment." Luke 23:56.

That was a never-to-be-forgotten Sabbath to the sorrowing disciples, and also to the priests, rulers, scribes, and people. At the setting of the sun on the evening of the preparation day the trumpets sounded, signifying that the Sabbath had begun. The Passover was observed as it had been for centuries, while He to whom it pointed had been slain by wicked hands, and lay in Joseph's tomb. On the Sabbath the courts of the temple were filled with worshipers. The high priest from Golgotha was there, splendidly robed in his sacerdotal garments. White-turbaned priests, full of activity, performed their duties. But some present were not at rest as the blood of bulls and goats was offered for sin. They were not conscious that type had met antitype, that an infinite sacrifice had been made for the sins of the world. They knew not that there was no further value in the performance of the ritual service. But never before had that service been witnessed with such conflicting feelings. The trumpets and musical instruments and the voices of the singers were as loud and clear as usual. But a sense of strangenes pervaded everything. One after another inquired about a strange event that had taken place. Hitherto the most holy place had been sacredly guarded from intrusion. But now it was open to all eyes. The heavy veil of tapestry, made of pure linen, and beautifully wrought with gold, scarlet, and purple, was rent from top to bottom. The place where Jehovah had met with the high priest, to communicate His glory, the place that had been God's sacred audience chamber, lay open to every eye,—a place no longer recognized by the Lord. With gloomy presentiments the priests ministered before the altar. The uncovering of the sacred mystery of the most holy place filled them with dread of coming calamity.

Many minds were busy with thoughts started by the scenes of Calvary. From the crucifixion to the resurrection many sleepless eyes were constantly searching the prophecies, some to learn the full meaning of the feast they were then celebrating, some to find evidence that Jesus was not what He claimed to be; and others with sorrowful hearts were searching for proofs that He was the true Messiah. Though searching with different objects in view, all were convicted of the same truth,—that prophecy had been fulfilled in the events of the past few days, and that the Crucified One was the world's Redeemer. Many who at that time united in the service never again took part in the paschal rites. Many even of the priests were convicted of the true character of Jesus. Their searching of the prophecies had not been in vain, and after His resurrection they acknowledged Him as the Son of God.

Nicodemus, when he saw Jesus lifted up on the cross, remembered His words spoken by night in the Mount of Olives: "As Moses lifted up the serpent in the wilderness, even so must the Son of man be lifted up: that whosoever believeth in Him should not perish, but have eternal life." John 3:14, 15. On that Sabbath, when Christ lay in the grave, Nicodemus had opportunity for reflection. A clearer light now illuminated his mind, and the words which Jesus had spoken to him were no longer mysterious. He felt that he had lost much by not connecting himself with the Saviour during His life. Now he recalled the events of Calvary. The prayer of Christ for His murderers and His answer to the petition of the dying thief spoke to the heart of the learned councilor. Again he looked upon the Saviour in His agony; again he heard that last cry, "It is finished," spoken like the words of a conqueror. Again he beheld the

reeling earth, the darkened heavens, the rent veil, the shivered rocks, and his faith was forever established. The very
event that destroyed the hopes of the disciples convinced
Joseph and Nicodemus of the divinity of Jesus. Their fears
were overcome by the courage of a firm and unwavering
faith.

Never had Christ attracted the attention of the multitude as now that He was laid in the tomb. According to
their practice, the people brought their sick and suffering
ones to the temple courts, inquiring, Who can tell us of
Jesus of Nazareth? Many had come from far to find Him
who had healed the sick and raised the dead. On every
side was heard the cry, We want Christ the Healer! Upon
this occasion those who were thought to show indications
of the leprosy were examined by the priests. Many were
forced to hear their husbands, wives, or children pronounced leprous, and doomed to go forth from the shelter
of their homes and the care of their friends, to warn off
the stranger with the mournful cry, "Unclean, unclean!"
The friendly hands of Jesus of Nazareth, that never refused to touch with healing the loathsome leper, were folded on His breast. The lips that had answered his petition
with the comforting words, "I will; be thou clean" (Matt.
8:3), were now silent. Many appealed to the chief priests
and rulers for sympathy and relief, but in vain. Apparently
they were determined to have the living Christ among
them again. With persistent earnestness they asked for
Him. They would not be turned away. But they were driv-
en from the temple courts, and soldiers were stationed at
the gates to keep back the multitude that came with their
sick and dying, demanding entrance.

The sufferers who had come to be healed by the Saviour
sank under their disappointment. The streets were filled
with mourning. The sick were dying for want of the healing touch of Jesus. Physicians were consulted in vain;
there was no skill like that of Him who lay in Joseph's
tomb.

The mourning cries of the suffering ones brought home
to thousands of minds the conviction that a great light had
gone out of the world. Without Christ, the earth was
blackness and darkness. Many whose voices had swelled
the cry of "Crucify Him, crucify Him," now realized the
calamity that had fallen upon them, and would as eagerly
have cried, Give us Jesus! had He still been alive.

When the people learned that Jesus had been put to

death by the priests, inquiries were made regarding His death. The particulars of His trial were kept as private as possible; but during the time when He was in the grave, His name was on thousands of lips, and reports of His mock trial, and of the inhumanity of the priests and rulers, were circulated everywhere. By men of intellect these priests and rulers were called upon to explain the prophecies of the Old Testament concerning the Messiah, and while trying to frame some falsehood in reply, they became like men insane. The prophecies that pointed to Christ's sufferings and death they could not explain, and many inquirers were convinced that the Scriptures had been fulfilled.

The revenge which the priests had thought would be so sweet was already bitterness to them. They knew that they were meeting the severe censure of the people; they knew that the very ones whom they had influenced against Jesus were now horrified by their own shameful work. These priests had tried to believe Jesus a deceiver; but it was in vain. Some of them had stood by the grave of Lazarus, and had seen the dead brought back to life. They trembled for fear that Christ would Himself rise from the dead, and again appear before them. They had heard Him declare that He had power to lay down His life and to take it again. They remembered that He had said, "Destroy this temple, and in three days I will raise it up." John 2:19. Judas had told them the words spoken by Jesus to the disciples while on the last journey to Jerusalem: "Behold, we go up to Jerusalem; and the Son of man shall be betrayed unto the chief priests and unto the scribes, and they shall condemn Him to death, and shall deliver Him to the Gentiles to mock, and to scourge, and to crucify Him: and the third day He shall rise again." Matt. 20:18, 19. When they heard these words, they had mocked and ridiculed. But now they remembered that Christ's predictions had so far been fulfilled. He had said that He would rise again the third day, and who could say that this also would not come to pass? They longed to shut out these thoughts, but they could not. Like their father, the devil, they believed and trembled.

Now that the frenzy of excitement was past, the image of Christ would intrude upon their minds. They beheld Him as He stood serene and uncomplaining before His enemies, suffering without a murmur their taunts and abuse. All the events of His trial and crucifixion came back to them with an overpowering conviction that He was the Son of God. They felt that He might at any time stand before them, the accused to become the accuser, the condemned to condemn, the slain to demand justice in the death of His murderers.

They could rest little upon the Sabbath. Though they would not step over a Gentile's threshold for fear of defilement, yet they held a council concerning the body of Christ. Death and the grave must hold Him whom they had crucified. "The chief priests and Pharisees came together unto Pilate, saying, Sir, we remember that that deceiver said, while He was yet alive, After three days I will rise again. Command therefore that the sepulcher be made sure until the third day, lest His disciples come by night, and steal Him away, and say unto the people, He is risen from the dead: so the last error shall be worse than the first. Pilate said unto them, Ye have a watch: go your way, make it as sure as ye can." Matt. 27:62-65.

The priests gave directions for securing the sepulcher. A great stone had been placed before the opening. Across this stone they placed cords, securing the ends to the solid rock, and sealing them with the Roman seal. The stone could not be moved without breaking the seal. A guard of one hundred soldiers was then stationed around the sepulcher to prevent it from being tampered with. The priests did all they could to keep Christ's body where it had been laid. He was sealed as securely in His tomb as if He were to remain there through all time.

So weak men counseled and planned. Little did these murderers realize the uselessness of their efforts. But by their action God was glorified. The very efforts made to prevent Christ's resurrection are the most convincing arguments in its proof. The greater the number of soldiers placed around the tomb, the stronger would be the testimony that He had risen. Hundreds of years before the death of Christ, the Holy Spirit had declared through the psalmist, "Why do the heathen rage, and the people imagine a vain thing? The kings of the earth set themselves, and the rulers take counsel together, against the Lord, and against His anointed. . . . He that sitteth in the heavens shall laugh: the Lord shall have them in derision." Ps. 2:1-4. Roman guards and Roman arms were powerless to confine the Lord of life within the tomb. The hour of His release was near.

Chapter 43

"AFTER THREE DAYS"

THE NIGHT of the first day of the week had worn slowly away. The darkest hour, just before daybreak, had come. Christ was still a prisoner in His narrow tomb. The great stone was in its place; the Roman seal was unbroken; the Roman guards were keeping their watch. And there were unseen watchers. Hosts of evil angels were gathered about the place. Had it been possible, the prince of darkness with his apostate army would have kept forever sealed the tomb that held the Son of God. But a heavenly host surrounded the sepulcher. Angels that excel in strength were guarding the tomb, and waiting to welcome the Prince of life.

"And, behold, there was a great earthquake: for the angel of the Lord descended from heaven." Clothed with the panoply of God, this angel left the heavenly courts. The bright beams of God's glory went before him, and illuminated his pathway. "His countenance was like lightning, and his raiment white as snow: and for fear of him the keepers did shake, and became as dead men."

Now, priests and rulers, where is the power of your guard? Brave soldiers that have never been afraid of human power are now as captives taken without sword or spear. The face they look upon is not the face of mortal warrior; it is the face of the mightiest of the Lord's host. This messenger is he who fills the position from which Satan fell. It is he who on the hills of Bethlehem proclaimed Christ's birth. The earth trembles at his approach, the hosts of darkness flee, and as he rolls away the stone, heaven seems to come down to the earth. The soldiers see him removing the stone as he would a pebble, and hear him cry, Son of God, come forth; Thy Father calls Thee. They see Jesus come forth from the grave, and hear Him

This chapter is based on Matt. 28:2-4, 11-15.

proclaim over the rent sepulcher, "I am the resurrection, and the life." As He comes forth in majesty and glory, the angel host bow low in adoration before the Redeemer, and welcome Him with songs of praise.

An earthquake marked the hour when Christ laid down His life, and another earthquake witnessed the moment when He took it up in triumph. He who had vanquished death and the grave came forth from the tomb with the tread of a conqueror, amid the reeling of the earth, the flashing of lightning, and the roaring of thunder. When He shall come to the earth again, He will shake "not the earth only, but also heaven." "The earth shall reel to and fro like a drunkard, and shall be removed like a cottage." "The heavens shall be rolled together as a scroll;" "the elements shall melt with fervent heat, the earth also and the works that are therein shall be burned up." But "the Lord will be the hope of His people, and the strength of the children of Israel." Heb. 12:26; Isa. 24:20; 34:4; 2 Peter 3:10; Joel 3:16.

At the death of Jesus the soldiers had beheld the earth wrapped in darkness at midday; but at the resurrection they saw the brightness of the angels illuminate the night, and heard the inhabitants of heaven singing with great joy and triumph: Thou hast vanquished Satan and the powers of darkness; Thou hast swallowed up death in victory!

Christ came forth from the tomb glorified, and the Roman guard beheld Him. Their eyes were riveted upon the face of Him whom they had so recently mocked and derided. In this glorified Being they beheld the prisoner whom they had seen in the judgment hall, the one for whom they had plaited a crown of thorns. This was the One who had stood unresisting before Pilate and Herod, His form lacerated by the cruel scourge. This was He who had been nailed to the cross, at whom the priests and rulers, full of self-satisfaction, had wagged their heads, saying, "He saved others; Himself He cannot save." Matt. 27:42. This was He who had been laid in Joseph's new tomb. The decree of heaven had loosed the captive. Mountains piled upon mountains over His sepulcher could not have prevented Him from coming forth.

At the sight of the angels and the glorified Saviour the Roman guard had fainted and become as dead men. When the heavenly train was hidden from their view, they arose to their feet, and as quickly as their trembling limbs could carry them, made their way to the gate of the garden.

Staggering like drunken men, they hurried on to the city, telling those whom they met the wonderful news. They were making their way to Pilate, but their report had been carried to the Jewish authorities, and the chief priests and rulers sent for them to be brought first into their presence. A strange appearance those soldiers presented. Trembling with fear, their faces colorless, they bore testimony to the resurrection of Christ. The soldiers told all, just as they had seen it; they had not had time to think or speak anything but the truth. With painful utterance they said, It was the Son of God who was crucified; we have heard an angel proclaiming Him as the Majesty of heaven, the King of glory.

The faces of the priests were as those of the dead. Caiaphas tried to speak. His lips moved, but they uttered no sound. The soldiers were about to leave the council room, when a voice stayed them. Caiaphas had at last found speech. Wait, wait, he said. Tell no one the things you have seen.

A lying report was then given to the soldiers. "Say ye," said the priests, "His disciples came by night, and stole Him away while we slept." Here the priests overreached themselves. How could the soldiers say that the disciples had stolen the body while they slept? If they were asleep, how could they know? And if the disciples had been proved guilty of stealing Christ's body, would not the priests have been first to condemn them? Or if the sentinels had slept at the tomb, would not the priests have been foremost in accusing them to Pilate?

The soldiers were horrified at the thought of bringing upon themselves the charge of sleeping at their post. This was an offense punishable with death. Should they bear false witness, deceiving the people, and placing their own lives in peril? Had they not kept their weary watch with sleepless vigilance? How could they stand the trial, even for the sake of money, if they perjured themselves?

In order to silence the testimony they feared, the priests promised to secure the safety of the guard, saying that Pilate would not desire to have such a report circulated any more than they did. The Roman soldiers sold their integrity to the Jews for money. They came in before the priests burdened with a most startling message of truth; they went out with a burden of money, and on their tongues a lying report which had been framed for them by the priests.

Meanwhile the report of Christ's resurrection had been

carried to Pilate. Though Pilate was responsible for having given Christ up to die, he had been comparatively unconcerned. While he had condemned the Saviour unwillingly, and with a feeling of pity, he had felt no real compunction until now. In terror he now shut himself within his house, determined to see no one. But the priests made their way into his presence, told the story which they had invented, and urged him to overlook the sentinels' neglect of duty. Before consenting to this, he himself privately questioned the guard. They, fearing for their own safety, dared not conceal anything, and Pilate drew from them an account of all that had taken place. He did not prosecute the matter further, but from that time there was no peace for him.

When Jesus was laid in the grave, Satan triumphed. He dared to hope that the Saviour would not take up His life again. He claimed the Lord's body, and set his guard about the tomb, seeking to hold Christ a prisoner. He was bitterly angry when his angels fled at the approach of the heavenly messenger. When he saw Christ come forth in triumph, he knew that his kingdom would have an end, and that he must finally die.

The priests, in putting Christ to death, had made themselves the tools of Satan. Now they were entirely in his power. They were entangled in a snare from which they saw no escape but in continuing their warfare against Christ. When they heard the report of His resurrection, they feared the wrath of the people. They felt that their own lives were in danger. The only hope for them was to prove Christ an impostor by denying that He had risen. They bribed the soldiers, and secured Pilate's silence. They spread their lying reports far and near. But there were witnesses whom they could not silence. Many had heard of the soldiers' testimony to Christ's resurrection. And certain of the dead who came forth with Christ appeared to many, and declared that He had risen. Reports were brought to the priests of persons who had seen these risen ones, and heard their testimony. The priests and rulers were in continual dread, lest in walking the streets, or within the privacy of their own homes, they should come face to face with Christ. They felt that there was no safety for them. Bolts and bars were but poor protection against the Son of God. By day and by night that awful scene in the judgment hall, when they had cried, "His blood be on us, and on our children," was before them. Matt. 27:25.

Nevermore would the memory of that scene fade from their minds. Nevermore would peaceful sleep come to their pillows.

When the voice of the mighty angel was heard at Christ's tomb, saying, Thy Father calls Thee, the Saviour came forth from the grave by the life that was in Himself. Now was proved the truth of His words, "I lay down My life, that I might take it again. . . . I have power to lay it down, and I have power to take it again." Now was fulfilled the prophecy He had spoken to the priests and rulers, "Destroy this temple, and in three days I will raise it up." John 10:17, 18; 2:19.

Over the recent sepulcher of Joseph Christ had proclaimed in triumph, "I am the resurrection, and the life." These words could be spoken only by the Deity. All created beings live by the will and power of God. They are dependent recipients of the life of God. From the highest seraph to the humblest animate being, all are replenished from the Source of life. Only He who is one with God could say, I have power to lay down My life, and I have power to take it again. In His divinity, Christ possessed the power to break the bonds of death.

Christ arose from the dead as the first fruits of those that slept. He was the antitype of the wave sheaf, and His resurrection took place on the very day when the wave sheaf was to be presented before the Lord. For more than a thousand years this symbolic ceremony had been performed. From the harvest fields the first heads of ripened grain were gathered, and when the people went up to Jerusalem to the Passover, the sheaf of first fruits was waved as a thank offering before the Lord. Not until this was presented could the sickle be put to the grain, and it be gathered into sheaves. The sheaf dedicated to God represented the harvest. So Christ the first fruits represented the great spiritual harvest to be gathered for the kingdom of God. His resurrection is the type and pledge of the resurrection of all the righteous dead. "For if we believe that Jesus died and rose again, even so them also which sleep in Jesus will God bring with Him." 1 Thess. 4:14.

As Christ arose, He brought from the grave a multitude of captives. The earthquake at His death had rent open their graves, and when He arose, they came forth with Him. They were those who had been colaborers with God, and who at the cost of their lives had borne testimony to the truth. Now they were to be witnesses for Him who had raised them from the dead.

During His ministry, Jesus had raised the dead to life. He had raised the son of the widow of Nain, and the ruler's daughter and Lazarus. But these were not clothed with immortality. After they were raised, they were still subject to death. But those who came forth from the grave at Christ's resurrection were raised to everlasting life. They ascended with Him as trophies of His victory over death and the grave. These, said Christ, are no longer the captives of Satan; I have redeemed them. I have brought them from the grave as the first fruits of My power, to be with Me where I am, nevermore to see death or experience sorrow.

These went into the city, and appeared unto many, declaring, Christ has risen from the dead, and we be risen with Him. Thus was immortalized the sacred truth of the resurrection. The risen saints bore witness to the truth of the words, "Thy dead men shall live, together with My dead body shall they arise." Their resurrection was an illustration of the fulfillment of the prophecy, "Awake and sing, ye that dwell in dust: for thy dew is as the dew of herbs, and the earth shall cast out the dead." Isa. 26:19.

To the believer, Christ is the resurrection and the life. In our Saviour the life that was lost through sin is restored; for He has life in Himself to quicken whom He will. He is invested with the right to give immortality. The life that He laid down in humanity, He takes up again, and gives to humanity. "I am come," He said, "that they might have life, and that they might have it more abundantly." "Whosoever drinketh of the water that I shall give him shall never thirst; but the water that I shall give him shall be in him a well of water springing up into everlasting life." "Whoso eateth My flesh, and drinketh My blood, hath eternal life; and I will raise him up at the last day." John 10:10; 4:14; 6:54.

To the believer, death is but a small matter. Christ speaks of it as if it were of little moment. "If a man keep My saying, he shall never see death," "he shall never taste of death." To the Christian, death is but a sleep, a moment of silence and darkness. The life is hid with Christ in God, and "when Christ, who is our life, shall appear, then shall ye also appear with Him in glory." John 8:51, 52; Col. 3:4.

The voice that cried from the cross, "It is finished," was heard among the dead. It pierced the walls of sepulchers, and summoned the sleepers to arise. Thus will it be when the voice of Christ shall be heard from heaven. That voice will penetrate the graves and unbar the tombs, and the dead in Christ shall arise. At the Saviour's resurrection a few graves were opened, but at His second coming all the precious dead shall hear His voice, and shall come forth to glorious, immortal life. The same power that raised Christ from the dead will raise His church, and glorify it with Him, above all principalities, above all powers, above every name that is named, not only in this world, but also in the world to come.

Chapter 44

A STONE UNTURNED

THE WOMEN who had stood by the cross of Christ waited and watched for the hours of the Sabbath to pass. On the first day of the week, very early, they made their way to the tomb, taking with them precious spices to anoint the Saviour's body. They did not think about His rising from the dead. The sun of their hope had set, and night had settled down on their hearts. As they walked, they recounted Christ's works of mercy and His words of comfort. But they remembered not His words, "I will see you again." John 16:22.

Ignorant of what was even then taking place, they drew near the garden, saying as they went, "Who shall roll us away the stone from the door of the sepulcher?" They knew that they could not remove the stone, yet they kept on their way. And lo, the heavens were suddenly alight with glory that came not from the rising sun. The earth trembled. They saw that the great stone was rolled away. The grave was empty.

The women had not all come to the tomb from the same direction. Mary Magdalene was the first to reach the place; and upon seeing that the stone was removed, she hurried away to tell the disciples. Meanwhile the other women came up. A light was shining about the tomb, but the body of Jesus was not there. As they lingered about the place, suddenly they saw that they were not alone. A young man clothed in shining garments was sitting by the tomb. It was the angel who had rolled away the stone. He had taken the guise of humanity that he might not alarm these friends of Jesus. Yet about him the light of the heavenly glory was still shining, and the women were afraid. They turned to flee,

This chapter is based on Matt. 28:1, 5-8; Mark 16:1-8; Luke 24:1-12; John 20:1-18.

but the angel's words stayed their steps. "Fear not ye," he said; "for I know that ye seek Jesus, which was crucified. He is not here: for He is risen, as He said. Come, see the place where the Lord lay. And go quickly, and tell His disciples that He is risen from the dead." Again they look into the tomb, and again they hear the wonderful news. Another angel in human form is there, and he says, "Why seek ye the living among the dead? He is not here, but is risen: remember how He spake unto you when He was yet in Galilee, saying, The Son of man must be delivered into the hands of sinful men, and be crucified, and the third day rise again."

He is risen, He is risen! The women repeat the words again and again. No need now for the anointing spices. The Saviour is living, and not dead. They remember now that when speaking of His death He said that He would rise again. What a day is this to the world! Quickly the women departed from the sepulcher "with fear and great joy; and did run to bring His disciples word."

Mary had not heard the good news. She went to Peter and John with the sorrowful message, "They have taken away the Lord out of the sepulcher, and we know not where they have laid Him." The disciples hurried to the tomb, and found it as Mary had said. They saw the shroud and the napkin, but they did not find their Lord. Yet even here was testimony that He had risen. The graveclothes were not thrown heedlessly aside, but carefully folded, each in a place by itself. John "saw, and believed." He did not yet understand the scripture that Christ must rise from the dead; but he now remembered the Saviour's words foretelling His resurrection.

It was Christ Himself who had placed those graveclothes with such care. When the mighty angel came down to the tomb, he was joined by another, who with his company had been keeping guard over the Lord's body. As the angel from heaven rolled away the stone, the other entered the tomb, and unbound the wrappings from the body of Jesus. But it was the Saviour's hand that folded each, and laid it in its place. In His sight who guides alike the star and the atom, there is nothing unimportant. Order and perfection are seen in all His work.

Mary had followed John and Peter to the tomb; when they returned to Jerusalem, she remained. As she looked into the empty tomb, grief filled her heart. Looking in, she saw the two angels, one at the head and the other at the foot where Jesus had lain. "Woman, why weepest thou?" they asked her. "Because they have taken away my Lord," she answered, "and I know not where they have laid Him."

Then she turned away, even from the angels, thinking that she must find someone who could tell her what had been done with the body of Jesus. Another voice addressed her, "Woman, why weepest thou? whom seekest thou?" Through her tear-dimmed eyes, Mary saw the form of a man, and thinking that it was the gardener, she said, "Sir, if thou have borne Him hence, tell me where thou hast laid Him, and I will take Him away." If this rich man's tomb was thought too honorable a burial place for Jesus, she herself would provide a place for Him. There was a grave that Christ's own voice had made vacant, the grave where Lazarus had lain. Might she not there find a burial place for her Lord? She felt that to care for His precious crucified body would be a great consolation to her in her grief.

But now in His own familiar voice Jesus said to her, "Mary." Now she knew that it was not a stranger who was addressing her, and turning she saw before her the living Christ. In her joy she forgot that He had been crucified. Springing toward Him, as if to embrace His feet, she said, "Rabboni." But Christ raised His hand, saying, Detain Me not; "for I am not yet ascended to My Father: but go to My brethren, and say unto them, I ascend unto My Father, and your Father; and to My God, and your God." And Mary went her way to the disciples with the joyful message.

Jesus refused to receive the homage of His people until He had the assurance that His sacrifice was accepted by the Father. He ascended to the heavenly courts, and from God Himself heard the assurance that His atonement for the sins of men had been ample, that through His blood all might gain eternal life. The Father ratified the covenant made with Christ, that He would receive repentant and obedient men, and would love them even as He loves His Son. Christ was to complete His work, and fulfill His pledge to "make a man more precious than fine gold; even a man than the golden wedge of Ophir." Isa. 13:12. All power in heaven and on earth was given to the Prince of life, and He returned to His followers in a world of sin, that He might impart to them of His power and glory.

While the Saviour was in God's presence, receiving gifts

for His church, the disciples thought upon His empty tomb, and mourned and wept. The day that was a day of rejoicing to all heaven was to the disciples a day of uncertainty, confusion, and perplexity. Their unbelief in the testimony of the women gives evidence of how low their faith had sunk. The news of Christ's resurrection was so different from what they had anticipated that they could not believe it. It was too good to be true, they thought. They had heard so much of the doctrines and the so-called scientific theories of the Sadducees that the impression made on their minds in regard to the resurrection was vague. They scarcely knew what the resurrection from the dead could mean. They were unable to take in the great subject.

"Go your way," the angels had said to the women, "tell His disciples and Peter that He goeth before you into Galilee: there shall ye see Him, as He said unto you." These angels had been with Christ as guardian angels throughout His life on earth. They had witnessed His trial and crucifixion. They had heard His words to His disciples. This was shown by their message to the disciples, and should have convinced them of its truth. Such words could have come only from the messengers of their risen Lord.

"Tell His disciples and Peter," the angels said. Since the death of Christ, Peter had been bowed down with remorse. His shameful denial of the Lord, and the Saviour's look of love and anguish, were ever before him. Of all the disciples he had suffered most bitterly. To him the assurance is given that his repentance is accepted and his sin forgiven. He is mentioned by name.

"Tell His disciples and Peter that He goeth before you into Galilee: there shall ye see Him." All the disciples had forsaken Jesus, and the call to meet Him again includes them all. He has not cast them off. When Mary Magdalene told them she had seen the Lord, she repeated the call to the meeting in Galilee. And a third time the message was sent to them. After He had ascended to the Father, Jesus appeared to the other women, saying, "All hail. And they came and held Him by the feet, and worshiped Him. Then said Jesus unto them, Be not afraid: go tell My brethren that they go into Galilee, and there shall they see Me."

Christ's first work on earth after His resurrection was to convince His disciples of His undiminished love and tender regard for them. To give them proof that He was their living Saviour, that He had broken the fetters of the tomb, and could no longer be held by the enemy death; to reveal that He had the same heart of love as when He was with them as their beloved Teacher, He appeared to them again and again. He would draw the bonds of love still closer around them. Go tell My brethren, He said, that they meet Me in Galilee.

As they heard this appointment, so definitely given, the disciples began to think of Christ's words to them foretelling His resurrection. But even now they did not rejoice. They could not cast off their doubt and perplexity. Even when the women declared that they had seen the Lord, the disciples would not believe. They thought them under an illusion.

Trouble seemed crowding upon trouble. On the sixth day of the week they had seen their Master die; on the first day of the next week they found themselves deprived of His body, and they were accused of having stolen it away for the sake of deceiving the people. They despaired of ever correcting the false impressions that were gaining ground against them. They feared the enmity of the priests and the wrath of the people. They longed for the presence of Jesus, who had helped them in every perplexity.

Often they repeated the words, "We trusted that it had been He which should have redeemed Israel." Lonely and sick at heart they remembered His words, "If they do these things in a green tree, what shall be done in the dry?" Luke 24:21; 23:31. They met together in the upper chamber, and closed and fastened the doors, knowing that the fate of their beloved Teacher might at any time be theirs.

And all the time they might have been rejoicing in the knowledge of a risen Saviour. In the garden, Mary had stood weeping, when Jesus was close beside her. Her eyes were so blinded by tears that she did not discern Him. And the hearts of the disciples were so full of grief that they did not believe the angels' message or the words of Christ Himself.

How many are still doing what these disciples did! How many echo Mary's despairing cry, "They have taken away the Lord, ... and we know not where they have laid Him"! To how many might the Saviour's words be spoken, "Why weepest thou? whom seekest thou?" He is close beside them, but their tear-blinded eyes do not discern Him. He speaks to them, but they do not understand.

Oh that the bowed head might be lifted, that the eyes might be opened to behold Him, that the ears might listen to His voice! "Go quickly, and tell His disciples that He is risen." Bid them look not to Joseph's new tomb, that was closed with a great stone, and sealed with the Roman seal. Christ is not there. Look not to the empty sepulcher. Mourn not as those who are hopeless and helpless. Jesus lives, and because He lives, we shall live also. From grateful hearts, from lips touched with holy fire, let the glad song ring out, Christ is risen! He lives to make intercession for us. Grasp this hope, and it will hold the soul like a sure, tried anchor. Believe, and thou shalt see the glory of God.

Chapter 45

PROMISE OF FIRE

STANDING BUT a step from His heavenly throne, Christ gave the commission to His disciples. "All power is given unto Me in heaven and in earth," He said. "Go ye therefore, and teach all nations." "Go ye into all the world, and preach the gospel to every creature." Mark 16:15. Again and again the words were repeated, that the disciples might grasp their significance. Upon all the inhabitants of the earth, high and low, rich and poor, was the light of heaven to shine in clear, strong rays. The disciples were to be colaborers with their Redeemer in the work of saving the world.

The commission had been given to the twelve when Christ met with them in the upper chamber; but it was now to be given to a larger number. At the meeting on a mountain in Galilee, all the believers who could be called together were assembled. Of this meeting Christ Himself, before His death, had designated the time and place. The angel at the tomb reminded the disciples of His promise to meet them in Galilee. The promise was repeated to the believers who were gathered at Jerusalem during the Passover week, and through them it reached many lonely ones who were mourning the death of their Lord. With intense interest all looked forward to the interview. They made their way to the place of meeting by circuitous routes, coming in from every direction, to avoid exciting the suspicion of the jealous Jews. With wondering hearts they came, talking earnestly together of the news that had reached them concerning Christ.

At the time appointed, about five hundred believers were collected in little knots on the mountainside, eager to learn all that could be learned from those who had seen

This chapter is based on Matt. 28:16-20.

Christ since His resurrection. From group to group the disciples passed, telling all they had seen and heard of Jesus, and reasoning from the Scriptures as He had done with them. Thomas recounted the story of his unbelief, and told how his doubts had been swept away. Suddenly Jesus stood among them. No one could tell whence or how He came. Many who were present had never before seen Him; but in His hands and feet they beheld the marks of the crucifixion; His countenance was as the face of God, and when they saw Him, they worshiped Him.

But some doubted. So it will always be. There are those who find it hard to exercise faith, and they place themselves on the doubting side. These lose much because of their unbelief.

This was the only interview that Jesus had with many of the believers after His resurrection. He came and spoke to them saying, "All power is given unto Me in heaven and in earth." The disciples had worshiped Him before He spoke, but His words, falling from lips that had been closed in death, thrilled them with peculiar power. He was now the risen Saviour. Many of them had seen Him exercise His power in healing the sick and controlling satanic agencies. They believed that He possessed power to set up His kingdom at Jerusalem, power to quell all opposition, power over the elements of nature. He had stilled the angry waters; He had walked upon the white-crested billows; He had raised the dead to life. Now He declared that "all power" was given to Him. His words carried the minds of His hearers above earthly and temporal things to the heavenly and eternal. They were lifted to the highest conception of His dignity and glory.

Christ's words on the mountainside were the announcement that His sacrifice in behalf of man was full and complete. The conditions of the atonement had been fulfilled; the work for which He came to this world had been accomplished. He was on His way to the throne of God, to be honored by angels, principalities, and powers. He had entered upon His mediatorial work. Clothed with boundless authority, He gave His commission to the disciples: "Go ye therefore, and teach all nations," "baptizing them into the name of the Father and of the Son and of the Holy Ghost: teaching them to observe all things whatsoever I commanded you: and lo, I am with you always, even unto the end of the world." R. V.

The Jewish people had been made the depositaries of

sacred truth; but Pharisaism had made them the most exclusive, the most bigoted, of all the human race. Everything about the priests and rulers—their dress, customs, ceremonies, traditions—made them unfit to be the light of the world. They looked upon themselves, the Jewish nation, as the world. But Christ commissioned His disciples to proclaim a faith and worship that would have in it nothing of caste or country, a faith that would be adapted to all peoples, all nations, all classes of men.

Before leaving His disciples, Christ plainly stated the nature of His kingdom. He called to their minds what He had previously told them concerning it. He declared that it was not His purpose to establish in this world a temporal, but a spiritual kingdom. He was not to reign as an earthly king on David's throne. Again He opened to them the Scriptures, showing that all He had passed through had been ordained in heaven, in the councils between the Father and Himself. All had been foretold by men inspired by the Holy Spirit. He said, You see that all I have revealed to you concerning My rejection as the Messiah has come to pass. All I have said in regard to the humiliation I should endure and the death I should die, has been verified. On the third day I rose again. Search the Scriptures more diligently, and you will see that in all these things the specifications of prophecy concerning Me have been fulfilled.

Christ commissioned His disciples to do the work He had left in their hands, beginning at Jerusalem. Jerusalem had been the scene of His amazing condescension for the human race. There He had suffered, been rejected and condemned. The land of Judea was His birthplace. There, clad in the garb of humanity, He had walked with men, and few had discerned how near heaven came to the earth when Jesus was among them. At Jerusalem the work of the disciples must begin.

In view of all that Christ had suffered there, and the unappreciated labor He had put forth, the disciples might have pleaded for a more promising field; but they made no such plea. The very ground where He had scattered the seed of truth was to be cultivated by the disciples, and the seed would spring up and yield an abundant harvest. In their work the disciples would have to meet persecution through the jealousy and hatred of the Jews; but this had been endured by their Master, and they were not to flee from it. The first offers of mercy must be made to the murderers of the Saviour.

And there were in Jerusalem many who had secretly believed on Jesus, and many who had been deceived by the priests and rulers. To these also the gospel was to be presented. They were to be called to repentance. The wonderful truth that through Christ alone could remission of sins be obtained was to be made plain. While all Jerusalem was stirred by the thrilling events of the past few weeks, the preaching of the gospel would make the deepest impression.

But the work was not to stop here. It was to be extended to the earth's remotest bounds. To His disciples Christ said, You have been witnesses of My life of self-sacrifice in behalf of the world. You have witnessed My labors for Israel. Although they would not come unto Me that they might have life, although priests and rulers have done to Me as they listed, although they have rejected Me as the Scriptures foretold, they shall have still another opportunity of accepting the Son of God. You have seen that all who come to Me, confessing their sins, I freely receive. Him that cometh to Me I will in nowise cast out. All who will, may be reconciled to God, and receive everlasting life. To you, My disciples, I commit this message of mercy. It is to be given to Israel first, and then to all nations, tongues, and peoples. It is to be given to Jews and Gentiles. All who believe are to be gathered into one church.

Through the gift of the Holy Spirit the disciples were to receive a marvelous power. Their testimony was to be confirmed by signs and wonders. Miracles would be wrought, not only by the apostles, but by those who received their message. Jesus said, "In My name shall they cast out devils; they shall speak with new tongues; they shall take up serpents; and if they drink any deadly thing, it shall not hurt them; they shall lay hands on the sick, and they shall recover." Mark 16:17, 18.

At that time poisoning was often practiced. Unscrupulous men did not hesitate to remove by this means those who stood in the way of their ambition. Jesus knew that the life of His disciples would thus be imperiled. Many would think it doing God service to put His witnesses to death. He therefore promised them protection from this danger.

The disciples were to have the same power which Jesus had to heal "all manner of sickness and all manner of disease among the people." By healing in His name the diseases of the body, they would testify to His power for the healing of the soul. Matt. 4:23; 9:6. And a new endowment was now promised. The disciples were to preach among other nations, and they would receive power to speak other tongues. The apostles and their associates were unlettered men, yet through the outpouring of the Spirit on the day of Pentecost, their speech, whether in their own or a foreign language, became pure, simple, and accurate, both in word and in accent.

Thus Christ gave His disciples their commission. He made full provision for the prosecution of the work, and took upon Himself the responsibility for its success. So long as they obeyed His word, and worked in connection with Him, they could not fail. Go to all nations, He bade them. Go to the farthest part of the habitable globe, but know that My presence will be there. Labor in faith and confidence, for the time will never come when I will forsake you.

The Saviour's commission to the disciples included all the believers. It includes all believers in Christ to the end of time. It is a fatal mistake to suppose that the work of saving souls depends alone on the ordained minister. All to whom the heavenly inspiration has come are put in trust with the gospel. All who receive the life of Christ are ordained to work for the salvation of their fellow men. For this work the church was established, and all who take upon themselves its sacred vows are thereby pledged to be co-workers with Christ.

"The Spirit and the bride say, Come. And let him that heareth say, Come." Rev. 22:17. Everyone who hears is to repeat the invitation. Whatever one's calling in life, his first interest should be to win souls for Christ. He may not be able to speak to congregations, but he can work for individuals. To them he can communicate the instruction received from his Lord. Ministry does not consist alone in preaching. Those minister who relieve the sick and suffering, helping the needy, speaking words of comfort to the desponding and those of little faith. Nigh and afar off are souls weighed down by a sense of guilt. It is not hardship, toil, or poverty that degrades humanity. It is guilt, wrongdoing. This brings unrest and dissatisfaction. Christ would have His servants minister to sin-sick souls.

The disciples were to begin their work where they were. The hardest and most unpromising field was not to be

passed by. So every one of Christ's workers is to begin
where he is. In our own families may be souls hungry for
sympathy, starving for the bread of life. There may be children to be trained for Christ. There are heathen at our
very doors. Let us do faithfully the work that is nearest.
Then let our efforts be extended as far as God's hand
may lead the way. The work of many may appear to be
restricted by circumstances; but, wherever it is, if performed with faith and diligence it will be felt to the uttermost parts of the earth. Christ's work when upon earth appeared to be confined to a narrow field, but multitudes
from all lands heard His message. God often uses the simplest means to accomplish the greatest results. It is His
plan that every part of His work shall depend on every
other part, as a wheel within a wheel, all acting in
harmony. The humblest worker, moved by the Holy Spirit,
will touch invisible chords, whose vibrations will ring to
the ends of the earth, and make melody through eternal
ages.

But the command, "Go ye into all the world," is not to
be lost sight of. We are called upon to lift our eyes to the
"regions beyond." Christ tears away the wall of partition,
the dividing prejudice of nationality, and teaches a love for
all the human family. He lifts men from the narrow circle
which their selfishness prescribes; He abolishes all territori-
al lines and artificial distinctions of society. He makes no
difference between neighbors and strangers, friends and
enemies. He teaches us to look upon every needy soul as
our brother, and the world as our field.

When the Saviour said, "Go, . . . teach all nations," He
said also, "These signs shall follow them that believe; In
My name shall they cast out devils; they shall speak with
new tongues; they shall take up serpents; and if they drink
any deadly thing, it shall not hurt them; they shall lay
hands on the sick, and they shall recover." The promise is
as far-reaching as the commission. Not that all the gifts
are imparted to each believer. The Spirit divides "to every
man severally as He will." 1 Cor. 12:11. But the gifts of
the Spirit are promised to every believer according to his
need for the Lord's work. The promise is just as strong
and trustworthy now as in the days of the apostles. "These
signs shall follow them that believe." This is the privilege
of God's children, and faith should lay hold on all that it
is possible to have as an indorsement of faith.

"They shall lay hands on the sick, and they shall recover." This world is a vast lazar house, but Christ came to heal the sick, to proclaim deliverance to the captives of Satan. He was in Himself health and strength. He imparted His life to the sick, the afflicted, those possessed of demons. He turned away none who came to receive His healing power. He knew that those who petitioned Him for help had brought disease upon themselves; yet He did not refuse to heal them. And when virtue from Christ entered into these poor souls, they were convicted of sin, and many were healed of their spiritual disease, as well as of their physical maladies. The gospel still possesses the same power, and why should we not today witness the same results?

Christ feels the woes of every sufferer. When evil spirits rend a human frame, Christ feels the curse. When fever is burning up the life current, He feels the agony. And He is just as willing to heal the sick now as when He was personally on earth. Christ's servants are His representatives, the channels for His working. He desires through them to exercise His healing power.

In the Saviour's manner of healing there were lessons for His disciples. On one occasion He anointed the eyes of a blind man with clay, and bade him, "Go, wash in the pool of Siloam. . . . He went his way therefore, and washed, and came seeing." John 9:7. The cure could be wrought only by the power of the Great Healer, yet Christ made use of the simple agencies of nature. While He did not give countenance to drug medication, He sanctioned the use of simple and natural remedies.

To many of the afflicted ones who received healing, Christ said, "Sin no more, lest a worse thing come unto thee." John 5:14. Thus He taught that disease is the result of violating God's laws, both natural and spiritual. The great misery in the world would not exist did men but live in harmony with the Creator's plan.

Christ had been the guide and teacher of ancient Israel, and He taught them that health is the reward of obedience to the laws of God. The Great Physician who healed the sick in Palestine had spoken to His people from the pillar of cloud, telling them what they must do, and what God would do for them. "If thou wilt diligently hearken to the voice of the Lord thy God," He said, "and wilt do that which is right in His sight, and wilt give ear to His commandments, and keep all His statutes, I will put none of these diseases upon thee, which I have brought upon the

Egyptians: for I am the Lord that healeth thee." Ex. 15:26. Christ gave to Israel definite instruction in regard to their habits of life, and He assured them, "The Lord will take away from thee all sickness." Deut. 7:15. When they fulfilled the conditions, the promise was verified to them. "There was not one feeble person among their tribes." Ps. 105:37.

These lessons are for us. There are conditions to be observed by all who would preserve health. All should learn what these conditions are. The Lord is not pleased with ignorance in regard to His laws, either natural or spiritual. We are to be workers together with God for the restoration of health to the body as well as to the soul.

And we should teach others how to preserve and to recover health. For the sick we should use the remedies which God has provided in nature, and we should point them to Him who alone can restore. It is our work to present the sick and suffering to Christ in the arms of our faith. We should teach them to believe in the Great Healer. We should lay hold on His promise, and pray for the manifestation of His power. The very essence of the gospel is restoration, and the Saviour would have us bid the sick, the hopeless, and the afflicted take hold upon His strength.

The power of love was in all Christ's healing, and only by partaking of that love, through faith, can we be instruments for His work. If we neglect to link ourselves in divine connection with Christ, the current of life-giving energy cannot flow in rich streams from us to the people. There were places where the Saviour Himself could not do many mighty works because of their unbelief. So now unbelief separates the church from her divine Helper. Her hold upon eternal realities is weak. By her lack of faith, God is disappointed, and robbed of His glory.

It is in doing Christ's work that the church has the promise of His presence. Go teach all nations, He said; "and, lo, I am with you alway, even unto the end of the world." To take His yoke is one of the first conditions of receiving His power. The very life of the church depends upon her faithfulness in fulfilling the Lord's commission. To neglect this work is surely to invite spiritual feebleness and decay. Where there is no active labor for others, love wanes, and faith grows dim.

Christ intends that His ministers shall be educators of the church in gospel work. They are to teach the people how to seek and save the lost. But is this the work they are doing? Alas, how many are toiling to fan the spark of life in a church that is ready to die! How many churches are tended like sick lambs by those who ought to be seeking for the lost sheep! And all the time millions upon millions without Christ are perishing.

Divine love has been stirred to its unfathomable depths for the sake of men, and angels marvel to behold in the recipients of so great love a mere surface gratitude. Angels marvel at man's shallow appreciation of the love of God. Heaven stands indignant at the neglect shown to the souls of men. Would we know how Christ regards it? How would a father and mother feel, did they know that their child, lost in the cold and the snow, had been passed by, and left to perish, by those who might have saved it? Would they not be terribly grieved, wildly indignant? Would they not denounce those murderers with wrath hot as their tears, intense as their love? The sufferings of every man are the sufferings of God's child, and those who reach out no helping hand to their perishing fellow beings provoke His righteous anger. This is the wrath of the Lamb. To those who claim fellowship with Christ, yet have been indifferent to the needs of their fellow men, He will declare in the great judgment day, "I know you not whence ye are; depart from Me, all ye workers of iniquity." Luke 13:27.

In the commission to His disciples, Christ not only outlined their work, but gave them their message. Teach the people, He said, "to observe all things whatsoever I have commanded you." The disciples were to teach what Christ had taught. That which He had spoken, not only in person, but through all the prophets and teachers of the Old Testament, is here included. Human teaching is shut out. There is no place for tradition, for man's theories and conclusions. or for church legislation. No laws ordained by ecclesiastical authority are included in the commission. None of these are Christ's servants to teach. "The law and the prophets," with the record of His own words and deeds, are the treasure committed to the disciples to be given to the world. Christ's name is their watchword, their badge of distinction, their bond of union, the authority for their course of action, and the source of their success. Nothing that does not bear His superscription is to be recognized in His kingdom.

The gospel is to be presented, not as a lifeless theory. but as a living force to change the life. God desires that the receivers of His grace shall be witnesses to its power. Those whose course has been most offensive to Him He freely accepts; when they repent, He imparts to them His divine Spirit, places them in the highest positions of trust, and sends them forth into the camp of the disloyal to proclaim His boundless mercy. He would have His servants bear testimony to the fact that through His grace men may possess Christlikeness of character, and may rejoice in the assurance of His great love. He would have us bear testimony to the fact that He cannot be satisfied until the human race are reclaimed and reinstated in their holy privileges as His sons and daughters.

In Christ is the tenderness of the shepherd, the affection of the parent, and the matchless grace of the compassionate Saviour. His blessings He presents in the most alluring terms. He is not content merely to announce these blessings; He presents them in the most attractive way, to excite a desire to possess them. So His servants are to present the riches of the glory of the unspeakable Gift. The wonderful love of Christ will melt and subdue hearts, when the mere reiteration of doctrines would accomplish nothing. "Comfort ye, comfort ye My people, saith your God." "O Zion, that bringest good tidings, get thee up into the high mountain; O Jerusalem, that bringest good tidings, lift up thy voice with strength; lift it up, be not afraid; say unto the cities of Judah, Behold your God! . . . He shall feed His flock like a shepherd: He shall gather the lambs with His arm, and carry them in His bosom." Isa. 40:1, 9-11. Tell the people of Him who is "the Chiefest among ten thousand," and the One "altogether lovely." The Song of Solomon 5:10, 16. Words alone cannot tell it. Let it be reflected in the character and manifested in the life. Christ is sitting for His portrait in every disciple. Every one God has predestinated to be "conformed to the image of His Son." Rom. 8:29. In every one Christ's long-suffering love, His holiness, meekness, mercy, and truth are to be manifested to the world.

The first disciples went forth preaching the word. They revealed Christ in their lives. And the Lord worked with them, "confirming the word with signs following." Mark 16:20. These disciples prepared themselves for their work. Before the day of Pentecost they met together, and put away all differences. They were of one accord. They believed Christ's promise that the blessing would be given, and they prayed in faith. They did not ask for a blessing for themselves merely; they were weighted with the burden for the salvation of souls. The gospel was to be carried to the uttermost parts of the earth, and they claimed the endowment of power that Christ had promised. Then it was that the Holy Spirit was poured out, and thousands were converted in a day.

So it may be now. Instead of man's speculations, let the word of God be preached. Let Christians put away their dissensions, and give themselves to God for the saving of the lost. Let them in faith ask for the blessing, and it will come. The outpouring of the Spirit in apostolic days was the "former rain," and glorious was the result. But the "latter rain" will be more abundant. Joel 2:23.

All who consecrate soul, body, and spirit to God will be constantly receiving a new endowment of physical and mental power. The inexhaustible supplies of heaven are at their command. Christ gives them the breath of His own spirit, the life of His own life. The Holy Spirit puts forth its highest energies to work in heart and mind. The grace of God enlarges and multiplies their faculties, and every perfection of the divine nature comes to their assistance in the work of saving souls. Through co-operation with Christ they are complete in Him, and in their human weakness they are enabled to do the deeds of Omnipotence.

The Saviour longs to manifest His grace and stamp His character on the whole world. It is His purchased possession, and He desires to make men free, and pure, and holy. Though Satan works to hinder this purpose, yet through the blood shed for the world there are triumphs to be achieved that will bring glory to God and the Lamb. Christ will not be satisfied till the victory is complete, and "He shall see of the travail of His soul, and shall be satisfied." Isa. 53:11. All the nations of the earth shall hear the gospel of His grace. Not all will receive His grace; but "a seed shall serve Him; it shall be accounted to the Lord for a generation." Ps. 22:30. "The kingdom and dominion, and the greatness of the kingdom under the whole heaven, shall be given to the people of the saints of the Most High," and "the earth shall be full of the knowledge of the Lord, as the waters cover the sea." "So shall they fear the name of the Lord from the west, and His glory from the rising of the sun." Dan. 7:27; Isa. 11:9; 59:19.

"How beautiful upon the mountains are the feet of him that bringeth good tidings, that publisheth peace; that bringeth good tidings of good, that publisheth salvation; that

saith unto Zion, Thy God reigneth! . . . Break forth into
joy, sing together, ye waste places: . . . for the Lord hath
comforted His people. . . . The Lord hath made bare His
holy arm in the eyes of all the nations; and all the ends of
the earth shall see the salvation of our God." Isa. 52:7-10.

Chapter 46

GOING AND COMING

THE TIME had come for Christ to ascend to His Father's throne. As a divine conqueror He was about to return with the trophies of victory to the heavenly courts. Before His death He had declared to His Father, "I have finished the work which Thou gavest Me to do." John 17:4. After His resurrection He tarried on earth for a season, that His disciples might become familiar with Him in His risen and glorified body. Now He was ready for the leave-taking. He had authenticated the fact that He was a living Saviour. His disciples need no longer associate Him with the tomb. They could think of Him as glorified before the heavenly universe.

As the place of His ascension, Jesus chose the spot so often hallowed by His presence while He dwelt among men. Not Mount Zion, the place of David's city, not Mount Moriah, the temple site, was to be thus honored. There Christ had been mocked and rejected. There the waves of mercy, still returning in a stronger tide of love, had been beaten back by hearts as hard as rock. Thence Jesus, weary and heart-burdened, had gone forth to find rest in the Mount of Olives. The holy Shekinah, in departing from the first temple, had stood upon the eastern mountain, as if loath to forsake the chosen city; so Christ stood upon Olivet, with yearning heart overlooking Jerusalem. The groves and glens of the mountain had been consecrated by His prayers and tears. Its steeps had echoed the triumphant shouts of the multitude that proclaimed Him king. On its sloping descent He had found a home with Lazarus at Bethany. In the garden of Gethsemane at its foot He had prayed and agonized alone. From this mountain He was to ascend to heaven. Upon its summit

This chapter is based on Luke 24:50-53; Acts 1:9-12.

His feet will rest when He shall come again. Not as a man of sorrows, but as a glorious and triumphant king He will stand upon Olivet, while Hebrew hallelujahs mingle with Gentile hosannas, and the voices of the redeemed as a mighty host shall swell the acclamation, Crown Him Lord of all!

Now with the eleven disciples Jesus made His way toward the mountain. As they passed through the gate of Jerusalem, many wondering eyes looked upon the little company, led by One whom a few weeks before the rulers had condemned and crucified. The disciples knew not that this was to be their last interview with their Master. Jesus spent the time in conversation with them, repeating His former instruction. As they approached Gethsemane, He paused, that they might call to mind the lessons He had given them on the night of His great agony. Again He looked upon the vine by which He had then represented the union of His church with Himself and His Father; again He repeated the truths He had then unfolded. All around Him were reminders of His unrequited love. Even the disciples who were so dear to His heart, had, in the hour of His humiliation, reproached and forsaken Him.

Christ had sojourned in the world for thirty-three years; He had endured its scorn, insult, and mockery; He had been rejected and crucified. Now, when about to ascend to His throne of glory,—as He reviews the ingratitude of the people He came to save,—will He not withdraw from them His sympathy and love? Will not His affections be centered upon that realm where He is appreciated, and where sinless angels wait to do His bidding? No; His promise to those loved ones whom He leaves on earth is, "I am with you alway, even unto the end of the world." Matt. 28:20.

Upon reaching the Mount of Olives, Jesus led the way across the summit, to the vicinity of Bethany. Here He paused, and the disciples gathered about Him. Beams of light seemed to radiate from His countenance as He looked lovingly upon them. He upbraided them not for their faults and failures; words of the deepest tenderness were the last that fell upon their ears from the lips of their Lord. With hands outstretched in blessing, and as if in assurance of His protecting care, He slowly ascended from among them, drawn heavenward by a power stronger than any earthly attraction. As He passed upward, the awe-stricken disciples looked with straining eyes for the last glimpse of their ascending Lord. A cloud of glory hid Him from their sight; and the words came back to them as the cloudy chariot of angels received Him, "Lo, I am with you alway, even unto the end of the world." At the same time there floated down to them the sweetest and most joyous music from the angel choir.

While the disciples were still gazing upward, voices addressed them which sounded like richest music. They turned, and saw two angels in the form of men, who spoke to them, saying, "Ye men of Galilee, why stand ye gazing up into heaven? this same Jesus, which is taken up from you into heaven, shall so come in like manner as ye have seen Him go into heaven."

These angels were of the company that had been waiting in a shining cloud to escort Jesus to His heavenly home. The most exalted of the angel throng, they were the two who had come to the tomb at Christ's resurrection, and they had been with Him throughout His life on earth. With eager desire all heaven had waited for the end of His tarrying in a world marred by the curse of sin. The time had now come for the heavenly universe to receive their King. Did not the two angels long to join the throng that welcomed Jesus? But in sympathy and love for those whom He had left, they waited to give them comfort. "Are they not all ministering spirits, sent forth to minister for them who shall be heirs of salvation?" Heb. 1:14.

Christ had ascended to heaven in the form of humanity. The disciples had beheld the cloud receive Him. The same Jesus who had walked and talked and prayed with them; who had broken bread with them; who had been with them in their boats on the lake; and who had that very day toiled with them up the ascent of Olivet,—the same Jesus had now gone to share His Father's throne. And the angels had assured them that the very One whom they had seen go up into heaven, would come again even as He had ascended. He will come "with clouds; and every eye shall see Him." "The Lord Himself shall descend from heaven with a shout, with the voice of the Archangel, and with the trump of God: and the dead in Christ shall rise." "The Son of man shall come in His glory, and all the holy angels with Him, then shall He sit upon the throne of His glory." Rev. 1:7; 1 Thess. 4:16; Matt. 25:31. Thus will be fulfilled the Lord's own promise to His disciples: "If I go and prepare a place for you, I will come again, and receive

you unto Myself; that where I am, there ye may be also."
John 14:3. Well might the disciples rejoice in the hope of
their Lord's return.

When the disciples went back to Jerusalem, the people
looked upon them with amazement. After the trial and crucifixion of Christ, it had been thought that they would appear downcast and ashamed. Their enemies expected to'
see upon their faces an expression of sorrow and defeat. Instead of this there was only gladness and triumph. Their
faces were aglow with a happiness not born of earth. They
did not mourn over disappointed hopes, but were full of
praise and thanksgiving to God. With rejoicing they told
the wonderful story of Christ's resurrection and His ascension to heaven, and their testimony was received by many.

The disciples no longer had any distrust of the future.
They knew that Jesus was in heaven, and that His sympathies were with them still. They knew that they had a
friend at the throne of God, and they were eager to present their requests to the Father in the name of Jesus. In
solemn awe they bowed in prayer, repeating the assurance,
"Whatsoever ye shall ask the Father in My name, He will
give it you. Hitherto have ye asked nothing in My name:
ask, and ye shall receive, that your joy may be full." John
16:23, 24. They extended the hand of faith higher and
higher, with the mighty argument, "It is Christ that died,
yea rather, that is risen again, who is even at the right
hand of God, who also maketh intercession for us." Rom.
8:34. And Pentecost brought them fullness of joy in the
presence of the Comforter, even as Christ had promised.

All heaven was waiting to welcome the Saviour to the
celestial courts. As He ascended, He led the way, and the
multitude of captives set free at His resurrection followed.
The heavenly host, with shouts and acclamations of praise
and celestial song, attended the joyous train.

As they drew near to the city of God, the challenge is
given by the escorting angels,—

> "Lift up your heads, O ye gates;
> And be ye lift up, ye everlasting doors;
> And the King of glory shall come in."

Joyfully the waiting sentinels respond,—

> "Who is this King of glory?"

This they say, not because they know not who He is, but because they would hear the answer of exalted praise,—

> "The Lord strong and mighty,
> The Lord mighty in battle!
> Lift up your heads, O ye gates;
> Even lift them up, ye everlasting doors;
> And the King of glory shall come in."

Again is heard the challenge, "Who is this King of glory?" for the angels never weary of hearing His name exalted. The escorting angels make reply,—

> "The Lord of hosts;
> He is the King of glory." Ps. 24:7-10.

Then the portals of the city of God are opened wide, and the angelic throng sweep through the gates amid a burst of rapturous music.

There is the throne, and around it the rainbow of promise. There are cherubim and seraphim. The commanders of the angel hosts, the sons of God, the representatives of the unfallen worlds, are assembled. The heavenly council before which Lucifer had accused God and His Son, the representatives of those sinless realms over which Satan had thought to establish his dominion,—all are there to welcome the Redeemer. They are eager to celebrate His triumph and to glorify their King.

But He waves them back. Not yet; He cannot now receive the coronet of glory and the royal robe. He enters into the presence of His Father. He points to His wounded head, the pierced side, the marred feet; He lifts His hands, bearing the print of nails. He points to the tokens of His triumph: He presents to God the wave sheaf, those raised with Him as representatives of that great multitude who shall come forth from the grave at His second coming. He approaches the Father, with whom there is joy over one sinner that repents; who rejoices over one with singing. Before the foundations of the earth were laid, the Father and the Son had united in a covenant to redeem man if he should be overcome by Satan. They had clasped Their hands in a solemn pledge that Christ should become the surety for the human race. This pledge Christ has fulfilled. When upon the cross He cried out, "It is finished," He addressed the Father. The compact had been fully carried out. Now He declares: Father, it is finished. I have done Thy will, O My God. I have completed the work of redemption. If Thy justice is satisfied, "I will that they also, whom Thou hast given Me, be with Me where I am." John 19:30; 17:24.

The voice of God is heard proclaiming that justice is satisfied. Satan is vanquished. Christ's toiling, struggling ones on earth are "accepted in the Beloved." Eph. 1:6. Before the heavenly angels and the representatives of unfallen worlds, they are declared justified. Where He is, there His church shall be. "Mercy and truth are met together; righteousness and peace have kissed each other." Ps. 85:10. The Father's arms encircle His Son, and the word is given, "Let all the angels of God worship Him." Heb. 1:6.

With joy unutterable, rulers and principalities and powers acknowledge the supremacy of the Prince of life. The angel host prostrate themselves before Him, while the glad shout fills all the courts of heaven, "Worthy is the Lamb that was slain to receive power, and riches, and wisdom, and strength, and honor, and glory, and blessing." Rev. 5:12.

Songs of triumph mingle with the music from angel harps, till heaven seems to overflow with joy and praise. Love has conquered. The lost is found. Heaven rings with voices in lofty strains proclaiming, "Blessing, and honor, and glory, and power, be unto Him that sitteth upon the throne, and unto the Lamb forever and ever." Rev. 5:13.

From that scene of heavenly joy, there comes back to us on earth the echo of Christ's own wonderful words, "I ascend unto My Father, and your Father; and to My God, and your God." The family of heaven and the family of earth are one. For us our Lord ascended, and for us He lives. "Wherefore He is able also to save them to the uttermost that come unto God by Him, seeing He ever liveth to make intercession for them."